POST–INDUSTRIAL CITIES

POST-INDUSTRIAL

CITIES · POLITICS AND

PLANNING IN NEW YORK,

PARIS, AND LONDON

H. V. Savitch

PRINCETON UNIVERSITY PRESS ▪ PRINCETON, NEW JERSEY

Copyright © 1988 by Princeton University Press

Published by Princeton University Press, 41 William Street, Princeton, New Jersey 08540
In the United Kingdom: Princeton University Press, Guildford, Surrey

All Rights Reserved

This book has been composed in Linotron Bembo type

Clothbound editions of Princeton University Press books are printed on acid-free paper, and binding materials are chosen for strength and durability. Paperbacks, although satisfactory for personal collections, are not usually suitable for library rebinding

Printed in the United States of America by Princeton University Press, Princeton, New Jersey

Library of Congress Cataloging-in-Publication Data

Savitch, H. V.
Post-industrial cities.

Includes index.
1. City planning—Political aspects—New York (N.Y.)
2. City planning—Political aspects—France—Paris. 3. City planning—Political aspects—England—London. I. Title.
HT168.N5S28 1988   307.1'2   88-2548
ISBN 0-691-07773-8 (alk. paper)

For Susan

Contents

Illustrations

Tables

Preface

LIKE ANYONE ELSE, authors are guided by personal values, tacit assumptions, and underlying motivations. These factors constitute the most fundamental of choices and make up an invisible spine of a book. In this project, one of the first choices I made was to attempt a book that addressed certain theoretical questions. I have tried to inform content with theory and to put the politics of urban planning in perspective. I have not, however, turned to grand theory, nor have I gone too far astray from the subject matter in order to attain perspective. I believe it is worthwhile to keep theory grounded in the actual experience of cities and to gear theory to an explanation how those cities work.

Post-Industrial Cities uses theory to illuminate differences in both process and outcome. This is a book about the politics of planning in New York, Paris, and London. It seeks to inform the reader about these cities and to extrapolate comparative propositions from their experience. It is also a book about how these cities plan, make decisions, deal with interest groups, and treat their populations.

In doing the research for this volume I toyed with a good many theories. In the end, I settled on an application and adaptation of what has come to be known as power structure theory. This, too, was a fundamental choice, based on my own appreciation for the richness of the literature and its capacity to pry through the endless threads that connect government to the social order. Understanding the competing explanations that fall under the rubric of power structure theory was a first step that helped me pinpoint the linkages between interest groups and public actors. I then explored these linkages through concepts that clarified different patterns of political leadership, different combinations of power, and different planning strategies.

Still another choice I made was a commitment to detail. As it turns out, this is a "meaty" book. Although theory should inform content, I believe there is equal virtue in substance—not only because substance informs, but because it allows each of us to test theory against the case at hand. Without substance we drift into countless generalizations that may seem appropriate in some instances but are altogether implausible in others. With substance, we validate theory and give it momentum.

For these lessons I am indebted to the work of scholars like Wallace Sayre, Marcel Roncayolo, and William Robson. It was Robson who first broached the idea for a book of this kind. My acquaintance with the professor from the London School of Economics began in 1971. At the time I was on my first trip to England, and I met him as I went about London trying to find out what made it tick. He introduced me to politicians in the boroughs, to academics at the LSE, and to a new world of urban politics. Our contact grew into a friendship, carried on across the Atlantic via telephone and mail. On one occasion Robson visited me in America. Then in his late seventies he set a formidable pace as we hiked through the Westchester woods, talking about cities, their politics, and how to compare them. Robson exhorted me to begin a comparative study, but I resisted.

Ten years after our first meeting, I made another trip to Europe, hoping to fulfill the promise of our conversations. Though my friend had passed on, his words and his example were with me. As a feeler, I presented a methodological paper to his colleagues at the LSE. It met varying degrees of praise, criticism, encouragement, and skepticism. The most striking remark—one that heartened me and set my sights— was that this was the kind of work William Robson would have liked. I hope this volume will do justice to his memory.

There are others to whom I owe a great deal of thanks. Alan Altshuler, Dean of the Graduate School of Public Administration at New York University, went through part of the manuscript with a fine-toothed comb. His incisive remarks, his criticisms, and his suggestions were of immense benefit to me. They not only guided the revisions of the latter half of the book but also stirred up ideas for a new draft of the introductory chapter. Martin Schain, of the Department of Politics at New York University, helped me find my way through the world of French politics. Our conversations were amply bolstered by good French wine and a good friendship. Other scholars and friends also helped me with their ideas—among them Doug Muzzio and Bob Percorella. Elsewhere in New York, Herbert Sturz and Marcy Benstock gave me the benefit of their time and experience.

Paris proved to be a marvelous resource and a wonderful place to work. My friends in the Fourth Arrondissement—Pascal and Gisele Petit, Michel and Babette Duflos, Vincent and Claude Thibault, Georges Léopold and Annie Olhagary—were always generous and warm. I shall always value their friendship. Nathan Starkman of the Atelier Parisien d'Urbanisme, both a friend and a capable professional, gave me a first-class tour of French planning. Paul Delouvrier, Maurice Doublet, Pierre Ligen, and Jean-Claude Dumont were some of the other outstanding professionals who shared their wisdom. I am grateful also to the staffs at the Institut d'Aménagement d'Urbanisme de la Région d'Ile-de-France and to the librarians at the Préfecture de la Région Parisienne for their help.

As always, London and its people were friendly, capable, and ever ready to lend a helping hand. John Hollis (former officer of the Greater London Council), George Nicholson (former member of the GLC), Robert Prestwood (former officer at the GLC), Bob Colenut (Southwark), R. Maxwell (Southwark), Reg Ward (London Docklands), and the late Edmund Lewis (London Planning and Advisory Committee) shared their expertise and their perspectives. James Simmie (Bartlett School, University of London) and John Shepherd (Birkbeck College, University of London) introduced me to important lines of inquiry. Derek Diamond, George Jones, Brendan O'Leary, and Patrick Dunleavy (all of the London School of Economics) graciously gave their time. Jim Monahan and Sebastian Loew (veterans of the struggle for Covent Garden) provided me with valuable material. I hope that Richard Woods, who helped me carry weighty boxes of documentation, made his way strumming his guitar in the Paris Métro.

At Princeton University Press, my appreciation goes to Gail Ullman, who shepherded the manuscript through the editorial process, and Elizabeth Gretz, who, with a deft hand, healed my lame prose. Readers Peter Hall and Oliver Williams pointed up areas where the work needed improvement and gave me the right kind of advice. The illustrations, under the aegis of Wiebe and Squibb, were done superbly, and I want to thank Gina Federico at Wiebe and Squibb and Susan Bishop at the Press for their talents.

This work was made possible by leave time and a Faculty Support Award afforded me by the State University of New York at Purchase, by travel opportunities provided by the Fulbright Scholar Program, and, by the courtesy of the Chancellerie des Universités de Paris.

Closer to home, I want to thank my son Adam for his artistic talents and for taking the photographs of Manhattan. My son Jonathan, always a great companion, rendered a different service. On wintry mornings he would turn up the heat in my study by adjusting a kerosene burner. One day he overdid the job, which shrouded my research in a thick blanket of smoke. Here is a lad, I say, who set his father's thoughts ablaze. Jonathan more than made up for this with his ability at the computer. I thank him for taking me by the hand and showing me the wonders of that technology. Most of all, I am grateful to my wife Susan, whose care and love makes my work meaningful. It is with understatement that I dedicate this book to her.

As is the custom I absolve all those I have mentioned from any blame. I would not want any of them to be thought guilty by association.

Mount Kisco, New York
February 1987

Illustration Credits

Sources of previously published figures are acknowledged in the captions. In addition, acknowledgment is made to the following individuals, agencies, and enterprises who have permitted the reproduction of materials in this book: Atelier Parisien d'Urbanisme, Ville de Paris; Claude Abron, Photographer; Ena Bodin, Photographer, and the Oxford Press Limited; Clive Boursnell, Photographer; Jeremiah Bragstand, Photographer; Etablissement Public pour l'Aménagement de la Région de la Défense; Journal of the American Planning Association; London Docklands Development Corporation; the London Residuary Body, Successors to the Greater London Council; the late Tucker Ashworth, of the New York City Planning Department; New York City Public Development Corporation; Foster Beach III and Robert Brakman, of the New York State Department of Transportation; Harry Oster, of the New York State Urban Development Corporation; Park Tower Realty; Skyview Survey, Inc., Westbury, N.Y., 150,000 air views of the New York Metropolitan Area and the Eastern Seaboard; Jeannine Serco of the Société Anonyme d'Economie Mixte d'Aménagement de Rénovation et de Restauration du Secteur des Halles; and Bill Wilkinson, Architectural Illustrator, whose photo appeared in *New York Magazine* on April 2, 1984, p. 30. The epigraph in Chapter 4 from "God Bless the Child" (Billie Holiday, Arthur Herzog, Jr.) is used by permission (© 1941—Edward B. Marks Music Company; copyright renewed; all rights reserved).

POST–INDUSTRIAL CITIES

Introduction: A Tale of Three Cities

No conceptual scheme ever exhausts social reality. Each conceptual scheme is a prism which selects some features, rather than others, in order to highlight historical change or, more specifically, to answer certain questions.—Daniel Bell, *The Coming of Post-Industrial Society*

Approach: Politics, Planning, and Post-Industrialism

THERE ARE many ways to write about a great city. It can be treated from the vantage point of its territorial and geographic features; it can be viewed as the outcome of economic relationships and as a container for wealth; it can be studied as an object of planning or as a repository of architecture; or it can be analyzed as a legal entity that administers services. There are, of course, still other perspectives—the city's social and class dynamics, its style of life and culture, its power configurations, and its evolution through history.[1]

Any single volume that embraces one or a combination of these perspectives may be faulted for omitting the others or for taking too narrow a gauge. Writing about a single dimension makes the great city appear all too limited, yet a singular dimension can discipline the analysis and allow the subject to be treated with depth. By the same token, only the inclusion of multiple dimensions can do justice to the variety and rich tapestry of the great city, yet too broad a scope may lead to a superficial result.[2] We face a dilemma either way. In one case, we may have an in-depth probe of a single aspect, but we may miss a sense of the whole—a sense of what the city is really like. In the other case, we may be able to read about the whole city, but the understanding is much too fleeting and the treatment too vague—here we miss as much as we gain.

This book takes a middle course. As its subtitle suggests, it is about politics and planning in New York, Paris, and London. The subject matter is organized by focusing on two dimensions—politics and planning. The fundamental questions asked are: (1) What changes have taken place in the demographic and industrial order of New York, Paris, and London over the past twenty years? (2) How have planning and development responded to demographic and industrial change? (3) What kinds of political struggles occur behind planning choices? (4) What do these events tell us about the politics of the built environment? (5) How can we understand the relation between politics and planning, once it is cast in comparative perspective?

The setting for this examination of politics and planning is the post-industrial transformation through which New York, Paris, and London have passed since the 1960s. By this I mean the type and level of production that predominate in each city. In his exemplary study of industrial transformation, Daniel Bell describes three levels of development: (1) a pre-industrial type, which is primarily *extractive* and rests on agriculture, fishing, timber, and mining; (2) an industrial type, which is concerned with the *fabrication* (manufacture) and conversion of raw materials into finished products; and (3) a post-industrial type, whose main activity is the *processing* of information and knowledge.[3]

We might add that each of these societies is driven by different needs and works on different principles. Pre-industrial society was locked in a struggle with nature and relied on human or animal muscle. Industrial society mastered natural threats through the power of the machine. Its overriding objective was to harness machinery and human power. For the industrial era, the challenge was not mere survival but how productive that survival could be made. Post-industrialism transcends the world of production to deal with its effects. It is organized around the dissemination of information for purposes of social control, business efficiency, demand management, and scientific innovation. Its challenge is not just well-being, but the exploration of new modalities (telecommunications, genetic engineering) in order to enlarge that well-being.

Still another way to understand development is to view it through changes in employment as they occur from one level to another. Industrialism relied on blue-collar workers to turn the wheels of production; post-industrialism uses a white-collar force to deal with people and manipulate information. Industrialism counted on manual labor and the artisan trades to build things; post-industrialism relies on finance and marketing to see that new things are built and to promote their trade. As a goods-producing economy, the indices of industrialism can be found in the number of lathe operators, seamstresses, and assemblers. As a processing or service-oriented economy, the indices of post-industrialism are best located among those who sustain business (managers, brokers, researchers), among those who render personal services (health professionals), or among those who engage in regulation (legal workers, public administrators).

Moreover, post-industrialism means not only a change from pushing goods on the assembly line to pushing paper at the desk but also an orientation toward human services.[4] To use Bell's words, post-industrialism involves "a game between persons."[5] This can be seen in the burgeoning business between those who perform and those who watch (theaters, concerts, athletic events) or between service providers and service recipients (schools, sports clubs, hospitals).

Finally, post-industrialism should be seen as a transformation of the built environment. This can entail social upheaval: factories are dismantled, wharves and warehouses are abandoned, and working-class neighborhoods disappear. Sometimes there is replacement of one physical form by another—the growth of office towers and luxury high rises or the refurbishing of old waterfronts. Cafés and boutiques arise to feed and clothe the new classes. At other times the transformation is truncated and nothing but an empty shell is left behind. Housing falls into disuse, stores are boarded up, and streets are desolate.[6]

Boiled down, post-industrialism is a broad phenomenon that can be gauged along multiple dimensions. It encompasses a change in *what* we do to earn a livelihood (processing or services rather than manufacture) as well as *how* we do it (brains rather than hands) and *where* we do it (offices rather than factories). As will be seen in later chapters, these components can be translated into indices on employment or social classes and into assessments of the built environment (office towers, cultural centers).

It is at the juncture of planning, politics, and post-industrial transformation that we make our exploration. To begin, a consideration of what the literature says about the subject and how this book's themes relate to the ongoing debate may be useful.

Contextual Themes: Politics and the Many Faces of Capitalism

There is no dearth of investigations and viewpoints concerning the relationship between political economy and the built environment. In all probability there are as many views on the subject as there are investigators.[7] Most of the works published in the United States draw their conclusions from American cities, yet they tend to generalize about capitalist political economies as if they were of a single order.[8]

One kind of study draws its inspiration from a faith in unregulated capitalism.[9] It defends the free-market system as the best way to allocate resources and decide on matters of public choice. According to one free-market advocate, the principal forces operating on local political economies are scarcity, individualism, self-interest, and individual rationality.[10] By its sheer cumbersomeness, the state is incapable of dealing with these complexities, which means that we need to "place stringent limits on (state) policy."[11]

5

For free-market scholars, individuals making private choices, rather than states, make the best decisions about the urban environment. The way to do this is by multiplying and fragmenting local government. Multiple governments allow individuals to choose among competing and diverse public services. Fragmentation is good because it hampers government's ability to interfere with an open marketplace.

In his book *The Public Economy of Metropolitan Areas*, Robert Bish points up the virtues of multiple governments that foster individual choice. He writes:

> The variety of local political units in the United States political economy provides a wide range of alternatives for collective action to solve problems and to provide goods and services. . . . Because this rich environment offers every chance to examine the manner in which individuals seek solutions to collective problems, it deserves considerably more study than it has generally been accorded.[12]

Contraposed to this view is the neo-Marxist interpretation of the urban political economy. Neo-Marxist scholars also take a dim view of the state, but for very different reasons. For Marxists the state is at fault not because it is inept, but because it is all too adept at protecting and preserving capitalism. Without the state, capitalism would falter, and without capitalism, the bourgeoisie could not perpetuate itself. The state ensures this system's survival by continuing the flow of private profit (capitalist accumulation) and by managing mass discontent (through legitimation).

The state saves the free market from its own demise. Note, for example, these propositions from a leading neo-Marxist anthology on the urban political economy:

> . . . government is shaped in order to serve the functions of rationalizing capital accumulation and managing dissent.

> The function of the professional urban planner today is to plan the restructuring of urban space in such a way that the process of capital accumulation is rationalized; that is, so that the urban environment is an arena in which profits can be maximized.[13]

Another neo-Marxist account views capitalism as creating massive imbalances, much of it abetted by the state:

> Instead of moving towards equilibrium, market forces produce cumulative advantages and disadvantages. Profit depends upon (class) segmentation within housing and commercial property markets, . . .

. . . "improvement" in one city or neighborhood leads to "decline" in another, since the process depends upon the spatial displacement of lower-income and minority groups.[14]

The underlying themes of this book differ from those of both the free market and the neo-Marxist schools. First, we find that there are many different kinds of capitalism that treat urban populations and their environments differently. Capitalism has many faces that are sharply distinguishable under different political, social, and cultural conditions.

Second, the state is neither incapable of efficient planning nor necessarily a handmaiden for capitalism. Contrary to free-market expectations, the state can work effectively to shape individual (and collective) behavior in accomplishing public ends. In some instances it accomplishes this with a combination of market incentives and persuasion. In other instances, by monopolizing economic resources it leaves the major actors with little choice. Nor is the neo-Marxist view of the state as a mere technician for capitalist accumulation an adequate explanation for a very diverse set of processes.[15] There are multiple cases where capitalist accumulation has not been fostered and where territories of immense value have been used for relatively nonprofitable ventures.

Stemming from these observations, the third theme of this book is that the state often possesses a definable will of its own. Politicians and technocrats who represent the state do pursue an autonomous path. That path is not always free from the winds of capitalism, but it has been insulated against its most forceful gusts. The upshot is that politicians and technocrats, rather than capitalists, have a strong hand on the tiller of urban development. As representatives of the state, these public actors exercise great discretion in what is built, how it is built, and who are the likely beneficiaries.

Fourth, in saying that public actors can pursue an autonomous path and exercise great discretion, I mean that they establish public priorities and enlist resources to realize their objectives. This does not mean that public actors can ignore social pressures. Power is reciprocal, and public actors receive as well as exert it. Sometimes public actors have exerted power without much regard for social pressure. More often, there has been a pulling and tugging between public actors who want one thing and interest groups that want another. At other times, public actors have persuaded, coopted, neutralized, or bypassed the opposition. Occasionally public actors have lost to coalitions of interest groups.[16] When the tallies are in, however, public actors stand as the

7

most compelling single force in controlling and directing the flow of capital.

Fifth, in each of the three cities there are differences in the degree to which capital flow is controlled and the manner in which it is directed. Yet despite these differences, New York, Paris, and London are joined by the commonality of state-influenced or -managed economies. Decisions are initiated by politicians and technocrats who make the state their career. Politicians and technocrats make decisions with an eye toward maximizing different kinds of public benefits.

Given the experience of three cities, neither the free-market nor the neo-Marxist denial that public actors can pursue long-term state interests is warranted. Free-market theorists argue that it is not possible to identify a state or a public interest.[17] Neo-Marxists have an easier time recognizing the short-term supremacy of state interests, but explain it as an effort to achieve the long-term survival of capitalism. Some neo-Marxists see public actors as "state managers," who use public policy to save capitalism from the excesses of individual capitalists.[18]

Sixth, under capitalism the state's response to the interests of different classes has been variable. The major reasons for this relate to the previous point that (a) the state pursues its own interests, which are different from those of a single social class, and that (b) under conditions of post-industrialism it may not be easy to find that the interests of one social class are antagonistic to the interests of another. For example, the fall of the old industrial bourgeoisie in New York and London also had dire consequences for blue-collar workers. In contrast, the rise of a post-industrial bourgeoisie has meant jobs for individuals across the social spectrum. Admittedly, the pains of dislocation and the pleasures of prosperity do not embrace all classes equally. The consequences may be disproportionate, but this negates neither the fact nor the significance of interclass linkage.[19]

Seventh, although politics involves conflict, it is not necessarily a zero-sum game. It can be an add-sum game or even a zero-zero game. Applying this to tangibles, I find no necessary validity in the neo-Marxist claim that "improvement in one city or neighborhood leads to decline in another." Indeed, the post-industrial boom of Manhattan has led to add-sum results in other areas of New York. Without that prosperity, much more of New York would be awash in unemployment and disinvestment. London is in a different situation. To some extent it has been caught in a zero-zero game in which upper, middle, and lower classes have been economically hurt.

Eighth, in all three cities investor-developers have tried to push residents out of valuable terrain. When it comes to capitalist motives, the neo-Marxists are correct. Private developers do behave as if "profit depends upon class segmentation." But the state often steps in to safeguard the interests of residents and curtail private profit. This is particularly true in two post–industrial cities, where a political-technocratic elite either preserved the existing community (London) or shaped the built environment for a larger public (Paris). In New York governing elites have been less willing to curtail private profit. But they have exacted a steep price from investor-developers, and those revenues are used for public facilities.

Apart from this contextual response, there are additional themes underlying *Post-Industrial Cities*. As a ninth point, I claim that the urban political system is crucial in determining both how economic resources are applied and how the built environment is shaped. To be sure, national politics and economics condition the actions of all localities. Cities are not sovereign, and, as other writers have pointed out, urban policies are subject to variable external pressures.[20] But it must be recognized, too, that all political systems, including nation-states, face external pressures (for example, international competition over trade, capital investment, or weapons superiority). As political systems which make certain policy choices, cities are no different. In some ways New York, Paris, and London represent a particular class of city, which transcends the limitations faced by smaller cities. As I elaborate later, this status enlarges their political scope. National, state, or regional actors participate in many of their policy decisions and often lend them additional autonomy.

One way to interpret this issue is to envision national conditions as setting up the pieces on the urban chessboard, so that one player may be subject to more external pressure than another. One player may be better off than another. But the players have latitude. They can tap great amounts of wealth, they can control some of the most valuable land in the world, and most important, they can change things through political discretion. This discretion has been used to choose between giant office towers and community preservation, between suburbs and green space, and between additional jobs and a more humane environment.

Tenth, urban political systems can be understood in terms of how they combine power. The major actors within each system are politicians, technocrats, and interest groups. These actors are put together in different ways to form different combinations of power. Some of the factors involved in a combination of power are the timing that determines when interest groups enter the political process, the discretion enjoyed by technocrats in making decisions, and ultimately, the

9

influence wielded by politicians, technocrats, and interest groups on each other.

Eleventh, when analyzed from the planning perspective, politicians, technocrats, and interest groups function as fairly homogeneous clusters of political forces. Each cluster behaves in its own particular way, setting priorities and pursuing them for its own advantage. Top politicians seek to put the best face on a project and win broad approval. Technocrats opt for intelligibility and try to integrate development into a larger rationale. Most interest groups want to disaggregate larger projects and reduce them to immediate concerns. Only London, of the three cities studied here, showed significant diversity within the internal ranks of its politicians, technocrats, and interest groups. This diversity was due to the salient role of political parties in providing cues for the response to post-industrialism and how to plan for it.

Twelfth, in New York and Paris political parties played an insignificant role on land-use decisions, and they played only a minor role on the broader issue of post-industrialism. In both of these cities, personal leadership, individual contacts, and the authority of official position were far more important than partisan affiliations. In New York party labels counted for little, as politicians from the city and state promoted radical post-industrial growth, largely for its economic benefits. In Paris, partisan debate meant one thing and governance another. As Gaullists and Socialists attacked each other in public, they privately collaborated to plan the post-industrial transformation of the city, largely to spearhead their national ambitions. London stands as the exception. There, political parties set the ideological tone for debate and staked out positions for most actors. Conservatives pushed for aggressive post-industrial growth and sought to limit planning. Labourites took the opposite path by trying to limit post-industrialism through aggressive planning. The Alliance Party has tried to strike a balance between the two major parties and draws voters from each side.

The thirteenth and final theme below relates to the costs and benefits of post-industrialism. There is no question that public actors either have managed to place substantial costs onto private investors (New York) or have been able to generate benefits for broad strata of the population (Paris and London). When we focus more closely on a particular stratum, the issue is complex. Costs and benefits are mixed and the results are not always easy to untangle. Though wealthy classes are induced to absorb the costs of post-industrial change, they do so with the expectation of reaping profits. Conversely, though large numbers of the population enjoy the benefits of post-industrial conversion, they are paying its costs in higher prices and impacted environments. Not surprisingly, the very weakest, unorganized portion of the citizenry gains nothing. The long-term unemployed and local transients have not been able to take advantage of post-industrial jobs. Only sometimes have they gotten better housing. Although post-industrial change deals harshly with these people, neither can it be said that the status quo treats them well.

Above all, post-industrialism ought not be evaluated by a sole score-card. It must be seen as a socially dynamic and interactive process. Post-industrialism fosters new industry, creates new classes, and furnishes new opportunities for those ready to enter a new economic order. As much as people act upon it, it acts upon people. Thus, the experience of post-industrialism owes as much to new classes and future generations as it does to those presently shaping its course.

Typologies: Elitism, Pluralism, and Corporatism

In the grand scheme of things, the transformation from industrial to post-industrial city may very well be due to technological advancement and economic development. Once the process is under way, however, the city assumes a certain autonomy—no longer playing a passive role but deciding on the composition, extent, and limits of post-industrialism.[21] In the nitty-gritty of decision making, politicians, technocrats, and interest groups are decisive. To examine this, conceptual guideposts, as "ideal types" or pure constructs, are used.[22] Not all aspects of a complex situation will fit into these types. The real world is a muddle—a skein of events and contradictions that is difficult to unravel, much less to conform perfectly to scientific generalizations. Nonetheless, ideal types can help focus on the gravamen of power relations. Once we have settled on a typology for each city, we use it to probe further into how these relations work.

Three principal theories of power distribution best serve these objectives and can accurately be distilled into distinct typologies. These are elitism, pluralism, and corporatism. Each possesses its own intellectual tradition and criteria for evaluating social conditions.[23]

Elitist theory bases its claim on the assertion that there are very distinct differences between the rulers and the ruled. Society, it contends, is divided into sharp stratifications of social class and power. Those at the uppermost reaches of society have economic, social, and political interests in common. This group constitutes an elitist class and is able to exercise a disproportionate amount of influence on governmental actions. Elites, rather than popular democratic will, govern society. These elites are defined by their wealth, education, economic position, and social status.[24]

Elites are clearly distinct from the rest of society, though they may sometimes act in concert with other strata. Those elites who establish relationships with other classes are considered to be far sighted. Still, the theory stresses that elites will ultimately retain consciousness of their own needs and class interests. In doing so, elites constitute a relatively cohesive class. Subgroups of the elite interlock with one another in order to protect their long-term interests. The quality of interlocking membership within an elite class is an important component of the theory. For without the unity of action that sets the elite apart from other social strata, the theory may waffle and meld with competing explanations.[25] Thus cohesive class membership and coherent interests are necessary conditions that enable elites to maintain one or multiple "pyramids of power."[26] Although the elite class is not invariably monolithic, it is usually cognizant of its vital interests. Both the existence of an identifiable class and its actions on its own behalf to bring about a superior-subordinate relationship are central features of elite theory.

The elitist relationship to the state is variable. Members of the elite may sometimes serve directly in high governmental posts—noblesse oblige is by definition a form of elitist behavior. Nonetheless, the formal government is viewed as a distant entity that is apart from the elitist class. Government is seen as a mechanical object that can be influenced, enticed, threatened, manipulated, or forced to conform to the elite's vital needs. The theory also holds that elites have a great deal of power over the actions of government and that they will use this power when vital, long-term interests are at stake. One reason elites are supposed to prevail over the will of the majority is because they have unique access to the levers of power. Unique access means that the elite can use special, exclusive, or covert methods to influence decisions.[27]

The result of this conception is a state whose actions are dominated by a single class. Policy making is not an objective governmental task, but a refraction of class relationships. Though some elite theorists might be chary of using the phrase, many would uphold the Marxist maxim that "the executive of the modern state is but a committee for managing the common affairs of the whole bourgeoisie."[28]

On a completely opposite trajectory is the pluralist conception of the political system. For pluralists, the emphasis is on "the group" rather than on class structure. Society is conceived as a multitude of diverse, competing, autonomous, and nonhierarchical groups.[29] These groups are spread across the social spectrum. Dominance by any single group is rare. More often, society is kept in rough equilibrium by the mutual contention of groups.[30] Labor counteracts business, tenants offset landlords, consumers pressure retailers, and when matters are seriously amiss, a sense of fair play moderates conflict. Moreover, membership in one group frequently overlaps with membership in another.[31] Overlapping membership promotes contact with a broad variety of citizens; it makes individuals more tolerant of one another and encourages moderation. Groups, then, are neither monopolistic nor always cohesive. The pluralist vision consists of floating bunches of individuals, counteracting one another and fed by a fluid social structure.

The idea of access is an important one for pluralists. Pluralists recognize that not all groups have equal influence or power. Resources are distributed unevenly and so too is skill, time, knowledge, and good fortune. Given the imperfections of society, there are likely to be flaws in the political system, and this is why access to government is not always equal. Some groups do, in fact, wield more influence than others. Unlike the elitists, however, pluralists maintain that the political field is competitive. The reasons for this lie in the very nature of dispersed inequalities between groups. Although some groups may be wealthy, others may be resourceful and have more motivations; when some groups have the status of name, others have time and the diligence to work things through. For the pluralist the system may pose difficulties, but channels of access are available to any group that is persistent, legitimate, and tries hard enough.[32]

One reason the political system is relatively open is that it is characterized by a multiplicity of decision points to which most alert and motivated citizens can appeal. These points include the legislature, the courts, the bureaucracy, and political parties. In pluralist parlance the system is "permeable," meaning different groups can gain entry at one point or another. Government is sometimes likened to a sponge whose many pores accommodate the competitive entreaties of groups.

Contrary to the notion that the state is a tool of bourgeois interests, pluralists see the state as a popular institution that registers a diversity of demands. The pluralist state is largely impartial. On this score the logic is inexorable. Recall that pluralism postulates a society of mobility, freedom, and competitive interaction. The state stands apart from these processes and intervenes only to maintain social equilibrium. In effect the state is like an umpire who keeps some distance from the players.[33] Impartial administration forged under objective rules of law

13

is the modus operandi of the state—otherwise the game could not go on.*

Pluralists see policy as the outcome of compromise between groups. The state frequently "brokers" between contending groups, and though every group may not get what it wants, most get something. Thus the "best solution" is the negotiated solution. Policies are like barometers that show the highs and lows of group influence.

Corporatism is an entirely different way of looking at power relations.[34] From elitism, it accepts the notion of a social order divided by class but rejects its assertion that a single class can dominate that order. From pluralism, it takes the idea that citizens can express themselves through groups but denies that those groups should randomly interact.

Instead of a pyramidal class structure or a floating congeries of groups, corporatists envision society as composed of vertically segmented organizations. Each organization acts as an authority for a distinct socioeconomic sector. Elitist domination and pluralist competition are replaced by organizational collaboration, guided by a mutual agreement to cooperate. The importance of established organizations entails restraint and recognition by leaders that their more exuberant followers ought to be tamed. Limits are placed on the quantity of organizations. Responsibility and accountability hedge the quality of organizational behavior.

Political linkages between state and organization are made possible by a series of trades. For its part, the state furnishes the organization with special political status. Licensing, franchises, recognition, subsidies, and privileged access are some of the means through which an organization gains this status. In return, the organization must concede something to the state. Curtailing member demands, leadership screening, limits on permissible action, and tithes paid to the public purse are ways in which an organization can reciprocate.[35] In effect

---

* More and more, scholars see the American state as captured by interest groups and parceling away its sovereignty. Yet most observers continue to define this as pluralism. I too see this as a very real occurrence, but claim that this shift entails a qualitative change in pluralism. That is, when American political scientists describe interest groups as robbing the state of its sovereignty, they may be describing not pluralism but a version of a corporatist state. This may not be corporatism full blown, but the American state may have begun to adopt its elements. More than thirty years ago David Truman described fragments of this in *The Governmental Process* (New York: Alfred Knopf, 1951). Theodore Lowi's contemporary account, *The End of Liberalism* (New York: W. W. Norton, 1969), shows the dominance of select interest groups and the development of institutionalized bargaining. Lowi too resists the possibility that this can be seen as truncated corporatism and, instead, calls the new politics "interest group liberalism."

each party gives up something it ordinarily possesses in exchange for greater gains elsewhere. Organizations become incorporated into the formal decision-making apparatus, while the state delegates administrative authority. We can think of corporatism as an arrangement of limited monopolies that are given to private organizations on a discriminatory basis, in exchange for the cooperation and support they give to the state.

For the corporatist looking at others systems, a political order that excluded nonelite groups would not necessarily be elitist, nor would a system that included nonelite groups necessarily be pluralist. Rather, much would depend on what kinds of groups are brought into the decision-making process (are they established organizations that represent differing shades of the social spectrum?), what the nature of group access is (is it privileged?), and how institutionalized the bargaining arrangements are (do select organizations meet regularly with decision makers?).*

Under corporatism the state is partial, but its partiality spans the social structure. The state does not so much "oppress" or "broker" as it does "orchestrate" and "direct." This must be the case, because the state is the sole institution that works between the vertical divisions of society. It is the sole institution that can link the intricacies of means to the greater design of ends.†

---

* Thus, in New York City after the fiscal crisis, the Municipal Union Financial Leaders group (MUFL) was formed. MUFL consisted of the heads of New York's labor unions and leading bankers, who worked in collaboration with leading politicians to influence public policy. Since many of MUFL's members were drawn from labor, it could hardly be considered to conform to the elitist model. Nor could MUFL be considered to conform to a pluralist schema, because it possessed privileged access to government and its bargaining arrangements with politicians occurred regularly and exclusively. MUFL is an example of an organization whose activities wove a fine thread between elitist and pluralist conceptions. In theory and in fact, MUFL was a corporatist solution to a very vexing set of interclass problems. For a description of MUFL, consult Martin Shefter, *Political Crisis/Fiscal Crisis* (New York: Basic Books, 1985), pp. 163-66.

† On this account there are differences among corporatist theorists. Some scholars see the sovereignty of the corporatist state evaporating into different organizations that take over different public functions. Others see corporatism as a more directive institution, where the state emerges to orchestrate and control. I have chosen the latter (strong state) definition, for several reasons. First, a corporatism that features a strong state better enables us to draw a contrast between corporatism and pluralism. Second, there are strong precedents for this kind of corporatism in modern history. Among these are Salazar's Portugal and Franco's Spain. Third, although corporatism should be distinguished from fascism (which featured nationalist, one-party, undemocratic politics), Mussolini's Italy did use corporatist elements under the guidance of strong political leadership. For a discussion that analyzes corporatism in its various forms, see *Comparative Political Studies* 10, no. 1 (April, 1977), edited by Philippe Schmitter.

Policy outcomes are the results of coordinated state planning. Policy is neither a passive prize of interest groups nor made on behalf of a dominant class. Rather, it is an expression of public objectives, planned and executed by servants of the state.[36]

To further sharpen the elitist-pluralist-corporatist trichotomy, the distinction hinges on how each system manages the interaction between society and the state. Does the state respond to a cohesive class (elitism) or to multiple, free-floating groups (pluralism)? Or does the state orchestrate and direct a limited number of select organizations (corporatism)?

To restate the issue differently, elitism, pluralism, and corporatism posit different theories of who or what moves the wheels of state power. For elitists power is surreptitious. When it can be found, power is usually located in economic relations, where the wheels turn by the energy of wealth. Writing on contemporary Paris, the French scholar Jean Lojkine advances the argument that

> Urban politics is a reflection of class relations. It condenses and sharpens contradictions which are derived from the segregation and occupation of space by the dominant class.[37]

Jack Newfield and Paul Dubrul offer a more journalistic explanation of how elitist power works in New York:[38]

> Ultimate power over public policy in New York is invisible and unelected. It is exercised by a loose confederation of bankers, bond underwriters, members of public authorities, the big insurance companies, political fund raisers, . . .[39]

For pluralists, power is hardly exercised by the state or by practically anyone else. The wheels move by *arcana imperii*. The key words are not so much power but "negotiation" and "mutual accommodation." Note Wallace Sayre and Herbert Kaufman's well-known characterization of New York:

> In a broad sense it may be said that nobody 'runs' New York. It runs by a process of negotiation and mutual accommodation, with all the virtues and weaknesses such a process entails.[40]

The pluralist state is a facilitative state. Its theories are essentially explanations about the processes of power rather than about its substance. Political leaders merely maintain a machinery that seems to work by itself. Again we turn to Sayre and Kaufman, who in describing the mayors of New York say that most mayors find themselves compelled by the nature of the office, their political posture and their personalities to be mediators more often than arbitrators, and to be arbitrators more than innovators.[41]

Corporatism is the only explanation that really bites the bullet of state power. It alone offers a theory about public authority, that is, about how the state uses power to realize public ends. J. T. Winkler captures this when he comments that

directive state intervention is the principal defining characteristic of corporatism.[42]

Corporatist leadership seeks control by taking private organizations under its wing. In doing this, politicians and technocrats expand the scope of their authority. Writing about corporatism in Oxford, James Simmie remarks:

The trend has therefore been towards the development of formal state control of land uses, [and] the incorporation of major landowning, industrial and commercial organizations into this decision making process, . . .[43]

In sum, elitism, pluralism, and corporatism are theories of power relations that can be compared to the real world of decision making. To facilitate application, a typology demarcates how each theory compares on (1) social perspective, (2) access to decision making, (3) theory of the state, (4) policy making, and (5) policy outcomes (see Table 1.1).

Typologies Applied to New York, Paris, and London

The politics of post-industrialism transformation is best explained by corporatism in Paris and London and by a corporatist-pluralist hybrid in New York. The kernel of what we call "the corporatist impulsion" is the relative autonomy of public actors (politicians and technocrats) and the role played by them. In all three cities public actors set priorities, manage them through implementation, and shape the course of post-industrialism. In most cases, private-interest groups are recruited by public actors and put under governmental aegis. When there are differences between interest groups, public actors arbitrate; when there are deadlocks, they intercede.

Yet except for this similarity, corporatism manifests itself in different ways and actors behave differently. The genus of corporatism yields different species in Paris and London, and its cross-fertilization with pluralism in New York produces still another result.

One difference between Paris and London stems from the way in

Table 1.1.   A Typology of Elitism, Pluralism, and Corporatism

Summary Concept	Elitism
Social Perspective	The class is key. Society is stratified according to class and in pyramidal order. Class conflict is pervasive. A cohesive and interlocking elite is socially ascendent.
Theory of the State	Rule by a dominant social class that uses manipulation, unique access, wealth, or power to retain its position. The state is largely an instrument of class rule.
Access to Government	A cohesive upper class enjoys unique access. This social elite or its representatives work with government officials on vital issues. The system is biased against weaker classes.
Policy Making	A cohesive upper class shapes the broad contours of crucial policies. Politicians and technocrats carry out those policies. Public policy is designed to protect and maintain economic dominance.
Policy Outcomes	Retain and preserve vital elite interests. Those interests can sometimes mesh with the interests of other classes, but elite interests remain paramount. Accordingly, policy results reflect disproportionate advantages that accrue to the elite class. Other classes may gain residual benefits.

which the political-technocratic elite interacts with interest groups. In Paris, politicians and technocrats at both local and national levels coalesce at an early state of decision making. Not only do they face interest groups as a cohesive block, but they monopolize political discretion. In effect, the Parisian political-technocratic elite absorbs private organizations into a publicly dominated power bloc. Private organizations are recruited into this bloc only after the major decisions have been taken. Their function is not to decide fundamentals but to carry out objectives. We call this *mobilizing corporatism.*

In London, public actors are segmented in several important ways.

Pluralism	Corporatism
The group is key. Cross-cutting and over-lapping groups mitigate cleavage. Social relations are free flowing and relatively mobile.	The organization is key. Class distinctions are modified by vertical organizations that cooperate with one another. Class tensions are eased by functional representation of socioeconomic sectors.
Competition in an imperfect society. Political leaders are "brokers" trying to maintain social equilibrium. The state is impartial.	An ordered framework of organizations works in concert to bring about specified objectives. Political leaders orchestrate and direct these organizations. The state is partial when it chooses select organizations. These organizations are located along different points of the social spectrum.
Pluralist groups are openly competitive. There are multiple points of access. Any group with stamina, sense, and skill can be heard and often listened to.	A variety of corporatist organizations have privileged access. Organizations have become incorporated into the decision-making process. They are accorded limited public monopolies.
Policy is not so much made as emerges. Policy comes into being as a consequence of group rivalry. Like barometers, politicians and technocrats register the pressures of group interaction.	Policy is initiated, orchestrated, and directed by government. Politicians and technocrats work with organizations to establish policy. The state has its definable interest, and it collaborates with organizations to realize its goals.
The best solution is the negotiated solution. Compromise between groups is a valuable policy end because it is difficult to define the public interest.	Coordinated planning and scientific policy objectives can be established. The state posits its own objectives, and these can be consonant with the objectives of incorporated or privileged organizations.

To begin with, the three-tiered government that ran London between 1965 and 1986 drew sharp theoretical distinctions among functions that belonged to the localities (boroughs), those that belonged to the metropolitan authority (the Greater London Council or GLC), and those that belonged to the central government. In practice, this caused rifts in the decision-making process. Each tier saw the issues differently, and sometimes coalitions of government would form alliances against other coalitions of government.

Public actors compound this segmentation by differentiating between tasks that belong to politicians (matters of value) and tasks that belong to technocrats (matters of technical expertise). Londoners take these distinctions seriously, and there is a tendency for politicians and technocrats to act separately—at least in the initial stages of a decision.

One result of the London system is that although interest groups are incorporated into a public apparatus, the apparati may be different. The incorporating governments may be at odds and the political-technocratic elites may be dissimilar. London's corporatism is something like monopolistic competition. In order to fight city hall one must join its organization. But there is more than one city hall. Governmental segmentation creates slack and augments organizational choice. We call this *liberal corporatism*.[44]

In theory, New York politics is fragmented and its governing structures are pulverized into multiple fiefdoms. In practice, the system has more cohesion than is generally recognized. This cohesion stems largely from the pulling power of two politicians who have risen to top positions since the late 1970s: Governor Mario Cuomo and Mayor Edward Koch.[45] Together Koch and Cuomo have cemented ad hoc coalitions to initiate development. Their coalitions combine public and private actors, which supply the city with a potent admixture of planning and money.

What then gives New York its qualities as a *corporatist-pluralist hybrid*? On the one hand, the city's corporatism is rooted in strong public actors who lead coalitions of recognized interest groups. Granted, New York's political-technocratic elite does not enjoy the same freedom as its Parisian counterparts. Nonetheless, public actors have leeway—they can choose between diverse interests and they can manipulate external pressures. Private organizations are given privileged access in exchange for concessions they provide to the public.

On the other hand, New York also contains a strain of pluralism. Though not always on the surface of land-use decisions, pluralism is embedded in the social and political structure. Given enough time, it will spring into action.

At the crux of this pluralism are the multiple, free-flowing and unrecognized interests that have never become part of the system. As well as accommodating corporatist organizations, New York also responds to nonestablished groups that are open and that influence decisions by dint of competitive ability. They have no unique or privileged access to government. Pluralist groups have few material resources and must depend on the resourcefulness of their leaders. This, however, makes them no less formidable. In Paris and London, pluralist groups surface and soon wither. In New York they thrive.

Although there are parallels between the post-industrial experience of cities in Europe and North America, there are also dissimilarities. In general politicians and technocrats on both sides of the Atlantic lead organized interests. Organizations are incorporated into the political machinery—voluntarily or because they have little choice or by governmental cooptation. In New York, this corporatist fiber is entwined with pluralism. Interest groups remain stubbornly outside the system to challenge it. What is more, they sometimes succeed.[46]

These differences may be summarized in an illustration built around the unity of political-technocratic elites and the type of access accorded to interest groups (see Table 1.2).

In Paris, mobilizing corporatism comes from cohesive public actors, who harness private organizations. Decision making resembles a chain of hierarchical collaboration led by the public sector. In London, liberal corporatism is the outcome of divisible public actors, incorporating separate private organizations. Decision making flows through channels of communication between one set of public-private actors and another. New York's corporatist-pluralist hybrid mixes cohesive public actors and privileged organizations with openly competitive groups. Decisions depend upon public actors recruiting select organizations and keeping the pluralist opposition at bay.

Note too that New York's pluralism has varied between a divisible politics (type 1 pluralism) and a tighter structure (type 2 pluralism). Type 1 occurred intermittently through the 1950s and 1960s, when land-use decisions were left to a competitive private sector. Politicians played a lesser role and did more reacting to private decisions than initiating of them.[47] Douglas Yates describes this as "street-fighting

Table 1.2. Political-Technocratic Elites and Interest Groups: New York, Paris, and London

| | | Interest-Group Access | |
		Privileged	Open/Competitive
Unity of Political-Technocratic Elite	Indivisible	Mobilizing Corporatism PARIS	Pluralism: Type 2 NEW YORK (1980s)
		corporatist-pluralist hybrid NEW YORK	
	Divisible	Liberal Corporatism LONDON	Pluralism: Type 1 NEW YORK (1950s)

pluralism"—a condition of fragmented government at all levels that produces anarchic demands and policy conflicts.[48]

At least in land-use politics, this sort of pluralism has not been apparent through the 1980s. It may be that with less forceful leadership, type I pluralism will reemerge. New York politics is more fickle than its sister cities abroad. Top politicians are more easily replaced, more vulnerable to scandals, and more easily lose favor with the electorate. For the moment, New York's leaders—Koch and Cuomo—are secure.

Political systems normally generate a leadership that can satisfy social and industrial needs. As will be pointed out later, post-industrialism is no exception, and it has demanded a proactive leadership. That leadership may vary in style and operation, but it must rise to the fore.

Finally, public actors and the combinations of power they manage make a great deal of difference to a city. New York, Paris, and London look, feel, and behave differently. They do different things with their people and their built environments. Green meadows are maintained in one city; another permits "sliver buildings" on the slightest gutter of space. Public housing is treated as essential in one city; in another it is a nuisance. Coincidentally, the centerpieces of each city—New York's Times Square, Paris's Les Halles, and London's Covent Garden—have all been ripe for redevelopment in the last twenty years. Each city has rebuilt, or is rebuilding, those areas in dramatically different ways and with profoundly different financial and social implications. These differences are not the result of monolithic capitalist economy. They are the product of conscious systems of decision making that grow out of indigenous circumstances.

Even the patterns of development surrounding the post-industrial core are consonant with each city's decision-making system. Industrial and social growth are bounded by political parameters. New York's development as an inverted doughnut—rich in Manhattan and depleted at the fringes—is a product of public actors working with separate interests to funnel investment into the urban center. Parisian development is much smoother and extends in continuous bands around the urban center. It is the product of a centralized political-technocratic elite that controls resources in the wider region. For the past twenty-five years, London's development has been anchored in physical conservation, social stasis, and a quest for identity. This was made possible by the countervaillance of three-tier government. Since the Greater London Council's late abolition, three-tier government has been modified and London broken into pieces. Most of those pieces have yet to change, while a few are in a whirlwind of development.

Method: The Comparative Study of Urban Decision Making

This is a comparative study of urban decision making in three cities. The key words here are *comparative, decision making,* and *cities.* In comparing political phenomena the focus is on process and behavior. I am primarily interested in how actors respond to one another when deciding matters of public policy. Many of those actors are public actors, from different sections and levels of government. These actors invariably mix with one another, so that outcomes are derived from a mélange of governmental units. For our purposes it makes little difference whether those actors are drawn from central government or from regional and local authorities. The fact that these are public actors who can be reasonably identified and evaluated is critical to our analysis, and the asymmetry of institutional comparison is not. Put another way, we are mostly concerned with analyzing "functional equivalents" (actors who do the same kinds of things) and not the particular nomenclature of the actors (prime ministers, governors, mayors).[49]

Recognizing that actor overlap exists does not in the least hamper our analysis. To the contrary, this occurrence provides a rich source of data that casts light on why New York, Paris, and London pursue different policy paths. The degree to which actors from different levels of government meld together or take opposing positions is important to decisional outcomes. Institutions also play a fundamental role in shaping the interaction of all actors. Among other things, institutions are opportunity structures. Governmental units in New York are more hospitable to interest-group intercession than they are in Paris, and this tells us a great deal about why interest groups are so effective in New York as well as why technocrats are so powerful in Paris.

In New York, the major governing units concerned with land use are the city, the state, and public authorities. National government plays an intermittent role. In Paris, the national government (the state) is far more consistent in its interaction with the city. Until 1986, London's three-tier system accorded major roles to national government (central government), to a metropolitan-wide authority (Greater London Council or GLC), and to the localities (boroughs). Since the GLC's abolition in April of that year, as will be discussed in Chapters 6 and 7, a *de jure* two-tier system has prevailed, although the third tier refuses to disappear and has played a role through a number of institutions commonly called, "GLCs-in-exile."

Another feature of the comparative approach is that it allows for the relative assessment of political categories. It allows for "contrast

23

models" that can posit standards, thereby illuminating the qualities of a particular system. The conclusion, for example, that Paris is a mobilizing corporatist system, says that it is more tightly corporatist than London and certainly more so than New York. Similarly, when we say that New York is a hybrid, a blend of corporatism and pluralism, we make these observations in relation to what is analyzed elsewhere.

Stated differently, the comparative approach enables us to get a better hold on the meaning of things. It provides a better understanding of the way in which public actors may centralize power or the extent to which the state may control local markets. The more ideas are cast into different contexts, the more dimensions are added to them. To say, for example, that New York's government intervenes in the marketplace means one thing in an American context. But comparing New York's intervention with what Parisians do makes it possible to see how Europeans treat the same idea.

Decisions and the politics emanating from them are the targets of this analysis. A total of nine case studies—three in each city—have been selected. Each case represents a "crucial issue," which is defined as a political struggle involving the shaping of the built environment or the disposition of material resources having a substantial effect on the built environment. Crucial issues are major questions that emphasize a struggle or a significant political effort to get something built, demolished, remade, or preserved. Although crucial issues contain the potential for conflict, they do not always engender it. Political conflict depends on the willingness of an opposition to form and mobilize for or against a political action.

Crucial issues are not trivial, routine, or of parochial concern to a limited number of people. The shaping of the built environment affects all people within a given terrain, whether they like it or not. If classes, groups, or organizations do not act in opposition to a crucial issue, it is not assumed that they are content with the situation or that they are suppressed by hidden biases. We simply observe those actions that are observable. The approach is positivist and assesses those classes, groups, or organizations that did, in fact, respond to a crucial issue. That assessment is then compared with the elitist-pluralist-corporatist typology and the appropriate conclusions are drawn.[50]

This notion of a crucial issue differs from Peter Bachrach and Morton Baratz's conception of a "key issue."[51] Their key issue is one "that involves a genuine challenge to the resources of power or authority of those who currently dominate the process by which policy outputs are determined." As Bachrach and Baratz subsequently explain, a "key issue . . . involves a demand for [an] enduring transformation" by which values are allocated.

Our experience shows that key issues are rare in the politics of post-industrial nations. They are especially rare when it comes to end-of-the-century urban problems. In addition, the selection of such a "genuine challenge" says nothing about the political system during "normal times" or during periods of gradual transformation. These are the times that constitute the stuff of urban politics. Put succinctly, a crucial issue is intended to capture the manner by which a political system copes with nonviolent change.

Finally, in any book of this sort the very meaning of "the city" is at issue. At first blush, this may seem like a simple, even a trivial question. But it is a debatable subject. Does "the city" mean its legal-political bounds? Or is the city a "functional" entity that includes all those individuals who commute to it for work? Is the city a product of technocrat-planners, who have mapped out its boundaries and subsections? Or is the city a combination of all of those things, including urban central areas, legal bounds, regions, and so forth?[52] Because this book stresses the relationship between post-industrialism, planning, and politics, the city is explored in five territorial parameters.[53] These are (1) the municipality, (2) the central business district (CBD), (3) the urban core, (4) the first ring, and (5) the second ring.

The Municipality   This consists of political boundaries defined by legislative or executive enactment. Each of the three cities is referred to by its official name—New York City, La Ville de Paris (or Paris), and Greater London. New York City consists of five counties (Bronx, Kings, Manhattan, Queens, and Richmond).[54] La Ville de Paris is divided into twenty *arrondissements* or small wards. Greater London consists of thirty-two boroughs plus the tiny and ancient City of London (or simply "the City").

The Central Business District (CBD)   Within the political bounds of each city there is a small knot of concentration in commerce and business. Office buildings, retail outlets, and various services (banking, legal, government, transport) dominate the CBD, though it also has a significant amount of multiple-family housing. Millions of workers pour into the district each work day.

In New York the CBD consists of approximately nine square miles lying on the southern half of Manhattan Island. This area concentrates business development in two major clusters: one in Midtown, surrounding the major railway terminal of Grand Central Station, and the other in lower Manhattan, which holds Wall Street and the World Trade Center. In La Ville de Paris, the CBD is within the inner ten of the city's twenty arrondissements. Like New York, the Parisian CBD is roughly nine square miles. In Greater London, the heart of the CBD is the "City of London," where the Bank of England conducts business. Another important borough of the CBD is Westminster, which holds the Houses of Parliament and other governmental institutions.

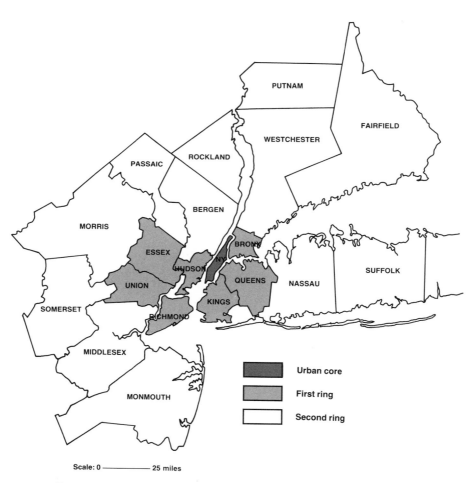

Scale: 0 ——————— 25 miles

Fig. 1.1. The New York Standard Consolidated Area: Urban Core, First and Second Rings

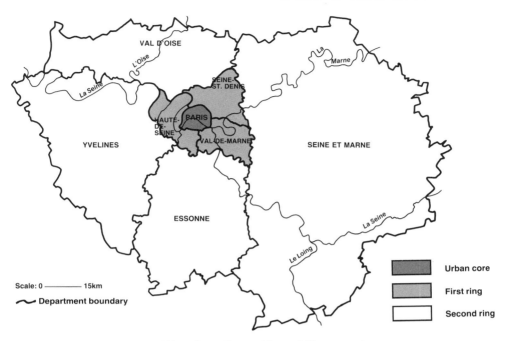

Fig. 1.2. The Ile-de-France: Urban Core, First and Second Rings

The Urban Core This consists of the most densely settled part of the metropolis and encompasses the CBD. It is in the urban core where the city's fabric is the tightest. Residences are finely interwoven with business, commercial, and sometimes industrial activity. Cultural research and higher educational facilities are an integral part of this area. The urban core is characterized by an interspersion of mutliple-family housing, office towers, museums, universities, and theaters. Easy access is made possible by an extraordinary concentration of mass transit—buses, trams, underground stations, and railway terminals.

In New York, the urban core consists of the island of Manhattan. In Paris, the urban core is coterminous with La Ville de Paris (twenty arrondissements). In Greater London, the urban core consists of fourteen boroughs. This area is otherwise known as "Inner London."[55]

The First Ring This territory immediately bounds the urban core. Though it is considered to be part of the city, it is generally less populated and contains a larger proportion of single-family dwellings. The urban fabric is also less tightly knit here. Compared to the urban core,

27

Fig. 1.3. Greater London: Urban Core and First Ring

there is a greater separation between residential, commercial, and recreational space.

In New York City this ring consists of seven counties: The Bronx, Kings, Queens, Richmond, Hudson, Union, and Essex. In Paris the first ring consists of the three departments that are closest to La Ville de Paris: Haut-de-Seine, Val-de-Marne, and Seine-St. Denis. In Greater London the first ring consists of the eighteen boroughs not in the urban core and is known as "Outer London."

The Second Ring   This ring is characterized by considerably lower densities and an abundance of open space. Activities tend to be separated from one another and most people rely on the automobile for transportation. In contradistinction to the first ring, the second is clearly apart from the urban core. Agricultural activity is common in parts of the second ring and urban development tends to have taken place in the last decade.

In New York the second ring embraces twelve counties in the states of New York, New Jersey, and Connecticut. This ring extends approximately seventy-five miles from the heart of the urban core, Times Square. In Paris the second ring consists of four departments laid in a concentric circle at the furthest edge of the region. These departments are Yvelines, Essone, Val-d'Oise and Seine-et-Marne. This ring extends approximately sixty miles from the Parisian center, Notre Dame. In Greater London the second ring is called the Outer Metropolitan Area (OMA). It is approximately fifteen miles wide and straddles an area of open farm land called the Green Belt. London's second ring extends approximately forty miles from the London center, Charing Cross.

The larger regions of New York, Paris, and London are respectively called the New York Standard Consolidated Area (NYSCA), the Ile-de-France, and Greater London. In New York and Paris, these regions encompass the urban core and the first and second rings. In Greater London, the regional bounds are limited to the urban core and the first ring. The maps in Figures 1.1, 1.2 and 1.3 lay out the regional bounds and their territorial subdivisions for each city. See also the Appendix.

These regions are the terrain on which post-industrial politics is played. The next six chapters discuss these areas and their subdivisions. New York, Paris, and London are dealt with separately in Chapters 2 through 7. The discussion of each city begins by turning to the larger urban region and examining how each region developed in its own fashion. The focus then narrows to a discussion of the municipality and the first rings, until the most strategic area of the post-industrial city—the urban core—is reached.

The urban cores of New York, Paris, and London furnish the sites for eight of the nine crucial issues. Only La Défense, in the Ile-de-France, lies outside the urban core. Its creation as a new CBD just outside Paris is a comment on the character of French politics and planning.

Chapters 8 through 10 bring New York, Paris, and London together again. Chapter 8 analyzes how the elitist-pluralist-corporatist typology compares to the reality of land-use decisions. It also compares the corporatist-pluralist hybrid in New York to mobilizing corporatism in Paris and to liberal corporatism in London. Chapter 9 applies the idea of power combinations to each city and examines how different systems are formed and why different decisions emerge from those systems. Finally, Chapter 10 discusses the post-industrial conditions, the post-industrial future, and why corporatism is an integral part of it.

CHAPTER 2

New York: Unbalanced Development and Social Fragmentation

Them that's got shall have / Them that's not shall lose / So the Bible says / And it still is news—Billie Holliday, "God Bless the Child"

Robert Moses as a Power Centralizer in a Fragmented Region

IF ANY single phrase captures the essence of the New York region, it is "polarized development and economic contradiction." For the New York Standard Consolidated Area (NYSCA), the result is a bundle of trends and countertrends that often work at cross-purposes. Centripetal forces agglomerate economic activity into the urban core and central business district (CBD), at the same time spinning off industry in a centrifugal pattern around the distant suburbs. Evidence of these contradictions can be seen in the region's patchwork of economic "booms" in some counties and "busts" in others; in the rubble-strewn emptiness of the South Bronx and the congestion of mid-Manhattan; in the squalid poverty of central Brooklyn and the astonishing wealth of Fairfield; and in the abandoned wharves of Jersey City and the posh corporate parks of Westchester. There are whole swatches of territory within the NYSCA that have been deserted for lack of capital; others are overheated because of a surfeit of dollars.

This description should be considered in the context of the region's political institutions. More than anything else, the New York area is a loose federation of separate and fragmented jurisdictions. The American tradition of local prerogatives runs strong, and control over land use and development is mostly vested in local governments. Zoning regulations, construction permits, and property taxes are decided upon by many small governments (townships, counties, cities, villages, special districts, etc.) rather than by any kind of regional or centralized government.

Moreover, these localities compete with one another for the sources of wealth and production. Taxes are lowered to attract certain industries, zoning regulations are adjusted to bring in office complexes, special leasing privileges are given to developers, and training programs have been provided by counties to attract corporations. There is also competition for state or federal aid, and public officials run for reelection on the record of how much they have gotten for their constituencies.

The diffuse and competitive nature of the region contributes to its checkered development. Although the states of New York, New Jersey, and Connecticut theoretically possess the capacity to redress these disparities, they have never really done so. Power and local rights are too heavily vested and would upset the delicate political balance upon which state governors retain office. Even Nelson Rockefeller, the most powerful Governor of New York in this century, failed to bring coordinated development to the region, though he placed the great weight of his influence and prestige behind that attempt.[1]

One man, however, functioned especially well in the New York environment. That man was Robert Moses. In power for nearly forty years, he was the predominant figure in building the region in and around New York City. His influence outlasted that of eight mayors of New York City and five governors of New York State, a list that includes the most powerful and prominent in the region's history—mayors like Fiorello LaGuardia and governors like Al Smith, Herbert Lehman, Thomas E. Dewey, and Nelson Rockefeller.

Moses endured because his power was built out of New York's fragmentation, not over it. He rose from a confusing morass of petty rivalries, and his influence swelled as he was able to bring some order to that chaos. He was a man who knew that the key to power in New York lay at the interstices of the region's many governments. Although he could not wholly possess that power, he did the next best thing—he coordinated its many pieces.

The cement for putting those pieces together was public works—parkways, bridges, tunnels, housing, parks, and impressive complexes for culture, recreation, and politics. Public works knew no bounds. Bridges connected urban to suburban areas, parkways brought together a string of localities, and city residents came to appreciate the beaches that Moses built for them in the countryside.

The mechanisms for his power were the public authority, the committee, and the commission. To most people these were innocuous bodies that carried out technical chores. To Moses they were vital linchpins that could operate at the nexus of the region's multiple governments. A special commission could function among several localities, between the locality and the state, and between the city and the federal government. Best of all, the public authority could function with relative autonomy. It relied neither upon the state legislature for approving its actions nor upon the state treasury for providing it with revenue.

Public authorities received their capital from investment bankers and large bondholders, who gave them that credit based on their potential for generating revenue once the project was completed. The vast bridges that spanned New York's waterways were Moses' favorites, because they were "self-liquidating" projects: they not only repaid the interest and principal on their debt but were a steady source of revenue.

At the height of his power, Moses held a bewildering number of titles. The titles were not grand, but they reflected the scope of his coordinative authority and ultimately his command. His major post was that of Chairman of the Triborough Bridge and Tunnel Authority, and to that he added chairmanships of the Emergency Housing Committee, the Jones Beach and Bethpage Parks, and the State Council of Parks. In addition, he was city Construction Coordinator, held the presidency of the Long Island State Park Commission, and was a member of the New York City Planning Commission.

Little could be accomplished in public works without in some way touching on his network of authority, which was held together by the force of his personality. It was virtually an interlocking directorate in which assorted bodies appeared to undertake separate tasks. In reality, they all functioned under the guiding hand of Robert Moses, who was among the first to recognize that one project could engender another. Highways required the demolition of housing. Housing demolition entailed the construction of new dwellings. Bridges required rights of way and elaborate surveys. Parks, stadiums, and causeways brought on accompanying commitments in bricks and mortar. Moses did it all, and for a time he won the gratitude of investors who earned profits, laborers who were put to work, and the middle class who enjoyed the facilities. After it was all done, he was castigated for ignoring mass transit, breaking up stable neighborhoods, and wrecking the urban environment.[2]

Robert Moses left a lasting imprint, whether one lauds it or not, upon New York's built environment. He built seven of the city's major bridges, over four hundred miles of highway for its motor vehicles, and housing for hundreds of thousands. He built the great magnets of the city—the United Nations, Lincoln Center, Shea Stadium. Outside the city he contoured a region. With the help of the automobile, he made the suburbs possible. His work would ultimately replace the potato farmers and Back Bay fishermen of Long Island with the mass-produced housing of Levittown. A new industrial order and culture grew up in the region.

Although the physical changes Moses effected in the built environment remain, his political legacy was far less durable. After he left office, the interlocking directorate among his organizations was quickly disbanded. His seat of power, the Triborough Bridge and Tunnel Authority, was merged into another organization, and public works fell into decline. The political fragmentation that always characterized planning in the NYSCA became more apparent as population began to spread and farmlands were converted into suburbs. What has that transformation meant for the region in the 1980s?

The New York Standard Consolidated Area: The 1980s

To answer this question, we will examine the twenty counties of the NYSCA in the context of their economic growth during the last decade or two. This perspective will then be narrowed to the outer city and urban core, and finally to the Manhattan CBD. Afterward, the social consequences of this development, as well as the source of its political impetus, will be discussed.

The larger New York Standard Consolidated Area may be thought of in terms of its (1) urban core and CBD, (2) its first ring, and (3) its second ring, comprising both near and distant suburbs (see Fig. 2.1).

A popular way of assessing the vitality of a region is to look at population growth and decline. Population change is also supposed to tell us where people choose to live, where they place their wealth, and where the opportunities lie.

In 1960 the NYSCA held 15.8 million people. Twenty years later that number had modestly increased by less than a million. Although the region's population stagnated, there were intraregional shifts. Counties in the urban core and the first ring lost population amounting to 800,000 residents. Manhattan, the Bronx, Kings, Hudson, and Essex bore the brunt of the decline.[3] Like other parts of the country, people in the NYSCA moved out of the older cities to the newer and more distant suburbs. Second-ring counties like Suffolk, Putnam, and Rockland nearly doubled in population. Meanwhile, near suburbs like Westchester and Nassau remained unchanged.

These shifts need to be noted, but their magnitude should not be exaggerated. Though the urban core and first ring lost 800,000 people, it was a loss that drew from a population base of nearly 10 million. This amounted to a drop of just 8 percent. Similarly, although counties in the distant suburbs doubled in size, these gains occurred in a small population base. In sum, the losses were real, but they were not dire. The gains were meaningful, but they were not massive.

In 1960 slices of population skewed toward the urban core and first ring (see Fig. 2.2). By 1980 the slices were more symmetrical.

What, then, has been dramatic about the changes since the 1960s?

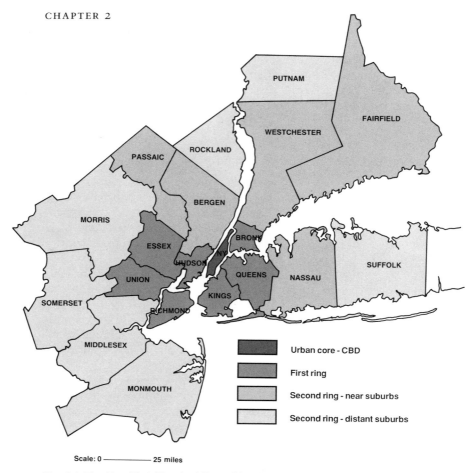

Fig. 2.1. The New York Standard Consolidated Area

One key factor has been the continued prominence of Manhattan's urban core and the CBD as a source of wealth, jobs, and white-collar employment. In contrast to Manhattan, a group of counties in the first ring have experienced real declines, not only in jobs but in their inability to attract compensating employment in what is often called "white-collar" employment. The second ring of counties has continued to grow at a modest rate.

Put another way, centripetal pulls within the urban core and CBD remain strong and Manhattan continues to be a powerful magnet. At the same time, there have been centrifugal pulls into the second ring

34

and these will continue, though perhaps with a reduced attraction. In the first ring, however, the urban fabric is disintegrated particularly in the Bronx, Kings, Essex, and Hudson counties. Another key factor to keep in mind is that the social class and condition of a territory change with redistributions of employment. In the NYSCA, the urban core and second ring have undergone an infusion of social prosperity and physical enhancement. Less fortunate areas in the first ring have become reservations for the poor and unwanted.

As we shall see, development in the NYSCA has taken the form of an inverted doughnut, with the urban core and CBD filled with large accretions of white-collar workers, high-rise apartment complexes, and office towers. In the meantime, the first ring of the doughnut has deteriorated and gone through a process of spilling out its population and industry into both near and distant second-ring suburbs. What lies behind this is an economic and developmental phenomenon attributed to the "post-industrial" revolution.

Post-Industrial Transformation and Corporate Leapfrogging

Post-industrialism is a broad term encompassing a variety of ideas. As discussed in Chapter 1, it involves employment shifts that emphasize white-collar rather than blue-collar work, managerial and technical services rather than manual labor, and the professions rather than

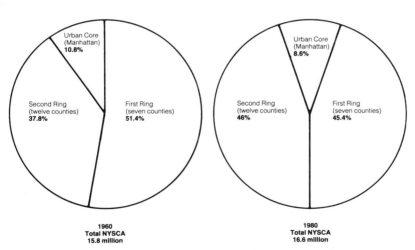

Fig. 2.2. Distribution of the Population in the New York Standard Consolidated Area: 1960 and 1980. Source: *Population Abstract of the United States* (Maclean, Va.: Androt Associates, 1980) and U.S. Bureau of the Census.

artisan trades.[4] The most apparent indices of post-industrialism can be found in the growth of careers in accounting, advertising, and management. The fields of finance, insurance, and real estate (FIRE) are also major ingredients of a post-industrial economy. In addition, post-industrialism has stimulated business in a host of auxiliary services in health, recreation, culture, and cosmetics.

In New York, employment and industrial patterns have been especially influenced by the arrival of the post-industrial era. Jobs in blue-collar industries such as manufacturing and construction declined during the 1970s and 1980s. By the same token there has been an upsurge in the categories of FIRE, services, and administration. We may consider these trends for the NYSCA by comparing employment across its four sectors in 1971 and 1981 for five basic economic sectors—*manufacturing*, FIRE, *services, contract construction*, and *transportation* (see Table 2.1).

Taking the NYSCA as a whole, it is apparent that the region has continued its post-industrial shift through the 1970s. In every ring manufacture has fallen as a share of the economy. In the urban core of Manhattan there was a drop of nearly 8 percent and in the first ring there was a still higher fall of almost 11 percent. Even through the second ring, there were drops in the vicinity of 10 percent.

The dynamics of post-industrial transformation have generated a shift from blue-collar jobs, which are "manual" and "heavy machine" intensive, to white-collar tasks, which are "paper" or "high technol-

Table 2.1. Employment by Sector in the NYSCA: 1971 and 1982 (by place of work; in percentages except for Total Employed)

Sector	Urban Core		First Ring		Second Ring (near)		Second Ring (distant)	
	1971	1982	1971	1982	1971	1982	1971	1982
Manufacturing	27.2	19.3	45.4	34.5	48.1	38.9	52.9	42.4
FIRE	23.2	28.1	8.6	8.6	7.8	10.1	6.3	8.6
Services	34.7	41.1	22.9	36.9	28.1	37.3	24.4	32.7
Transportation and Public Utilities	11.8	9.2	16.8	14.0	8.4	7.3	9.0	10.2
Construction	3.1	2.3	6.3	6.0	7.6	6.4	7.4	6.1
Total Employed								
1971	1,632,066		1,411,358		923,972		431,207	
1982	1,573,068		1,272,587		1,168,311		725,323	
% Change	−4%		−10%		+26%		+68%	

Source: Adapted from *County Business Patterns: 1971 and 1982* (Washington, D.C.: Department of Commerce, Bureau of the Census).

ogy" intensive. This can be seen in all parts of the region in which manufacture was replaced by a combination of FIRE and service jobs. The most dramatic change occurred in the urban core of Manhattan, where a combination of FIRE and service employment accounted for over 69 percent of the total. Although the first ring saw no growth in FIRE, it did increase its service sector so that by the beginning of the 1980s it too depended on nonmanufacturing employment. The transformation in the direction of a FIRE–service economy also affected the second ring. In both the near and distant suburbs there were increases ranging from a few percentage points in FIRE to almost 10 percentage points in services.

Compared to the decline in manufacture and the rise in FIRE and services, there was little dramatic change in construction or transportation and public utilities. High interest rates brought marginal declines in construction, and transportation was spotty.

Total employment in the region was a split picture. Manhattan, which has a base of more than 1.5 million jobs, was not seriously damaged when it lost 3.6 percent of its total force (mostly in manufacture). The first ring also has a substantial base, but its losses were nearly 10 percent and a number of counties were badly hurt. The near and distant suburbs of the second ring experienced an appreciable growth of several hundred thousand jobs. Though the increase of 68 percent in the distant suburbs looks spectacular, the base was relatively small.

Overall, jobs were moving from the first ring to the near and distant suburbs. But what kind of jobs were moving where and how did they affect different areas? We can get a better idea of this by continuing to examine three key sectors—manufacture, FIRE, and services. As we have seen, manufacture has fallen off in both the urban core and first ring of the NYSCA. The losses in absolute numbers are not shown in Table 2.1, but these figures are significant.

Between 1971 and 1982 Manhattan lost over 139,000 manufacturing jobs. The first ring lost even more—almost 202,000 jobs, which accounted for nearly one-third of the industrial base. For Manhattan, however, the decline was alleviated by job replacement in post-industrial sectors. Thus in the all-important category of FIRE, Manhattan added over 62,000 jobs, or better than a 16 percent jump in its existing base. This occurred at just about the same time that manufacture was leaving. In contrast, the first-ring counties actually lost 13,000 FIRE jobs, thereby reducing their job base by 10 percent. It is this simultaneous loss of existing blue- and white-collar jobs that so badly hurt counties like the Bronx, Kings, Essex, and Hudson.[5]

In mentioning these statistics, it should be noted that FIRE is particularly important because it provides lucrative positions in banking, international finance, brokerage, and the burgeoning business of real estate. It is also important to keep in mind that it is not just the quantity of employment but its quality that determines the fortunes of the city. Disposable income in FIRE is appreciably greater than in most kinds of employment. The multiplier effect from FIRE can have an enormous impact on hotels, recreation, and retail trade. It is this quality that enables Manhattan to retain its preeminence as the nation's international banker, and it has continued to attract 80 percent of new banking activity in the United States.[6]

It is true that as Manhattan has increased service jobs, so too has the first ring. But there is a world of difference in the kind of services each has attracted. Manhattan has absorbed an influx of high-priced professionals (physicians, lawyers, therapists, and assorted professionals). In the first-ring counties, service jobs are more commonly taken up by domestic servants, hospital orderlies, cooks, and hairdressers.[7]

Turning to the second ring, the employment picture was as bright as it was consistent in the years between 1971 and 1982. Near and distant suburbs gained in the three sectors of manufacture, FIRE, and service. In the near suburbs the increase in manufacture was slight—a mere 10,000 jobs. But there was a steady growth in FIRE and service jobs of almost one-quarter million.[8]

The distant suburbs did even better. In manufacture these counties gained over 90,000 jobs. In FIRE, over 167,000 positions were added to their roles.[9] Although it is apparent that all kinds of jobs moved into counties like Rockland, Putnam, and Monmouth, the effect of these jobs should not be exaggerated. Given the negligible base in these counties, a gain of 20,000 or 30,000 positions can send the percentages skyrocketing. In these young, low density areas, if experience is any guide, rates of growth will flatten out by the 1990s.

Given these patterns of development, there is little doubt that the near and distant suburbs have become the beneficiaries of the region's wealth and talent. Young professionals who might have settled in the first ring (Bronx, Kings, Essex, or Hudson) choose to set up shop in the second ring (Nassau, Suffolk, Morris). The urban core of Manhattan remains strong, though changed in a profound way.

Another theme to be drawn from statistical evidence is that business has decided either to establish itself in the urban core or to "leapfrog" over the first ring into the second. Those businesses that choose Manhattan are not manufacturing operations. Other data suggest that they tend to be corporations that have a national or international clientele and are not tied to a local market.[10] Professional services that choose the urban core tend to be larger and to hire only white-collar workers. In the 1970s there was an actual increase in the number of large professional firms, while smaller firms moved out of the CBD.[11]

Those firms that "leapfrog" the first ring into the second tend to be light-manufacturing operations (distant suburbs) or smaller professional firms (near or distant suburbs). In many cases such firms have a local- or middle-market clientele rather than an international one. Another aspect of this leapfrogging is that many firms split their activities between the CBD and the second ring. For example, publishing houses are known to keep their central offices in Manhattan while moving their technical and manual operations out to the distant suburbs of the second ring.

Why does leapfrogging occur? Why do the CBD and second ring remain attractive, while the first ring decays? These are complicated questions and no single response can serve as an adequate explanation. To begin with, Manhattan has always had an enormous investment of private and public capital in its buildings, streets, piers, and infrastructure. It has been the business hub of the region as well as the nation, and the urban core has enjoyed the continual attention of the business community. Thus the momentum of its economic agglomeration has carried Manhattan forward. Public and private investment continue to pour into Manhattan Island, particularly its CBD. This has been no miserly investment in working-class tenements (though that has existed too) but an investment in luxurious brownstones, high rises, hotels, and office towers. The sheer design and architectural fabric of the urban core reflects the priorities that will continue to be given to it in the future.

Moreover, Manhattan is the transportation center of the region. Rail, subway, bridge, postal service, and street patterns put Manhattan at the center of communications—something like the hub that is served by numerous spokes of the wheel. The psychological value of locating at an existing center cannot be underestimated. It is the place that is most identifiable, easiest to reach, and most prestigious. Possessing an address in the urban core continues to be worth a great deal of money. Architects and developers go to great lengths not only to locate in the CBD but to place exactly the "right address" on the corporate letterhead.

Though the explanation is less than scientific and well worn, "nothing succeeds like success." Once the infrastructure and business were concentrated in the urban core, other investments followed to create additional centers such as Lincoln Center, Rockefeller Center, the World Trade Center, and the Convention Center. The geography that

39

made the urban core in the first instance—an island surrounded by navigable waters yet accessible to other land masses—continued to reinforce the magnitude of its built environment.

In contrast to the urban core, the first ring was built as an adjunct to Manhattan. It formed the spokes—scattered, apart, and lacking in prestige—that could only be united through the hub. In addition, much of its fabric and design lacked the expensive and enduring quality of the urban core. Most neighborhoods in the Bronx and Kings were built for the working classes who commuted to Manhattan. Jersey City, which is in Hudson County, developed as a backyard for the urban core. The same could be said of Newark, which is located in Essex County. At best, these were locations for heavy industry and business that could not afford to settle in the urban core. Those that succeeded often moved to Manhattan.

As industrial and production needs changed after World War II, the first ring became less desirable. Manhattan could still keep its place as the center of the region by attracting more white-collar firms. But the infrastructure and design of the first ring never contained the same quality and appeal. Why stay in an aging and dilapidated periphery of the region, when one could move to modern facilities in the open spaces of the second ring? The choice was clear. If a firm could afford it and did not require large tracts of land for manufacturing operations, the likely selection was Manhattan. On the other hand, if the cost of space was an important factor or if large-scale production required more space, a logical choice was the second ring.

There were other considerations that prompted leapfrogging. The construction of a massive highway system made the second ring accessible. Thus, although a rail trip to Grand Central or Penn Station was still plausible, a subsequent transfer to an outlying spoke in the Bronx was not looked upon with favor—especially if one could take an easy drive to Westchester.

These considerations interacted with a host of well-known reasons attributed to the rise of the suburbs: lower taxes, low interest rates, federally subsidized mortgages, income-tax benefits, etc.[12]

On top of this, the worse things appeared in the first ring, the worse they became. Once poverty and welfare hit the South Bronx, central Brooklyn, and Jersey City, the trek outward became an exodus. Manhattan could tolerate Harlem, because Manhattan also had Park Avenue, Wall Street, and Greenwich Village. But what was there in Brooklyn to offset the filth and depression of Brownsville?

It should also be recognized that large capital investment protects itself against intrusions of poverty and deterioration. If the West Side of Manhattan was in danger of becoming another Harlem, Lincoln Center could be built to serve as a focal point for the middle class. The tawdriness of Times Square could be offset by a new and fashionable East Side. Real estate and other investments could be made all over the urban core and CBD, but how many investors are willing to take a chance on the Bronx?

The alternatives soon became obvious. Remain in the urban core and contribute to its boom or leapfrog out to the second ring and take advantage of the new speculation in land and development. Meanwhile the first ring fell into a depressing spiral of bust.

New York City: A Contrast in the Urban Core and First Ring

It was not just a change in jobs that altered the New York region during the 1970s. There were also shifts in social class, ethnicity, and race. The 1980 census shows that virtually all the population loss in the NYSCA was white, and this often meant that the middle class was departing. Yet the departure did not mean that middle and upper classes were abandoning all of New York City. The urban core is extraordinarily valuable and its social composition is increasingly upper middle class. (See Table 2.2.)

Manhattan has by far the largest number of managers and professionals residing in it. If technical and administrative occupations are

Table 2.2. Employment by Occupation in New York City: 1980 (by residence; in percentages)

	New York (Manhattan)	Bronx	Kings (Brooklyn)	Queens	Richmond (Staten Island)
Managers and Professionals	41.7	17.6	20.0	22.5	24.6
Technical and Administrative Support	30.0	37.6	38.0	39.1	38.4
Services	13.4	18.1	15.0	13.7	14.5
Skilled Manual	4.3	9.3	9.5	10.0	10.6
Unskilled Manual	10.4	17.1	17.3	14.4	11.4
Farming, Forestry, and Fishing	.2	.3	.2	.3	.5

Source: Adapted from *1980 Census of Population, Characteristics of People and Housing*, New York State Data Center, New York State Department of Commerce, Summary Tape, File 3.

included as part of a white-collar middle class, 70 percent of Manhattan's population fall in that category. In contrast, Bronx and Kings counties have the fewest managers and professionals residing in them. The inclusion of technical and administrative occupations bring the totals in the Bronx and Kings to little more than a majority of their populations. As newer parts of the city, Queens and Richmond have a larger middle class, although they are a significantly lower proportion than in Manhattan.

Note too that Manhattan has a lower proportion of its population in either the skilled or manual occupations. In all cases the other boroughs exceed Manhattan percentages for blue-collar workers.

To understand this profound social imbalance it must be linked to other social conditions, such as patterns of ethnic migration, neighborhood deterioration, and racial segregation. The years between 1960 and 1980 were a transitional time. As we have seen, manufacture was moving out. The housing stock was aging and in a state of incipient deterioration. Manhattan held, because the departing manufacture had begun to be replaced by office towers, professional and financial services, and a resurgence in the theater. All this attracted a middle class that invested in its neighborhoods.

For the Bronx and Kings, the matter was altogether different. Like the old immigrant population, new waves of immigrants came into those counties searching for work and a place to live. Most of these immigrants either came from the American South and were black or

Table 2.3. New York City's Five Counties: Selected Characteristics, 1980

County	Income Per Capita 1980	Population Total 1980	Black and Hispanic 1980	%	% Change in Black and Hispanic, 1960-1980
New York (Manhattan)	$10,863	1,427,000	645,000	45%	+25%
Bronx	4,502	1,169,000	769,000	66	+175
Kings (Brooklyn)	5,779	2,230,000	1,114,000	50	+138
Queens	7,596	1,891,000	616,000	33	+267
Richmond (Staten Island)	7,706	352,000	44,000	13	+4

Source: Compiled from New York City Planning Commission, "Neighborhood Profiles and Neighborhood Statistical Profiles," second edition, August 1978; New York Times, April 12, 1981; "Characteristics of

had migrated from the Caribbean and were predominantly Puerto Rican. For many of the newcomers there was no work to be found. Blue-collar jobs were leaving the city, and the migrants were not equipped to take on employment in post-industrial occupations.

Other ethnic groups once had an industrialized New York to take up their labor and the time to get an education and assimilate. Blacks and Hispanics in the 1960s and 1970s, however, remained segregated. Whole counties went through a massive social shift. The Bronx lost almost half of its white population. Kings lost over a quarter of its white population.

The significance of this social upheaval is not entirely a matter of skin color or ethnic difference. Poverty and class composition are involved as well. Black and Hispanic populations fall disproportionately into the poorest classes and as a consequence have higher rates of unemployment, dependence on public assistance, and incidence of crime and criminal victimization. Another aspect of this poverty is lower rates of home and business ownership, savings, and disposable income. Yet it is precisely safe, prosperous, and stable neighborhoods that make a city viable. The absence of such qualities within whole counties has a depressing effect on every aspect of urban life.

Table 2.3 provides a sketch of the social characteristics of all five of New York City's counties. The data, presented in terms of income, education, and ethnicity or race, aid our analysis of New York's ethnic and racial transformation.

Educational achievement

Completed 4 years high school	% aged 25+	Completed 1-3 years college	% aged 25+	Completed 4+ years college	% aged 25+
210,765	21%	120,401	12%	336,370	33%
211,877	31	73,251	11	61,785	9
429,695	32	148,512	11	154,408	12
423,064	34	170,474	14	192,969	16
82,404	39	30,401	15	31,025	15

New York City's Population," Department of Commerce, U.S. Bureau of the Census, 26 Federal Plaza, New York, N.Y., 1982.

Between 1970 and 1980 the transformation was in its final stages of completion. By 1980 66 percent of the Bronx population was black or Hispanic, half of Kings was black or Hispanic, and one-third of Queens held "nonwhite" populations. Over a twenty-year period, the ethnic/racial change in the Bronx amounted to a turnover of 175 percent. In Kings the turnover was 138 percent and in Queens 267 percent. Manhattan's turnover was only 25 percent, most of which took place between 1960 and 1970.

The transformation suggests a pattern of migrant poor initially moving into aging areas that have not been renewed or physically rehabilitated. Housing is well worn though not destroyed; subway stations and streets begin to have an exhausted look about them. Areas in the Bronx, Brooklyn, and parts of Queens were ripe for this transition. By the time poor populations had inhabited these neighborhoods for one decade, the deterioration was no longer incipient. Corrosion and depression were manifest and spreading. Like a heavy weight on a weak plank, the society collapsed and the people who were left behind suffered the consequences.

The social results of this transformation are found in Table 2.3. Note, for example, that Manhattan holds more than twice the percentage of college graduates as does its nearest competitor (Queens). The Bronx and Kings have the lowest percentage of college graduates in the city. Moreover, less than a third of the population in the Bronx and Kings have completed high school.

The category of income reveals the same disparity between Manhattan and the other counties. Manhattan holds approximately twice the per capita income of the Bronx or Queens. It is also well ahead of Queens and Richmond. Not shown in the table is the exclusivity of Manhattan as the location of upper-income households. Manhattan has the highest cluster of upper-income earners in the city.[13]

This is not to say there is no poverty in Manhattan. Pockets of deep poverty exist in Harlem and in the vicinity of the Lower East Side. In 1980, 14.6 percent of Manhattan's population lived close to or below the poverty line.[14] A similar percentage of Manhattan residents received public assistance.[15] Still, Manhattan's poor reside in particular areas, and these have not grown since 1960. If anything, impoverished neighborhoods are subject to pressures of gentrification. This is particularly true of the Lower East Side, where tenement houses are converted into condominiums and renovated railroad flats are put up for sale at prices beginning at $170,000.

There is another phenomenon associated with Manhattan's newly won status. This is dedensification. In and of itself population loss does

Fig. 2.3 Average Household Size in New York City: 1980. Source: *Capital Needs and Priorities for the City of New York*, 1982 Capital Needs Statement of the New York City Planning Commission, Pursuant to Section 214(d) of the City Charter, map 2-16, pp. 44-45.

not mean urban decline. Between 1970 and 1980 Manhattan lost 7.3 percent of its population.[16] That county's residential mass is thinning out yet growing more prosperous.

A comparison of the size of households in each of the city's counties in 1980 is useful here (see Fig. 2.3). Note that Manhattan stands out as the single county with an average household size of 2.25 or less. Richmond to the southwest and the Bronx to the northeast have large chunks of territory whose average household size is 2.75 or more. Kings and Queens, to the east, are in much the same position as their

first-ring sister counties. Note too that Manhattan's smaller households are at or below Central Park (represented by the small rectangle).
This area includes neighborhoods in Midtown, the East and West
Sides, and in the vicinity of Greenwich Village. Smaller households
are associated with affluent, double-income families or with young
professionals who remain single. This new class of "Yuppies," as they
are sometimes called, occupy the sleek, high-priced neighborhoods of
the city. They are also the site of building booms, gentrification, and
real estate speculation.

Land and Office Towers

The symbol of New York is its skyline, which is confined to Manhattan. The skyline is so well known that Manhattan has acquired the
status of a verb: cities that experience a massive surge of office construction are said to be "Manhattanized," and the process of "Manhat-
tanization" has impinged on such urban treasures as San Francisco and
Jerusalem.

Within Manhattan, office construction and land value have surged
even more since the onslaught of post-industrial transformation. This
is because post-industrialism places a premium on personal interaction. Higher buildings not only facilitate interaction but make more of
it possible. The urban core is the strategic terrain on which post-industrialism builds its foundation. Close attention should thus be paid
to the pressures that make Manhattan's boom so formidable. If Manhattan is already there, can Paris or London or any great city be very
far behind?

With just a tiny fraction of the region's land mass, Manhattan has
absorbed over one quarter of the office construction, a trend that is
likely to continue through the 1990s.

As Figure 2.4 shows, the amount of office construction in Manhattan has risen sharply since 1977. This rise has taken place on a substantial base created between 1960 and 1980, when 77 million square feet
was built.[17] In construction circles, Manhattan continues to be a mine
of employment.

The capital invested in CBD real estate has reinforced Manhattan's
preeminence. In communications, a move to Manhattan is a sure sign
of a promotion; in law, a location in Manhattan means work from top
corporate clients; in the arts, Manhattan is the mecca for talent. The
dramatic post-industrial transformation of the urban core has sparked
international interest of it.[18] In 1979 New York City contained 277
Japanese-owned businesses, 213 British enterprises, 175 French companies, 80 Swiss, 74 German, and 53 Swedish, with many other na-

tions represented in smaller numbers. A survey of 2,000 major firms revealed that almost half of them were foreign owned.[19] The Japanese, in particular, have been avid purchasers of real property and heavy contributors to the rise in Manhattan land prices.

Data on international communications and transportation are a good indication of how important a city may be to the world economy. In the last decade, 21 percent of all international telephone calls made in the United States took place in New York. The shift of New York toward international business and the world economy is unmistakable.[20]

What is also unmistakable is the impact of CBD development on the urban core and on parts of adjacent counties. The cutting edge of this transformation is the construction of a whole new generation of skyscrapers, which have been built in vacant spaces or have replaced older buildings. In some cases historic brownstones are razed and glass towers are shoehorned into a sliver of space. In still other instances "air rights" are sold above existing buildings, and fifty-story towers built

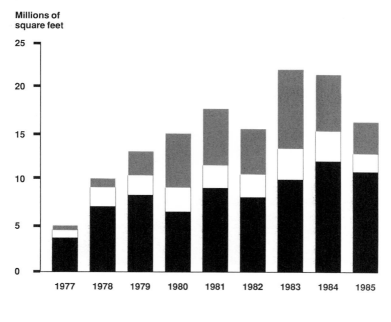

Millions of square feet

- ■ Rest of Region
- □ Rest of NYC
- ▨ Manhattan

Fig. 2.4 Contract Awards for Office Construction in the New York Region: 1977-1985. Source: Port Authority of New York and New Jersey.

47

in the once open spaces. Years ago it was possible to glimpse the Manhattan skyline from atop a fifteen-story building. Today a view from fifty stories would not suffice, as Manhattan itself becomes "Manhattanized."[21]

Beyond this first edge of change is the phenomenon of "gentrification."[22] White-collar workers and professionals from the post-industrial sector seek out residential space and in the process transform whole neighborhoods with new tastes, habits, and purchasing power. Factory lofts have been converted into fashionable apartments; warehouses have been gutted and divided into cooperative apartments to be put up for sale in an expensive market; a new surge of speculation has occurred in nineteenth-century "brownstone" and "graystone" townhouses; simple shops have been remade into high-priced boutiques.

Although gentrification has increased the attractiveness and the wealth of the city, it has also exacted its toll on those who can no longer afford to live in their old neighborhoods. The sons and daughters of working-class families who have found social mobility do what many small businesses have done—either they find comfortable quarters in Queens or Richmond or they "leapfrog" over the first ring into the near or distant suburbs of Long Island, upstate New York, or New Jersey. Less fortunate families find themselves moving into undesirable neighborhoods in the first ring. This is particularly true for the elderly and for black or Hispanic families, who move into the Bronx or Brooklyn.

The CBD boom, gentrification, and the displacement of working-class households have worsened existing imbalances. The CBD is saturated with investment, the remainder of the urban core is overcrowded due to excessive demands placed upon it, and much of the first ring

Table 2.4. Property Assessments in New York City: 1969 and 1987 (in thousands of dollars, unless otherwise indicated)

County	1969	1987	1987 % Share of Total	% Change 1969-1987
New York (Manhattan)	14,938,102	36,032,321	59%	+141%
Bronx	3,764,031	3,574,031	6	−5
Kings	6,637,049	8,131,267	14	+23
Queens	7,789,785	10,517,952	17	+35
Richmond	1,163,096	2,424,620	4	+96

Source: New York City Department of Finance, Bureau of Real Property Assessment.

falls into deeper poverty and deterioration.[23] Just how skewed this relationship has become may be seen by considering land values in each
of New York's five counties (see Table 2.4). Within a mere twenty-
two miles of the city, constituting just 7 percent of its land mass, lies
more than half of the property value. Working from an enormous base
of nearly $15 billion, Manhattan increased its property value by 141
percent in less than two decades. During this same period, the Bronx
dropped by 5 percent and Kings and Queens enjoyed moderate increases. Richmond was the only other county to register a substantial
gain, but this occurred on a tiny base. To be sure, Manhattan property
values are based on commercial buildings, which are assessed at a
higher rate than residential dwellings, but the differences remain significant.[24]

Significance

For the past quarter century the NYSCA has gone through a post-
industrial transformation equal to the one that made New York an
industrial giant at the turn of the century. Manhattan has pulled
through this transformation richer and more powerful than before. It
has replaced blue-collar losses with burgeoning white-collar employment, and it has rebuilt its terrain with mighty office towers. Despite
problems in the first ring, the Manhattan urban core gives sustenance
to the region around it. It provides commuters with jobs, it gives fin-
anciers an enormous field of investment, and it gives many others a
reason to live in the region. Indeed, Manhattan is the hot sun around
which other bodies may shine.

Because Manhattan is so critical, so too is its planning. Economic,
social, and physical descriptions achieve meaning in the context of
their underlying dynamics and the choices that make them operational. And if planning is anything, it is the selection of critical choices.
It is this combination of planning and choice that provides the seedbed
for land-use politics. From that seedbed sprouts the geopolitics of
New York.

New York: Geoplanning, Geopolitics, and the Corporatist-Pluralist Hybrid

I'd like to think that I have created a climate that says to people, this is a place to create jobs and make a buck.—Mayor Edward I. Koch

WE HAVE SEEN how uneven development in New York has promoted radical economic swings and social fragmentation. This is acutely manifest in the booms and busts that characterize the region. The urban core grows with affluence and its built environment is packed with bricks and mortar, while the first ring decays.

This outcome is often attributed to the aggregate behavior of landlords, investors, and businessmen. Yet, as we shall see, technocrats and politicians shape that behavior through zoning, taxation, and public spending.

Geoplanning: Strategic Development in the Urban Core

Manhattan is a veritable nucleus of post-industrial growth for the region. Offices, white-collar jobs, and luxury housing are crowded onto its terrain. For New York bigger is always better, and the city spares no effort to make the "big apple" the best. Zoning laws that are supposed to ensure that enough sunlight reaches the sidewalks are amended in order to promote development. The "sky plane" is a way of calculating how much light and sky a tall structure must leave to its surrounding environment. To preserve an open feeling, a builder is required to step a building's mass backward after it reaches a certain height. Yet zoning variances and special provisions have allowed office buildings to loom well above their intended heights. The city has granted "bonus zoning" rights to developers who agree to establish public space at the base of a building. This allows builders to increase the height of a building as long as a plaza or additional room is allocated for pedestrians. In theory, "bonus zoning" was a fine idea that was supposed to relieve street congestion. In fact, developers left spaces that were inhospitable or uncongenial to the public while they took advantage of additional heights and compromised the sky plane. In some cases developers even placed metal spikes on concrete railings that marked off their plazas, in order to prevent outsiders from sitting on them. In other instances developers simply built public spaces as elaborate lobbies for their own buildings.[1]

The city has also allowed developers and owners to transfer or purchase "air rights" from one building to another. Historic theaters and other structures that are built on a smaller scale can sell unused air space to other sites, so that whatever slack is left in the environment is quickly snapped up. The result is a territory that is heavily built, with columns of multistory towers growing taller and taller. The enormous gusts of wind that swoop down the manmade canyons of Manhattan during the winter are a testimony to compromised zoning laws; so too are the long shadows that descend upon the central business district to shorten sunny afternoons.

All this has been undertaken in the belief that New York City must continue to grow lest it slowly die. The momentum for growth is so strong that little is sacred when it comes to matters of architectural preservation. Newer buildings replace older ones and, on occasion, they are built on top of them.

As if to pardon itself for not having enough space available in the CBD, the city has filled in a section of the Hudson River in order to construct another huge complex, Battery Park City. This has been built on ninety-two acres at the southwestern tip of Manhattan, just astride the World Trade Center. It consists of 16,000 units of luxury residential housing and a complex of office buildings. As an economic venture it is designed to be a high quality, high-rent neighborhood for the elite of post-industrial New York, and it is supposed to encourage others to invest in the area, despite the high costs of development.

A sister project to Battery Park City is located well to the north, on the same western edge of Manhattan. Dubbed Lincoln West because of its proximity to New York's foremost cultural complex, Lincoln Center, this project as originally planned would have cost one billion dollars to complete and would have added thousands of people to the already dense West Side.

We should add that these are not isolated and uncoordinated patches of construction. Much of this development will be linked by an auto route that is planned for the western shore of Manhattan. The original project, known as Westway, also entailed large-scale real estate development and would have tied lower Manhattan's CBD to Midtown. Beyond Midtown, Westway would have been continued by a smaller parkway that passes along the site of Lincoln West and the scenic banks of the Hudson. Westway itself would have been partially underground so that parks, housing, and other facilities could be built above it.

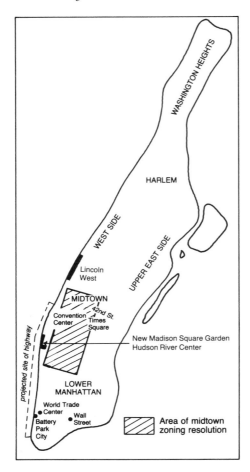

Fig. 3.1. The Manhattan
Urban Core

The map in Figure 3.1 shows existing areas of development in the urban core that are concentrated in Lower Manhattan, Midtown, and the West Side. Areas of future development are to be concentrated on the Lower West Side running northward into the West Side of the urban core.

A number of planning issues stem from having concentrated so much of the city's resources in the urban core. The first is that there is no room left for expansion in the financial quarters of Lower Manhattan, in the office complexes of Midtown, or in the high-rent district of the Upper East Side. The theater district around Times Square is also

52

filled, except for the parking lots that are scattered on its western edge. Lower Manhattan, Midtown, and the Upper East Side have absorbed the great construction boons of the past twenty years. These areas were targets of attention during the early phase of post-industrial transformation, especially when it came to bonus zoning and other types of variance.

Second, now that these areas are saturated, there are planning initiatives to move just astride them. The idea is to take advantage of the existing momentum for development by diverting it westward. To bring this about, the city and state have created investment catalysts, which can be seen in Figure 3.1. These are a projected highway, once called Westway, and large commercial or residential tracts labeled in Figure 3.1 as Battery Park City, Times Square, the Convention Center, and Lincoln West. The development of these areas is planned as an expanding oil slick. Having succeeded in other parts of the urban core, the city wants to re-create that slick where there is still vacant space.

Third, turning our attention to a key element of the strategy—Westway—we can conceive of it as a unified corridor of transportation, commerce, housing, and other development.[2] As originally planned, it would have held at least six lanes of traffic, connected to bridges, tunnels, and every major artery of the urban core.

The rendition in Figure 3.2 looks northward from the lower West Side. Note the extensive development planned for the tier above the proposed highway.

Fourth, it becomes clear that Westway, or any major route along Manhattan's western rim, would be of inestimable worth to Battery Park City, Times Square, and Lincoln West. Such a route would magnify their viability, visibility, and value. A journey north would take travelers past Battery Park City and the Convention Center, place them at 42nd Street and within blocks of Times Square, before finally driving them alongside Lincoln West.

Without Westway or a suitable alternative, the value of western rim development would be diminished and the western rim would remain as it is today—rows of dilapidated piers, unsightly parking lots, and sleazy taverns. With a major auto route, the western rim will pioneer a new surge of interest in housing, real estate, and commerce. Battery Park City, the Convention Center, Times Square, and Lincoln West would no longer be islands of investment in a sea of neglect, but continuous links in a rich chain.

Assisting the force of catalytic investment is another planning prong, the Midtown Zoning Resolution of 1982. Technically, Midtown Zoning is supposed to lay out three areas of the urban core for

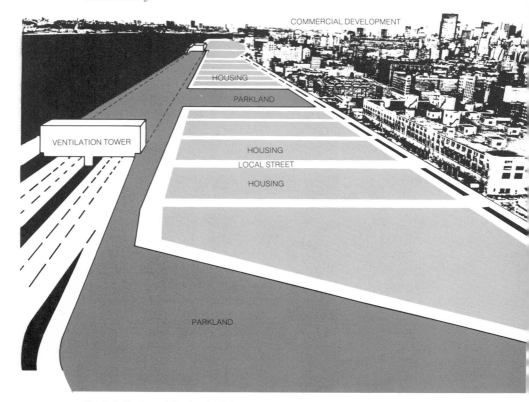

Fig. 3.2. Projected Design for Westway

stabilization, preservation, and growth. In fact, the sections of Midtown Zoning that are designated for growth are keys to New York's post-industrial strategy. Zoning and tax policies are being liberalized within these growth sections, and it is there that the geopolitical struggle is waged.

Figure 3.3 presents a map of the Midtown Zoning Strategy as it pertains to stabilization, preservation, and growth. Also depicted are the Times Square/42nd Street project and connecting improvements along Eighth Avenue.

Note that the growth areas on the map protrude westward in an elongated north and south corridor. The dark areas are sieves for reinvestment that are supposed to fertilize the adjoining neighborhoods. The intent of Midtown Zoning is to push growth westward. A report by the City Planning Commission concedes this, when it states:

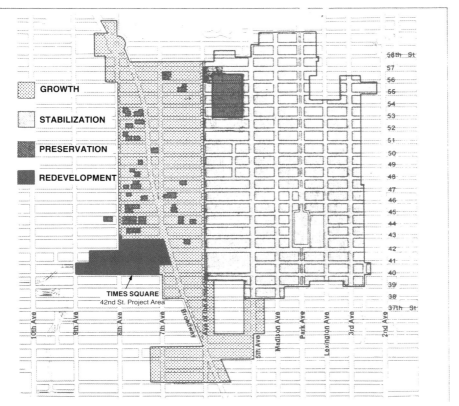

Fig. 3.3. Midtown Development Strategy. Source: Department of City
Planning, City of New York.

The overall development strategy is to facilitate the expansions of
Midtown from the prestigious, densely developed high value East
Side office core to the west and to the south where there is room to
grow, where sites and development opportunities are available,
where congestion is less and mass transit more available.[3]

Further on, the same document reveals how planners perceive redevelopment and how they choose to go about it:

Builders will not build nor will bankers advance mortgage loans if
the market does not bring in profitable rents. A building in a less
desirable area will have to offer a bargain to attract tenants. To in-
duce office construction on the West Side, rents must come in substantially below East Side rents.[4]

To stimulate this cooperation, planners have turned to a number of financial carrots. These include (1) zoning western portions of Manhattan to accommodate higher densities, (2) reducing taxes to encourage property investment, and (3) furnishing public funds to bring about catalytic investment. Apparently Midtown Zoning does nothing to limit or redirect growth out of Manhattan, and it increases allowable densities to the urban core's west, where land is still vacant. City planners hoped that developers will see the profits to be made on the western portion of Manhattan, where buildings can contain nearly 17 percent more space for office rentals. In a city where office space costs as much as $50 per square foot, the additional amounts gleaned from monthly rentals can be hefty.

Should zoning incentives be an insufficient attraction, the city is offering a large tax incentive program. As finally adopted, the incentives consist of a 50 percent reduction on real estate taxes, which decrease by 5 percent each year for a period of ten years. In some areas tax exemptions are automatic ("as of right"); in others special application has to be made. The tax exemption, in conjunction with increased office densities, is supposed to make rents 25 percent lower than those in the CBD.

The centerpiece of planning strategy in Midtown is in Times Square and 42nd Street. The potential for Times Square is enormous. It is the best juncture for transportation in New York City. It is at the seam of New York's major industries—to the north is the theater district and to the south is the garment center. Few locations in the world can rival Times Square for its strategic placement, and city planners know this.

In 1980 they unveiled a plan whose scope, planners believed, would befit New York's reputation as the greatest commercial magnet in the world.[5] The new plan called for more than a billion dollars in investments for office towers, theaters, a hotel, and various facilities. Millions of square feet in office space would be lodged in towers rising more than fifty stories into the air.[6] Times Square's bright lights would glow even brighter in a revitalized theater district. Like its sister projects in Midtown, the new Times Square would be a product of a private-public partnership.

These, then, are the crucial projects designed to redevelop the western rim and Midtown section of Manhattan. For the most part, they are contiguous, abundantly supported by a public-private partnership and rationalized through zoning and tax policies. They are the substance over which city politics is fought and represent elaborate policy choices. Before examining these choices, we turn to the institutions and practices of New York politics.

Geopolitics: Making Policy amid Pluralist Structures

A glance at New York City's political institutions confirms its multicentered character.[7] The chief executive of the city is the mayor, and though he enjoys latitude in running the bureaucracy and making up the budget, his powers are offset by two other citywide officials (the Comptroller and the President of the City Council) as well as five other executives who are elected from each of the city's counties or boroughs. All eight officials sit on the Board of Estimate, a quasi-legislative body that decides a host of questions, including zoning and the disposition of city-owned land. There is also a City Council, and although the 35-member Council occasionally sparkles, it has never shorn its reputation as an assemblage of political ghosts who are anxious to avoid controversy and be reelected.[8]

Like most American cities, the prerogatives accorded to New York on matters of land use and zoning are substantial. The city has the power to buy, sell, and rezone land, and only the courts have sometimes stepped in to curtail this power. The Board of Estimate is the major institution that decides questions of land-use policy. For more than eighty years the Board has made decisions through differential voting, in which at-large officials (Mayor, Comptroller, President of the City Council) each held two votes and the Borough Presidents from the five counties each held one vote. This system played on historic divisions within the city, which pitted the neighborhood interests of the counties (commonly called boroughs) against the broader constituencies of the Mayor, Comptroller and City Council President.[9]

Within the bureaucracy, the major agency dealing with land use is City Planning. This agency counts among its team seven individuals, who vote on policy (the Commission), plus a sizable professional staff, who do research and planning (the Department). Important personalities in New York politics have served as Chair of the Commission. As mayoral appointees, they have become conduits of information between the Mayor, members of the Board of Estimate, interest groups, and developers.

Added to this system are fifty-nine community boards, which represent the neighborhoods. Over the years, community boards have become formidable institutions, especially on land-use decisions. One study reports that in 98 percent of the cases tallied, City Planning went along with community board recommendations.[10] What gives community boards clout as sounding stations for neighborhood sentiment is a planning requirement entitled the Uniform Land Use Review Procedure, known inelegantly as ULURP. Under ULURP, community boards are given sixty days to comment on land-use applications. After that, the applications are forwarded to the City Planning Commission, which issues a formal report. The last step in the ULURP process involves a hearing before the Board of Estimate, which votes on the final action to be taken.[11]

There are developers who do not share much enthusiasm for the community boards or the ULURP process. Builders who are in short supply of patience, time, or resources find these institutions frustrating. When faced with a resistant community board the choices, they say, are simple—don't build, build elsewhere, or build to the letter of the law.

Nonetheless there are ways of making the choices easier and faster. Public authorities are one set of institutions that possess the prerogatives of either circumvention or overrule. These alphabetocracies include the Urban Development Corporation (UDC), the Public Development Corporation (PDC), the Battery Park City Authority (BPC), and the Port Authority of New York and New Jersey. In New York City, the two most salient public authorities are the UDC and the PDC. The UDC is a state institution that is capable of bypassing zoning laws and other kinds of local restrictions. It operates neither as a conventional builder nor as a property owner, but as a catalyst for land development. As such the UDC acquires land, puts up an initial investment, and plans or "packages" a project. Its objective is to recruit private capital in the service of public purpose. Top politicians see the UDC as an indispensable tool in assembling land and making end runs around the political process. The PDC functions primarily as an economic and job developer for the city. It also engages in land development and assembles large tracts of property. The PDC does, on occasion, work closely with the UDC to plan an area comprehensively.

The courts are another of the institutions that expedite certain choices. The courts play an altogether different role than public authorities do. Their purpose is not to coordinate or catalyze development, but to determine whether or not it is undertaken with due process. They function at either the state or federal level, and they entertain appeals from proponents and opponents alike. The courts are frequently used by developers who seek redress from municipal restrictions. More recently, community groups and citizens have turned to the judiciary to seek relief from the pains of post-industrial transformation.

These are the institutions to keep in mind. From the grass roots up they consist of the community boards, City Planning, the mayor, the

Board of Estimate and those institutions that work alongside the process—the UDC, the PDC and the courts.

The Geopolitics of Lincoln West, Times Square, and Westway

In examining development and land use inside the urban core of New York, no single theory fully explains the dynamics of decision making, though some do it more adequately than others. There is very little in elitist theory that corresponds with the facts of major land-use decisions. No single, interlocking, ruling class emerged to dominate the wishes or interests of other classes, nor did politicians act as the pawns of such a class. If anything, there appears to be collaboration among different parties (politicians, big business, labor), which would lend some credence to the corporatist view of the political system. The corporatist typology does answer some questions about how land use is decided, but it can be applied only with major qualifications and only on certain kinds of issues. The pluralist view also has limited applications, both in the initiation of a project and after it is brought to public attention. For this reason New York has been analyzed as a hybrid political system, containing a blend of corporatism and pluralism. Corporatism appears to be a common thread, woven into the tapestry of New York politics. Pluralist strands, however, are visible and appear in select aspects of the decisional process.

To better frame the analysis, I offer the following propositions:

▶ There is an impulsion toward corporatism, which stems from the city's perceived need to attract investment, increase the value of land, augment tax revenues, provide jobs, and advance toward a post-industrial order. This corporatist organization is composed of groups that have a stake in the city and crosses into a variety of social strata.

▶ The corporatist impulsion is led by top politicians who enlist business, labor, interest groups, and community boards. Top politicians provide the mandate and set the pace for development. These politicians rely on technocrats in City Planning and in the public authorities to furnish the strategy for development, to determine what kinds of development packages are feasible, and to pilot development through the shoals of planning and investment.

▶ Public authorities, like UDC, PDC, and BPC are cocoons for corporatist intermediation. They are convenient shelters for recruiting private investors. Public authorities insulate politicians, planners, and developers, from outside pressure; they allow projects to incubate with "start up" money; and they provide time so that disputes can be worked out or additional players recruited. UDC and PDC were instrumental in recruiting developers for Times Square, and both now continue to be major mechanisms for rebuilding Times Square. In Lincoln West II, the developer tried to use UDC as a shield against tax, zoning, and ULURP requirements. Public authorities will undoubtedly play a role in Westway II. This time, BPC is likely to try what others have failed to do—to develop the city's western waterfront.

➤ By European standards, New York's political parties are weak and amorphous. Party primaries and public referenda have given much influence to interest groups, which are capable of mounting their own campaigns on behalf of particular issues and specific candidates. Because of this, political parties are not effective mechanisms for aggregating interest groups, for framing issues, or for solidifying support.

➤ Although political parties may be weak, political leaders are not necessarily hampered. Indeed, top leaders have been able to maneuver between different groups, patch together agreements, and lead the city toward economic growth. The ingenuity of these leaders and their willingness to cooperate are critical factors in evaluating the system's performance.

➤ When top politicians act quickly and flexibly in uniting select organizations, their initiatives can be successful. The development of Times Square illustrates how top politicians can create corporatist intermediation between themselves and private organizations. When Times Square was on the verge of collapse, top politicians interceded to negotiate directly with developers and settle differences. Under the guiding hand of a political/technocratic class, Times Square is being rebuilt with the use of private monies drawn from several key developers and large corporations.

➤ Nonetheless, corporatism is not an exclusive model for interpreting New York politics. It can be modified by institutions and procedures that foster pluralist competition, which means that issues can get caught in a process that opens them up to broader types of conflict. Westway is an example of how institutions (community boards, legislatures, the courts), legal procedures (environmental requirements), and ad hoc interest groups can thwart the establishment.

➤ The longer an issue remains in the political process and the longer it is unresolved, the greater are the chances that pluralism can influence the outcome. At times nonestablished groups, with few resources and no privileged access, have made the difference between a project's success and its failure.

➤ Thus, the corporatist and pluralist features of the system will vary with the issue at hand. Issues that are settled out of the limelight and with relative dispatch fall closer to the corporatist end of the spectrum. Those issues that require a lengthier time frame or are held up in a legal web are closer to the pluralist schema. Nonestablished groups recognize this feature of the system. On occasion, they have learned to use its biases for newsworthy stories and litigation in order to broaden the arenas of conflict.

Lincoln West   New York's West Side is the most ordinary and the most extraordinary neighborhood. Its sights and its feel are typically "New York." Its people are a great mélange—natives, Cubans, blacks, students, intellectuals, vagabonds. All of these mix in an unconscious stirring of the melting pot. The bustle of its main streets is compounded by merchants who offer everything from pastrami on rye sandwiches to stolen watches. Passersby are welcome to visit its bookstores, bric-a-brac shops, newstands, tobacconists—even a gypsy palmist and an astrologer are available for the mystically minded. These social delicacies can be found in most big cities, but to have them within a fifteen-minute walk is extraordinary.

The neighborhood is already in the throes of gentrification. The façades of its turn-of-the-century "brownstones" and "greystones" have come alive. Their angled steps kneel down to newly asphalted sidewalks. The signs of social invasion are everywhere. The Irish tavern has been taken over by a café and the hot dog stand has been replaced by "quiche alley" and fancy wine bars.

Time was when the West Side was home for Irish dock workers and Jewish unionists from the "needle trades." The Irish commuted further crosstown toward the Hudson; the Jews took the subway downtown to labor in the garment center.[12] Toward the west, sinking below grade level to the river shores, were the great Penn Central railyards. The yards were the base point for industrial freight, and in their day were the industrial artery to the rest of the nation. Almost everything originated from Penn Central. The croaking engines of its trains and the whine from its winches could be heard up and down the riverside.

Today the yards are a noiseless field of garbage. Except for the rodents who feed on the debris and an occasional tramp seeking shelter, the Penn Yards are lifeless. Its tracks are rusted and overgrown with weeds. Much of it is submerged in polluted waters. The Penn Yards' most visible use now is as an enormous trash can for careless automobilists who pass overhead.

Since the bankruptcy of Penn Central, the land has been available for

Fig. 3.4. The West Side of Manhattan and Site for Lincoln West. Photo/Skyview Survey Inc.

sale. Realtors have seen its potential but have been discouraged by the costs of reconstruction as well as by a community known for its fiery populism. The West Side's political progeny has always cast a suspicious eye on developers. The great majority of its population are tenants who dislike business adventurism. Apparently this did not stop one New York businessman, Abe Hirschfield, who made a fortune flattening land for parking lots. On this occasion Hirschfield wanted to promote something more than a parking lot and got in touch with an Argentinian, Carlos Varsavsky. "I have a nice piece of land for you—76 acres in Manhattan," Hirschfield is purported to have said. "I know exactly what you mean," Varsavsky joked, "it's called Central Park and it's beautiful."[13] Hirschfield explained that it was the next best thing to Central Park, and persuaded Varsavsky to join in developing the land. Varsavsky represented the majority partner, financed by Argentine money, while Hirschfield was the New York connection. By

62

1982 the project was ready for the ULURP process and had been named Lincoln West.

In conception Lincoln West was designed as a boulevard running parallel to the Hudson River from 59th to 72nd Street. Much of the land was still under water and a heavy investment was needed to reclaim it. The dimensions and layout of the project may be seen in Figure 3.4, an aerial view of the West Side and the contours of the Lincoln West site, and in Figure 3.5, a close-up view of the site as it appears today. As proposed, Lincoln West would fill this space with 4,850 housing units, one million square feet of office space, an abundance of retail outlets, a hotel, and parking facilities. Its eight residential towers would climb as high as forty-one stories and hold over 10,000 people. In order to blend with the existing street grid, Lincoln West would have to be built on a massive thirteen-block platform that would lift it above the Hudson, giving some tenants a spectacular view.[14]

Hirschfield and Varsavsky were elated. They believed their plan brought civilization to a wasteland, opened up a new waterfront, and gave New Yorkers badly needed housing. Even more significant, Lin-

Fig. 3.5. The Lincoln West Site. Photo/New York State Department of Transportation

coln West promised the city higher property taxes, which were estimated by the developers to run as high as $45 million per year.

West Siders had an altogether different perception. Led by local politicians and community activists, they at first resisted and then attacked. Their front lines were in the two community boards which,
under ULURP, would pass on the project.

In a series of successive motions both community boards voted their
resounding disapproval (25 to 0 and 20 to 6).[15] The boards were not in
diehard opposition to all development. What they disliked was Lincoln
West's development. Its high densities, the boards felt, would clog already congested streets. Its high towers would block existing riverfront views. If the community boards had their own way, they too
would prefer development. But it would be development at much
lower densities, with much reduced building heights. In the opinion of
the boards, the seventy-six acres should be developed as parks, espla-
nades, and recreational docks.[16]

Another item that aroused local passions was the railyards. West
Siders had seen manufacture leave the area—the old industrial fabric
was worn away, and the demise of the railroad meant an eventual death
for the remaining industry. A politician who spearheaded the opposition claimed that the city "was cut off from the nation's rail freight"
and that New York was reduced to "the most truck dependent major
city in America." Manufacturers supported the claim, saying that if
"the railyards are not reconstructed, the garment industry and its
600,000 jobs will disappear in the next 10 years."[17]

Railyard proponents cited studies that showed that a rejuvenated
Penn Central would lower costs for manufacturers and attract more
than 75 percent of heavy freight traffic.[18] Their idea was to put up a
"Trailer on Flat Car" (TOFC) terminal on part of the site. Such a terminal would allow truck trailers to drive into the yards and hoist their
containers onto flat rail cars for easy transport elsewhere.

For the West Side this was all well and good. From the standpoint
of the larger city, matters were not so simple. The Penn Yards were a
wasteland. The city contended it did not have the resources to develop
the land by itself. Not only could private capital do the job effectively,
it would yield hefty taxes, increased values, and an estimated 11,000
jobs.[19] Furthermore, a TOFC terminal on the West Side was viewed
askance by city planners. To be sure they wanted a terminal, but they
wanted it for the still industrialized Bronx, not for a post-industrial
Manhattan. Planners took heart in the knowledge that it would be up
to citywide institutions, not the community boards, to decide the issue.

Following ULURP, the City Planning Commission soon received the Lincoln West proposal. By July 1982 its verdict was prepared and its voting complete. By unanimous vote the community boards were overruled. The Planning Commission's rationale was summed up in a succinct conclusion when it called Lincoln West

> a rare opportunity to return a portion of the City's land mass to constructive, primarily public use. This could not be accomplished by the City itself without the expenditure of hundreds of millions of dollars. The history of this site suggests that if this opportunity is lost, the site is likely to remain in its present deteriorated condition well into the future.[20]

The Planning Commission also made the most of its opportunity to extract concessions from the developers, thereby showing that a good favor deserved a favor in return. In exchange for the right to proceed with Lincoln West, the developers promised to supply $7 million toward the construction of a TOFC facility in the South Bronx. The promise was symptomatic of New York's development strategy, which was to build one way in the urban core and another way outside of it. And politicians and planners had a sense of how far they could press developers to put up extra dollars in exchange for zoning modifications.[21] They often resorted to this tactic on the high-priced East Side, and they saw no reason why it could not be applied to an anticipated boom on the West Side.

The Planning Commission's action was portentous. The city's folkways meant that Commission members were in touch with City Hall. Bargaining with the Commission was a kind of surrogate bargaining with the Mayor's office. The Planning Commission would begin the negotiation, squeeze what it could, and then announce that its vote was only advisory. The decisive battle would take place in the ornate chambers of the Board of Estimate.

By the time Lincoln West reached the Board of Estimate, groups were dug in on both sides of the issue. Against Lincoln West were local politicians, a garment worker's union, two community boards and an ad hoc neighborhood association. For Lincoln West were the developers, the construction unions, and members of the City Planning Commission. Lincoln West also had several influential personalities promoting its cause. The developers were represented by John Zuccotti, a former Planning Commissioner and newly turned zoning lawyer. Another lawyer, Judah Gribetz, was close to Governor Hugh Carey and well connected politically. Still another operative for Lincoln West had been a key member of the Koch administration.

The decision was clouded by an accusation of influence peddling. Mayor Koch was singled out as having received an $18,000 campaign contribution from the developers. Editorials in the local press charged Koch with a clash of interests and asked that he abstain in the Board's vote.[22] Koch refused, claiming he had always been for Lincoln West and that the campaign contribution was inconsequential. Whatever one might think about the Mayor's position on the issue, he did speak the truth. The Koch administration was unabashedly pro-development and went out of its way to encourage it.[23] Sometime earlier, the Mayor had been reported as being anxious to show "a positive signal to the business community."[24] During the Board's deliberations, the Deputy Mayor openly negotiated on behalf of the project. So close were the relationships between the Mayor and Lincoln West's developers that on the evening of the decision, Zuccotti and Gribetz were using mayoral offices and telephones as if they themselves were staff members.[25]

Board of Estimate members prepared for a late evening session. Crowded into the chambers were community residents, wearing buttons with the caption "Vote against Lincoln West." They faced a boisterous band of construction workers who wanted Lincoln West built. Operating more quietly was a phalanx of lawyers, including some from the banks that had promised financial backing for the project. There were still Board members who were undecided about the project, and at least one had announced his opposition. The huddling and bargaining were constant, much of it centered around the President of the City Council, Carol Bellamy, who commanded two votes. Bellamy had her eyes fixed on the mayoralty and she was anxious to replace Koch. Resistance to Lincoln West would earn electoral points with West Siders and, at the very least, she wanted to extract more concessions from the developers. Much of the negotiating took place in her office, with the Deputy Mayor, lawyers for the developers, and local politicians whispering around large desks.[26]

As the deliberations stretched passed midnight, the bargaining turned into a row. One Borough President called it government "at its worst" and complained that City Planning officials were still negotiating Lincoln West "after it passed and it was before the Board of Estimate." He added in astonishment, "I've never seen this before."[27]

The Deputy Mayor was not sure that Lincoln West rated a superlative for bad government and phrased his opinions in more circumspect language. He described the issue "as a kind of paradigm of the process. It has every kind of policy issue," he continued, "community involvement and interest versus the city's interests, the political needs of all actors on the Board of Estimate, the developer caught up with the bankers on one side and the city on the other. It really is perfect."[28]

The Board's vote was finally taken in the early morning hours. By a majority of 10 to 1 the Board of Estimate passed on the project. The dissenting vote came from the Mahattan Borough President, who reflected the sentiments of West Siders.[29] There may have also been some doubts about the depth of the Borough President's dissent, because he took few pains to convince his colleagues that his was the correct course. Speculation was that his own dissent made for a good public show, and there was a gentlemen's understanding that political posturing was sometimes allowable. As for Carol Bellamy, she finally conceded that Lincoln West was good for the city and that the Board had struck a fair deal.

Were Lincoln West's developers an elite who imposed their wishes on the city? It is difficult to sustain such a theory. The political clamor behind the issue might be written off as showmanship and part of New York atmospherics. But the final package and the concessions made by developers are not as easily dismissed. The fact of the matter is that the political process exacted some very tough concessions from the developers.

As finally adopted, the scale of the project was reduced by one apartment tower and by five hundred residential units. A hotel was scratched from the plan and there was a substantial increase in the costs to the builder for "public amenities."

Most telling were the increments of amenities borne by the developers—over $130 million, according to some estimates. These included a 26-acre park, football fields, swimming pools, and rebuilt subway stations.[30] There was also a modest concession made for low and moderate rental apartments. As a result of the Board's hearing, the $45 million originally projected for real estate taxes was reestimated at $90 million. This was as much of a surprise to the developers as it was to the politicians. As one political aide remarked, "If they underestimate taxes by half, what does that mean about the other numbers. . . . can they afford it?"[31] Reflecting on the events, John Zuccotti later told a group, "I think the city extracted more from the developer than the developer will be able to deal with in the context of financial capability."[32]

These remarks were prescient. Lincoln West won the political battle only to lose the financial war. The costs of building a whole neighborhood upon a thirteen-block platform became acute. To be sure, the amenities guarantees and design criteria weighed on Hirschfield and Varsavsky. In 1984 another weight was added to the developer's scale and finally tipped it. The Argentine economy went into a tailspin. Shortly afterward, Lincoln West's developers defaulted on their initial loan and the Chase Manhattan Bank foreclosed. The death of Lincoln West came more quickly than its birth. Sloppy finances and overblown costs were held to blame.

City Hall is aware of the problem and is hopeful about getting Lincoln West II started. A new developer, Donald Trump, bought the land for $95 million, which is about three times the price paid for it by Varsavsky and Hirschfield. Trump believes Lincoln West is a risk worth taking. Meanwhile, Hirshfield has held onto 20 percent of the land and has become Trump's silent partner. As for Trump, the young millionaire is known as an exceptional "packager" of high-priced real estate. He is an aggressive builder who has run newspaper advertisements showing the Lincoln West site as a pile of rubbish, with a caption reading "One hundred acres of New York's wild west is about to become Manhattan's most vital community."[33]

Trump is trying to live up to his claim. In 1985 he unveiled his plan for Lincoln West II, nearly twice the size of its predecessor. Trump hopes to construct a platform over the thirteen-block site and plant high rises, parking lots, and commercial and green space upon it. This already formidable project is to be capstoned by the erection of the world's tallest building, whose spire would pierce the Manhattan skyline. If built, the project would blanket the West Side with 60,000 new residents and workers. Trump's tower would cast a shadow across the width of the Hudson that would, in the afternoon sun, rotate onto Harlem.

With over a million square feet of studio, Lincoln West II is supposed to furnish a new home for media, and Trump christened his project "Television City." To make "Television City" work, the developer sought to attract the National Broadcasting Company. When NBC threatened to relocate out of Manhattan, Trump thought he could marry his own interests with those of the Mayor, nervous about NBC's departure. The cost of such a union was high, with Trump asking for thirty years free from taxes. When Koch's aides told him the offer was "ridiculous," Trump submitted another bid. This time, the developer suggested that the UDC buy the land from him for one dollar, then lease the land back to the Trump Organization. At the end of the lease period, the property would revert back to Trump for the same dollar. In return, the Mayor could claim that he kept NBC in New York and Trump would brighten the city's fiscal horizon by sharing with the city one-fifth to one-quarter of his profits.[34]

The strategic benefits for development were enormous. The UDC would shield Trump from ULURP, give him loose rein over zoning requirements, free him from twenty years worth of taxes, and allow him to recapture title to the land. The political tactics were also clever. Trump had put the Mayor in what seemed the untenable position of either assenting to his proposal or turning away the largest television network in the nation.

Koch refused the alliance and shot back, saying "what's good for Mr. Trump isn't necessarily what's good for the people of . . . New York." The mayor also took a swipe at the size of Lincoln West II by indicating that he was not disposed to supporting a project of such unreasonable dimensions. At this Trump exploded, calling the mayor a "moron," his aides "jerks," and the city a "cesspool of corruption."[35] Never one to shy away from trading insults, Koch held back and instead outflanked Trump by making a direct offer to NBC. The Mayor told the network that it could transfer tax abatements to any locale within the city, including, if it so wished, Lincoln West II. Within a short time NBC took up the Mayor's offer (sweetened with more tax benefits) by deciding to refurbish its existing headquarters. In a few brilliant strokes Koch portrayed himself as above parochial interests and as a "can do" politician, while leaving "Television City" without a major network.

Whatever happens to Lincoln West II, it is not likely to escape the conditions of Lincoln West I. Trump may be pumping up his plans so that he can give away what he never intended to keep, but politicians will not see this as a clean slate. There are expectations about what the site is reasonably capable of absorbing, and Trump's altercation with the Mayor underscored these. Lincoln West I also made sure that development would be accompanied by "amenities," and anyone interested in the site will have to meet its restrictive declarations—or explain throughout the ULURP process why this is impossible.

West Siders still resist large-scale development and are readying themselves for another fight. They have already taken up collections and resurrected a neighborhood pressure group. Mimeographed handouts bespeak the exuberant support West Siders give to the cause. In slightly exaggerated language the handouts claim

> [We] took Lincoln West to court on your behalf. We slowed the developer down. . . . We delayed start of construction long enough to expose weaknesses in the developer's financial structure, long enough that the banks had to foreclose on loans they had given to him.[36]

On the streets of the West Side, buttons reading "Stop Lincoln West" are being worn again. They did not even have to be remade.

Times Square/42nd Street   Times Square is the most famous district in New York City—some would say in the world. It was intended that way by those who pioneered its development. Two hundred years ago the larger tract surrounding Times Square and 42nd Street was a solitary farm. John Jacob Astor came along and bought it for $25,000. Like much of Manhattan, the property was divided and sold into building lots. The city adopted a gridiron plan to hasten construction,[37] and streets running from river to river were carved out at precise intervals. In the other direction, from the uppermost tip of the island down past its midriff, avenues were built at still larger intervals. Much of Manhattan became a grate of thoroughfares; Times Square became the major axis. Trolleys and elevated lines crisscrossed its intersections. Boarding houses sprang up along the way. Many of the city's carriage makers located their businesses in the neighborhood. Drawing on the name of the area where their London counterparts also made carriages, the artisans called their section Longacre Square.[38] Other businesses occupied the burgeoning neighborhood. Light industry rented the uppermost floors of some buildings; restaurants, cafés and general stores took over at street level.

By 1904 the city had constructed its first subway. It ran northward and traversed 42nd Street at the juncture of Broadway. Property values soared in the area and so too did the construction of commercial buildings, hotels, and theaters. Adolf Ochs, who started the *New York Times* crowned 42nd Street by purchasing a triangular plot at its intersection with Broadway. On it he built one of the tallest buildings in the city and named it Times Tower. Ochs's newspaper and his building were about to become one of New York's great landmarks. The City Council later affirmed that distinction by naming the site Times Square.[39]

Times Square was a local wonder. The Tower contained more steel than any other building of its era and could be seen for twelve miles around. Ochs assured its reknown by dedicating the Tower to a public celebration each New Year's Eve. From 1908 on, the New Year was welcomed by lowering a lighted ball down the Tower's seventy-foot flagpole, an event that has since become a national spectacle.

It was not long before a bevy of theaters appeared around Times Square. One after another opera, burlesque, and play houses lined the streets. Oscar Hammerstein built some of the first grand theaters, which were linked by a glass-enclosed bar, a dance hall, fountains, waterfalls and a live menagerie. Up above there were rooftop gardens. Times Square's Broadway became the code word for legitimate entertainment. The city's aristocracy frequented its fine plays, its cabarets, and its bawdier comedy.

By the Roaring Twenties, Times Square was at its peak. George M. Cohan inspired the Square's mood by setting it to music. His statue is not far away, inscribed with the titles "Over There," "Give My Regards to Broadway," and "You're a Grand Old Flag." No fewer than nine train lines, twelve surface lines, and a ferry stopped somewhere along the 42nd Street corridor.[40] For those traveling a longer distance, Grand Central Station was on the east side of 42nd Street and Penn Central just blocks away to the southwest.

The neighborhood around the bright lights was a world apart. A veritable shantytown of Irish immigrants popped up along the western fringes. Later, these shacks were replaced by dour-looking tenements, whose new luxuries included a bathroom for each floor's families. The Irish worked in New York's docks, railyards, and stockyards. Fathers and sons were a tough, beer-drinking, feisty lot, whose neighborhood was nicknamed "Hell's Kitchen." Like many of New York's immigrants, the Irish of Hell's Kitchen took charge of their own affairs. Politicians, bureaucrats, and priests were raised on its streets.

By the Depression, the high life of Times Square had begun to dwindle. The theaters and fancy cabarets were displaced by a honkytonk town. Pinball arcades, gun-shooting galleries, and tacky souvenir stands arose to cater to a different kind of crowd. At first the change was gradual and given scant mention. But when pornography was added to the list of Times Square's varieties, the transformation became all too conspicuous.

By the early 1970s Times Square's social nosedive was well under way. Though its physical structure was intact, its streets were seedy and run down. Every other storefront was either a topless bar, a sex shop, or had a window that featured the latest in street weaponry and sadistic torture. Its corners and alleyways were nesting places for drugs and prostitution. Its theaters were converted into sleazy entertainment that featured "action films." The garish atmosphere attracted an assortment of loiterers, derelicts, and petty thieves, who by posture or action threatened ordinary pedestrians. What was once hailed as the "crossroads of the world" was now too dangerous for tourists.

Yet Times Square has its saving graces. Whatever its streets have turned into during the years of decline, they have retained their identity and a certain attractiveness. The short streets and human-scale environment afford a relief from the rest of Midtown's skyscrapers. The bright lights amid the airy skyline give Times Square a unique and thrilling presence. Even its sleaziness has added to the color. On any given day, evangelists preach to sinners and hawkers sell messianic newspapers.

Given its intrinsic virtues, most New Yorkers felt Times Square could be reclaimed. It has been the object of countless police sweeps. The words "clean up Times Square" were familiar, but they were unfulfilled promises. No sooner had the street hustlers been packed into police vans than bail was posted and the area filled with the same crowd. It was obvious that Times Square would need something more than police raids. Physical renovation would have to pave the way for social reformation.

The first proposals to come out of this new realization were generated by government, private enterprise, and leading foundations. These organizations came up with their own plan, "The City at 42nd Street." Their idea was to rebuild Times Square and 42nd Street as an avenue of recreation, culture, and commerce, all of which would advertise the marvels of urban life. The plan included a large museum, a theme park, and a fashion center. There was also provision for a hotel and office towers. Topping off "The City at 42nd Street" was an amusement ride that simulated movement through layers of New York, from the subway to the tip of a skyscraper.[41]

The Mayor was dismayed. Aside from the alleged infeasibility of "The City at 42nd Street," Koch disliked its tone. Never one to equivocate, the Mayor rebuked the entire idea, saying, "New York cannot and should not compete with Disneyland—that's for Florida. We've got to make sure we have seltzer instead of orange juice."[42]

Besides these objections, Koch added that he had difficulty with the way in which the plan was formulated. It was too monopolistic and too closed. Although he was committed to doing something about Times Square, he wanted it done "publicly" with city guidelines, community comment, and agency participation. The key to making sure the process was open, Koch opined, was to rely on competitive bidding.[43]

So the Mayor turned to the state to help make the new choices for Times Square. In 1980 Koch and Cuomo signed a Memorandum of Understanding in which the UDC and City Planning were asked to prepare a program for development and find suitable developers.[44] UDC and City Planning became the lead agencies in the rebuilding of Times Square, joined soon afterward by the PDC. As an arm of the state, the UDC represented the Governor; PDC and City Planning reflected Koch's priorities. Translated, the arrangement meant that the future of Times

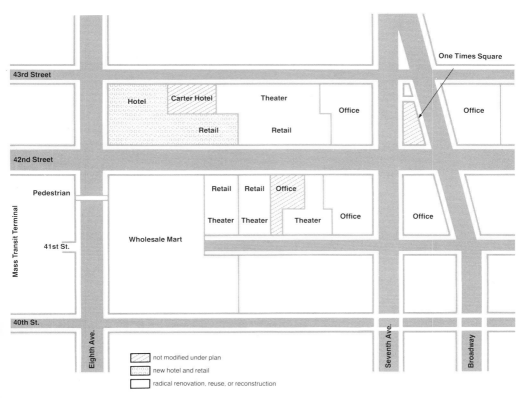

Fig. 3.6. The Plan for Times Square/42nd Street. Source: New York State Urban Development Corporation.

Square depended on the good fellowship of Ed Koch and Mario Cuomo.

Incorporated into the competitive bidding was an elaborate set of guidelines that were supposed to ensure that any new design would do justice to Times Square's open qualities and distinct vista. Of great concern was the height and bulk of buildings. People feared that Times Square could be overshadowed by more skyscrapers.

To guard against abuse, the guidelines stressed the integrity of the streets, the area's low roofline, and the characteristics that gave it fame eighty years ago. These requirements, it was pointed out, were "not discretionary."[45] Twenty-six proposals were received and over two years lapsed before a decision was made.

Given the concern over ecological values, the eventual choice came

73

as a surprise to New York's architectural buffs and landmark lovers. Instead of conservation, more concrete and glass would loom into the sky. The new plan was formidable. It called for the construction of four office towers, a wholesaler's merchandise mart, a hotel, and the renovation of nine theaters. Over four million square feet of office space would be built in towers rising from twenty-five to fifty-six stories high.

Figures 3.6 and 3.7 portray the uses, scope, and content of the Times Square/42nd Street Plan. Figure 3.6 is a planning scheme laying out how the area is to be used. Figure 3.7 is an architectural rendition of buildings that will surround the new Times Square. The highlighted buildings are those proposed for construction.

Each of the buildings is located at a strategic corner of Times Square. Once built, they will shroud the historic site in a quartet of megastructures. A tiny triangular island that bears the marking Number 1 Times Square might remain, but as a speck at the bottom of a well. The fate of Adolf Ochs's landmark, Times Tower, is uncertain. At best it might coexist with its flat, high-rise neighbors.

If this was Ed Koch's version of "seltzer," he would have to do more to please the critics than offer them a 2 cents plain. The former architectural critic for the *New York Times*, Ada Louise Huxtable, described the new towers as "enormous pop-up buildings with fancy hats."[46] A journalist from the *Village Voice* called them "dark hulking slabs."[47] A historian at New York University lamented that the new plan violated Times Square's past and said it was "contemptuous of the public character of the streets."[48]

Koch shot back at the critics, calling them "idiots."[49] When asked why the new plan ignored his own guidelines, Koch retorted, "I for one have never felt it necessary to explain why we improve something."[50]

The real explanation had little to do with architecture, the environment, or historic preservation. More than anything else, Times Square was built upon economics. Its planning was shaped by its financial feasibility and by what the city could get out of its redevelopment. The founding stones of the towers were investment obligations and potential revenues.

From the short-term vantage point, the city came out on the right side of the investment and revenue scale. Private investors put up almost all of the cash and assumed nearly all of the risks. These investors were to pay the costs for acquisition, demolition, renovation, and reconstruction. Meanwhile they would not hold title to the land. For at least fifteen years, UDC would be the landlord.[51]

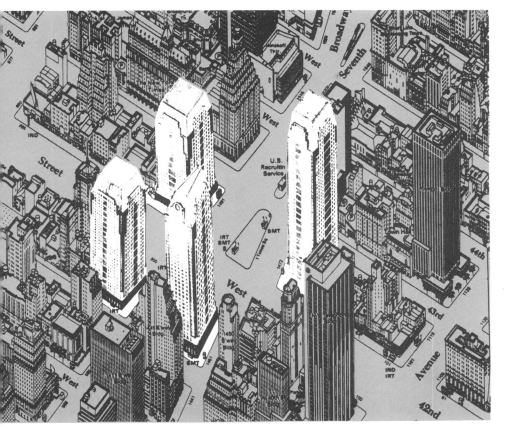

Fig. 3.7. New Buildings for Times Square/42nd Street, Bill Wilkinson, Architectural Illustrator.

The financial particulars are contained in an elaborate leasing agreement, through which the developers pay a stipulated rent plus a percentage of net revenue to UDC. This is known as a "payment in lieu of taxes," or PILOT. Under PILOT, leases can be granted to developers for as long as ninety-nine years, and payments can be reduced if the costs of acquisition exceed a prearranged limit. Because the UDC is a public agency and exempt from municipal taxes, all payments derived from PILOT are turned over to the city.[52]

From one perspective the city is supposed to reap a harvest. By the year 2005 the project is estimated to yield several hundred million in direct revenues.[53] Furthermore, the investment costs for remaking the public's land will cost the developers an estimated $2.4 billion.[54] Not only is the land underneath the new megastructures to be prepared for renewal, but so too is Times Square's midblocks of theaters, whose renovation cost, estimated at $15 million, is borne by the developers. A final touch of gold for the city is an "amenities package" worth roughly $90 million.[55] These amenities include the costs of subway reconstruction, improvements along Eighth Avenue, and the building of a pedestrian bridge across it.

And these are just the direct, hands-on rewards that would accrue to the public. There are supposed to be other delights for New Yorkers, including a projected 21,000 jobs, new streets, more commerce, and lots of middle-class workers to saturate the streets.[56] If the city could not excise Times Square's sleaze, the jobs and new people most certainly would smother it.

The city's harvest is not without its exactions from the urban soil. Developers are not public philanthropists. They are adept at making profits, and they do this by adding height and bulk to buildings as well as by speculating in the value of land. By most accounts, the developers have done well. The new buildings contain more than twice the allowable limits on internal space. Although the developers have their own PILOT payments fixed at a low level, they will be able to sublet that space at some of the highest rents in the world.

Moreover, Times Square's new face will be enhanced by a temporary reprieve from city taxes, and part of that face may eventually belong to private investors. During its fifteen-year building period, the project will be under the UDC umbrella, and its developers will enjoy a sizable tax abatement. After that, those same developers can exercise an option to purchase any of the skyscrapers. The formula for purchase is generous and would allow developers to take title at bargain rates.[57]

Another exaction would have been levied from New York's older industry in the garment center. The city has opted for post-industrial change, and those to pay the price were to be smaller manufacturers. A rebuilt Times Square was supposed to feature a wholesale market, and garment manufacturers were supposed to take advantage of a new central locale. But smaller firms unable to pay the steep rents would have been left in the cold. The UDC's own study confirmed this, projecting a loss of about fifty firms and five hundred jobs.[58]

These financial underpinnings were compounded by the politics of making it all work. The hinge between public and private interests was the UDC As a public corporation, UDC could swing past the ordinary process of government, thereby circumventing all kinds of local opposition. But the hinge was fastened by the tenuous glue of politicians and developers. There were disagreements between public and private parties. There were rivalries between developers. Not least, the city and the state were at odds over which developers to choose and over how much control would be accorded to the principals.

When UDC took a vote against Koch, the Mayor walked out and told reporters that the city would not be treated as "a vassal."[59] Times Square's redevelopment had practically collapsed when, on a Sunday evening, Mario Cuomo met Ed Koch in the empty lobby of the World Trade Center.[60] They had come to work out their differences, and it was the Governor who made concessions. As Cuomo tells it, the two men sat in the Governor's office and Cuomo laid out the priorities:

> "One, we must do the project. Everybody else had failed. Two, the city must be respected. Three, nobody has an agenda other than getting the best developers. Four, we should not give any group too much control over the project."[61]

Having heard that Cuomo was willing to respect the city, Koch reentered the negotiations. Eventually a consortium of developers was chosen. The leading sponsors still needed to be convinced to settle for a smaller piece of the project, and UDC, PDC, and City Planning worked together to persuade investors to settle for a much reduced role. The negotiations were difficult because noncooperation by one developer could have meant the collapse of another investor's interest. Public officials used economic threats to win their point ("If you don't work toward the Governor's compromise, the deal's off—we're going to kick you out").[62] Warnings and implicit promises were made to prospective investors ("You have a long life to live in this city—don't be a warrior").[63] And eventually the major investors relented and agreed to cooperate (said one unhappy realtor, "If you want to get along, you've got to go along").[64]

Eventually the matter was settled. No one developer would control the project. The lead agency would be the UDC, working in close conjunction with PDC and City Planning.

Now that Koch and Cuomo had struck the deals, there was still the hurdle of the Board of Estimate. Although the UDC could make end runs around ULURP, the Koch-Cuomo Memorandum of Understanding required that the Board of Estimate approve leases connected to the plan.

As the decision came to a head in the spring of 1984, the opposition organized. Over the years Hell's Kitchen had changed. Ethnic pockets of Hispanics, Greeks, and blacks had replaced the Irish. Parts of the area were gentrified with young, white professionals. The new status brought a new name; Hell's Kitchen became Clinton. Despite outward differences the people of Clinton were united in their dislike for the plan. They feared its success and the commercial invasion that was sure to come. Joining the popular opposition was a commercial class threatened with displacement. This included local merchants, manufacturers, unions from the garment center, and owners of entertainment houses. A majority of this opposition conceded the need for some change. They agreed with Mario Cuomo's plea that Times Square needed to "save its soul,"[65] but they were worried about the price of its redemption.

Once again the Board of Estimate would stand between top politicians, developers, and the unarticulated consensus of the larger city on one side and local politicians, the Clinton community, and neighborhood business on the other. The Board's vote would be crucial. Anywhere along the way, the project could be wounded or dealt a fatal blow. For the first time in five years, Mayor Koch presided over the Board. For the first time in thirty-five years, the Governor of New York State made a personal appearance. The senior Senator from New York appeared.[66] Also appearing to applaud the new plan were two former mayors.

Opponents were in an awkward position. They were caught in the trap of either going along with the plan or defending Times Square as it was. "Frankly, it appears that the votes are there for 42nd Street," said one Borough President who questioned the plan. "It's a place everyone wants cleaned up."[67] A carpenter expressed the inexorable tide of opinion when he called Times Square "a cancer" and then told the Board, "the project means to me and my family the difference of eating and not eating."[68]

By the time of the Board's vote in November of 1984, the outcome was little in doubt. In near vacant chambers surrogates for Board members cast their ballots. Their vote was unanimously in favor.

City Council President Carol Bellamy and the Manhattan Borough President held out, but ultimately, as expected, voted for the project. Koch and Cuomo knew something had to be given to the opposition. That turned out to be $25 million to Clinton for "neighborhood stabilization." Garment manufacturers and workers were promised a study and further consideration of their problems.

Though lost in a sea of approval, the opposition searched for a friendly beacon. After the vote was taken, one local politician appealed to his constituents:

We've been told many times with other projects that it's over.
You've lost. There's nothing you can do about it. . . . and Lincoln
West, that was passed by the Board of Estimate two years ago and
we fought it. . . .

We were told to make your peace. Sit down with the developers.
Well, it ain't been built and in fact, the developers had to sell out.
Just because the Board of Estimate approved this project our fight is
not over. . . . Our fight is just beginning.[69]

There was more to these remarks than political bluster. Like many
other public projects, Times Square is a patchwork of collaboration
between City Hall, the Governor's Mansion, public authorities, and a
number of major investors. The patchwork is fragile and can be pulled
apart by internal dissension, financial crisis, or external opposition. A
stalemate between public agencies, a sudden pullout by investors, or
judicial blockage can unravel these threads of collaboration.

When the municipal scandals of 1986 shook the city, they also tore
at the Times Square project. Revelations that one developer was im-
plicated in the scandals brought the entire project into question. Still
another developer, facing financial difficulties, waivered. Booming
real estate prices added to the public cost and the project seemed less
feasible. Critics wondered whether Times Square could not rejuvenate
by itself and might be better off without government intervention. On
top of this, over two dozen lawsuits put the project in jeopardy. The
legal complaints covered a multitude of sins. They ranged from property owners faced with dispossession to the elderly suffering the loss
of "familiar and reassuring sites." Added to the list of plaintiffs were
sex shop proprietors, who complained that the project prejudiced their
business, and environmentalists, who contended that it would bring
more air pollution.[70]

For a while, it looked as if Times Square's sponsors could never be
brought together. Politics and land development are creatures of perception, and the mere perception that one party was pulling out threatened to accelerate into the stinging reality that others would pull out.
But the Mayor and the Governor held on, the technocrats from UDC
and PDC renegotiated PILOT and other payments in relation to higher
land prices, and new developers joined the venture. The idea for a mass
garment center exodus to a single building was quietly dropped and
replaced by other possible uses for a wholesale mart. Over a two-year
period the major suits were dismissed. By 1988 most of Times
Square's supports had been rewoven.

Westway An automobile ride up the western rim of Manhattan is a scenic exploration. The rim's high bluffs look out on the Hudson and across to the Palisades. As the shoreline snakes northward it burrows into the woods of the Cloisters and then climbs up to the pastures of Westchester.

It was not always a pleasant or an easy trip. In the early part of the century, ferry boats were needed to carry people to the mainland. The shoreline was strewn with piles of rotted timber and freight trains bellowed black smoke as they clanked up and down the riverbank. By 1936, the trip from Manhattan to the mainland was made possible by bridges and roads that Robert Moses had built.[71] Those roads connected to the old West Side Highway.

The West Side Highway was built as an elevated roadway. It began at the tip of Manhattan and ran to 72nd Street, where it connected to another parkway. Built for cars only, it was a magnificent though treacherous route. Its cobblestone surface and left-sided exits gave unfamiliar motorists palpitations. Others more accustomed to the ride were reminded of a time when cars were fewer and roadways were built as ornate pieces of architecture.

Fifty years after its completion, the West Side Highway was obsolete. Its rickety supports and tortuous lanes could not bear up to the legions of automobiles that besieged the city each day. At rush hours the highway choked with bumper-to-bumper traffic. When hordes of motorists flocked to leave the city during the summer months, the West Side Highway became one huge parking lot. The scenery was still there, but few motorists could enjoy it. Their eyes were fixed on a sooty windshield and on the endless rows of bumpers before them.

In 1969, state transportation planners recommended that the highway be torn down and rebuilt for integration into a network of interstate auto routes. The idea was the brainchild of two technocrats who had made their careers soliciting urban renewal funds from the Federal Government.[72] Once again, Washington was happy to cooperate. Planners in the federal highway bureaucracy wanted to extend the interstate system. Only an interstate could carry trucks and heavy commercial traffic, and this was a perfect way to link New York's industry with Boston, Philadelphia, and Washington.

New York's top politicians soon took the lead in pushing the idea for a new highway. By 1971 Nelson Rockefeller made himself the most powerful Governor in the state's history. One big project after another added to Rockefeller's popularity, and he was especially enthusiastic about this one. The Mayor at the time, John Lindsay, was cautious. He was concerned that the state would gobble up the work and the credit for a new superhighway. He wanted his own agencies to control planning.

Lindsay and Rockefeller finally agreed. City Hall would take charge; the Governor would furnish the backup. City Planning would prepare the design that laid out the possibilities associated with a new highway.[73] The plan did more than contour a path for motor vechicles; it proposed a full-scale land-use plan with houses, factories, and playgrounds.

In the meantime a key operative, Lowell Bridwell, was hired to head what was to become the West Side Highway Project.[74] Bridwell was an imposing and intense figure. As an experienced Washington hand, he knew how to put a project together. His first priority was not engineering but politics.

Bridwell knew that whatever else happened, he was likely to be sued. In readying himself for the occasion he turned to the public pulse, rather than to lawyers. "We are in a period of intense public participation," he said. "The level of involvement of interest groups and the . . . consideration given to their views has risen dramatically."[75] Bridwell began contacting neighborhood groups almost immediately. About seventy-five separate groups were involved, each with from twenty-five to fifty people. The project had an extensive network and its staff participated in more than six hundred meetings, briefings, and workshops.

The strategy was purposeful. By meeting with many small groups, Bridwell hoped to avoid their coalescence into a large bloc. Further, by coming onto neighborhood turf, Bridwell prevented aggressive West Siders from invading his.

The strategy also had advantages that fed into the planning process. It enabled Bridwell to feel his way around the social landscape, and in doing so, he developed alternatives for the new highway. Initially, these ideas were formulated into seventeen different alternatives. Sifting and revision whittled this number down to five.[76] The remaining alternatives spanned a continuum from the most conservative approaches:

1. Maintain the existing highway.

2. Reconstruct the existing highway.

To a single mid-range suggestion:

3. Build an arterial highway at grade level and keep it small.

To two radical choices:

4. Construct an inboard highway at grade level and make it a six-lane

interstate autoroute. Parts of this highway would be depressed and 21 acres of new land would be created through landfill operations.

5. Construct an outboard highway beyond the existing shoreline, using landfill, and make it a six-lane interstate autoroute. Most of the waterfront would be replaced and over 240 acres of new land would be reclaimed for extensive redevelopment.

The choices were prepared with plans and mock-ups. By this time a new Mayor–Governor team was in office. Abe Beame had replaced John Lindsay at City Hall and Hugh Carey had moved to Albany. Besides new personalities, new circumstances were shaping decisions and narrowing the field.

The first of these circumstances was physical. In December 1973, a truck making repairs to the West Side Highway fell through its roadbed. Like a child's toy it dangled over the streets below before rescue workers arrived. The incident was no mere fluke or the result of an isolated weak spot on the road's surface. Years of neglect finally led to a dramatic casualty. Much of the highway was on the verge of collapse; half of it was shut down and motorists were forced onto Manhattan's gridlocked streets.

The second and third circumstances were financial. Federal highway law makes it extremely attractive for cities to build interstate routes rather than repair existing ones. Funding for interstates is provided by Washington at $90 for every $10 put up by the states. Big projects bring in big bucks, and clever planners can combine highways with other kinds of development, thereby getting Washington to pay for a huge proportion of the improvement. These considerations weighed heavily with Beame and Carey, but when the fiscal crisis of 1974-1975 left both New York State and City dry, interstate funding looked like an oasis in the desert.

Paradoxically, the simplest alternatives (maintenance, reconstruction, a small arterial road) turned out to be the most financially troublesome. Given Carey and Beame's calculations, the most expensive route for Washington was the cheapest for them. They were convinced that the most feasible successor was some kind of interstate auto route.

By the spring of 1975 Carey and Beame had reached a decision. Major features of the outboard route were linked to the inboard proposal to produce Westway. A partially depressed highway, Westway was only 4.2 miles long and ran from the tip of Manhattan up to 42nd Street. Westway was designed as a six-lane highway, though service roads broadened it to eight lanes. In order to make way for inland development, Westway would be built on landfill deposited in the Hud-

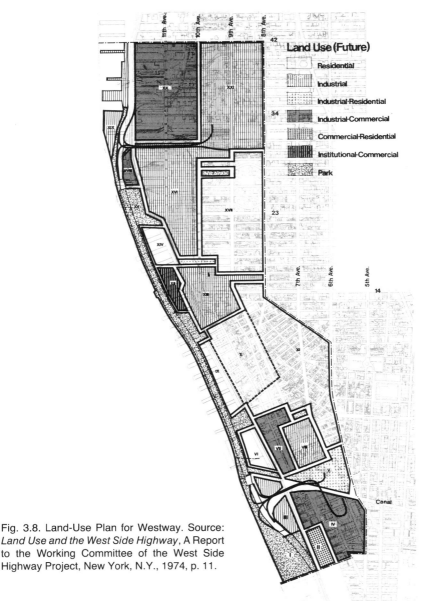

Land Use (Future)

◻◯ Residential

▦ Industrial

⸬ Industrial-Residential

▩ Industrial-Commercial

▥ Commercial-Residential

▮ Institutional-Commercial

⣿ Park

Fig. 3.8. Land-Use Plan for Westway. Source: *Land Use and the West Side Highway*, A Report to the Working Committee of the West Side Highway Project, New York, N.Y., 1974, p. 11.

son River. The ultimate costs of this scheme varied, though experts put it at $4 billion, or $7,500 per inch.[77] For its size, Westway would have been the most expensive highway in the world. Figure 3.8 presents a land-use map of the Westway project. Figure 3.9 shows the highway in panoramic view.

83

Fig. 3.9. Westway: A View from Lower Manhattan. Photo/New York State Department of Transportation

For a highway of little more than four miles, the development scheme is dazzling. Residence, commerce, industry, parks, and waterfront are piled on almost every side of Westway. The entire project was supposed to generate over $7 billion in private investment. Another 7,300 jobs were supposed to be created through the next decade. If built, billions more in property values and taxes would have been added to the ledgers of municipal accountants—and still more to the region's gross national product.[78]

It was not surprising that Westway garnered an impressive following. Its supporters were a "who's who" of New York and included the leading business people, bankers, and planning associations. Personalities like David Rockefeller, Felix Rohatyn, the publishers of the *New York Times*, and experts from the Regional Planning Association took up the cause of Westway. Three Presidents of the United States and their Secretaries of Transportation have supported Westway. Not only big business and big politics, however, backed the plans. Big labor was also solidly behind it. The state's AFL–CIO, the Teamster's local, municipal employee unions, and construction workers supported Westway.

In 1976 business and labor joined together in a Business–Labor Working Group. The group represented 150 organizations and began under the joint leadership of David Rockefeller (Chase Manhattan Bank) and Harry Van Arsdale (Central Trades and Labor Council). Rockefeller and Van Arsdale lobbied for Westway at the highest levels in Washington.[79] They tried to sell Westway on the basis of its economic potential, its job-creating possibilities, and its tax revenues.

On at least this issue, organized labor and organized finance were in accord. Both acknowledged that "Westway is essential to preserving the substantial investment already made by the public and private sector . . . in lower Manhattan." Both had pledged "their collective efforts" to ensure Westway's success.[80]

Yet despite the enormous head of organizational steam that propelled Westway, its future was always in doubt. Since that day when a truck fell through the old highway, Westway has been mired in one obstacle after another. The delays have been brought on by the numerous decision points that are the logos of New York politics. For Westway these include appropriations by the state legislature, studies by the Army Corps of Engineers, dredge and fill permits by federal agencies, court challenges, and even action by the Congress.

An alert and motivated group can make the most of these moments by converting them into stumbling blocks and permanent pitfalls. Westway's opposition was small but effective. What it lacked in mass or inside political clout, it made up in energy and sagacity. Much of the fight was spearheaded by a crusading *pro bono* community organizer, Marcy Benstock. For ten years Benstock, together with friendly lawyers, waged an uphill fight. She buttonholed local politicians, won them over as allies, and cobbled together a formidable coalition.[81]

Benstock's struggle was made easier by the West Side of New York, whose population is fertile ground for political resistance. Like Br'er Rabbit in the briar patch, Benstock thrived in this community. Benstock's natural allies were the community boards, whose influence is lodged in a string of neighborhoods along the western rim of Manhattan. Despite Bridwell's earlier efforts to win support for the superhighway, West Siders were apprehensive. They feared that its access ramps would slice through their neighborhoods and bring a deluge of trucks and automobiles. They also worried about the growing pressures of capital investment on residential neighborhoods, and wondered whether Westway would add to their troubles.[82]

Benstock collaborated with the community boards and provided them with information and arguments against the highway. In between her trips to Albany and Washington, she traveled to local boards urging them to join the fight.[83]

Although the community boards held no formal role in the process, they did express their sentiment. In one resolution after another, boards registered their opposition. On the lower West Side, the community board voted its unalterable opposition and met with local legislators to garner their support. On the upper West Side the community board convinced state legislators that Westway should not reach past 42nd Street. In Midtown, the board was divided over the superhighway and put off the most controversial vote.[84]

This opposition was confined to neighborhood pockets and said little about the rest of the city. But it was effective in forcing top politicians into a protracted conflict. Top politicians initiated action only to have it challenged at critical points of the political process. Leading politicians then became consumed in meeting the challenge, and opponents took advantage of the pause by bringing their arguments to the public.

The opposition also managed to put some of New York's most powerful politicians on the defensive. Opponents discredited Westway in the press (calling it "Wasteway")—thus casting politicians into the embarrassment of cradling a "white elephant."[85] Opponents persuaded the state legislature to deny funding for the superhighway—until the Governor finally rescued it with a veto. Opponents succeeded in getting the Army Corps of Engineers to delay permits for dredging and left the Governor to unravel the red tape.

After Koch became Mayor, he backed off on a promise that, if he were elected, Westway would not be built. Koch soon joined Hugh Carey and later Mario Cuomo in coming to Westway's defense.[86] Mario Cuomo was even more forceful in trying to pull Westway out of a political morass. Apparently unsuccessful in getting the Army Corps of Engineers to act quickly, a frustrated Cuomo turned to the White House. In a letter to Ronald Reagan, he wrote, "Your administration has committed itself to the streamlining of [the] regulatory process," and then complained, "Surely the Army Corps of Engineers can deal with the narrow issues [of Westway] in a more timely fashion."[87]

One by one the Governor and the Mayor worked to remove the obstacles and, for a time, they appeared to succeed. But the opposition persisted, the questions gnawed, and each delay crippled the project's momentum. Using the political process, the opposition bogged down the superhighway in a public debate. The opposition blocked, critiqued, and tried to show there was a better way. Benstock and her allies argued that a smaller, cheaper highway should be built; that Westway was an environmental hazard; and that federal funds for an interstate could be traded in to support subways and buses.

The Westway dragon could not be felled by a single blow, but it was vulnerable to sniping. The longer Westway could be delayed, the greater the chances to question its credibility and muster allies.

The most effective way to do this was through the courts.[88] Evironmental Impact Statements gave opposition groups a new platform from which to launch legal appeals. Initial results were not definitive, but they were encouraging. By 1982 a federal judge ruled that the environmental impact of the project had not been adequately examined. At issue was the survival of striped bass, which apparently had grown accustomed to the river's piers and used them as spawning nests. Significantly, the courtroom gave opponents the chance to put Westway on trial.

New studies and new trials continued through the fall of 1985. Allegations were made that consultants and lawyers who worked for Westway had withheld vital information in order to obtain landfill permits. The episode mushroomed into charges of a Watergate-type cover-up. Adding to the scandal was the admission by Bridwell that he had not told the complete truth because "that would have been an absolute bomb . . . [for] the state's case."[89]

Westway's landfill permits were voided. The state appealed. Although the Appeals Court left the door open for a "fresh look at the collected data," a pall was cast over the project.[90] On the same day that the U.S. Court of Appeals rendered its judgment, the House of Representatives voted to withdraw interstate funding for landfill operations. Koch called the House's action "a blow" to Westway, but he insisted that it was "not a body blow."[91] The Mayor still hoped the U.S. Senate would restore the funding. When New York's senior Senator reported that restoration was not possible, Koch admitted the project might not see the light of day. Koch told reporters, "you can hear the death rattle."[92] A day later a crestfallen Mayor conceded, "It's dead," and added ". . . those responsible for its death carry a heavy burden."[93]

Westway may be deceased, but the issue of its replacement is very much alive. The city is scheduled to receive $1.7 billion in federal trade-in funds. Both Koch and Cuomo have agreed that only 40 percent will go toward another highway and the remaining 60 percent will go toward mass transit. Guidelines specify that any substitute roadway cannot encroach upon the river, that Westway's replacement must be a boulevard-type facility (with traffic signals, intersections) and that any plans for the western rim must take mass transit into account.[94] To lay the new groundwork, Koch and Cuomo appointed a West Side Task Force, whose composition was heavily weighted with technocrats and public officials.

Judging from these concessions, it would appear that victory might be in the hands of Westway's opponents. It would seem that the remaining choices might be more technical than controversial and that the costs for a new highway would be relatively modest. We also might expect that Westway's ending might be more like a minor skirmish in an anticlimax than a fresh adventure.

New York is not a city given to easy expectations. Within a few months of the superhighway's demise, there was a whiff in the political air that Westway I might turn into Westway II. The West Side Task Force made its recommendations, confirming the fears of anti-Westway stalwarts. Though the Task Force accepted a boulevard-type facility, it dressed the idea in some of Westway's old garb. The new highway will not, as expected, cost a few hundred million dollars, but closer to a billion dollars. The new roadway will not be an ordinary boulevard, but will rise above and fall below grade level at key intersections.[95]

On the sticky question of the waterfront, the recommendations were evasive. In carefully phrased language, the Task Force stated that it was "neither recommending nor rejecting the use of landfill or platforming" over the Hudson.[96] Apparently the Task Force has kept a distance from this irresistible asset. This reluctance has not stopped other public agencies. Planners from the UDC talked long ago about promoting "phased construction" beside the riverfront.[97] More recently, the head of BPC began percolating ideas about filling in more sections of the Hudson. His idea is to extend Battery Park City northward by using the filled-in portions of the Hudson for parks and office development.[98] Keeping an eye on its sister agencies, City Planning is studying how development would generate additional traffic along the waterfront.[99] There are also proposals for a light rail system that would reach from lower Manhattan up to the site of Lincoln West. Still other city agencies see the unused piers of the Hudson as sites for housing.[100]

Thus, what Westway I could not bring in through the front door in one fell swoop, may be attempted through the back door, piece by piece. Koch and Cuomo have approved the Task Force's recommendations. Westway II and a fight over the waterfront could create new political contests. Analysts of the city politic know there are few permanent victories in New York, but they had not counted on so fast a replay. Mario Cuomo once referred to Westway I as "a walnut in the batter of eternity"—big at the moment, but destined to be drowned by newer memories.[101] Westway may not be quite so episodic. A different vision might picture Westway as a schooner, first devastated by a storm, luffing for a while, then dispatching smaller crews to take different tacks toward port.

Summary Analysis

As mentioned, crucial decisions in New York are propelled by corporatist politics that unite politicians with different kinds of organized interests. Top politicians or technocrats took the lead in promoting two projects (Times Square and Westway), and in one (Lincoln West) they lent active support. In each case, public and private spheres produced a package of mutual benefits and costs. In Lincoln West investors obtained special zoning rights, but the city was also to profit from taxes and "amenities" to be paid by the developers. In Times Square politicians arranged for an elaborate trade-off that gave developers land and allowed the city investment dollars and future revenues. Westway was also a product of corporatist initiation. There, too, organized interests (the state, the city, the Business-Labor Working Group) arranged a package of mutual advantage and worked together in promoting the project.

By and large the opposition to this corporatist impulsion has been scattered. The strongest bastions of resistance are in specific neighborhoods threatened by post-industrial change. These local interests are legitimated through the community boards. Though the boards have been successful in smaller land-use decisions, they have not been able to prevail on crucial decisions. Community boards have succeeded in extracting concessions, but when top politicians are united and want to build, the boards can be dealt with in any number of ways (concessions, compromise, or circumvention).

Yet for all its corporatist impulsion, the system is laden with pluralist tracks, any one of which can be used by the opposition. Often the opposition arises spontaneously and relies on a neighborhood base of support. As a rule these groups consist of political novices. This does not stop them from winning the support of local politicians. Together this opposition can derail a decision (Westway I) or inflate the costs of its implementation (Lincoln West I). Thus, although the corporatist locomotive moves, it is more like the rattling caboose than the express.

In pointing out the differences between corporatist organizations and pluralist groups, we should note that citywide sentiment was generally more supportive of the "establishment" than it was of the local "populists." The remaking of Times Square was endorsed in every county outside of Manhattan, and Manhattan's opposition was confined to particular pockets (Clinton, affected businesses, intellectuals). In the end not even Carol Bellamy (Koch's natural opponent) voted against the project. Times Square was a decision waiting to happen for ten years, and still it was not easily realized. Only through the active intercession of a popular Governor and equally popular Mayor was Times Square put together.

As a corollary, we should observe that it was neither developers nor land speculators who began boosting Times Square, but politicians and planners. All the plans for Times Square may not be in good taste and all of them may not be good for the local ecology. They may arouse the ire of urban afficionados who, in Times Square's remaking, see elephants dancing among the chickens. But, after all, Times Square's plan makes good business sense—it is good for the city's pocketbook. In all likelihood the plan will reduce crime in the area. Apart from the critics, however valid their criticisms, these facts hearten millions of New Yorkers.

Westway provides a still sharper profile between corporatist organizations and pluralist groups.[102] Westway too may have been an instance of questionable ecology—but it was good finance. For most New Yorkers, it was good politics. During the peak of its political salience, 53 percent of city residents favored the superhighway; 29 percent were opposed.[103] Westway was supported by the broadest citizenry but resisted in some of the affected neighborhoods. This sentiment was reflected among the political elite. Leading officials (governor, mayor) fought on behalf of the highway; local politicians (legislators, members of the community boards) opposed it.

If, as Dahl says, pluralism signifies that an intense minority can make its weight felt, then Westway confirms the pluralist proposition.[104] But it is a proposition in need of limits and qualifications. Westway was amenable to blockage because there are times when decisional junctures are not easily bypassed. It is true that intense minorities can succeed in blocking a decision, but this does not mean they can operate effectively in initiating a decision. And positive results are at least as important as negative power when evaluating group strength. The larger lesson is that although blockage is a product of pluralism, initiation depends upon corporatist organization led by top politicians.

Still another question is the ability of top politicians to push projects through the system. Politically and legally, two out of three decisions were successful. This success may be attributed to the galvanizing capacity of political leadership. New York furnishes substantial flexibility to the skilled and popular leader. Its loose political parties, its multiplicity of interest groups, and its fluid environment provide for a variety of opportunities.

Still, this capacity to organize support remains a potential to be realized by special people working under favorable circumstances. Cuomo and Koch color the city's politics with a combination of skill and popularity, harnessed to a common vision. Lesser talents working with diminished support have produced fewer results.

Although the system can work for radical change, it can also work against it. Coalitions of mayor-governor, public authorities, developers, and unions can fall apart. Overall, the corporatist-pluralist hybrid can be fickle. All too easily, decisions can get caught in a thicket. Top politicians managed to steer Lincoln West and Times Square around the densest parts of that thicket, but in Westway they failed. Cuomo and Koch underestimated the ability of the opposition to turn decisions into the thorniest impasses. The impasses were not simply delays, but entrapments into what one planner called a "procedural infinity,"[105] decision rounds that can go on and on, in which the possibility of victory may be worth neither the price nor the gamble.

Put another way, New York is a city where decisional closure does not come easily. There are always ploys or gambits that can be used by one side or another. Even after a decision is resolved, there exists a chance to resurrect the issue in another form. Lincoln West's financial collapse may well be recovered by Lincoln West II. Westway's political failure can be partially recouped by Westway II.

Finally, although the results of this process are not easy to predict, there is little doubt about the intention of New York's leaders. They have opted for radical post-industrial conversion, centered in Manhattan. Though policy makers have tried to shift blue-collar industry into the first ring, those who cannot adapt are nudged aside. Manhattan steadily acquires a newer, sleeker look and top politicians show no hesitation about continuing the trend. The path is clearly laid out.

Fig. 3.10. Midtown. Photo/Adam Savitch

Fig. 3.11. 42nd Street Today. Photo/Adam Savitch

Fig. 3.12. Times Square Today. Photo/Adam Savitch

Fig. 3.13. Times Square: Proposal for the 1990s. Park Tower Realty

Fig. 3.14. West Side Highway at Midtown. Photo/New York State Department of Transportation

Fig. 3.15 (*at top*). West Side Highway at Battery Park City. Photo/Adam Savitch

Fig. 3.16. West Side Highway Extended: Henry Hudson Parkway. Photo/New York State Department of Transportation

Paris: Concentric Development and Embourgeoisement

Paris is nothing but an immense hospitality.—Victor Hugo, appeal to the German Army to spare Paris, 1870

Paul Delouvrier and Forging the Ile-de-France

URBAN development is always carried out in some kind of context. In France, the major contexts are the historical preeminence of Paris relative to the rest of the country and the fear that that city could fall into the hands of a left-wing working class. Although Paris bears striking resemblances to New York and London, it is different in one profound respect. Its power is not derived from being a great port, but from its political stature as the heart and capital of the nation. In this sense Paris holds a position closer to that of Berlin or Vienna.

To be sure, the political role held by Paris has reinforced its economic and cultural predominance. As the capital of a highly centralized state, roadways and rail lines converged upon the city, making it the transportation hub for all of France. By virtue of this position, construction and manufacture also burgeoned in Paris and it quickly became the commercial and cultural core of France. Napoleonic centralization added to this powerful combination of forces by making Paris the seat of the national bureaucracy. So rigid was the central direction that it was popularly said that every child in France studied the same topic, on the same day, during the same hour, and at precisely the same moment. To do otherwise would apparently be a breach of national unity.

Paris has occupied a role in the nation that has been both unique and supreme. As such it has been the quintessential prize of national sovereignty to be won by whoever captured power. The French Revolution of 1789 set off a chain of events that confirmed this fact. Subsequent uprisings and revolutions throughout nineteenth-century France made Paris a fiery battleground. The revolution of 1870 resulted in a Seine streaked with blood and in the destruction of the city's greatest monuments. The Paris Commune, which the revolutionary Left held for days, symbolized the political struggle between orthodoxy and radicalism that marked French history. That struggle reemerged almost a century later when, in 1968, a revolutionary coalition took up arms in the streets of Paris against President Charles de Gaulle.

Recently, the struggles between Left and Right have worn a more peaceful cloak and have been settled through elections. But feelings are still sharp, and these are tied to the symbols of the Parisian landscape. The Left celebrates victories at the Bastille—testimony to the collapse of the *ancien régime*; the Right stages its festivities at the Arc de Triomphe—monument to the glory of military conquests.

It was the force of such events that gave La Ville de Paris its special political structure.[1] As a nation given to a high degree of centralization, all French cities were subject to the ultimate control of their respective departmental prefects. Places like Lyon or Marseilles could ease the heavy-handedness of the state by having their mayors negotiate with the departmental prefect. However, except for brief interludes between 1789 and 1871, Paris had no mayor. For most of its history Paris was a city subject to the unassuaged supervision of two prefects operating from the Department of the Seine. One prefect administered civil matters; a second was in change of police and security. The arrangement kept Paris tightly within the clutches of the state, which more often than not was controlled by the Right. Violent threats to the regime could be identified at an early stage and dealt with by the Prefect of Police. Political challenges could be warded off by placing municipal services and resources under the watchful eye of the civil prefect.

As long as Paris remained a compact trading or industrial city, this system of uncomplicated direct rule accomplished its purpose. But the Parisian region grew in the throes of the post-industrial revolution, and La Ville de Paris changed its character. Surrounding departments and communes in the region also went through a transformation, becoming more urbanized and taking on the industrial complexion that once had characterized the eastern end of Paris. Paris itself began to lose its working-class character and absorbed still more white-collar employees through the 1960s. The three departments that composed metropolitan Paris prior to 1964 (Seine, Seine et Oise, and Seine et Marne) became more interdependent with the urban core and connected to it by a city-suburban commute. Not the least of these changes was a decisive political alteration in the urban core. La Ville de Paris tilted more strongly toward the Right with each additional influx of prosperity and became safer for the bourgeoisie.

By the middle of the twentieth century, radical demographic and industrial shifts made Paris ripe for some kind of regional association and comprehensive planning. The ensuing years brought to the region great changes that would shape its governance and planning for generations to come. The catalyst for many of these changes was a high-level functionary, Paul Delouvrier. Like Baron Haussmann a century earlier, Delouvrier relied upon a national leader to bolster his position. As Haussmann had used Napoleon III, Delouvrier took advantage of his ties with Charles de Gaulle. Delouvrier had worked as the General's top administrator in Algeria during its stormy days of French rule. Most people assumed he had de Gaulle's unqualified approval to push ahead with radical changes in the Paris region.

This was all rather ironic, because neither man was enthusiastic about encroaching upon the status quo of the 1950s. Upon hearing that La Ville de Paris should be treated as part of a larger region, de Gaulle frowned and called the idea "a kind of fantasy."[2] For his part, Delouvrier was an unwilling candidate for the job.

Early in 1961 Delouvrier received a telephone call from the Prime Minister, Michel Debré, who announced that a special district for the region was about to be created. The new district would leave the three existing departments of Seine, Seine et Oise, and Seine et Marne unchanged and simply respond to their individual or collective needs. Debré then mentioned that the district would need a chief executive (Délégué Général) and offered Delouvrier the post. A skeptical Delouvrier responded that he preferred some other post, away from the capital, in Brittany. Moreover, he had aspirations for a still higher post than the one offered and would prefer to bide his time. Debré, however, persisted. "Before tending the garden," he told Delouvrier, "one must tend to the heart of the house. In France the heart is the Paris region."[3]

Despite the poignancy of the metaphor, Delouvrier still resisted and continued asking questions. Debré demurred, claiming that he could not be any more specific and that he had other matters of state that pressed on his time. "In that case," Delouvrier replied, "my answer is no."[4] Believing the matter settled, Delouvrier left for a vacation. Several days later he learned from the newspapers that he had been nominated as Délégué Général for the District of the Paris Region.

So began a new era for metropolitan Paris—hatched on a skeptical de Gaulle and on a flimsy telephone call to an unsure candidate. Delouvrier soon found out he had had reason to doubt. The new district was more of a coordinating body than a regional government. As such it facilitated arrangements between the Seine, Seine et Oise, and Seine et Marne. These departments had legal prerogatives that were common to all the departments of France. By contrast the district was an unusual entity, ambiguously designed to realize an ill-defined mission. As a district it could act only for the ostensible benefit of its constituent departments, and not on its own behalf. Yet it did not take orders from those departments, nor could it command a department to take an action against its will.

The very ambiguity of the district was reflected in the title of its chief executive. As Délégué Général, Delouvrier was not a prefect, a minister, or a mayor. He appeared to play a little of each role (representing the state qua minister or administering services qua mayor) and also to play still other roles (e.g., a regional innovator).

Whatever his role, he was going to have to define and defend it himself. He would also have to compete with the department prefects who jealously guarded their own prerogatives. This was especially true of the Prefect of the Seine, who counted La Ville de Paris within his domain. Delouvrier's task was complex. It required that he forge a regional identity while imbuing his own role with command and authority. At one and the same time, he would have to be a master planner and a master politician. He had neither the time nor the inclination to finish one task before starting the other. Planning and politics would mesh in countless permutations as the new Délégué Général went about his job.

The major issue to confront Delouvrier in 1961 was industrial decentralization. France was said to be suffocating from the overconcentration of capital and industry in Paris. Francois Gravier's *Paris et le désert français*, published in 1947, had dramatized the problem, and there was a general feeling that something needed to be done about it. By the time the district was established, a plan was already in effect to disperse the Parisian monopoly out to the provinces. The plan, known as PADOG (Plan d'Aménagement et d'Organisation Général de la Région Parisienne), was the beginning in a string of proposals to transfer people and industry out of Paris and its environs.[5]

Delouvrier and his team were uncomfortable with PADOG, because too little was being done to prepare Paris for post–industrial change. As an experienced administrator, Delouvrier turned his attention to emerging trends and a future plan. By the year 2000 the Paris region was expected to triple its population to more than 14 million people. The composition of the region's industry was expected to change: people would have different kinds of jobs, buying power was already on the increase, and leisure time was consuming a larger portion of daily life.

Paris was said to be one of the most densely packed cities in the West; the baby boom of the 1950s would squeeze the population even more. Comparisons with the historical progression of other cities suggested that something needed to be done about dwelling space. In Washington, D.C., the population had grown 2½ times while the land available for its population had increased 5 times; in New York the population had risen by one-third while its land mass had doubled; and in Copenhagen, where the population had climbed 70 percent, the terrain available for settlement had tripled.[6]

A glance at the trends and a map of the Paris region furnished Delouvrier with his opportunity. True, Paris was a dense and compact nucleus; but much of the land around it was open and still unsettled. Delouvrier could make his mark in Paris by working outside of it. This could be done by establishing new patterns of settlement in the rest of the region to which Parisians could move and from which they could commute.

Early in his administration Delouvrier dispatched two associates to investigate "new town" development in the London region. Their report indicated that British new towns were built some 60 to 80 kilometers from London, beyond the Green Belt. The French saw little use in such an approach, because it cut off the urban core from satellite settlements. As Delouvrier saw it, new settlements should complement the urban core by interacting with it. British new towns were isolated rural implantations; the French would make different use of the new town idea. Rather than a reimplantation of the urban root in the remote countryside, French new towns would be extensions of the urban core, built only 30 kilometers away and connected to the city's center by a bundle of public transportation and auto routes. Indeed, the term "new town" was not the best to describe what Delouvrier intended and was adopted for its publicity value.[7] The word "new" conveyed something fresh, innovative, and belonging to the next century. "Town" (*ville*) connoted an urban settlement built to human scale and embellished with neighborhood familiarity. In conjunction with new towns Delouvrier also planned *centres restructurateurs*, or suburban growth poles. In contrast to new towns, suburban growth poles contained few residents. They were essentially built out of existing low-density industrial areas that were located just outside the urban core. Delouvrier converted these drab industrial basins into nuclei for the growth of light industry and offices.

In effect Delouvrier sought new ways to expand Paris. New towns and suburban growth poles were a method of channeling population and development into designated locales. The French approach should not be mistaken for American suburban development, which rises helter skelter around a central city. Far from that, Delouvrier promoted the concentration of resources and people within confined spaces. Apart from these spaces, land was left relatively open for either farming or recreation. Planning was the decisive and directive edge for in-augurating a new region. In the nineteenth century Georges Hauss-mann had built Paris as a unique center. In the twentieth century Paul Delouvrier would build La Région Parisienne as polycentered. Al-though each of Delouvrier's centers would have an industrial base, its umbilical cord to Paris would nourish it with population and capital.

Delouvrier set out his ideas in the Schéma Directeur (master plan) of 1965. Eight new towns were laid out in a radial pattern around Paris. Like a belt linking buckles to one another, suburban growth poles pro-vided urban continuity by tying the new towns to the urban core. All of this would be enhanced by a dense network of auto routes and rail-roads.[8]

For a time the master plan was kept confidential and shown to only a handful of technocrats (prefects, ministers, top planners, and archi-tects). To do otherwise might trigger a rash of land speculation around the proposed sites. Once the master plan was adopted, the government could put restrictions into effect that would control real estate prices.

While Delouvrier's planners were marking up the regional map, he was remaking the political map. Like all power, that of the Délégué Général could be magnified or diminished by the personality of the person holding the position. Through his presence and initiative De-louvrier imposed an iron will on the region. There was, as well, an authoritarianism and an ambition in Delouvrier that was apprehended by his rivals. Soon after his appointment, Delouvrier met with the Pre-fect of the Seine, who told him, "My position is a powerful one. I would advise you not to touch it."[9] Yet within three years Delouvrier was orchestrating events that did just that. Between 1964 and 1968 a series of national decrees converted the former departments of the Pa-risian metropolis into a politically manageable region. The District of the Paris Region was formally replaced and given the more prestigious title of La Région Parisienne. By a law of July 10, 1964, the three de-partments were reorganized into eight new departments. Paris itself took on the legal dimensions of both a municipality and a department. No longer was it a commune within a larger Seine; in 1964 it became a distinct and unified piece of geography. Its elective body could sit as representatives of the City of Paris or as representatives of the Depart-ment of Paris. The group took the name Le Conseil de Paris, reflecting its unique status. The other new departments followed standard prac-tice, electing a General Council within each department and a City Council within each commune or city.[10]

By these acts the metropolitan region came closer to political unity, at least as that unity was conceived by the state and by Delouvrier.

Leftist strongholds in the communes around Paris were diluted within the more heterogeneous departments. Presumably the new geographical composition was less likely to favor a leftist opposition and would have a broadening influence on smaller cities.

The most important blow to the Left was in La Ville de Paris. No longer would it be represented in the General Council of the Seine. Its politicians were now cordoned off from the outlying Red Belt, where the Communist Party could amass a loyal cadre of activists. The Gaullists correctly reasoned that a city rapidly on its way to embourgeoisement could be differentiated from its suburbs and treated to a larger measure of autonomy.

There was a problem, however, that struck one minister as serious. Just before the territorial reorganization was about to be implemented, the Minister of the Interior, Roger Frey, expressed concern that the Department of Seine-St. Denis would surely fall to the Communists. Frey wanted to delay implementation until he could strengthen the presence of the state within the localities. Frey then went to de Gaulle and presented his ideas. Delouvrier, who was present at the meeting, recounts de Gaulle's cool reply:

> Mr. Minister of the Interior, in what time are you living? We will have to live with the Communists for 50 or even 100 years. What do you think, that they are going to rush across the plains of St. Denis down the King's road to retake the Bastille. Mr. Frey, the Bastille is already taken, it is taken.[11]

Unfazed by the Minister's objections, de Gaulle and Delouvrier pushed ahead with the construction of a new region. There were other means for ensuring control. By 1966 Delouvrier's hegemony was bolstered by formal authority and he was appointed Prefect of the Paris Region. He became the linchpin between the new departments and the central ministries, and he alone commanded the access points between the central authorities and the localities. The formula for Delouvrier's position was simple. Because the state had created the new region, the state would also have to make it work, through Delouvrier's political craft.

From his position Delouvrier could wield the formidable resources that were put at his disposal. He had control over the region's budget, directed its administrative services, and was in charge of its overall development. Most important, Delouvrier was a "super Prefect" for the eight departments. The other Prefects were tethered to his supervision because of his liaison with the central ministries. As such, he could influence or even control their actions. Until 1977, for example, it was the Prefect of Paris who provided the agenda and presented the budget to the Council of Paris. And when the Council was constituted to act on departmental matters, it was the omniscient Delouvrier whose weight was felt during the deliberations.

There were other advantages that accrued to the Prefect of the Paris Region. After 1966 he was no longer confined to servicing constituent units, but could act directly. This meant that he could acquire land and build housing in the name of the region. As it turned out, this power was instrumental in putting together the new towns.

In sum, Delouvrier's planning and politics were an impressive beginning toward regionalization. By 1968 that beginning could be seen on the map and felt by the construction of new roads, new rail lines, and new towns.[12] The eight new departments stretched over more than 6,000 square miles. La Région Parisienne (later named the Ile-de-France) consisted of Paris, Hauts-de-Seine, Val-de-Marne, Seine-St. Denis, Yvelines, Essonne, Seine et Marne, and Val d'Oise.

Figures 4.1 and 4.2 illustrate how the regional map was remade. The first figure shows the Metropolis as it existed prior to 1964; the second shows the eight departments as they exist today. The eight departments are shown as the urban core of Paris, the departments of the first ring, and the departments of the second ring.

Note that the political geography of the Ile-de-France continues to place La Ville de Paris at the hub of the region. Departmental boundaries have been drawn in radial fashion around Paris. As Chapter 5 will discuss, political lines have strongly interacted with planning priorities so that transportation and construction have been designed around the Parisian focal point.

Delouvrier's strategy of building around Paris and providing mass access to it through auto and rail lines profoundly influenced the development of the urban core. Those who could afford it would settle in the urban core and remold it. Those who could not afford to remain in Paris would move into the new towns and suburban growth poles or still further out, to the provinces of France.

To be sure, the region continued to grow and change. Political challenge and the passage of time dimmed Delouvrier's impact. Like other great builders, (Haussmann, Robert Moses) Delouvrier abruptly fell from the pinnacle of power. The blow came in 1968, when he crossed swords with an influential minister, Albin Chalandon. Chalandon wanted the Paris region to develop by force of the "free market" rather than by technocratic direction. He initiated Operation "coup de poing" or "clenched fist" and began lifting restrictions against construction and investment. Although Chalandon wanted to retain a strong urban nucleus, he was strongly influenced by the dynamism of American society. "Surely urban development in America is not perfect," he wrote, "because their cities have no centers. But in France we have strong city centers . . . around those centers we would allow the freest development."[13]

Delouvrier, the precise planner, was Chalandon's natural enemy. The Prefect fought his battle in the press, where he had the sympathy of journalists and intellectuals. Chalandon took his case to higher political circles (by this time de Gaulle had been succeeded by Pompidou) and won. After more than seven crucial years, Delouvrier was forced out. Yet despite Chalandon's victory, he left only the faintest imprint on the region's development. If anything lessened Delouvrier's legacy, it was in the political realm and occurred well after he left the Prefecture.

In 1975 the national government passed a statute granting Paris the right to its own mayor. Two years later the City Council elected the first mayor of Paris since the bloody days of the Commune. The new

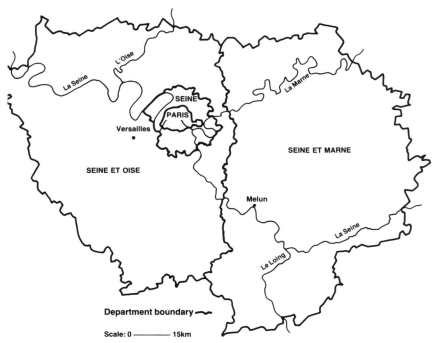

Fig. 4.1. Metropolitan Paris before 1964 (three departments)

official, Jacques Chirac, was supposed to share responsibility with the Prefect of Paris on matters of urban development. Chirac, however, was a powerful figure, a leader of the Gaullists and heir apparent to the Presidency. He was not about to be overshadowed by a *haute fonctionnaire* like a prefect.

Ironically, Chirac's standing as mayor was bolstered by the Socialists' rise to power in 1981. After the Left won control of the national government, Chirac dramatized the Gaullist opposition from his office at the Hotel de Ville. When, in 1984, the Socialists tried to undercut Chirac's authority by proposing that Paris be divided into twenty self-governing neighborhoods, the Mayor took up the cudgels to protect a united city. He handily won the contest and, in the process, gained the admiration of many Parisians.

Other Socialist measures to decentralize authority were more successful, and these have diminished the authority of the prefects. In the early 1980s, decentralization laws were enacted that enhanced the authority of mayors and departmental councils. Decentralization has also

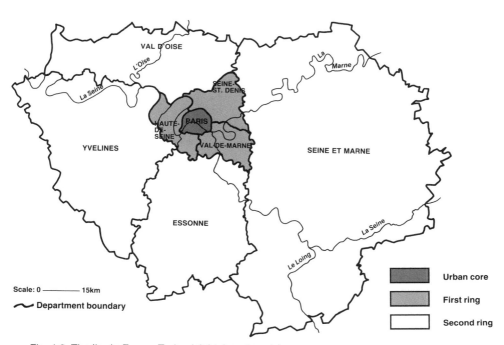

Fig. 4.2. The Ile-de-France Today (eight departments)

strengthened regional government to the detriment of the prefects throughout France. The Ile-de-France is still far from becoming a true regional authority, but it has come a long way since Delouvrier plowed the soil in 1964. The seeds of regional authority were planted in a council, which was indirectly elected.[14] Twenty years later, voters in twenty-two designated regions of France went to the polls to elect their regional councils directly. Thanks to decentralization, the presidents of these councils have soaked up executive powers that were once exclusively held by the prefects.[15]

It is one of those ironic twists of history that Delouvrier and his successors, who carved out the Parisian region, should come to have their power diminished by its growth. What cannot be diminished, however, is that Delouvrier took charge of a few historical moments to cast the die.[16] He set the stage in the Ile-de-France for decades to come. Other prefects might modify Delouvrier's plans, reduce his schemes, even rebut them. But they had to respond to his initiatives.[17] The thrust of innovation belonged to Delouvrier and consisted of (1) forging a regional identity, (2) moving people and industry to regional subcenters, and (3) connecting regional subcenters to the urban core by a vast network of transportation. Whether Delouvrier was simply reacting to economic imperatives that were about to burst asunder is another matter. Delouvrier could read statistics and discern trends better than most, and he may have been gracefully riding the waves of economic change to some extent. Those changes began to appear in the late 1950s, were still on the rise through the 1960s, and continued through the 1970s until a period of equilibrium was reached in the 1980s.

The Ile-de-France: The 1980s

According to the last French census there were 10 million inhabitants in the Ile-de-France, which represents a 22 percent increase over a twenty-year period. We can have a closer look at the details of regional development by examining the proportionate shares of the population held by each ring of the region (see Fig. 4.3). Briefly, this amounted to shrinkage in the urban core, stagnation is the first ring, and growth is the second ring.

Today, La Ville de Paris has the smallest population of any ring in the Ile-de-France. As a percentage of the regional population, Paris fell to 22 percent in 1982, a drop of 11 points in two decades. The population in the second ring climbed to a record level of 3.9 million in the same period. By 1982, the second ring contained almost twice the

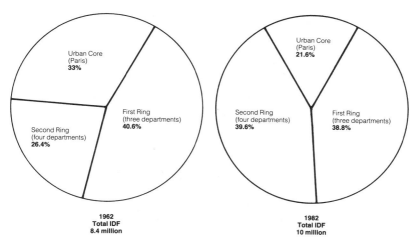

Fig. 4.3. Distribution of the Population in the Ile-de-France: 1962 and 1982. Source: *La Population de l'Ile-de-France: Résultats Provisoire du Récensement* (Paris: INSEE, 1982).

number of inhabitants as Paris, and its percentage of the regional population rose to almost 40 percent. Clearly the decentralist policies of Delouvrier and his successors were effective.

Employment trends throughout the Ile-de-France also reflected the potency of the decentralist strategy as it continued through the 1970s and 1980s. Table 4.1 presents a statistical profile of employment patterns by sectors in the Ile-de-France. The sectors include manufacture (automobiles, chemicals, heavy machinery, textiles); tertiary services (telecomunications, commerce, finance, management); construction and public works; and agriculture.

As in New York, a substantial change swept the economy of every department in the Ile-de-France. Post-industrial employment continued to replace manufacturing as the major source of the region's livelihood. A most pronounced change took place in Paris, where manufacturing fell from 26 percent to a mere 16 percent of the economy. In its stead tertiary or service jobs rose to commanding heights. By 1982 more than 80 percent of Parisian jobs were in services.

Similar trends occurred in departments of the first ring, though the fall of manufacture and the rise of service jobs was not as pronounced. In nearby Hauts-de-Seine manufacture fell to 36 percent while services climbed to 55 percent by 1982. Val-de-Marne saw a drop in its manufacturing base to 20 percent while services mounted to nearly 71 percent. Seine-St. Denis, which is primarily working class and the heart of the Red Belt, also saw its manufacturing base diminish. Manufacturing fell to just 30 percent while services grew to 61 percent.

In the second-ring departments the transformation continued, but the slopes of change were more gradual. Yvelines saw its manufacturing jobs fall just a few points to 31 percent, while its tertiary sector rose to 60 percent. In Essone manufacturing slid to 24 percent, while services mounted to 65 percent. In Seine et Marne and Val d'Oise manufacture went from holding approximately one-third of the employment to retaining just about a quarter.

Not only did the post-industrial economy replace older industry, but it more than compensated for losses in most departments. For instance, construction and public works also dropped as a proportion of employment in all departments, yet the employment picture throughout the region remained good. Of the eight departments, only Paris lost employment (9 percent), and advances in other departments ranged from a modest growth in Hauts-de-Seine (7 percent) to more spectacular results in Yvelines (46 percent) and Val d'Oise (56 percent).

Clearly great changes were occurring within the Ile-de-France, and this could be seen in radical shifts of people and work. The entire region was going through a post-industrial transformation as more and more people were changing their shirt collars from blue to white. The

Table 4.1. Employment by Sector in the Ile-de-France: 1968 and 1982 (by place of work; in percentages except for Total Employed)

| | Urban Core | | First Ring | | | | | |
| | Paris | | Hauts-de-Seine | | Val-de-Marne | | Seine-St. Denis | |
Sector	1968	1982	1968	1982	1968	1982	1968	1982
Manufacture	26.01	16.29	47.70	36.82	31.80	20.40	43.80	29.61
Tertiary								
Services	68.01	80.19	43.20	55.41	55.60	70.80	45.10	61.42
Construction and								
Public Works	5.90	3.49	8.90	7.71	12.00	8.60	10.70	8.91
Agriculture	0.08	0.03	0.20	0.06	0.60	0.20	0.40	0.06
Total Employed								
1968	1,991,932		666,504		367,192		428,368	
1982	1,813,160		715,840		444,700		460,760	
% Change								
1968-1982	−9%		+7%		+21%		+8%	

Source: Adapted from Institut de Aménagement et d'Urbanisme de la Région d'Ile-de-France, *Annuaire Statistique Sommaire, Avril 1978 et 1982* (Paris: IAURIF, 1982).

change was most pronounced in the urban core of Paris, but also occurred in its seven neighboring departments.

While the new order was being born, its birth pangs were mitigated
by refilling the emptying terrain with new industry and jobs. This occurred throughout the first and second rings; only Paris lost employment. And Paris could well tolerate the discomfort because it was
shedding population. The city even enjoyed a slight improvement in
the ratio of residents to jobs. Thus in 1960 Paris had 1.3 people for
every available position. By 1980 it had 1.2 residents for each job.[18]

The qualitative changes in social and physical surroundings were
just as profound. In Paris whole factories picked up and left for the
hinterlands. Between 1968 and 1982, La Ville de Paris lost 42 percent
of its factories. During the same period, departments in the second
ring increased their blue-collar jobs by more than one fifth.[19]

Some of the factories settled in new towns located in Essonne, Seine
et Marne, Val d'Oise, or Yvelines. Other blue-collar workers went to
designated areas in the industrial north or rural south. Still other factory jobs simply disappeared, as France converted into a service society.

Social change had been occurring in Paris for some time before the
1960s. The shift began as part of the post–World War II effort to de-

Second Ring

Yvelines		Essonne		Seine et Marne		Val d'Oise	
1968	1982	1968	1982	1968	1982	1968	1982
33.50	30.74	31.80	24.30	32.70	27.90	33.90	23.30
50.30	59.88	50.20	64.90	46.10	58.70	49.70	67.40
11.90	8.04	13.20	9.20	12.70	8.80	12.40	8.20
4.30	1.34	4.80	1.60	8.50	4.60	4.00	1.10
280,332		189,348		209,512		170,464	
409,260		263,430		279,240		265,401	
+46%		+39%		+33%		+56%	

centralize heavy industry. In the early years this could be seen in changes of a few percentage points between censuses. But these losses added up: by the late 1960s, the working classes had lost one quarter of their members.

Through the 1970s and 1980s the winds of economic change blew even harder, sweeping with them whole social classes. We can appreciate this transformation by consulting a statistical profile of changes in social class in the region (see Table 4.2). The categories are not always easy to translate into an American or British context. For example, the occupational group of upper management and intellectual professions is essentially upper middle class and well educated. Middle management and professionals have somewhat less demanding credentials and status but are white-collar and reasonably prosperous. The category of craftsmen, shopkeepers, and company foremen appears to most Anglo-Americans to contain a diversity of groups, yet the French concept refers to a class of mainly independent, self-employed individuals. The two categories of employees and manual workers are what most Americans would call lower middle or "working classes." Both these classes are wage earners and identify with labor unions.

The data of Table 4.2 confirm the trends outlined earlier. Throughout the region post-industrial or white-collar employment is on the rise, and blue-collar work is generally down. Within the region there are differences between departments. Paris continues to attract a new class of resident. In only a seven-year period, upper management increased its share of the population from 16 to 22 percent. Middle management gains are more modest, going from 18 to 19.6 percent. At the same time the proportion of the lowest two classes fall. Employees are down from 36 to 33 percent; workers slide from 21 to 17 percent.

The rest of the region also experienced an *embourgeoisement* of social class. In Hauts-de-Seine, upper management increased from 14 to 17 percent, Val-de-Marne also boosted its proportion of the same class from 9 to 11 percent, and there are similar rises throughout the Ile-de-France.

Without exception, middle-management categories also grew in every department of the region. Although there are clusters of class settlement, the extreme segregation so common in New York is not part of the Parisian picture. To be sure, La Ville de Paris profited most from the influx of riches, but other departments also rose with the post-industrial tide.

Where did the working classes go? Of all the departments, only Paris reduced its proportion of employees, clerks, and domestics. All the other departments absorbed modest but noticeable increments of this occupational category. We can only conclude that the first and second rings served as a sponge for the Parisian overspill. The greatest absorption occurred in nearby Seine-St. Denis, which is largely working class. Other departments, further out in the second ring, also took in this social class.

As for the manual workers, there was a steady decrease in their proportions throughout the Ile-de-France. We can assume that either they found different kinds of jobs, left the region, or became unemployed. Some workers followed the factories into the second ring, where blue-collar work could still be found. The movement of factories and other facilities into the second ring changed patches of its environment and its social composition. By 1982 the most rural departments, Seine et Marne and Val d'Oise, began to challenge the Red Belt of Seine-St. Denis as a habitat for French workers. The new settlements were quite different from the tawdry tenements of Paris or the apartment complexes and cottages of Seine-St. Denis. In the second ring there were the new towns; compact, low-density communities that were socially integrated. Middle managers, employees, manual workers, and a smattering of upper management could be found there. New towns were supposed to be the new France, where class distinctions were muted and everyone who worked was a "worker."

While other departments were building new towns, suburban growth poles, and a new infrastructure to absorb population, La Ville de Paris began to redo its own. In the wake of these changes, Paris prepared for new social classes that would bring new patterns of settlement, new habits, and different attitudes. Indeed, the new classes would change the social order and the physical fabric of the city.

Class and Ethnic Settlement in the Urban Core

The dichotomy of the opposing demographics of Paris has traditionally been between the western and eastern halves of the city. The western portions are generally newer and their housing and commercial fabric are attuned to the middle and upper classes. It is in the western arrondissements that one finds the great financial houses (First, Second, and Ninth arrondissements) and the large commercial centers (Eighth, Sixteenth, and Seventeenth). These arrondissements hold the most sumptuous and spacious housing of the city and the great boulevards built by Haussmann.

The eastern parts of the city are where Parisian industry first grew up. Heavy factories, metalworks, and assembly plants marked the

Table 4.2. Employment by Occupation in the Ile-de-France: 1975 and 1982 (by residence; in percentages except for Total Employed)

| | Urban Core | | First Ring | | | | | |
| | Paris | | Hauts-de-Seine | | Val-de-Marne | | Seine-St. Denis | |
Occupation	1975	1982	1975	1982	1975	1982	1975	1982
Upper Management, Intellectual Professions	16.2	22.2	14.1	17.7	9.1	11.5	5.7	6.8
Middle Management, Middle Professionals, Technical	18.0	19.6	20.5	20.8	19.9	20.9	18.3	18.2
Craftsmen, Shopkeepers, Company Foremen	7.4	7.4	5.3	5.5	5.8	6.3	5.3	5.6
Employees, Clerks, Domestic Service	36.4	33.2	31.9	32.7	33.3	35.2	31.8	35.7
Manual Workers	21.9	17.6	28.1	23.2	31.7	26.0	38.8	33.6
Farmers	.1	.0	.1	.1	.2	.1	.1	.1
Total Employed								
1975	1,168,855		713,620		579,980		635,585	
1982	1,098,980		692,980		580,520		640,840	
% Change 1975-1982	−6%		−3%		−1%		1%	

Source: Adapted from INSEE Observatoire Economique de Paris, *Récensement de la Population de 1975 et 1982: Région d'Ile-de-France* (Paris: INSEE, 1984).

eastern arrondissements and a strong working–class constituency took root. Families were often packed into inadequate quarters lacking bathrooms and hot water. These were among the most overcrowded neighborhoods in the industrial world. Though sometimes regarded as quaint by visiting tourists, they were often shabby and their inhabitants suffered a tubercular rate severalfold above the rest of the city. These arrondissements extended in a half-circular band around the northern and eastern periphery of the city and included parts of the Nineteenth, Twentieth, Eleventh, and Twelfth. See Figure 4.4.

Second Ring

Yvelines		Essonne		Seine et Marne		Val d'Oise	
1975	1982	1975	1982	1975	1982	1975	1982
13.7	17.8	11.1	13.2	7.3	9.6	8.4	10.6
21.5	21.6	22.2	23.0	18.6	19.6	20.6	21.7
5.1	5.5	5.1	5.4	7.5	6.9	5.5	6.0
28.9	30.9	30.0	32.5	25.9	30.7	31.6	33.6
30.0	23.6	31.0	25.3	39.1	31.2	33.3	27.7
.8	.6	.6	.6	1.6	2.0	0.6	.4
478,615		405,505		313,862		375,925	
554,600		466,000		407,980		435,320	
14%		13%		23%		16%	

Today the old dichotomy between west and east Paris has begun to fade. The new middle classes search for space in all parts of the city and they are not inhibited by imaginary lines. To be sure, eastern Paris is still a far cry from the elegance of the Champs Elysées and grand boulevards near the Avenue Foch. The Nineteenth and Twentieth arrondissements still belong to *la classe populaire* and their overcrowded streets are filled with Arab-speaking workers and cheap shops. But much of eastern Paris has been transformed for the middle class and young professionals. The social gap between eastern and western ar-

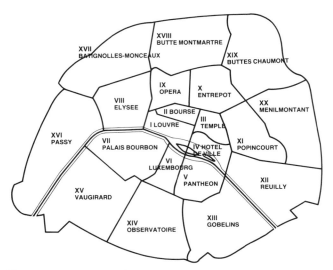

Fig. 4.4. The Arrondissements of Paris

rondissements still exists, but it has narrowed and is no longer accentuated by the polarities of class antagonism.

Post-industrialism has meant that the Parisian population has become smaller, multi-ethnic, more mature, and that it has drifted away from the extended family. Paris has also become a wealthier city, where married women are almost as likely to be holding down a job as their spouses and where single-person households are common.

Like other post-industrial cities, the population has shrunk. During the stormiest years of transformation, Paris lost more than 10 percent of its population, which stood at 2.1 million in the 1982 census. This was not terribly different from other major cities in France, such as Lyon, Bordeaux, and Lille, which also lost population through the 1960s and 1970s.[20]

Although the urban core lost residents during the last three decades, the number and proportion of foreigners increased. In 1962, 8 percent of the population was classified as foreign; by 1982 that had risen to 16 percent. The school-age population for ethnic groups is even higher, so that approximately one quarter of children in primary and nursery schools come from homes with at least one foreign parent.[21]

Of the nearly 355,000 foreigners who reside in Paris, the highest proportion come from North Africa and the Iberian Peninsula. Algerians, Tunisians, and Moroccans account for 5 percent of the population, Spanish and Portuguese for 4 percent, and black Africans for 1.4 percent. The rest of the ethnic population is scattered among immigrants from Southeast Asia and Asia Minor.[22]

Most of the Arab-speaking immigrants are concentrated in the northeastern arrondissements; immigrants from Iberia and the rest of Europe are integrated throughout the city. Arabs and black Africans take menial jobs and hope someday to return to their homelands. These people can often be found in pockets of substandard housing. Those from Iberia and the rest of Europe have an easier time and find jobs as taxi drivers, artisans, or in any of the numerous cafés.

Although the foreign population has made the city more cosmopolitan, its impact is still minimal. Immigrants do not vote and rarely do they speak out. They live in the cheapest housing and are not apt to organize into pressure groups in order to fight for better conditions.

A more telling indicator of social change is the growing maturity of the population. More and more, Paris is a city of adults. In just twenty years the number of residents under fifteen years of age fell by one third. During the same period, those sixty-five and over increased by 7 percent. In recent years the number of retirees has leveled off, so that Paris is not in danger of becoming a city of the aged.

Those who dominate the social structure are between thirty-five and sixty-four years old.[23] These individuals are independent and still strive for social mobility. When they are part of a married household, they tend to have fewer children; both husband and wife are likely to be breadwinners. Interestingly, the number of single individuals has increased over the decades. In 1982 nearly half the Parisian households consisted of single or divorced people. Household size is also related to geographical location and tends to decrease as one moves toward the center of the city (see Fig. 4.5).

Evidently big-city life has become more attractive to single people and childless couples. Couples that raise families often choose the suburbs and new towns of the second ring. One study of planning in the Paris region finds that the majority of those who settle in new towns consist of traditional families, in which the wife stays home and raises the children while the husband goes off to work. Most of the new-town households include young couples with children—there are relatively few unemployed and still fewer individuals on the fringe of social acceptability.[24]

Still another reason for the maturation of the Parisian population is that its socioeconomic composition has risen, and individuals who are well off tend to have fewer children. The shrinkage of working-class Paris started in an area very close to the epicenter of the city, in the

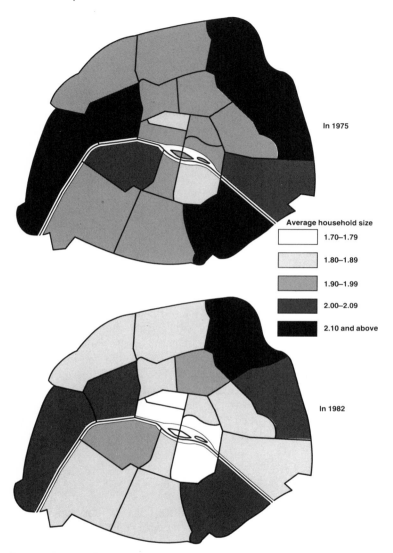

Fig. 4.5. Average Parisian Household Size: 1975 and 1982. Source: Atelier Parisien d'Urbanisme.

Fourth Arrondissement. The Fourth had once been a chic area for the families and mistresses of Royal France. Its streets were lined with seventeenth-century mansions, fronted by fancy French gardens and carriage houses. The area boasted the best of French architecture and hand-made window panes. With the arrival of the industrial revolution, the Fourth was turned into a working-class quarter. Its architectural heritage was ignored; the once stately mansions were broken up into multiple apartments for the poor, and carriage houses were converted into cottage industries. Later the Fourth became a Jewish quarter, packed with refugees from eastern Europe who brought their old ways with them.

By the 1960s the pendulum swung in another direction. The Fourth was rediscovered, first by young couples and intellectuals seeking a genuine urban community. Each succeeding influx of residents was more affluent than its predecessor. Developers invested in the area by gutting older buildings, maintaining their façades, and creating modern apartments. In some cases swatches of the Fourth were torn down and reconstructed in the old style. Small apartments sold for nearly a quarter of a million dollars and rents were among the highest in Paris. The Fourth had its old Metro station rehabilitated, its streets repaired, and a name resurrected for community identification—Le Marais (The Marshes). Along with this physical transformation, Le Marais lost nearly two-thirds of its population classified as "workers," nearly half of its population in the "unskilled services," and over 40 percent of moderate-income employees. In their place came business executives and professionals. This was "gentrification," or as some would call it, embourgeoisement.[25]

Gentrification pushed outward from this center of Paris through the inner arrondissements. The post-industrial bourgeoisie spread through arrondissements in the east (the Eleventh and Twelfth) to other arrondissements on both the right and left banks of the Seine. Social transformation was accompanied by dedensification. The average densities of La Ville de Paris fell from 330 inhabitants per hectare in 1954 to 300 in 1968, 267 in 1975, and finally 250 in 1982.[26] The historic center of Paris was particularly affected by dedensification. The quarter around Les Halles, the First Arrondissement, lost 30 percent of its population between 1968 and 1975. Other well-known areas, such as Bonne-Nouvelle (Second Arrondissement) and Enfants-Rouges (Third Arrondissement), lost 25 percent of their populations during this same period.[27] Figure 4.6 below shows the difference in densities in La Ville de Paris for 1954 and 1982.

Note that the western parts of the city went through very little change during this twenty-year period. The most dramatic changes occurred in the former working-class and older sections of the city. These neighborhoods are either in the historic center (roughly the First through the Sixth arrondissements), in the north (the Eighteenth) and in the east (the Tenth, Eleventh, and Twentieth).

Apparently the working classes either moved out in pursuit of jobs or could no longer afford to stay. Paris is a city where there is an ever diminishing stock of low-cost housing, and this has contributed to the exodus of workers. Despite the fact that Parisian streets are filled with renovation sites, the housing stock has remained constant. Thus, in 1962 the city counted approximately 1,235,000 housing units within its boundaries.[28] Twenty years later there was scarcely a change. Paris could count only 1,280,000 units, a net increase of 3 percent.[29] Evidently as much housing was torn down as was built or renovated.

Historically, the Parisian working classes have been all too accustomed to poorly kept, overcrowded housing. Once there was a rapid conversion to modern, expensive apartments, those who could not pay the price sought shelter elsewhere. The conversion of so much housing in so short a period of time meant that a sizable part of the new stock would be built by private developers. Despite government efforts to build affordable housing, the proportion of subsidized units slid downward. Thus, in 1962 approximately 74 percent of the housing units received some kind of public aid; between 1968 and 1975 this figure fell to 43 percent; and between 1976 and 1980 only 27 percent of the completed housing received public assistance.[30]

Having said this, it needs to be mentioned that in comparison with American cities, the public housing sector in France is a major force. To have 27 percent of new housing starts built with government assistance is quite substantial for a "down period."

Moreover, efforts were made to take in the Parisian working classes. Massive housing complexes were built on the Left Bank in the Thirteenth Arrondissement and in the northeast (the Nineteenth and Twentieth). The Parisian housing stock was sharply upgraded with "amenities" like hot water, toilets, and baths for each apartment, and elevators. In the last thirty years, the proportion of apartments in Paris without toilet facilities has been reduced by half.[31]

But not everyone could be accommodated. The post-industrial tide was too great, urban space too scarce, and zoning laws too rigid. Environmental and aesthetic concerns collided with the need for modern, residential high rises. Eventually the dam of publicly supported housing gave way to the pressure for high-priced, low-density shelter.

One study put its finger directly on the housing problem. The tran-

More than 500 inhabitants
per hectare

400–500

300–400

200–300

100–200

Fewer than 100

Fig. 4.6. Residential Densities in Paris: 1954 and 1982. Source: Atelier
Parisien d'Urbanisme.

sition to new housing was as much a matter of the life style and status of new residents as anything else. In a test of nearly one hundred renovations, it found that a disproportionate amount of new dwellers were professionals or worked for large corporations. White-collar workers and technicians replaced industrial and manual workers. Even the older bourgeoisie of merchants and small bosses (*patrons*) were left out of the renovated buildings.[32] In short, after the wrecking balls and masons did their work, the new apartments were turned over to small households or "singles" who belonged to the new middle class.[33]

Land and Office Towers

Behind the social changes of post-industrialism stood the physical transformation of the environment. This could be seen in the rise of Paris as one of the premier business sites in Europe. Office towers began to pop up in the city during the late 1960s and reached their apogee in the early 1970s.[34] Through the early 1970s, Paris added between three and five million square feet of office space per year. As a percentage of the region, Paris seemed to be doing extraordinarily well. Officials in the central ministries appeared more than happy to issue construction permits for office buildings and the numbers spoke for themselves.[35]

Year	% of permits for office space in the region
1970	27%
1971	33%
1972	30%

Aside from gobbling up additional construction, Paris had accumulated a handsome number of office buildings during the previous decades. The heady years of the 1970s and its earlier stock meant that the city was at the top of the region for available office space, and quite near the top of Europe.

Figure 4.7 depicts the division of new and renovated office space. The figure breaks down the first ring into three constituent departments (Hauts-de-Seine, Val-de-Marne and Seine-St. Denis). Separate categories are reserved for La Défense as well as for the second ring and the new towns.

Although Paris has a commanding lead in office space, the impact of post-industrialism has not been lost on the rest of the region. Other departments have also been able to accommodate this transformation. For example, Seine-St. Denis more than doubled its share of office stock in a six-year period, and by 1980 held 14 percent of the regional

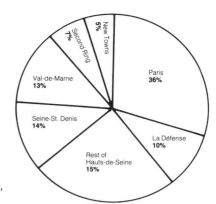

Fig. 4.7. Proportionate Share of New
and Renovated Office Space in the
Ile-de-France: 1980
Source: *Le Marché des Bureaux
en France en 1980* (Paris: IAURIF, 1980),
p. 30. Note: Figures are rounded.

supply. Hauts-de-Seine holds 15 percent of the region's office space, and when La Défense (which is part of Hauts-de-Seine) is added that proportion climbs to 25 percent, just about matching La Ville de Paris.

New towns have also arisen to take up the demand for offices and have succeeded in attracting large corporations. Thus the sweep of post-industrialism has affected the other departments of the Ile-de-France. Certainly, the first rings have absorbed some of the factories that once made up the industrial fabric of Paris. But the same areas have also diversified their economies, taken up the Parisian overspill, and, in some instances, competed with Paris for white-collar industry.

This is not to overstate the case. Much of the transformation has centered in Paris and the corporate elite continues to seek space there. This search can be seen in the market demand and in the escalating rents Parisian landlords charge. Office rents in the CBD are nearly twice as high as its nearest competitor and nearly three times as high as rents in other parts of the first and second ring. In 1980 the average rent paid per square meter in the Eighth Arrondissement of Paris was more than 1,100 francs ($220), the comparable price in Hauts-de-Seine was 600 francs ($120). In other parts of the first ring, such as Seine-St. Denis, the price per square meter dropped to 389 francs ($78), and in the region's new towns office space was the least expensive at 371 francs ($74).[36]

Office rentals vary in different parts of the urban core and the most expensive areas are in the central and western portions of the CBD. Figure 4.8 portrays the office marketplace.

The heart of the office market emanates from the center of Paris

123

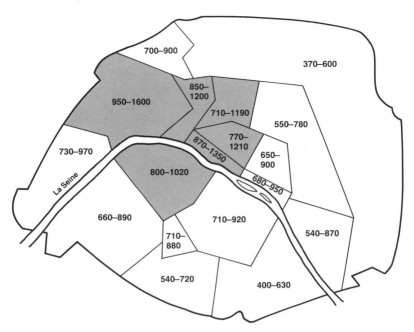

Fig. 4.8. The Cost of Office Space in Paris: 1981 (in francs per square meter).
Source: *Le Figaro* Magazine, March 23, 1981. Note: Shaded portions represent
areas of greatest cost.

(roughly the First through the Tenth arrondissements) and pushes
westward (Sixteenth and Seventeenth). This movement has spread
through parts of the Left Bank and into the eastern parts of the city.
Where possible, factory lofts and even apartment houses have been
converted for white-collar work. Though authorities now cast a suspicious eye on further corporate advances, the early 1970s gave business a chance to establish a beachhead in old industrial Paris.

In spite of the efforts to decentralize industry, France remains one of
the most centralized nations in the western world, and much of that
centralization still remains in Paris. It might well be argued that the
successful decentralization of blue-collar industry had the unintended
effect of concentrating more decision making in the urban core. In
some ways, Paris has become even more powerful than it was previously. It has substituted directorship for assembly plants and the craft
of high finance for the ways of the artisan. With the growth of an advanced world economy, Paris has emerged as a nerve center for the
nation and for the Common Market.

As long as the focus was on bringing jobs to other parts of France, there was little complaint. By the mid 1970s, however, state authorities recognized that the Parisian ascendence might be too much of a good thing. The state decided that the corporate grip on Paris should be loosened—at least as far as that grip clenched the built environment. The President, the Parisian Prefect, ministers, and other hautes fonctionnaires inaugurated measures that would stop the conversions and put a halt to the skyscrapers. Some of these measures tightened up on bureaucratic procedures (the issuance of construction permits); others were fiscal (differential taxes on overbuilt land). Overall, these policies worked, and the amount of office construction plummeted in the urban core. See Figure 4.9.

A sharp nosedive took place after 1974. From a high of over 400,000 square meters (4.4 million square feet), office activity has dropped to almost nothing. For more than a decade there had been a virtual moratorium on the construction of office towers in Paris, which has prompted protests by Mayor Chirac. The city put pressure on central authorities to soften their stand, but with scant success.

The state could not be budged because it had placed its construction chips elsewhere. Neither the state nor the region gave up on post-industrial aspirations. Rather, they shifted these aspirations to other parts of the region, mainly to nearby Hauts-de-Seine. There, an urban

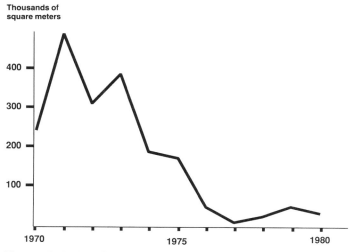

Thousands of square meters

Fig. 4.9. Authorized Office Construction in Paris: 1970-1980. Source: *Les Bureaux à Paris, 1970-1980* (Paris: Atelier Parisien d'Urbanisme, March 1981).

phoenix, La Défense, has arisen. This new complex is designed to rival
the megastructures of New York, Brussels, and Tokyo. French planners proudly compare La Défense to office complexes the world over.
They are also proud of how La Défense has been built—not as a suburb
that creeps from the Parisian limits, but as an integral, compact community that is a competing alternative to La Ville de Paris.

Significance

The Parisian transformation has been intense, exuberant and relatively well controlled. Despite the great movement of people and
work, the slopes of class distribution have not been skewed. A variety
of social classes has filtered into different departments of the region
and throughout France. New towns, suburban growth poles, and La
Défense are manifestations of that control.

To be sure, not all is perfect. Policy makers were unable (or unwilling) to stop the exodus of working classes from Paris. Parts of the
urban core still do remain for workers, but publicly assisted housing
has been insufficient to keep many of the old quarters intact. The
brakes on office development were applied too late, some ten years
after the boom had begun.

No doubt there has been slippage. One can also quarrel with the
wisdom of these objectives. Stopping growth in Paris did block what
might have been a spectacular growth in jobs for locals. Putting constraints on high-rise construction has made it more difficult for workers to find inexpensive apartments. But putting this aside, the French
have been effective in managing their post-industrial transition. We
could add that given the enormity of the task and the inherent clum-
siness of bureaucracy, policy makers have a right to signal this as an
achievement.

This achievement required planning, decisions, and organization.
Not least, it required that political choices be made. In the next chapter
we examine just how those choices were made and how they generated
a geopolitical momentum in the Ile-de-France.

Paris: Geoplanning, Geopolitics, and Mobilizing Corporatism

It was a very narrow street—a ravine of tall, leprous houses, lurching towards one another in queer attitudes, as though they had all been frozen in the act of collapse. All the houses were hotels and packed to the tiles with lodgers, mostly Poles, Arabs and Italians. At the foot of the hotels were tiny bistros, where you could be drunk for the equivalent of a shilling. . . . It was a fairly rackety place. And yet amid the noise and dirt lived the usual respectable French shop-keepers, bakers, laundresses and the like, keeping . . . to themselves and quietly piling up small fortunes.—George Orwell, Down and Out in Paris and London

BEGINNING with the 1960s, Paris went through its greatest transformation since Baron Haussmann's days. Manufacturing departed the city for other parts of the region or to the more distant provinces. A large part of the working class followed in its wake, as the bourgeoisie sought more space. New office complexes were built in parts of Paris, and a still larger amount of post-industrial space was allocated in nearby Hauts-de-Seine at La Défense.

The French undertook this transformation with unabashed pride. Paris had always been the jewel in the crown, and new planning initiatives would make it more so. Great men had always created grand schemes; planning was no different. Haussmann had re-created the city under Louis Napoleon. Working under de Gaulle, Delouvrier expanded the city into an urban region. There was no doubt that their successors would continue in the same tradition.

How were these schemes converted into bricks and mortar? A centralized government, the traditions of the prefect, and an elite bureaucracy made such schemes possible. They were given expression in a system that can best be described as mobilizing corporatism—that is, an assemblage of organizations working under the initiative of a unified political/technocratic elite.

Geoplanning: Strategic Development around the Urban Core

On the face of it one could attribute the Parisian transformation to a technological revolution that changed the role of the city and to laws of the marketplace that operated in the wake of this revolution. Much as the Bessemer steel converter and the sewing machine brought about the industrial city, so too has the electronic age and the computer produced the post-industrial city. French planners and officials have argued that Paris simply reacted to technological change through the free exchange of supply and demand.[1] Some claim that urban congestion hampered the operation of factories and that property itself became too valuable for people of modest means. Eventually the highest bidder was able to obtain property in the urban core; the factories, along with the working classes, were simply priced out of the market.

Officials claim that in addition to all of these reasons, those workers who were displaced found better, cleaner, and more spacious housing in the suburbs. Living in a dark, cold-water flat without a bathroom may be possible for university students, but it is not very glamorous or comfortable for a family of four. Post-industrial transformation enabled an overcrowded city to shed some of its population into unsettled green spaces and to upgrade its existing housing.[2] In many cases the government assisted those who were displaced with the costs of moving and with subsidized housing and new towns.

Although this is all true and there is a logic to the reasoning, it is also too facile and leaves too much unstated. For one, many individuals were compelled to leave neighborhoods they had known all their lives. Being forced out by a wrecking ball and by high rentals is still coercion, even if the state pays some of the costs. Second, old neighborhoods and social networks were, in fact, broken up by speculators and developers. Regardless of the fact that new apartments with bathrooms may have been provided, the Parisian quarter was the only place in which many individuals (particularly the elderly) felt comfortable and knew their neighbors. Being put into a huge residential tower such as the Grand Ensembles was like being locked into a rabbit hutch. Third, the same kind of public policies applied to many of the departing factories and artisan shops. Though some may have been glad to leave, others were not, and the resulting loss in neighborhood services, community identification, and traditional livelihoods could not be compensated.

Fourth, and significantly, the government was not neutral in this transformation. On the contrary, it was extraordinarily active and planned most of the movement and strategic building. It is therefore inconceivable that the transformation of Paris could be said to have been propelled by "market forces" or by a laissez-faire economic structure. Market forces may have exerted power and provided a financial impetus, but the government working in conjunction with private enterprise made it all possible.[3]

France has a very strong tradition of planning that is intricately mixed with the private sector. As the centerpiece of the nation, the Ile-de-France was to be a showcase for rational planning and economic coordination. The central ministries, the prefects, the regional governments, and the cities have a variety of tools that make regional planning possible.[4] A major tool is the master plan, designed by the regional prefect and carried out under the aegis of the central government in consultation with local authorities. As mentioned in Chapter 4, one of the earlier master plans, PADOG, was promulgated in 1960 and initiated a massive effort to decentralize factories out of Paris.[5] Five years later a new master plan, the Schéma Directeur of 1965, provided additional space and facilities for industries relocating from the urban core.

During the heady days of 1965 when growth seemed unlimited, French planners believed the Parisian overflow could be channeled into nearby suburban growth poles and new towns.[6] These areas were built on two axis points parallel to each other, passing along the north and south sides of the urban agglomeration. The idea was to make these axes into corridors of urban transportation and semicontinuous development that would run along the outskirts of the urban core. Figure 5.1 shows the placement of the new towns along the urban corridors as well as the suburban poles scattered around Paris.

There are five new towns shown in Figure 5.1: Cergy-Pontoise and Marne La Vallée along the northern corridor, and St. Quentin en Yvelines, Evry, and Melun-Sénart on the southern corridor. Placing the new towns within these corridors was supposed to stimulate independent subcenters and reduce the emphasis on Paris. The suburban growth poles in and around the corridors are supposed to "fill in" the distance between the new towns, providing additional coherence as an alternative to Paris.

The stagnation of the 1970s dashed the planners' most ambitious hopes for autonomous regional centers. The new towns grew to a fraction of their anticipated population, the corridors never really emerged in their own right, and the grip of Paris over the region became even stronger.[7] One reason the urban core retained its dominance was that Paris exchanged the industrial might of its factories for the political and administrative potency of its offices. As the outer suburbs grew just enough to become viable but not enough to challenge Paris, they became virtual satellites to the urban core. In many instances the new towns, in particular, served as dormitories for middle executives and clerks who traveled to Paris each day for their work. One study points out that in the mid-1970s, for the first time ever, more than half the

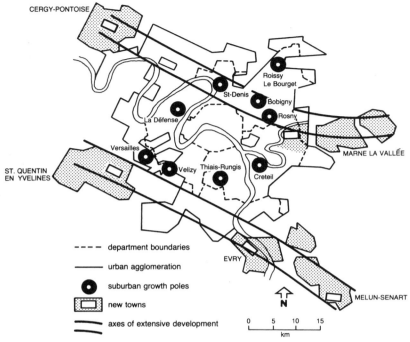

Fig. 5.1. New Towns, Urban Corridors, and Suburban Poles in the Ile-de-France. Source: Institut d'Aménagement et d'Urbanisme de la Région d'Ile-de-France.

jobs in Paris were held by those living outside the urban core. Over one million people commute into Paris each day and 97 percent of them do so from within the region.[8] This is made easier by the excellent mass transportation between the first ring and the Parisian urban core. All of the new towns are connected by rail and Métro service. Most of the suburban growth poles are also accessible to Paris through various modes of transportation (highways, rail, bus service).

Geoplanning: Strategic Planning within the Urban Core

Paris is a cramped city. Space is scarce and people are packed closely together. Until its recent period of dedensification, Paris held nearly three million people within the confines of forty-two square miles.[9] Open land in the urban core has always been scarce and it contains barely 15.5 square feet of parkland per inhabitant as compared to 100 square feet in London and 277.7 square feet in Vienna.[10] Because of the compact and tightly knit fabric, major construction projects have a magnified effect on the entire city. A project placed in one section of the urban core can tilt and shape human and business activity throughout, raising rents and changing demographic composition.

Because of this, the strategy of development within the urban core has been to engage in a limited number of large-scale projects. The objectives are multifold and they serve to (1) replace vacated sections of industrial Paris with post-industrial activity, (2) reinforce the importance of the center as a focal point of commerce, transportation, and culture, (3) redress the imbalances between the eastern and western portions of the urban core, and (4) renovate historic sections and preserve parts of the urban heritage for a new class of inhabitants. Figure 5.2 shows a number of sites within the urban core that have been or will be used for strategic development.

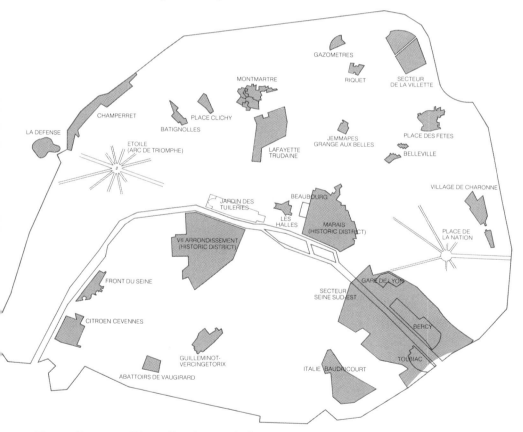

Fig. 5.2. Present and Future Development in the Parisian Urban Core

Most of the areas of renovation are scattered throughout the city, and their facilities have been made obsolete by departing industry. Citroën in the southwestern part of Paris was the former site of a large automobile factory. New plans call for the construction of housing, a park, and a hospital on its 75 acres. Just north of Citroën, at Front de Seine, are recently built office towers and apartment units. And on the northern periphery, at La Villette, there once existed slaughterhouses for cattle. Today La Villette is the site of a special museum for science and technology.[11]

These are substantial projects, but three developments have a particular significance. Imagine a line bisecting Paris and running almost parallel to the Seine. The line is anchored by La Défense in the west, Les Halles at the center, and Secteur Seine Sud-Est in the east. These three sites are crucial points on what has been called the Parisian spine of development.

Taken in conjunction, La Défense, Les Halles, and Secteur Seine Sud-Est furnish Paris with an enormous amount of catalytic investment. Public and private capital produce a synergism that makes these areas an international point of reference and commercial exchange. These sites are the leading edge for post-industrial transformation and the spine of development serves as a unifying axis.

Figure 5.3 delineates the geoplanning potential of this spine. Note, too, the size of the less developed Secteur Seine Sud-Est. The spine is a powerful thrust through the midsection of Paris. Along its length is a continuous line of commercial, cultural, and political investment. La Défense, Les Halles, and the Secteur are newly built environments that mesh with existing concentrations of capital. La Défense connects to the CBD along the Champs Elysées. Les Halles links up with the stock exchange and connects to eastern Paris. When fully developed, the Secteur will be a powerful attraction and complete this important axis.

Before discussing the political choices that brought about La Défense, Les Halles, and Secteur Seine Sud-Est, let us consider the basic tools and political character of French planning.

Geopolitics: Urban Policy and the Corporatist Impulsion

There are times when the form and content of policy provides an impulsion toward a particular type of power arrangement. Thus in New York, the fragmented and multicentered nature of the system allows a measure of pluralism to shape decisions.

In Paris, a different kind of apparatus impels decision making, and that apparatus is essentially corporatist. The roots of French corporatism are to be found in history, tradition, and in the machinery of pol-

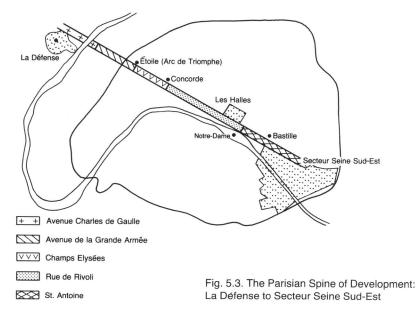

La Défense

Étoile (Arc de Triomphe)

Concorde

Les Halles

Notre-Dame

Bastille

Secteur Seine Sud-Est

| + + | Avenue Charles de Gaulle
| N N N | Avenue de la Grande Armée
| V V V | Champs Elysées
| ::::::: | Rue de Rivoli
| X X X | St. Antoine

Fig. 5.3. The Parisian Spine of Development:
La Défense to Secteur Seine Sud-Est

icy making itself. First, a strong centralized government is very much a part of the political fabric of the nation. The Napoleonic code laid out a system of rules and regulations that placed power in the hands of central institutions. Second, the strength of French institutions has been buttressed by the traditions of a professional bureaucracy led by a trained and loyal elite. When Baron Haussmann and Paul Delouvrier took action to remake Paris and the region around it, they were acting as delegates of extremely powerful national leaders. Third, in dealing with the private sector, the state has been active and forceful. Laissez faire may be a French phrase, but contemporary French actions belie its spirit. Going back to the Monnet Plan after World War II, the French have planned and directed private enterprise to achieve national ends. The line between what is the public and the private sphere is not as sharply demarcated in France as it is in Anglo-American (especially American) culture, and the French have not hesitated to embark upon extensive nationalization of private industry. This has taken place under both "rightist" and "leftist" governments. In some cases, collaborative partnerships were achieved between the two spheres; in other instances, government has imposed itself and directed private operations.

The implications of these traditions are profound for the development of the built environment. Private enterprise has had to deal with a strong, insulated, and centralized bureaucracy. It is not uncommon for French developers to behave as supplicants to a powerful class of technocrats.

As a consequence of these features, policy tends to be made along narrow lines of debate. Decisions have traditionally flowed down through hierarchical structures, and negotiations usually occur between a political-technocratic elite and representatives of select organizations. The French have composed a number of recognized organizations into official or semi-official bodies for the purpose of deciding public policy. Access is limited to designated organizations, policy is carried through by collaborating with select organizations, and there is a strong emphasis on rational planning.

Despite the decentralist laws of the early 1980s, centralism remains a valid force in French political life. Jacques Chirac's tenure as Mayor of Paris illustrates the centripetal forces of Parisian politics. Chirac was first elected in 1977 by the Paris City Council to a six-year term. Party cohesion and a strong Gaullist majority on the Council have ensured his control, and only a handful of Socialists and Communists actively oppose him.

In matters of urban development Chirac works closely with national leaders, regardless of political stripe. When the center-right party of Giscard d'Estaing held the central government in the late 1970s, Chirac traded mutual favors. When the left-wing coalition of François Mitterand won in 1981, Chirac continued a *sub rosa* collaboration. And when Chirac's own Gaullists took control of the National Assembly in 1986, Chirac became Prime Minister and also kept his job as Mayor. During that time, the collaboration between national and Parisian political elites was incestuous.

This is not to say there are no differences between national and local politicians. Indeed, as we will see, politicians at both levels struggle with one another over the control and design of projects. Those struggles, however, are tempered by the need to achieve, by interlocking political positions, and by a respect for the state. When national interests are at stake, the state can throw the trump card. All lines of authority stem from the state's mandate. Even the legislation granting Paris a mayor specifies that although the mayor is the chief executive of the city, he "is at the same time an agent of the state."[12]

There are a number of planning tools that keep political control intact and that ensure that urban development can be carried out along corporatist lines. One of these instruments is the Délégation à l'Aménagement du Territoire et à l'Action Régionale (DATAR). DATAR is a bureaucracy attached to the national government. Its powers to imitate public–private collaboration are formidable and consist of a number of "carrots" and "sticks" to realize national ends. Thus, it has the capacity to withhold permits for the construction of office space in Paris, and it has made extensive use of that power. Corporations seeking to build facilities must come before DATAR to plead their case. As well as "sticks," DATAR can offer inducements to corporations that are willing to cooperate. These include payments for corporate moving expenses, subventions to corporations for technical assistance, support for re-training employees, tax reductions, depreciation allowances, financial help for land acquisition, and aid for employee housing. DATAR has even intervened to establish telephone and telex services quickly for corporations that have agreed to decentralize.[13].

If DATAR's services are all too legalistic and financial, the French have devised more direct means of shaping the built environment. These can be found in the mixed corporation, which is an organization that combines public and private resources to develop predesignated sites. To make sure that public ends remain paramount, the controlling shares of mixed corporations are retained by the public sector. Hence the partnership is not fully equal and public policy can be pursued more energetically. Mixed corporations have been used extensively in the past to develop moderate income housing.

Another public body that works in tandem with private organizations is the Etablissement Public d'Aménagement (EPA). Though not a joint venture like the mixed corporation, EPAs work closely with firms to acquire land and prepare it for development. Invariably, they act as investment bridges between local government, the national ministries, and private developers. EPAs have collaborated with private organizations to build commercial and shopping centers.

In addition to an organizational framework to foster corporatist col-laboration, the French have a number of planning tools to control the disposition and price of land. Zones d'Aménagement Concerté (ZACs) have been used to designate a site where the government assembles land and pays for a certain amount of infrastructure (water mains, streets, sidewalks, utility lines) in return for private investment. The ZAC is essentially a contract between a public authority and a private developer to undertake a project and distribute costs and responsibili-ties. Once an area is designated as a ZAC, the public arm issues its own restrictions on density and building heights. This has proved to be a critical advantage for development in the urban core.

A final technique guards against speculation while sites are being developed. This is done by designating an area as a Zone d'Aménage-ment Différé (ZAD), which can be used to freeze the price of land in the vicinity of a heavily invested area. Once an area has been "ZADed" the price of land can be kept to a fair market value that existed before the site was selected for development. This freeze can last up to fourteen years. The ZAD is just one example of the way in which private interests can be submerged to rationally planned corporatist ends. It should not be interpreted as a "socialist" threat to the private sphere, but as a way of controlling and coordinating it with other activities. Thus, between the "carrots" and "sticks" of DATAR, the public–private partnerships of mixed corporations and EPAS, and the land prerogatives of ZACs and ZADs, the French have amassed a formidable array of instruments.

The Geopolitics of Les Halles, La Défense, and Secteur Seine Sud-Est

In the Paris region the politics of the built environment comes closest to mobilizing corporatism. The following generalizations can be made.

➤ Government is the dominant force in initiating and supervising major development. Hardly anything is done to the built environment without the overriding presence of the public sector. That presence is embodied in the actions of the national government, La Ville de Paris, or other local governments and public corporations.

➤ Lines of power usually extend from political elites, who make crucial decisions, to private organizations (banking, business, developers, community associations, etc.), which are legitimated by those elites. Led by representatives of the state (elected officials, ministers, hautes fonctionnaires), a chain of collaboration is established by using ZACs, ZADs, mixed corporations, and EPAS.

➤ The most important interactions take place within the political sector. Unlike New York, where negotiations continually cross between public and private spheres, the Parisian give-and-take is largely relegated to political elites who bargain among themselves. This occurs at the highest levels—between top officials (President, Prime Minister, Mayor), between a select number of ministers (Interministerial Council), and between technocrats (prefects, planners, or hautes fonctionnaires).

➤ Interaction among political elites carries with it cooperation, conflict, and sometimes stalemate between the state and local governments. The results are often influenced by the personalities and the vanities of top leaders. Once agreement is reached, the public sector is harnessed to specific objectives and its parts coordinated to ensure a project's success.

➤ Mass opposition to the political elite is surprisingly limited. In most cases the monopoly held by political elites has been accompanied by mass compliance, acceptance, or resignation. Relatively few decisions evoke the ire of the citizenry. Only in Les Halles did mass protest erupt, and this occurred at the eleventh hour just before the Baltard Pavilions were torn down. In neither the building of La Défense nor the remaking of Secteur Seine Sud-Est did citizen involvement attain any significance. This observation is supported by other decisions (new towns, industrial decentralization, building transport lines) that were not selected for case analysis here.

➤ When opposition does arise, it is often relegated to organizations within the public sphere such as legislative councils or political parties. The Communist Party, acting in coalition with the Socialists, spearheads the challenge against the uses to which land is put (as office towers rather than factories) or against the alleged misuse of public funds (for the benefit of private capital).

➤ Other types of opposition are coopted or incorporated into formal governmental bodies. French laws require that the state consult with localities before plans are approved, and this has cushioned a good deal of the opposition. In Les Halles, protest groups were made part of the governmental apparatus, supported by public funds, and given partial authority. In La Défense, the opposition was diffused when representatives from the local communes were incorporated into its operations.

➤ The lack of a forceful citizen opposition may seem curious for a nation that heralded the great revolutions of the modern age. It is doubly odd for the Ville de Paris, whose streets have been barricaded many times over. The paucity of mass protest may have more to do with the unique qualities of the subject matter than with the general nature of French politics. That is, decisions about the built environment have a different meaning to Parisians than do conflicts about religion, schools, wages, or foreign policy. The remaking of the built environment is more often perceived as a technical rather than a political issue. The French press treats decisions about the built environment under the less controversial captions of "urbanisme," "architecture," or "territorial development" rather than as a subject of political intrigue. Hence, the political consequences of redevelopment are not as consciously apprehended as they are in New York or London. Deference is more readily given to technocrats and planners, who are perceived to have the "correct solutions."

Les Halles   Les Halles has had a complicated and tortuous history. Some of the earliest accounts go back to the twelfth century, when the area served as a marketplace for pre-industrial Paris. By 1183, two large timber-framed structures sheltered the peasants and traders who came to ply their wares. The structures were sturdy, though crudely built, and open on all sides so they provided only overhead protection from rain and storm. Gradually Les Halles became the trading center for all of Paris, and migrants from the countryside occupied the housing around the market. They lived in cramped quarters and crowded the alleyways seeking some kind of living.

By the nineteenth century, Les Halles teemed with vendors, workers, and vagabonds. Its people were a nomadic underclass, who moved from one part of the quarter to another as conditions and work allowed them. Les Halles soon became a tinderbox for insurrection. In 1834 vicious street fighting and rioting enveloped the area. So intense was the conflict that troops had to retake the quarter street by street and much of it lay in ruins. Many of the residents were massacred and those who survived were deported to the provinces. The devastation was so complete that the Prefect was able to claim "I eliminated rue Transnonnain [a major street] from the map of Paris."[14]

Some of the streets of Les Halles were widened so that it would be more difficult to carry out guerrilla warfare. The marketplace, too, went through transitions. In 1845 the first buildings made of stone were erected. These structures failed to please Napoleon III, who asked the Prefect of the Seine, Baron Haussmann, to furnish plans for a new Les Halles. After considering several ideas, Haussmann turned to an architect friend, Victor Baltard.

Haussmann was a wily administrator who knew how to satisfy his superiors as well as cement the loyalty of friends. He instructed Baltard to draw up a number of spacious halls made of metal, instead of the conventional building materials of the day. Napoleon III would be reviewing the architectural sketches once again and the Prefect was sure these would please him. Haussmann's instincts were correct. Upon seeing the plans for buildings laden in iron, the Emperor burst out enthusiastically, "That's it. That's exactly it."[15]

With those drawings, Les Halles was defined for the next hundred years. Ultimately twelve pavilions were built—ten constructed during the nineteenth century and the last two completed in 1936. From the outside, the Baltard Pavilions looked like shiny rectangular blocks. Sitting atop each of them was a giant iron awning. From the inside, they resembled an ornate railroad station with embroidered archways delineating each subsection.

As Paris grew, so too did Les Halles. Between the construction of the Baltard Pavilions in the 1860s and the height of their activity, a century later, the Parisian population doubled. The consumption of fruit and vegetables grew from 7 kilos per person to 65 kilos by 1960. Meats, fruits, vegetables, flowers, and an assortment of goods were carried in from all over the countryside.[16] Les Halles was a virtual emporium for the produce of the region; Emile Zola dubbed it "the belly of Paris."

Unlike any quarter in Paris, Les Halles was mostly animated by its night life and by the workers and visitors who came to it. Commercial life started at eight in the evening and buzzed through the following day. Cafés, restaurants, and all-night bistros serviced its transient population. Prostitutes lined the streets to accommodate a different clientele.

By noon the work ground to a halt. Traders took down their wares and folded their stalls. Street cleaners arrived to collect the debris and hose down the sidewalks. The pavilions and the bistros fell silent.

There was, too, a residential side to Les Halles. During the 1950s and 1960s the neighborhood counted about 21,000 people who made it their home. Much as Les Halles' economic life was unusual, so was its social composition. Its inhabitants were a great mélange of Parisian society—professionals, workers, students, intellectuals, widows, families with children, the elderly living on the margins of the economy, and foreigners searching for Parisian adventure.

Narrow stone buildings, five- or six-story walkups, lined the streets of the quarter. Ground floors were often taken up by a small store, a café, or a workshop. First floors were rented to professional offices or to other services. As one trudged up the winding staircases, social class changed. Those who could pay the rent saved themselves the forced exercise by occupying second- or third-story apartments. The poorest residents lived on the uppermost floors. Despite the differences, everyone mixed and met on the streets, in the cafés, or on the building stairways. Class ties and social distance dissolved in the midst of jammed housing conditions and a spontaneous need for cooperation.

As one observer described it:

I was struck by the number of people who stopped on the streets to speak to one another; even whole families discussed things on the street. . . .

This was not just neighborly or small talk, but real frank discussion—done in good humor and in real freedom. Rarely does one hesitate to hail a friend or someone from the quarter. That isn't done in other neighborhoods. We can say practically anything in Les Halles without offending others. That's the mood of the quarter. We talk to customers at the market about rumors of a new crisis; we heckle one another in the pavilions. It's contagious and everyone expresses themselves in the same honest way.[17]

Another resident describes the ambiance and life style of Les Halles in terms of a small village:

Familiarity breeds friendliness. . . . One of the major factors in the neighborhood are the old timers who reside here. People here are like small villagers who always lived together. And that's the true character of Les Halles. We don't just know this to be so, but we see it all the time.[18]

Most outsiders saw the neighborhood in a different light. Les Halles may have been a quaint place to stop for wine or buy vegetables, but it was dirty, crowded, and unhealthy. Official records verified that impression. Sections of Les Halles had the highest rate of tuberculosis in France. Many of its buildings had burned down or had collapsed from age. Counting all of Les Halles, the living conditions were well below standard. Forty percent of the apartments consisted of one room, 30 percent of all apartments were overcrowded, and an equal proportion lacked running water.[19]

For those who made decisions about such matters, the course for Les Halles was inevitable. Les Halles was not only the "belly of Paris," it was also its very heart. The land on which the pavilions sat was immensely valuable. Each night over 10,000 trucks choked the streets for kilometers around the market, making traffic unbearable. The marketplace had clearly outgrown itself.

By 1959 the decision was taken by the de Gaulle government to move Les Halles to new facilities.[20] Most of the old market would be transferred to the outskirts of Paris, at Rungis. Meanwhile the pavilions were not touched, and there were no plans to fill the void that would be left after the marketeers departed.

Years passed before a plan for Les Halles was forthcoming. What emerged in 1966 was a radical proposal to remake practically all of the quarter. The plan would demolish 87 acres (34.8 hectares) and displace as many as 19,000 people. In that same year the Prefect of the Seine presented the plan to the Parisian City Council, which had a Gaullist majority. Party discipline was tight and showed in the 87 out of 90 votes cast to approve the plan.[21]

Though there was no doubt about the vote, there was a ray of hope for the opposition. The plan was still only a statement of intent; anything could be built within the specified area. Handfuls of citizens soon began to organize in order to salvage their quarter. One organization, the Union des Champeaux, took its name from the ancient field on which Les Halles was built. It included students, residents, and intellectuals. Another organization, COPRAS (Comité de Recherche et d'Action Sociale), formed a research group in order to critique the Prefect's proposals. Other organizations were composed of apartment owners and tenants, and most of these worked closely with either COPRAS or the Union. Meetings and expositions were held in an effort to alert the citizenry and rally an opposition. The expositions were particularly impressive and featured a history of the quarter, photographs, mock-up designs, and other plans. The largest of these expositions lasted several months and drew over 30,000 visitors from all over Paris. Petitions protesting the destruction of Les Halles were also passed out.

With these methods COPRAS and the Union succeeded in establishing some visibility and made a number of contacts with influential officials. The organizations were then invited by the Prefect to conduct studies of their own. The invitation was not an empty promise. COPRAS, in particular, was provided with space, materials, and minor support to carry out the work. Its studies dealt with the social composition of Les Halles and the financial implications of demolition and reconstruction.

In France and in Paris, 1968 was an important year. The Gaullist Presidency was confronted with a threat of a coup, there was rioting in the streets, and the Fifth Republic was on the brink of collapse. Government offices were closed and civil servants were on strike. For months COPRAS and its allies operated as a semi-official research staff and used government facilities freely. The leaders of COPRAS were even provided with keys to offices and access to records.

Cooperation soon turned into collaboration. The citizen associations of Les Halles were regrouped under one organization, CIAH (Comité d'Initiative pour l'Aménagement des Halles). The new organization was provided with enlarged quarters and supported by secretaries and a full-time staff.[22] Activists within the quarter were given executive posts. Along with this legitimacy there came an assumption of mission. Instead of critique, opposition, and protest, the task of CIAH was to prepare the quarter for the coming transition.

For Les Halles, 1968 was also an important year for decisions as well as deferment. In March, the City Council met to consider specific plans. In a session that began in the early evening and lasted through the early morning of the next day, the Council heard countless arguments. By the end, the sole decision taken was to appoint a commission to study the alternatives and report back to the Council.

Seven months later, in October, the commission issued its report and the Council duly approved it. The recommendations were general, later to be fleshed out by planners working for the Prefect. This again took months to prepare, but by 1969 everything was ready. The new plan reduced the area of redevelopment by more than half. To the credit of CIAH, the target area was reduced from 87 to 40 acres.[23] What was not mitigated, however, was the radical surgery slated for Les Halles. The area was divided into two sectors—one on the east, which held Les Halles' pavilions, and a second on the west, called the Plateau Beaubourg. Most of its housing was still to be gutted and renovated for new owners and tenants. The extent of the surgery may have been diminished, but the core of Les Halles was to be cut out and the rest of it treated to a cleansing and a face lift. The Baltard Pavilions were to be dismantled and sold for junk.[24] Most of the land was to be leveled and then a vast cavern was to be dug. Sunken into the cavern would be a Forum that contained underground facilities for shopping. Below the Forum, Métro and rail lines would be constructed. Les Halles would no longer be a truck stop, but a commuter shed for Paris and the region.

Many of the buildings and streets were also to be razed. In their place would stand the French answer to New York's World Trade Center, the Centre Français de Commerce International (CCI). The CCI would be located within minutes of the Parisian stock exchange and just a short walk to major banks. The ensemble would give Paris a *cité financière*, designed to rival Wall Street and the City of London as a world banking center. Finally, on Les Halles' western side, at the Plateau Beaubourg, would stand a great museum of contemporary art.

Figures 5.4 and 5.5 show the grand surfaces of Les Halles. Figure 5.4 is a planning scheme that shows both the eastern (Les Halles) and western (Plateau Beaubourg) sections. Note that the broadest perimeter marks an area designated as a ZAD. This land was to be "ZADed" and its prices frozen against excessive speculation. A smaller area is designated as a DUP (Déclaration d'Utile Publique), the targeted planning area. Running coterminous with the DUP is the ZAC, where infrastructure was to be concentrated. Figure 5.5 is an architect's rendition of Les Halles.

It did not take much imagination to see what would happen to old Les Halles. One glance at the plans showed the community that its way of life and its sights were about to disappear. The reduction in size was only a mild reprieve; what good was a smaller Les Halles when its

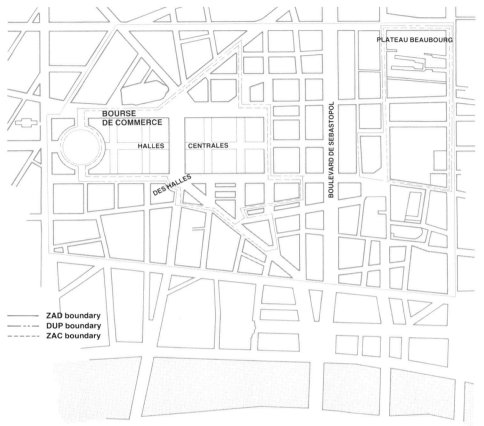

Fig. 5.4. A Plan for Les Halles: Circa 1969. Source: Société Anonyme d'Economie Mixte d'Aménagement de Rénovation et de Restauration du Secteur des Halles.

institutions and population would be scattered to the winds? CIAH and veteran warriors from the neighborhood protested. They even managed to obtain a stay of execution for the Baltard Pavilions. But what could they really do? They were now part of the state's apparatus and had unwittingly participated in Les Halles' demise.

As it turned out, the decisions taken in 1968–1969 were decisive.[25] They set the pattern for Les Halles. After that, there were modifications to the basic plan, but only in its political symbolism and in some of its architectural components. The frame of Les Halles' future was set; the best that could be done was to jockey for changes in detail.

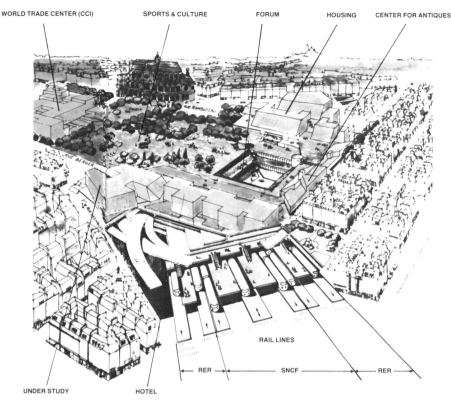

WORLD TRADE CENTER (CCI)   SPORTS & CULTURE   FORUM   HOUSING   CENTER FOR ANTIQUES

RAIL LINES

RER — SNCF — RER

UNDER STUDY   HOTEL

Fig. 5.5. Buildings and Development for Les Halles: Circa 1969. Source: Société Anonyme d'Economie Mixte d'Aménagement de Rénovation et de Restauration du Secteur des Halles.

Nonetheless, architecture can be an important emblem of power, especially in France, and the jockeying took place at the highest level of officialdom. When Pompidou was President, he had decided on a museum of contemporary art for the Plateau Beaubourg. After Pompidou's death the Presidency was held by a non–Gaullist, Giscard d'Estaing. Madame Pompidou continued to press for a national center as a tribute to her late husband. She worked through Jacques Chirac, who at the time was still Prime Minister. Chirac and Giscard reached an accord—Giscard would be left to develop the western sector as he wished if he gave the Gaullists free reign in the east, at the Plateau Beaubourg. Eventually a center for media and culture, bearing Pompidou's name, was built on the Plateau.

144

For his part, Giscard was anxious to promote himself as a progressive centrist who was sensitive to the Parisian heritage. He wanted to practice the politics of urban conservation rather than monumentalism, and soon modified the 1969 plan by scrubbing the World Trade Center. In its place Giscard planned a children's park—a shrewd maneuver, considering the awkwardness of demonstrating against green space for little tots.

Giscard's architectural tenure over Les Halles, however, was short lived. Once Paris elected its own mayor in 1977, Les Halles became subject to a review by the Hôtel de Ville (City Hall). The Les Halles shuttlecock was back in Chirac's court. By this time the area had been leveled, with nothing left of the pavilions. Chirac wanted complete discretion in designing the Forum and another trade was arranged with Giscard. Chirac offered a large site in northeastern Paris, La Villette, in exchange for the privilege of completing Les Halles. Giscard agreed. The parody of monarchical rule seemed to have escaped the Mayor as he triumphantly told a journalist "L'architecte en chef des Halles, c'est moi."[26]

Today Les Halles has one of the largest commuter terminals in the world. It is the major point of interchange for the Paris Métro. Deep in the recesses of its ground an elegant rail station accommodates passengers from the rest of the region. The Forum is now complete and is no mere hole in the ground. It is a sunken building, ziggurat in shape, and reaches four stories down.[27] On the eastern side at the Plateau is the Pompidou Center, which is one of the great attractions of the city.

Behind the various chic exteriors, a mass organization has been put together to make it all possible. The vehicle that has carried forth Les Halles is the mixed corporation. It is the quintessential corporatist instrument, in that it unifies a number of public and private organizations under a public umbrella. The City of Paris holds 51 percent of the mixed corporation's stock, followed by 22 percent belonging to the state, 14 percent to savings associations, and the remainder to banks and insurance companies. The announced mission of the mixed corporation is to join three different currents together: government (the state and La Ville de Paris), private enterprise (developers, architects, business), and the population of the new Les Halles.[28] The mixed corporation is thus the vital link in a chain of collaboration that stretches from the uppermost echelons of the state down to the grass roots.

For all this post-industrial upsurge, there is yet another story that lingers on about the old Les Halles. The wrecking of six pavilions took place in August of 1971, when most Parisians were on vacation. Recounting the episode one member of the Union said, "The authorities waited until vacation time when few people would be around. That's always their technique. But for us it was a summer's shock."[29] As un-believing spectators gathered to protest, the national police stood guard, riot gear in hand. Paddy wagons were parked on the far side of the pavilions, ready to whisk away anyone who interfered.

Until the actual demolition started, many residents did not believe old Les Halles would disappear. Some years earlier a survey showed that between 15 and 20 percent of the residents were unaware that the pavilions would be razed. An overwhelming majority of Les Halles' people were found to be "ill-informed" about the radical action planned by authorities.[30] This quiescence is striking, if we consider that over 1,400 households (3,000 to 5,000 individuals) were about to be dispossessed.[31]

The conclusion was inescapable. Another neighborhood was being transformed.[32] In the streets there was no pretense about who had won and who had lost. A hand lettered scrawl summed it up:

> The center of Paris will be beautiful. Luxury will be king. But we will not be here. The commercial facilities will be spacious and ra-tional. The parking will be immense. But we won't be here any-more. The streets will be spacious and the pedestrian ways numer-ous. But we won't be here anymore. Only the rich will be here. They have chosen to live in our quarter. The elected officials re-sponding to their wishes have decided the renovation is not for us.[33]

La Défense   When Napoleon began his Arc de Triomph, it bounded the edge of the city. Barely discernible on a clear day, beyond the Seine, is the hill of La Défense. Like the Arc, La Défense takes its name from the glories of war. It bears the monument commemorating the defense of Paris during the Franco-Prussian War.

La Défense was always a temptation to rulers who wanted to extend the Parisian domain. Its hill marked the culmination of an axis that began at the Tuilleries and continued through the Champs Elysées, the Etoile, and Port Maillot. Henry XIV replaced the ferryboats on the Seine with wooden bridges. Louis XIV talked about continuing the axis from the Tuilleries past the hill of La Défense. In an effort to com-plete the task of his forebears, Louis XVI replaced the rickety bridges with ones made of stone.[34] In the 1930s the Prefect of the Seine invited architects to submit ideas for La Défense's development. Among the contenders was Le Corbusier, who offered his own vista. But nothing came of those efforts, and World War II wiped away any hope that anything could be done in the near future.

The communes located in the area are Puteaux, Courbevoie, and Nanterre. Over the years they seemed unaffected by the planning and architectural chatter that had been brewing in Paris. The three stood as quiet country hamlets served by small shops and a few cinemas. Most of their land lay flatly sprawled before the edge of Paris in seeming defiance of its post-industrial revolution. Modest low-rise housing sat around the site of La Défense. Off to one side, large barracks housed the national gendarmes. On other sides, workshops and small factories were scattered on the landscape.

The communes could not ignore Paris forever. By the 1950s the city was feeling the first surges of an office boom. There was already a discernible drift toward the western arrondissements and pressure was mounting. Planners were faced with two problems: (1) how to alleviate the massive jams of traffic and commerce that were affecting the urban core, and (2) how to attract corporations from competitor cities like Brussels, London, and New York. Above all, they wanted to resolve these problems without jeopardizing the scale and architecture of inner Paris.

More important, President de Gaulle wanted to carve an independent and an international path for France. Defense and diplomacy were springboards for this kind of recognition, but so too was a formidable role in commerce and high finance. All the signs pointed to La Défense. On that side of the Seine, a national center for technical industries (CNIT) had just been established. CNIT was a natural lure for other industries and could be used to demonstrate the feasibility of the new site.

Soon after, some corporations showed an interest in coming to La Défense. Government ministers met with leading entrepreneurs and organized a syndicate of investors. The Minister of Construction, Pierre Sudrieu, was especially enthusiastic about prospects for La Défense. But Sudrieu was unable to work up equivalent interest from investors,[35] who were skeptical of Sudrieu's entreaties for several reasons.

For one, the conditions imposed by the state seemed too restrictive. Although Sudrieu wanted their money, he was unwilling to give investors full control over the land and insisted on putting limitations on building heights and population densities. Second, at that time there was still enough office space in the urban core and its potential for further development was formidable. The great tower at Montparnasse had just been built, conveying the impression that Paris would soon be turned into one large CBD. Having seen Montparnasse rise above the Parisian skyline, developers believed they could now build with limited governmental interference. Third, Montparnasse offered office space for the immediate future. Rents in the tower were still reasonable and corporations could always move west.[36]

In addition, there were risks at La Défense. Transportation networks were not in place, property would have to be expropriated, and land would have to be assembled. There were also political problems for big business. Representatives from Puteaux, Courbevoie, and Nanterre were suspicious of corporate interlopers. On the Left, local politicians had begun to talk about newcomers displacing townspeople. Politicians on the Right were more deferential (especially to a Gaullist government), but they too were becoming squeamish. Thus, despite the efforts of Sudrieu and others, the largest investors were unwilling to incur the financial and political costs of settling in La Défense. After all the conditions were laid down, Sudrieu was left with a handful of takers, almost all of which were publicly owned corporations.[37]

Several false starts and the sight of CNIT sitting alone on the plain roiled the political waters. The thought of La Défense turning into a white elephant instead of a "Manhattan sur Seine" was an embarrassment to planners who were fired up by projections on the growth of business and population. One of those people was a high-level functionary, André Prothin. He had worked on La Défense before and had witnessed its frustrations. Believing that the only way to create a new city was through strong and direct action by the state, he lobbied individual ministers on the need to make a full commitment to La Défense without promises of prior support from entrepreneurs. After a period of time the issue was put before the Interministerial Council. By 1958 the decision had been taken. A new center of post-industrialism would be built at La Défense and the state would take responsibility for its realization.

In France urban projects are frequently carried out via the mixed corporation. The development of La Défense, however, was too big and too complicated for standard procedures. The wedge used to open it up was the EPA, called in this instance l'Etablissement Public d'Aménagement de La Défense (EPAD). EPAD could do things faster and more efficiently than conventional organizations: land could be bought or expropriated more easily; special development zones could be established under EPAD's aegis; and limitations on construction could be cut in half by direct appeals to the Interministerial Council.

Moreover, EPAD could harness the presence and resources of the

state. From La Défense's network of transportation to controls on office construction, EPAD could move multiple levers and manipulate
conditions so they favored large-scale development. A complex infrastructure was quickly built in order to attract capital from the private
sector.

Should these carrots fail to lure investors, a suitable number of sticks
could also be wielded. DATAR was the most obvious ally. It began to
tighten up on permissions for office construction in the Parisian CBD.
Developers were blocked from building as frequently as they wished
or as high as they wished. Later on, as La Défense sought more clients,
the number of permissions to build in Paris dwindled to a trickle.[38]

Nor were officials at DATAR bashful about their intentions. Corporations seeking office space in the CBD were told about an excellent site
just five miles from the Parisian center. Brochures, information, and
offers to set up contacts at EPAD were freely given.

By 1958 the decisions were set into motion. La Défense was to be
transformed into a city for the twenty-first century. The Prefect of the
Seine and later Paul Delouvrier became de Gaulle's chief agent in the
creation of La Défense. The area was soon designated as a suburban
growth pole. Within a few short decades the land, contour, and character of old La Défense had been radically altered. Puteaux, Courbevoie, and Nanterre became bustling suburbs with new businesses,
housing, and a major university. Like a phoenix rising out of a desolate
plain, a new city was born, bringing in over 46,000 commuters to
work in ultra-sleek offices and 50,000 residents to occupy modern
apartments.[39]

It is not quixotic that the new La Défense is called "Manhattan sur
Seine." It looks much like smaller clones of New York's World Trade
Center. Its massive complex of more than thirty office towers is arrayed in columns that face toward the Etoile. The first towers were
influenced by American-styled architecture of the 1960s, typically
slabs of concrete banded by rows of glass. After that unhappy experience, the French added a touch of panache to newer buildings—sweeping rooflines that take on the curvature of a potato chip, circular structures, and lower-rise buildings stacked like blocks against the banks of
the Seine. All this is interspersed with greenery, concrete malls, and
fountains that spring up and dance in a pool of water.

In its fullest expanse La Défense covers 750 hectares (1,875 acres).
Of that total, 160 hectares (400 acres) are reserved for business. By
European standards, its amount of office space is mammoth—over 19
million square feet is available for its army of white-collar workers.[40]
Even more impressive, most of the space has been rented.

In configuration La Défense consists of two oblong bulges, bordered by an auto route that defines its perimeters. The entire area is fed by a complex of highways and public transportation that has few equals. Figures 5.6 and 5.7 show the basic plan for La Défense. Figure 5.6 shows La Défense's relation to Paris and the western portions of the region via its rail system. Figure 5.7 outlines the shape of the area as it impinges upon Puteaux, Courbevoie, and Nanterre. From Figure 5.6 we can envision La Défense as the transportation hub for the western part of the region. Eighteen bus lines converge at its terminal. A huge rail station accommodates mass transportation from most points in the region and is directly linked to the Paris Métro. Figure 5.7 reveals the two major zones of La Défense. The larger zone, located closer to the Seine, is the business district. This is where office and industrial space has been created. The zone on the western side of the map contains housing and green space.

Careful planning has paid off. Under the tutelage and organization of EPAD, hundreds of business organizations have come to La Défense to build in it, buy up its towers, or rent space in its buildings. Supported by large banks (Crédit Lyonnais) and insurance companies (Union d'Assurance), developers submitted their bids for construction rights. Large corporations soon followed, to buy up the towers or rent space in them. These firms came from the petroleum industry (Elf

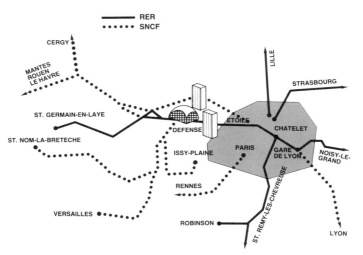

Fig. 5.6. The Strategic Position of La Défense: Rail and Métro Lines. Source: *Le Nouveau Journal*, May 26, 1978, p. xv.

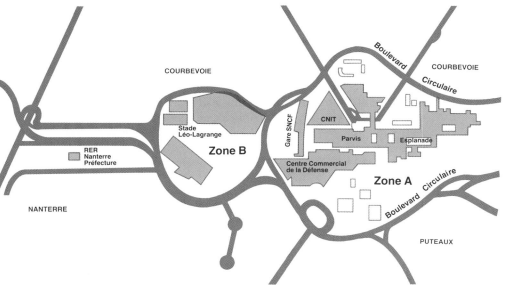

Fig. 5.7. The Plan of La Défense: Circa 1980s. Source: Etablissement Public pour l'Aménagement de la Région de la Défense.

Aquitane, Mobil, Esso), from international banking (Citibank, Worms, Société Générale), from the world of electronics and micro-chips (Sony, Xerox, IBM), and from transportation (British Airways, Fiat).[41]

In many instances business left adjacent arrondissements in the west of Paris to take advantage of cheaper and larger facilities at La Défense. By moving there, these enterprises were able to sell their properties in Paris at premium prices and set up shop at much lower cost. With these savings, the same firms were able to increase their investments in fac-tories located in the provinces of France or in other nations.[42]

La Défense has not been without its problems, and the state has shored up some of its crumbling pillars. One of those pillars has been financial, for during the mid- and late 1970s a crisis in the construction industry hit France. A declining market in the region's office space, coupled with overproduction at La Défense, sent finances tumbling. Between 1974 and 1978 EPAD's income fell by over 70 percent. As investors scurried for safer havens, EPAD was left with empty buildings and unsold construction rights.

The Interministerial Council met to discuss the crisis in September 1978. Led by Giscard d'Estaing, the ministers decided to trim construction and pump additional revenues into La Défense. The money was drawn directly from publicly owned savings banks.[43]

There were other actions taken by the state to assist La Défense. Rather than surrender to the vicissitudes of the marketplace, the ministers decided to manage it. Additional restrictions on allowable densities in Paris were enacted. Differential taxes were applied in Paris to dissuade business from settling in the CBD. All this was implemented by DATAR. Within a few years the competition that had crippled La Défense was broken. "Manhattan sur Seine" had recovered and newspapers were reporting that there would "hardly be a square meter of office space left" in the complex.[44]

State intervention is not confined to crisis. It is embedded in the everyday operations of La Défense. EPAD's lines of control extend down to private corporations and local governments. It assembles developers who buy construction rights and clients who rent space.[45] Most of the land is owned by EPAD, which designs the area, guides its architecture, and controls zoning and density.

EPAD's political relationships with the localities are forged differently. These are built around an Administrative Council. The Council is an unusual organization that acts as a bridge between the communes, the state, and EPAD itself. It is presided over by a president (nominated by the state) and is governed by eighteen members. Half of its membership is drawn from local government. The other half of the Council is nominated through the ministries and is composed mostly of high-level technocrats.

For a time representatives from Puteaux, Courbevoie, and Nanterre fought to give the Council a majority of political members. The brunt of the battle was waged by the Left (Communists and Socialists). They argued that La Défense was a public trust that affected the lives of tens of thousands. The Left called for the democratization of EPAD, the construction of more housing, and more emphasis on factories than on office towers.[46]

When that effort failed, local representatives tried to have one of their own nominated as Council President. Though newspapers and politicians wistfully speculate about the possibility, a Council President has never come from elected ranks. Though the state may listen and consult with local politicians, it is not willing to deal them a stronger playing hand. Political representation on the Council is more of an appearance than a reality of power.

By and large politicians on the Right have been compliant and willingly acknowledge their cooptation. They reason that it is better to have a Council President who speaks for the "boss" than one who merely represents the locals. Why dissent, they argue, when it is of no use. This reasoning may not be comfortable, but it has a basis in fact. The Council has been little more than a sounding board used to ratify ministerial decisions. The Left may speak eloquently about the need to bring more factories and workers into La Défense, but its arguments are drowned in the reality that La Défense is designed as a post-industrial city and little can change this. The majority of technocrats and politicians on the Right enjoy the mainstream and float with its tide.

Even when the Council has taken technical positions against the state, it has frequently been ignored. Decisions on the height and design of major structures are made at the highest levels, often by the President of the Republic himself. Pompidou opted for splendor and height, Giscard leaned toward a modest design, and Mitterrand has yet to decide. As one Gaullist member of the Council describes it:

> They [the Ministers and the President] don't even bother with us. And the Socialists are even worse. Any time there is a difference over a major item, the State decides. Sometimes they may call in a mayor to talk things over, but he is always on their side and agrees.[47]

Secteur Seine Sud-Est   The east of Paris has recently drawn the attention of policy makers. Always poorer than the western parts of the city, the eastern arrondissements have been the repository for most of the assisted housing (nearly two-thirds of the total), yet they have not attracted the more lucrative private developments (only one-fourth of the total).[48] These arrondissements are therefore places where many people make their homes, but where fewer jobs can be found. A 1983 report pointed out that although the east held 49 percent of the city's population, it offered only a quarter of its jobs.[49] Yet eastern Paris holds out opportunities for development. In a city where space is notoriously scarce, there is plenty of unused terrain in the east. The technocrats look longingly at land-use plans of the eastern arrondissements and call them "a new frontier of development."[50]

In a search for opportunities, the logical target in the east is the Secteur Seine Sud-Est. The Secteur straddles both sides of the Seine and covers parts of the Eleventh and Thirteenth arrondissements. It is the single largest empty space in all of the city; its 700 acres make up one-twentieth of the Parisian landscape (see Fig. 5.3).

The Secteur's strategic position makes it a real prize for anyone who can realize its potential. Lying within it are two of Paris' major railway stations (Gare de Lyon and Austerlitz), which account for 15 percent of the city's rail traffic. Secteur Seine Sud-Est is a gateway to the eastern suburbs and to new towns in that part of the region. Auto routes flow in and around it and it is accessible by Métro lines. Conditions of land ownership and territorial rights make the Secteur all the more attractive. Ninety percent of its land is publicly owned. The two leading proprietors are the national railway system and La Ville de Paris.[51]

The Secteur is not only sizable, it is lightly populated. Just 7,000 residents live there. Aside from the parks and woods of Paris, the Secteur has the lowest ratio of land to people.[52] Much of what has been built within the Secteur is dilapidated. Nearly one-third of the housing lacks central heating or hot water. Another half has no bathroom facilities.[53] Scattered throughout the area are shanty towns and temporary housing. Along one rail station the neighborhood is filled with hastily built shacks; its African population gives it a sober air of France's colonial past. All told, the Secteur contains the few eyesores that can be seen in Paris.

No single figure has shaped the Secteur's development. Its growth has been cumulative, catalyzed by a number of events. During the early 1970s, the Prefect of Paris brought the Secteur to the attention of politicians. At the Prefect's disposal is a staff of architects, planners, and mid-level functionaries. The staff, collectively called, l'Atelier Parisien d'Urbanisme (APUR), is the planning arm for Paris, and it carried out extensive studies on the Secteur. Eventually APUR came up with lines and points on the map it defined as the new Secteur.

The reports from APUR were made available to the City Council, where they were discussed with leaders and relevant committees. At the time Paris had no mayor, and leadership of the Council fell to a group of Gaullists who presided over its most important committees, such as Finance and Urban Affairs. Ideas for developing the Secteur took root as discussions proceeded between the Prefect, the Director of APUR, and leading Council members.

For a number of reasons private developers hardly took notice of the Secteur or its potential. Most of its land was in public ownership and the Secteur was not contiguous to the CBD or commercial projects. Moreover, there were plenty of diversions elsewhere. Office towers were sprouting at La Défense, the western arrondissements had just begun to ignite with investments, and the skyscraper at Montparnasse was captivating.

The team at APUR continued to work on the Secteur and by 1973 the Prefect presented his plan (Schéma) to the City Council. The Schéma was a sketch of what might be done, and, if approved, would establish an orientation for the use of the land rather than a set of hard prescriptions. Notwithstanding the French imagination, the Schéma also recognized that the Secteur was too large for any single development.

Instead, it proposed a number of separated though coordinated pieces of construction.

Among the suggestions were a 25-acre park, 11,000 housing units, a major office complex, and parcels of land that were to be used for light industry. There were other proposals that would glamorize the Secteur—a museum, a modern sports complex, and cultural centers. The Schéma recognized, too, that these projects would require access roads, sewer systems, and schools for the incoming population. That population was likely to reach 60,000 commuters who would find work in the Secteur and over 40,000 individuals who would make it their home. [54]

None of this impressed the Left, whose members were in the dark about the Prefect's work. They protested vigorously. In their eyes the Schéma was a conspiracy foisted on the Council by a bunch of technocrats and their Gaullist bosses. The Left accused them of wanting to rush the document through without popular consultation or extensive public debate. Seven hundred acres were about to be given over to big corporations and converted into an enclave for profiteers and a new bourgeoisie. For some of the less militant Socialists, the Schéma was an egregious wrong that needed amendment and modification. For the more militant Socialists and Communists, it was a nefarious idea that would cheat and disenfranchise *la classe populaire*. As one Communist member of the Council put it:

> the experience of Paris and its region proves what this research and this Schéma is all about. It's about maximizing the profit of the great financial houses and the corporations. It's about adapting the capital to the appetite of international business.
>
> They want to create a great office center for multinational corporations, which without that center, would run the risk of having to find another European capital. At this hour international capital increases its control over French business. That power enables them to take a royal seat in our city's heart, on free and cheap land given to them at public expense. [55]

This speaker was joined by his Socialist colleague, who rendered his own analysis of what was happening to the Secteur Seine Sud-Est:

> One time too many, the public is going to be sacrificed for private profit. One time too many, city land is going to be delivered to the insatiable appetites of the developers who are supported by the banks. One time too many, the law of the market place, . . . the law of profit, is going to contemptuously triumph over moral principles. One time too many these people will triumph over our prin-

ciples—the equilibrium between east and west, deconcentration, and decentralization, respect for the quality of life, the reduction of horrible commuter journeys, diversity of employment, the preservation of small business and trades.

One time too many, these principles that make for the good life are going to be abandoned for the profit of the privileged few. And when this comes to pass it won't be for lack of support by the political establishment.[56]

Whether this is political hyperbole or not, the Left had struck at least one chord that rang true. A close look at the Schéma showed that the Prefect and APUR had chosen to develop the Secteur as a post-industrial center. Although some space was put aside for factories and workshops, much of the area was put at the command of office development. The glossy pages and color-laden maps could not obscure the hard figures. Up to 10 million square feet of office space was planned, yielding jobs for 60,000 new petit bourgeosie.[57]

By comparison, the development for blue-collar labor was paltry. Specific amounts of industrial space were not mentioned, though the Schéma left more than a hint that industrial space would be limited. Only 2,000 to 3,000 industrial jobs were projected for the Secteur, a scant 5 percent of the total.[58]

Still, all was not bleak for the workers and people of Paris, and it would be foolhardy to believe the Schéma was a plot against them. More space was reserved for housing than for commercial activity. The number of housing units was scheduled to be quadrupled in comparison with what was already in the Secteur. One-third of the scheduled housing was to receive public subsidy, thereby allowing moderate-income families into the area. The creation of new green space, the planting of nine hundred trees, and the availability of cheap mass transportation were bound to be a boon for la classe populaire as well as for potential office developers.[59]

These were indeed substantial concessions to la classe populaire—but concessions they were, rather than core projects that would define the future Secteur. On balance the Schéma was written for a post-industrial Paris. It emphasized tertiary rather than industrial jobs and *haute culture* instead of soccer fields.

From the point of view of the Right, the Schéma was a realistic response to contemporary economics and to the necessities of technological progress. As one spokesperson for the Right pointed out, Paris would have to grow, would have to survive in a larger world, and could not exist by itself.

At the moment Brussels is trying to attract big corporations and

First National City Bank is setting itself up in Moscow. We ought to enter into this frank and friendly competition with the rest of the world.[60]

Furthermore, the Secteur was not in the grip of big business (which barely knew of its exsitence) nor was it likely to be given over to private interests to do as they might wish. The whole point of the Schéma was to establish the presence and direction of government. As one Gaullist leader put it:

there are three possible choices with regard to office construction in Paris. The first I spoke about yesterday with members of DATAR. . . . That is not to construct office towers anywhere in Paris, neither at Secteur Seine Sud-Est or elsewhere. This position is as clearcut as it is absurd, because it is impossible to freeze the current situation. . . .

The second choice is to rely on 19th-century economic principles, that is "laissez faire, laissez passer." It is the simple game of the free market. Who knows what that portends? It is the anarchical proliferation of office buildings, it doesn't matter where or how this comes about.

The third choice, I have reserved for the last because in my view it is the only good one. It entails some simple principles: that in the future there will be a need for office space in Paris, whether one wants that or not: that the public sphere must master that development, lest it escape from our control: and if there is office development, it is better to keep it along the narrow paths which we have chosen.[61]

Just before the vote, the Prefect of Paris added his own amen. He concluded by saying that the Schéma represented the best chance by the public to master urban development and to bring it "within governmental direction, thus avoiding a future of anarchical growth."[62] Shortly afterward, the votes were taken. The Left, which wanted to delay adoption and bring the Schéma before the public for more information and consultation, presented its motion. It failed by a vote of 47 to 43. Other motions by Communist and Socialist councillors also failed to carry. The Gaullists then made their proposals, arguing that the Schéma was the only way to harmonize public and private interests and the best way to bring jobs to Paris. The Schéma carried by a vote of 56 to 34.[63]

A decade passed before the Secteur emerged from the Council's debates. In the interim, Gaullists and Socialists quarreled over the Secteur's future and over who was to pay for its development. Mayor

Chirac played political chess with President Mitterrand over who was to control the Secteur and who was to take credit for its growth.[64] By the late 1980s those quarrels had faded, and the Secteur began to bloom with post-industrial revitalization. A number of ZACs were created to pave the way for housing, light industry, and office facilities. A wine warehousing district at Bercy was refurbished. Office towers already loom over the Gare de Lyon.

At Bercy an impressive sports complex (Palais Omnisports) has been built. The Palais Omnisports is designed to accommodate twenty-four activities, ranging from equestrian events to ice hockey. Paris intends to compete as the site of future Olympic Games and the Palais Omnisports will be the first bargaining chip in that competition, with the Secteur's open space held out as a lure for the Olympic Committee.

Another significant catalyst for development is the relocation of the Ministry of Finance into the Secteur. This decision, initiated by the Socialists and pursued by the Gaullists, adds new office buildings to an area where public and private interests have comingled. The decision to move an important ministry, like Finance, into the Secteur infuses it with a bevy of builders, bankers, restauranteurs, and other suppliers. Enlarged expressways and new bridges will be built to accommodate additional traffic.

Figure 5.8 shows an aerial view of the Secteur along with plans for its redevelopment. Note the strategic points of capital infusion that will be put into the Secteur. These points are along the northeastern bank of the Seine (Ministry of Finance, Palais Omnisports, ZAC Corbineau), on its southeastern bank (ZAC Tolbiac), and at refurbished bridges across the river (Nouveau Pont, Pont de Bercy, Pont de Tolbiac). Each of the railway stations (Gare de Lyon, Gare d'Austerlitz) also serves as a strategic locus. One can easily imagine the vast patches of unused land being filled in by private investors and mixed corporations.

The Secteur stands as an enormous magnet of public investment, drawing and directing private capital. Officials are embarrassed by the surfeit of riches pouring into a single locale and deny that Mitterrand and Chirac have struck a bargain to divide development between them. The common belief is that Socialists and Gaullists are not anxious to be seen working with one another, especially in the process of concentrating more activity in Paris. As one high-level planner remarked:

> The authorities are always talking about decentralization and the need to invest in the provinces. While they talk, they put everything in Paris. That's politics.[65]

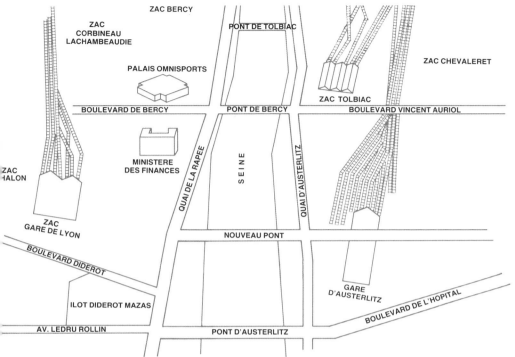

Fig. 5.8. Secteur Seine Sud-Est: Development and Plans

Summary Analysis

In Paris, land-use politics moves by the strokes of mobilizing corporatism. One element of mobilizing corporatism is the scope it af-
fords to a political-technocratic elite through extensive planning tools
and state resources. This scope enables planners to traverse political
boundaries as well as build bridges between public and private sectors.
Thus we have seen how new towns were built in the Ile-de-France for
demographic and industrial overflow; how Les Halles was rebuilt for a
new industrial order; how La Défense was created out of nothing to
become a new CBD; and how DATAR protected these ventures by influ-
encing the marketplace.

Another element of mobilizing corporatism is the potency it furnishes to public actors through "the plan" (ZACs, ZADs, and schémas).
Unlike New Yorkers, Parisians believe in the efficacy and worthiness
of "a plan." Planning is something the French do in order to plot their
future and determine their priorities. Its carryover into state and local
government is an integral part of the culture.

Public finance is the fuel that propels mobilizing corporatism. We have seen how state resources sustain mixed corporations or EPAS and how they further mass transit linkages between Paris and the region. Without state support, politicians and technocrats would be powerless. With it, they are able to fuel vast numbers of people and organizations. Public finance makes it possible for public actors to manage, direct, and synchronize a host of private organizations.

In comparison with the United States, there is little obfuscation in France. Parisian policy makers are more sure of themselves because they have greater assurance that their intentions will be fulfilled. Banks and financial institutions can be put at the disposal of the state. The marketplace can be regulated—frozen, if necessary—to accomplish policy objectives. Centralized politics and regionalization mitigate rivalry between local governments. There are always limits to what private enterprise can do vis-à-vis government. This, too, strengthens the potential of mobilizing corporatism.

In many ways the achievements of Parisian planning are reflections of its process. Thus it was the government that decided that Les Halles, La Défense, and Secteur Seine Sud-Est ought to be built. Once a decision is made, it is rare to see a project stumble. In comparison with judicial practices in America, the courts are constrained. In no case did judicial action modify a Parisian decision, much less halt development.

In and of itself achievement may not be a virtue. Planning without hesitation can be planning filled with mistakes and pain. For those whose fates were dealt with abruptly in Les Halles, the lack of recourse was a great shortcoming of the system. Drawings from the architect's table and calculations from the planner's desk are one thing—living with their results is quite another. The destruction of the Baltard Pavilions and the bleakness of La Défense bear a different kind of testimony about French achievements.

Similarly, mobilizing corporatism does not ensure dispassion in the use of power, nor does it mean that its application will be restrained. In comparison with the French, Americans are accustomed to muddier political waters. New York politicians always need to build their own power levers and garner interest group support from many corners. All this serves to restrain top leaders and inhibit them from personalizing their choices.* Under mobilizing corporatism the levers of power are more permanent and the lines of authority more clear. Di-

* This is not to say that personal choices do not affect decisions in New York. Ed Koch's decision to scrub the "City at 42nd Street" proposal is evidence of that. But Koch was restrained in the final plan adopted for Times Square by the Governor, the UDC, and a host of developers as well as the community of Clinton and local politicians. See Chapter 3.

rect access can also be less restrained access. Top politicians and planners are more apt to inject personal likes and dislikes into final choices. Giscard d'Estaing did away with the World Trade Center (CCI) at Les Halles simply by announcing its elimination. The Plateau Beaubourg was built in a particular manner because the Gaullists wanted a personal monument for a stricken president. Much of La Défense's design was at the personal behest of political leaders. Monumentalism is no longer what it was in the days of kings and emperors, but it does put important touches on projects. And it is made easier by the political process.

Both the tangibility of power and the paucity of restraint allow top politicians to horse-trade among themselves. Pieces of Les Halles went back and forth between Gaullists and Giscardiens as well as between the La Ville de Paris and the state. Still other pieces of Paris (La Villette) were traded in order to give Chirac his accolade as architect of Les Halles.

We have also noted the weakness of grass-roots opposition to government plans. The remaking of La Défense and Secteur Seine Sud-Est evoked hardly a wimper on their streets. Though these decisions were couched in partisan ideological debate, the outcomes were not in doubt. Compare the mobilizing corporatism of Paris with the hybrid of New York, where interest groups fought to the bitter end.

It is true that, in Paris, citizen opposition surfaced during the controversy over Les Halles. Resistence by a neighborhood group (CIAH) yielded rewards in that the size of the target area was reduced. But even these gains are uncertain. The CIAH was made part of the very apparatus that planned the changes and the genuineness of the reduction is questionable. The former prefect of the region, recounting the incident to the author, told a different tale. "Oh yes," he said, "they succeeded in reducing the size of the DUP [target area]. We knew all along they needed that. So that's why we made the DUP twice as large as we really intended."[66]

The Parisian vision is a grand one. Through mobilizing corporatism it has built a post-industrial order with vigor to match that of New York. But it is a different kind of vigor, which creates different kinds of results. La Défense was built out of a concern that Parisian densities and the Parisian skyline should be kept low. New towns and suburban growth poles were built to keep blue-collar industry within hailing distance of the urban core. Les Halles tells its own story. One look at it shows the difference between New York and Paris. The elimination of its World Trade Center tells us about a road that Parisians chose not to take.

Fig. 5.9 (*at left*). Old Les Halles:
The Baltard Pavilions. Photo/So-
ciété Anonyme d'Economie Mixte
d'Aménagement de Rénovation
et de Restauration du Secteur
des Halles

Fig. 5.10 (*above*). Looking Out-
ward from One of the Baltard Pa-
vilions. Source: From Jacques
Prévert and Romain Urhausen,
*Les Halles: L'Album du Coeur de
Paris* (Paris: Editions des Deux
Mondes, 1965), p. 106.

Fig. 5.11 (*above, top*). New Les Halles. Photo/Société Anonyme d'Economie Mixte d'Aménagement de Rénovation et de Restauration du Secteur des Halles

Fig. 5.12. New Les Halles (closeup). Photo/Société Anonyme d'Economie Mixte d'Aménagement de Rénovation et de Restauration du Secteur des Halles

Fig. 5.13 (*at right, top*). Old Plateau Beaubourg. Photo/Société Anonyme d'Economie Mixte d'Aménagement de Rénovation et de Restauration du Secteur des Halles

Fig. 5.14 (*at right, below*). New Plateau Beaubourg (Centre Pompidou). Photo/Jeremiah Bragstand

Fig. 5.15. Old La Défense. Photo/Etablissement Public pour l'Aménagement
de la Région de La Défense

Fig. 5.16. New La Défense. Photo/Jean-Pierre Salomon (EPAD)

Fig. 5.17. Secteur Seine Sud-Est with Palais Omnisports at upper right.
Photo/Claude Abron

London: Ambivalent Development, Ambivalent Result

If this is a country where few people take the trouble to learn other people's languages, it is also a country that has somehow managed, with a large population packed onto a small island to preserve vast tracts of pastoral beauty.

Such things may be impossible to quantify, unlike per capita income or gross national product. But such things make daily life in Britain far more rewarding than mere economic reality might suggest.—A newspaper article describing Britain's economic woes in 1985

The Search for Identity

ALTHOUGH there are marked similarities between New York, Paris, and London, there are also notable differences. One such difference has to do with the strong and stable identities of New York and Paris as opposed to the amorphous and vague identification of London. New York City has retained the same area and shape since its amalgamation in 1898. Paris has kept its fundamental form and contours since Haussmann remade the city in the nineteenth century. Though the farmlands around these two cities have become urbanized, New York and Paris still possess recognizable boundaries and remain indivisible.

But London is different. It is an intractable metropolis whose long-standing problem has been to define itself and find its true composition. The contours of London as well as its internal subdivisions have changed several times in the last hundred years.[1] In 1888 the Local Government Act gave one shape to London, by creating an administrative county out of a group of vestries and other subgovernments. This made both the county and municipality of London coterminous and established the London County Council (LCC) as a political focal point. Eleven years later, another act modified the political subdivisions of London by converting the vestries into twenty-eight metropolitan boroughs. Though the boroughs were vital subunits drawing the attention of the citizenry, the LCC earned a high reputation for efficiency and honesty. London was a relatively cohesive city, manageable in size, and the LCC presented a distinct and positive profile.

But London was to go through still more organizational change. In

170

1963 the Greater London Act abolished the LCC. In its place the Greater London Council (GLC) was established. At the time, the change was considered a stroke of genius, an example of Britain's willingness to accommodate the modern age. It was hoped the GLC would earn the same, if not greater, prestige as had its predecessor.

Creating the GLC, however, turned out to be a tidy theoretical innovation, flawed by practical politics. Under the new act the London area (now Greater London) nearly doubled in size. London was converted from a city to a region. The new authority was suddenly put to the test of harmonizing local interests and welding a regional loyalty. Thirty-two boroughs and the City also emerged as units of local government. The boroughs were supposed to function in different capacities than the GLC, but power is not easily shared. Borough and GLC interests were different and were bound to collide. Boroughs wanted to protect and serve their constituents; the GLC desperately needed to establish its legitimacy and its political credibility.

Shortly after the Greater London Act was implemented, a survey was commissioned to test public awareness of the change. The results were disappointing: 34 percent of the respondents either did not know what the initials GLC stood for or identified them incorrectly. When told what GLC meant, most respondents could not say what it did and a good many confused it with its predecessor, the LCC. Voting recognition was even poorer: only 2 percent of respondents could name their representative at the GLC though 58 percent could name their representative in Parliament.[2] Over the years recognition improved, but the disappointing surveys revealed just how incomplete the transition had been and how compromised the GLC would remain.[3]

London's identity problem is evident in the verbiage that attempts to describe it. Technically there is no London. There is Greater London, which encompasses a large sprawling land mass of over 600 square miles. There is also the City of London, which constitutes a tiny fragment of one square mile and houses fewer than 6,000 residents. In between Greater London and the City of London are the boroughs, which have become the real centers of gravity for local government. This has become so by tradition, sentiment, and legal fiat. Although there may be democratic virtue in the idea of borough government or rule at the grass-roots level, the virtue has contributed to the vice of a confused identity. And it is the search for identity that has consumed so much of London's developmental and political history. This history can be viewed through the efforts of two men—Sir Patrick Abercrombie and Professor William Robson. Abercrombie was a planner who tried to carve out concentric rings through which to define the physical environs of London. Robson was a political scientist who attempted to locate London's politics in a two-tiered system of government.

The Legacies of Patrick Abercrombie and William Robson

The issues dealt with by Abercrombie and Robson were neither discovered nor even brought to the public's attention by them. The difficulty of reconciling rational planning to democratic politics had long simmered in London's body politic and had been managed in typically British fashion—by gradual, piecemeal adjustments that respected traditions rather than by grand schemes.[4]

Soon after the LCC was created, it began to purchase land outside its boundaries in order to build "overspill housing" for London's excess population. Within a few decades, the amount of housing built for Londoners outside the geographical confines of the LCC was substantial. Between 1919 and 1929 over 46,000 houses were built in the adjoining counties of Essex, Hertford, Middlesex, Kent, and Surrey.[5] Thus, by the simple acts of land purchase, housing construction, and transferring population, the seedling of a Greater London had been planted.

In the mid-1930s the LCC was already taking steps to ensure the preservation of open land around the housing it had built. Inspired by Ebenezer Howard's prescription for a "garden city" and by Lewis Mumford's vision of an urban world without walls, the LCC began to cultivate a green background for its metropolis. By 1939 the LCC had already acquired and left vacant 13,000 acres of green land and had moved thousands of people to the countryside.[6]

Thus at the time Abercrombie was ready to promote his plans for a Greater London, an assortment of planners, politicians, and officials had already made a start. What Abercrombie did through the decades of the 1940s and 1950s was to give substance and fulfillment to the notion that London needed to be limited in its growth, made more habitable, and given careful definition. A major means for implementing these ideas was to create a Green Belt that would straddle an area around London at a distance of 10 to 15 miles from its center (Charing Cross). The Green Belt would be no ordinary sliver of land. Today it is close to the girth proposed by Abercrombie (about 5 miles) and covers 900 square miles of open space (one-third more than the size of Greater London).[7]

Over the years, the Green Belt has been painstakingly guarded and kept free of intrusions. Scattered residential enclaves do exist within the Belt, but they are limited and their growth is carefully monitored.

Government policies adopted through the 1960s and 1970s have respected its accomplishments and upheld the need to maintain and even enlarge it.

The Green Belt has in fact become a green, open wall around which to set the outer limits for Greater London. In doing so it states that this is the last frontier: limit urban sprawl and define yourselves within these bounds. There is, of course, a logic to this. The very act of self-recognition requires a degree of containment. It requires that a distinction be made between "we" and "they," between one mass of land and another, and between the institutions that govern different territories. In Abercrombie's day, self-recognition through containment had a strong appeal and was supposed to avoid the endless sprawl that had despoiled so many cities. But as we shall see, it also had unintended consequences and led to economic stagnation through many parts of Inner London.

On paper, economic stagnation could be avoided by providing for zones that could absorb overspill population and accommodate burgeoning industries. Abercrombie's idea was to establish concentric rings out of London's center, so that the metropolis might have the opportunity to adjust to the changing currents of demography. At the center an inner ring comprising the County of London would be declared an area of declining population and a policy of population dedensification would be implemented. A middle ring comprising an area up to the Green Belt would be adjudged an area of static population with no appreciable growth foreseen. And an outer ring comprising an area beyond the Green Belt would be designated as a zone of expansion intended for population absorption.[8]

Though radical on its face, Abercrombie's plan actually sought to stabilize and rationalize the predominance of London—not drastically change it. Inner London was still to possess a hierarchy of commerce, culture, politics, and status. A policy of dedensification would enhance the predominance of the center by beautifying and humanizing it. The remaining Inner London population would have more room, more amenities to share, and a metropolis that had reduced its heavy industrial smudge. This much was made clear by both the instructions given to Abercrombie by the LCC ("Full regard must be had to London as the seat of government . . . [as] an ancient city with established character [and] as a great industrial and commercial location").[9] It was also made clear by subsequent plans of the 1970s that clung to Abercrombie's initiatives (Everything should be done "to maintain London's position as the capital of the nation and one of the world's great cities").[10] London was to be renewed and not remade.

The growth around London, past the Green Belt, would be both a benefit to the countryside and to the metropolis. Industrial expansion could enrich new areas as well as unburden London. This expansion was to be accommodated in a series of new towns built on the outer edges of the Green Belt and in what now constitutes the Outer Metropolitan Area (OMA). Unlike the French new towns, however, the British versions were self-sufficient communities that were not intentionally linked to the urban core. The French emphasized urban integration and located their new towns in an urban corridor connected to Paris; the British stressed autonomy and placed their new towns at a longer distance away from the capital. The interposition of the Green Belt also served as a physical and psychological barrier to integration.

Like Abercrombie, Robson was the progenitor of an idea that went far beyond the confines of his métier. The scholar from the London School of Economics had been working on the problem of governmental reform since the 1930s. His book, *The Government and Misgovernment of London*, appeared in 1939 and in it he lambasted the "makeshift muddle" of hundreds of governments tripping over one another in their efforts to administer a vast metropolitan region.[11] For Robson, the solution lay in rationalizing the patchwork of local governments so there were fewer of them and so the remaining authorities could divide responsibilities that were appropriate to their function and to the size of their region. Under his scheme, the smaller jurisdictions would have the blessings of democracy at the grass-roots level while a regional government would provide them with the benefits of large-scale cooperation. To accomplish this, Robson grasped the idea of an elected two-tier government. One tier would be responsible for functions appropriate to regional government (such as long-distance transportation and long-range and strategic planning). Another tier would manage issues of local proportion (such as street traffic, social services, and community recreation).[12]

Robson's proposals were bold and sweeping. In them he was attempting to reorganize the governance of the LCC and the many governments around it by collecting authority from all of them and reassigning a portion of that authority to a lesser number of jurisdictions. This was no small task in a nation that after seven hundred years still called the one square mile of London's origin "the City."

The particulars of Robson's proposals called for more than one hundred local authorities to be abolished and consolidated to a mere twenty-nine. Each of the twenty-nine localities would contain a population of several hundred thousand and elect a council to run its affairs. The same localities would collectively be a larger Greater London and elect another body to care for regional concerns. All of this was contemplated for a metropolitan area of 700 square miles (more than five times the size of the LCC area) and for a population of over eight million (twice the number of the LCC population).

Despite the enormous difficulties of putting Robson's proposals into effect, his ideas had a fascinating, almost compelling, logic. They revolved around the assumption of placing functions where there was motivation, interest, and capacity to fulfill them. Thus local authorities, with populations of perhaps 300,000, would best be able to manage services that were typified by frequent interaction between service deliverers (i.e., civil servants) and service recipients (i.e., the local citizenry). Many of these services involve discretion, quick and reasonable judgments, and flexibility. They are what Michael Lipsky has called "street-level bureaucracies" and they require knowledge of local problems and rapport with residents.[13] Social services such as care for the elderly or crèche facilities for children are good examples of "street-level bureaucracies" because they entail intense interaction with citizens and practical judgment. The control of local traffic or parking regulations are other examples of "street-level" services, because they require sensitivity to the needs of motorists and flexibility in enforcing regulations. From a theoretical standpoint, these are types of services that are best administered by the government that is closest to the people.

On the other hand, there are problems that are unique to the needs of a broad region and that defy local boundaries. Mass transportation is one example of a service that should operate over vast stretches of territory, if it is going to be cost effective. Air pollution is another problem that pays no heed to local boundaries, and policies regarding its control are best set by a broader jurisdiction. Often functions that are unique to a region require long-range planning and coordination. Land preservation (Green Belts) and facilities for waste disposal are obviously services that require complicated preparations (land acquisition, zoning regulations) or coordination between smaller localities (a common dumping site or treatment plant).

For Robson it was not just efficiency but democratic virtue that counted. Years later he was to attack Abercrombie's proposal for an unelected Regional Planning Board as "an organ of Central Government . . . entirely unrelated to democratic self-government in London."[14] Abercrombie, the architect who sought clean efficiency, and Robson, the political scientist who valued participation, parted company over the issue of how to bring about a planned London. Where they stood together was in their search for order—both wanted a London whose functions would correspond to its different parts—and in their quest for synchrony—both wanted a London whose parts would work in harmony.

A Planned London: Realization and Contradiction

Abercrombie's influence took root earlier than Robson's. The Green Belt policy was formally in operation in the 1940s, his Greater London Plan of 1944 had already begun to shape future development, and by 1949 new towns had been designated outside of London.

Although time may have forced a divergence from Abercrombie's plans, its fundamental design remained intact from the 1940s to the present. London has been dedensified, much of its smokestack industry has left, an expanding Green Belt guards the perimeter of Greater London, and the new towns of the OMA are thriving. If anything, Abercrombie's expectations have been exceeded and this has caused problems. At the time Abercrombie was commissioned to do his work, the area that is comparable to today's Greater London held a population of more than 8 million. By 1981 that population had fallen to 6.8 million, a loss of 1.9 million or roughly 22 percent of the population base of the 1940s.[15] The OMA on which Abercrombie pinned his hopes also surpassed his objectives. By the mid-1970s and 1980s, it was growing apace and absorbing Greater London's population and industry. Today the OMA holds a population of six million, almost two million more than the "ultimate" figure Abercrombie had anticipated. As originally conceived, each of the new towns was supposed to hold a population of approximately 60,000. Later targets were revised upward to 100,000 each. Though more dense than anticipated, the new towns have kept their original design as low-density settlements and have been built in the English tradition of 14 to 16 multiple-family dwellings per acre.[16]

Although Abercrombie's design for London had its achievements, it also has had the unforeseen consequence of straining scarce facilities at the periphery and bankrupting abundant facilities at the center. New settlements within the OMA have converted sleepy hamlets into commuter sheds, which has resulted in clogged highways in and out of the CBD. In effect, the commuter trek in and out of London has expanded from 15 to 35 miles during earlier decades to 30 to 60 miles today.

Furthermore, many of the benefits that have accrued to the OMA have meant serious losses for Greater London. Dedensification of population has brought with it a disproportionate loss of jobs. Between 1965 and 1982, the unemployment roles have surged from a mere 35,000 to more than 376,000, amounting to a rise of 1,000 percent.[17] Since 1978, almost 300,000 jobs have been lost and 500 factories have closed. The stock of empty industrial buildings was at a record high in the 1980s.[18]

Parts of Inner London have been especially hard hit by the exodus to the hinterlands. Many of the docks on the East End have closed, leaving behind a depressing sight of boarded-up warehouses and broken piers. Between 1971 and 1981 more than 46 percent of Inner London's manufacturing jobs disappeared.[19]

Abercrombie wanted a London made beautiful by stopping and even reversing its growth. But his successors did not put in place substitutes for regenerating London's wealth or for rebuilding its abandoned sectors. In some instances hopes for beautification have turned into wretched emptiness.

The difficulty with the outcome of Abercrombie's design is that it relied upon a finite and static conception of London that was cast in the 1940s. Inner London was to be an area of population decline and Outer London one of stability. The most dynamic areas (the OMA and the new towns) were to be disconnected from the very base of the metropolis—its urban core and its first ring. As such the most dynamic region was discouraged from interacting with the static areas. The natural synergy that might have enlivened London was separated from it by a Green Belt, which acted as both the substance and the symbol for the limits of London. Everything that happened within that metropolis was to take place within clearly defined territorial bounds. But such a design denies the urban potential for cross-fertilization and growth, which requires a certain amount of spontaneous interaction with an outside environment so that population and innovation can move into the metropolis as well as out of it. As Jacobs so well illustrates, "chaos" and "planned disorder" are intrinsic to a lively city.[20] Yet the very idea of stability, containment, and limitation denies this potential. The effort to create self-recognition out of that containment was bound to a static process; ultimately it was also bound to a fruitless result.

As for the Green Belt, its critics charge that it has only succeeded in establishing an unused swath of land between Greater London and the OMA that prolongs the commute and creates traffic jams. One study, done in 1960, pointed out that only 5.4 percent of the Green Belt was used for recreation and only 3.4 percent was open to the public.[21] The belt also discouraged efficient farming because of the difficulty of putting land parcels together. Frustration with the results of preservation policy, coupled with concern over indistrial growth, have elicited proposals that the Green Belt be radically altered. Some have argued that a series of green wedges be put in its place, allowing housing and industry to grow around them. Others have proposed increased settlement within the Green Belt. Thus far, however, the Green Belt has been maintained and the GLC had taken pains to protect it. The major plan adopted by the Greater London Council argued:

> The Green Belt is an integral part of the metropolitan structure and an essential ingredient to the regional structure, for its separates London clearly from the outer Metropolitan Area. . . . limiting the continuous urban spread and preserving a Green Belt of open country surrounding it are fundamental to London planning policy, and indeed the plan envisages some additions to the Green Belt. The advantages which these measures confer on London living would be irreplaceable.[22]

Both the successes and difficulties of Abercrombie's design generated a new way of thinking about London in the late 1950s and early 1960s. A great deconcentration of population and industry throughout the region revealed the need to coordinate planning and services. Urbanization around the area of the LCC was changing its economic and physical composition; while new jobs were being created, so too were new problems. Moreover, as urbanization proceeded to gobble up nearby counties, there was a danger that political fragmentation would intensify. Should this come to pass, London was in danger of falling into the pattern of the American metropolis—formless, unplanned, and wastefully dependent upon the private motor car.

London's problems during this period also held out its promise, if London could act. What was needed was some kind of governmental institution that could better put planning into effect, could cope with the problems of fragmented services, and could shore up a common recognition of London. In short, if Abercrombie was to remain pertinent to new developments, he would need Robson. Robson's dictum that "planning was a problem of government" was indeed correct.[23] It simply neglected to mention that politics could block governmental action, as it did for nearly twenty years. By the late 1950s, however, the political circumstances were propitious and a confluence of other circumstances brought governmental reorganization to the fore.

The Conservative Party, which controlled the government, sensed its opportunity to redraw the boundaries of London and took advantage of discontent with the LCC's inability to control the situation. The LCC had been a Labour stronghold for many years and Conservatives looked upon London wistfully. Labour could count on Inner London to put it in power, but the suburbs around it were largely Conservative. Thus the Tories reasoned that reorganization could incorporate the suburbs, bring in Conservative votes, and put a new regional government in their hands.[24]

By the end of 1957 they had appointed a Royal Commission to examine the subject of reorganization, under the chairmanship of Sir Edwin Herbert (the Herbert Commission). Less than three years after the Herbert Commission's start it had issued its report, which was essentially a prescription for the reorganization of Greater London along lines that Robson had suggested twenty years earlier.

As it turned out, the Greater London Act of 1963 consolidated governmental authority in a sphere of 630 square miles. It also remade scores of local and county boundaries. The act embraced an elected two-tier government—one for the region called the Greater London Council or GLC, and another for small jurisdictions, or boroughs with populations in the vicinity of 250,000.

Although political compromise punctuated the act's provisions, its guiding principle was that functions should be placed where they could be best administered. This meant that responsibilities for intelligence gathering, coordination, and the distribution of resources belonged to the GLC. The administration of "routine services" belonged to the boroughs. The question of which governmental authority possessed more power was intentionally avoided, and it was pointed out that though the GLC was a "wider authority" it was not a "higher authority." By this reasoning the GLC was charged with strategic planning; it was given the responsibility of running the region's sprawling mass transportation; it was made a housing supplier of secondary resort ("overspill housing"); and it was given an assortment of "regional responsibilities" (fire fighting, land drainage, and the maintenance of large parks).

As for the boroughs, they took charge of a different kind of function. These included drawing up local plans; managing local transportation (parking, road maintenance); functioning as a primary housing supplier; and operating a variety of social services (day care, family welfare).

There were, of course, functions that did not fit so neatly between the GLC and the boroughs. Education for children in primary and secondary schools proved to be a special case, requiring different solutions for Inner and Outer London boroughs. Taxation and revenue raising were also thorny problems that were worked out by giving the boroughs the authority to collect property taxes (rateables) and allowing the GLC to impose a levy (precept) on the individual boroughs.

Last, control over the police was kept by the central government.

The police were organized for the whole of Greater London and constituted as a metropolitan force.

In theory, the Greater London Act of 1963 was a splendid instrument. Political scientists have long lauded the virtues of metropolitan government, regional planning, and local participation. The two-tier system appeared to accommodate all of these principles and London was held up as a model of good government and good planning. American scholars were particularly intrigued with London's arrangement. One article contrasted London and New York City under the caption "Local Government in Heaven and Hell." Another article referring to London used the title "The Governable City."[25]

A certain amount of myth has grown up about London's ostensible tidiness and its governability. The myth ignores the many difficulties and contradictions that have beset its politics and its planning. To begin with, the regional government or GLC has been caught between the watchful eye of the central government and the detailed and routine functions of the boroughs. At the time the Act was under consideration, Peter Self made the prescient comment that the GLC seemed "all too likely to find itself ground between the millstones of borough primacy and close government supervision." Thus, the so-called two-tier government of London might in reality be a three-tier government (central government, the GLC, and the boroughs) with, as Self put it, the GLC operating "as a sort of ghostly middleman between town hall and Whitehall."[26]

Once the theory was put into practice, Self's prognosis turned out to have validity. The GLC found itself either unable to make autonomous decisions or in such deep conflict with the boroughs that the central government had to intervene. Lacking its own teeth of implementation, the GLC became dependent upon other institutions. The GLC's strategic planning was dependent upon the boroughs for implementation, upon private industry for cooperation, and upon the central government for approval. The Greater London Development Plan of 1969 was so heavily criticized that it had to be sent back for a rewriting and did not emerge for seven years.

The GLC's most potent weapon for bringing about results has been its ability to build "overspill housing." Public housing is an issue of enormous consequence in London. More than a quarter of the population relies on it for shelter. Once built, it can have an impact upon the class status of an area, on its density, and on its physical development. Quite expectedly, many boroughs resented the intrusion of "overspill housing" into their neighborhoods. As the primary suppliers of housing, some boroughs felt usurped by GLC action and resisted it. In the face of this, the GLC was forced to seek the support of the central government. So fragile was the GLC position on "overspill housing" that it clung to vestigial powers (granted by the old LCC) in order to build public housing. These powers were exercised on a "temporary basis" for more than twenty years.

In the area of mass transportation, the GLC was supposed to have exclusive rights, yet even this brought it into conflict with some boroughs. In 1981, for example, the GLC raised its precept on the boroughs in order to reduce fares on the Underground. One outer borough objected and brought the matter to the courts. A protracted conflict ensued between the GLC and the outer boroughs over subsidizing Underground fares with rateables from Outer London property owners. Ultimately the House of Lords was brought into the fracas and ruled against the GLC.

When the GLC was not in conflict with the boroughs, it was accused of being unnecessary. Its formal authority to educate pupils in the Inner London boroughs was exercised by the Inner London Education Authority. Its formal authority to provide the water supply was exercised by a Metropolitan Water Board. Hospitals and port facilities were also run by special authorities or boards. Even the GLC's authority to maintain "regional parks" was circumscribed by the fact that London's giant parks have been adjudged national treasures for the central government to administer. Opponents of the GLC claimed that if the central government could run the parks, it could also manage the Green Belt, administer a system of precepts, and handle strategic planning.

The squeeze on the GLC by the boroughs and the central government was compounded by the GLC's own difficulty in finding a rightful place. In London the boroughs are regarded as the proper "localities" and the central government is regarded as "the Government." The GLC lacked any clear niche—except as an occasional interloper on local prerogatives.

In 1977 a movement to abolish the GLC took root in some outer boroughs. Angered by GLC housing policies, Conservatives began to field candidates who were pledged to GLC abolition. Not until the 1980s did the other side of Peter Self's twin millstones begin to turn. This time it was the central government that ground away at the GLC's legitimacy. Political ideology was the grist of conflict as the Labour-controlled GLC turned militantly leftist, while Margaret Thatcher's government moved to the far right. The GLC's leader, Ken Livingstone, shot off a flurry of criticism against Thatcher's policies. "Red Ken," as the Conservatives called him, attacked everything from Thatcher's domestic budget cuts to her foreign policy. Labourites on the GLC also embraced a more radical social policy by funding community action groups, supporting feminist causes, and declaring London a nuclear-free zone.

Thatcher responded by inserting a statement in the Conservative Manifesto that would do away with all metropolitan authorities in Great Britain, an obvious swipe at the GLC. At the time, most people dismissed her idea as political rhetoric. But in 1983 Thatcher began to act on her promise. A Conservative White Paper, "Streamlining the Cities," was published on the subject and bills were placed before Parliament. During the summer of 1984 the House of Commons passed the necessary measures for abolition.

As of April 1986 the GLC ceased to exist. Its operations have been scattered to different parts of London's political system. The boroughs have taken on responsibility for more miles of road, more parks, and more housing. In some instances boroughs have had to form joint committees and consortia in order to manage GLC functions. The central government has taken on more responsibility for strategic planning. A new statutory body, the London Planning Advisory Committee (LPAC) has been formed out of the boroughs to furnish the central government with strategic advice. When GLC operations could not be hived off to existing institutions, special authorities and quasi-autonomous non-governmental organizations (QUANGOS) were set up to do the job.

What was once, on paper, a neat and comprehensible metropolitan government is now a muddle. It takes several sheets of paper simply to list the names of the boards, committees, and temporary bodies that now carry out the GLC's work. It will take years to sort out responsibilities for running London—if they are ever sorted out.

Most Conservatives would rather contend with confusion than with the old GLC. During the election campaign of 1987, the Tories stood proudly for abolition and against a "wasteful and unnecessary tier of government." The opposition parties held high the banner of metropolitan government and saw abolition as a vindictive act that defied the traditions of local participation. Labour pledged to restore a "democratically elected strategic authority for London." The Alliance recalled that "London is now the only major capital city in the democratic world without a democratically elected local authority" and asked for the election of a regional assembly.[27]

Thatcher was not undone in 1987, and her victory sealed abolition for at least another five years. The Conservatives see this as a way of preventing "the far left" from controlling London, and just as significantly, as a first step toward reducing taxes. Meanwhile, citizens look around and ask, "where has London gone?"

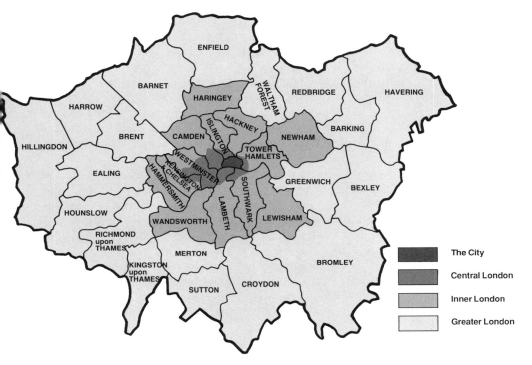

Fig. 6.1. Political Subdivisions of Greater London:
Central, Inner, and Outer Boroughs

*Demographics and Employment: Contrasting the Urban Core
and the First Ring*

The great planning initiatives and political innovations of the post-war era were written on the map of London and, in some ways, emblazoned on its social structure. Greater London was defined by a Green Belt and its strategic planning put in the hands of the GLC. Within London, the boroughs were made into "governments of first instance." Distinctions were made between "inner" and "outer" boroughs. Planners outlined four central boroughs whose parts comprised the CBD.

Figure 6.1 reviews these basic designations. All of London's thirty-two boroughs are portrayed along with the City. Also shown is the CBD as it splays across Camden, Kensington–Chelsea, Westminster, and the City.

183

Within this metropolis called Greater London, the population has undergone substantial change. As in New York and Paris, the urban core lost. Between 1967 and 1981, Central and Inner London fell by more than three-quarters of a million inhabitants. Even the "suburbs" of Outer London lost population. In 1981 Greater London held 6.7 million people, a drop of 13.5 percent from the previous fourteen years.[28] Figure 6.2 portrays the distribution of Greater London's population in 1968 and 1981. Note that while Greater London continued to shed population, Outer London absorbed a slightly larger proportion of the whole.

It is not clear why some parts of London incur heavier losses than others. The wealth or poverty of a community offers no sound explanation for the demographic falloff. Thus, some wealthy boroughs in Central London (Kensington-Chelsea, Westminster) lost more than one-fifth of their populations, yet by the same token the richest of the localities (the City) managed to increase its population by well over one-third.[29] To be sure, some of the poorest boroughs (Lambeth, Southwark) were heavy losers. But other economically damaged boroughs (Tower Hamlets, Newham) lost considerably fewer residents. The relationship between economic well-being and population loss is

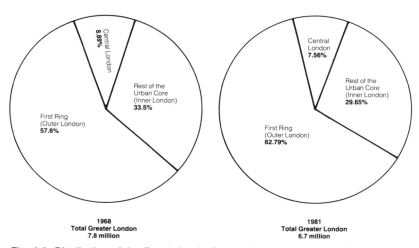

Fig. 6.2. Distribution of the Population in Greater London: 1968 and 1981. Source: Registrar General's Population Estimates, mid-1968 as cited in Gerald Rhodes and S. K. Ruck, *The Government of Greater London* (London: George Allen & Unwin, 1970), and *1981 Census Results for Greater London and the London Boroughs: Small Area Statistics and Historical Comparisons, Statistical Series, No. 19* (London: Greater London Council, 1983), Table 2.

also mixed for the boroughs of Outer London. Taken by itself, population loss can be associated with either wealth or poverty. It can be a signal of post-industrial investment (Kensington-Chelsea, Westminster) or the result of industrial decline (Lambeth, Southwark).

We can better glimpse the industrial and post-industrial condition of London by turning to the issue of jobs. Whatever might be said about London needs to be understood in the context of who, how many, and where people are gainfully employed. Today there are nearly 400,000 people in Greater London who are listed as unemployed, a figure that contributes to much of the debate over planning and politics. More than New York or Paris, unemployment is a primary issue among Londoners. The Labour Party, when it controlled the GLC, taunted the Conservative opposition with a large banner spread across County Hall, announcing the current number of unemployed. In the 1980s the rate of unemployment was highest among unskilled manual workers, where it reached 17 percent. It was also high in the construction industry, which also reached a 17 percent rate in Inner London, and it was high in the boroughs on the East End. Hackney, Islington, and Tower Hamlets were hard hit during the 1970s and they continue to suffer.

Post-industrial employment has absorbed an increasing proportion of the London economy over the last decade. Services and other white-collar jobs dominate the job market. However, though the percentages have climbed, the absolute numbers have fallen. For instance, the percentage of jobs in the service sector increased over the 1970s from 53 to 62 percent of Greater London's economy. At the same time there was an absolute loss of over 33,000 such jobs. The service sector both failed to hold its own and failed to compensate for losses in manufacture. The failure to catalyze the economy in the midst of post-industrial transition resulted in severe dislocations (unemployment, lack of investment, blight) that have plagued much of the urban core. It is the severity of this dislocation that distinguishes London from New York and Paris. While the urban cores of New York and Paris made a rapid transformation to post-industrial vitality, London's transformation has been ambivalent—partly one of post-industrial growth, partly industrial shrinkage, and partly stagnant.

Table 6.1 illustrates the proportional shifts among major sectors of the London economy between 1971 and 1981. Also given are the numbers and percentages of employment in different parts of Greater London. Looking across the table by sector, certain trends can be isolated. In every part of London there was a substantial decrease in manufacture. Central London lost over 4 percent of its manufacturing jobs.

Table 6.1. Employment by Sector in Central, Inner, Outer, and Greater London: 1971 and 1981 (by place of work; in percentages except for Total Employed)

	Central London		Inner London		Outer London		Greater London	
	1971	1981	1971	1981	1971	1981	1971	1981
Manufacture	14.2	9.6	22.3	16.2	29.7	20.7	26.6	19.0
Services, Distribution, and Government	68.4	76.4	54.2	65.0	51.6	59.9	52.7	61.7
Transport and Utilities	7.3	8.0	11.5	11.1	11.1	11.5	11.3	11.4
Construction	4.0	3.6	6.3	6.1	6.3	6.9	6.3	6.6
Agriculture	0.1	0.1	0.1	0.1	0.3	0.1	0.2	0.1
Total Employed (in thousands)								
1971	349.1		1518.6		2145.8		3664.4	
1981	232.6		1119.4		1959.3		3078.7	
% Change 1971-1981	−33%		−26%		−9%		−27%	

Source: Compiled and adapted from *YP 67 ECONDAT* (London: Greater London Council, 1984), Tables 18 and 19, pp. 55 and 56.
Note: Percentages do not add up to 100 because some categories are excluded.

Inner London was hit hard, losing more than 6 percent of its blue-collar work. Surprisingly, Outer London's losses were even greater, falling 9 percentage points in just a decade.

In comparison, the all-important sector called services, distribution, and government gained as a proportion of the economy. In the central boroughs there was a gain of 8 points; in Inner London there was a rise of almost 11 points; in Outer London there was an increase of 8 points. On its face this shift toward post-industrialism is impressive, but if we compare it to the total employed in London the picture is seriously flawed. Although post-industrialism has taken root, it has done so on a much smaller base of employment. As the figures show, every part of London decreased the number of persons employed over the last decade: Central London lost 33 percent of its jobs, Inner London was reduced by 26 percent, and Outer London fell by the least, 9 percent. Overall, Greater London's job base has declined by over 585,000 positions, a reduction of 27 percent. By itself job loss during a post-industrial transformation is not unusual; it has also occurred in

New York and Paris.★ In London, however, the amount was severe and cut across all sectors. Services may have incurred the least substantive damage, but its losses in actual numbers were equally telling.

Why is it that London suffered a diminution of business activity? Certainly a sluggish British economy since the 1970s limited London's ability to grow. This overlapped with earlier policies of industrial decentralization that transferred blue-collar jobs to other parts of Great Britain. Adding to London's woes were restrictive policies, which had begun in the mid-1960s and lasted a decade, on office development and other construction. The accumulation of obstacles prevented London from recouping its industrial losses with aggressive post-industrial vitality.

Far as this explanation may go, it does not account for all of London's difficulties. It has been estimated, for example, that only one-third of firms disappeared from London because they found other areas more attractive.[30] A majority of jobs were lost by firms that chose to remain in London and subsequently went bankrupt. This was especially true for small firms, which declined at a faster pace in Britain than in other parts of the industrial world.[31] Many Inner London boroughs were dependent upon these firms for economic sustenance; their collapse sent shock waves through working-class communities. During the 1970s almost half the manufacturing employment in the borough of Southwark was held by small firms. By 1981 it had an unemployment rate of 13.1 percent, 4 points more than the average for Greater London. In Islington almost all of the manufacturing plants in operation during the 1970s were considered in the category of "small." By 1981 firm deaths in that borough were widespread, and Islington had an unemployment rate of 13.4 percent.[32]

Once failed, most small firms could not rejuvenate themselves. Nor did enough new enterprises rise to take their place. Indeed, throughout Britain, large firms were taking up an increasing portion of the nation's employment and its output. For a variety of reasons Inner London has failed to incubate new enterprise and small businesses. One of these reasons is the considerable role played by the boroughs and the GLC in buying property to build public housing. Instead of being sold or rented at a cheaper price, abandoned buildings were held by their owners, who hoped that government would purchase them. The term "hope value" surfaced in the lexicon of realtors to show the potential land could bring in a future market. The resulting anomaly was that as firms died and land was left fallow, realty prices increased.

★ In the urban core of New York, the job loss for 1971-1981 was 3.6 percent; in the Parisian urban core, job loss for 1968-1982 was 9 percent. See Chapters 2 and 4.

Also bolstering the "hope value" of property was the expectation that the government would enter where private enterprise had failed. Many landlords expected that the government would buy up and redevelop land. They too held onto their property, basing their hopes on its speculative value. As it turned out, the bureaucracies were slow to act and the longer wait only heightened the anticipated price. Most affected were properties that were adjacent to "hope value" land, because they were seen as ripe for speculation. This made it difficult for people to move out of their dwellings for fear of not being able to find a suitable alternative. The least fortunate were prospective new businesses—more precisely, start-up firms that needed cheap rents, accessible markets, and low overhead. They were the kind of firms that once grew up in nooks around the Docklands and on the side streets of the East End. Paradoxically, as these areas became physically less attractive, their costs became more prohibitive.

Social Class and Ethnic Settlement in the Urban Core and First Ring

London is a metropolis of seeming social contradictions. It segregates social classes while also keeping them bound up within a proximate terrain. Although London may intersperse its economic classes, it does not integrate them. Integration implies an intermixing of economic class; interspersal suggests that different classes can inhabit a similar locale but they remain apart. Integration mixes different classes or ethnic groups; interspersal clusters them in proximate subsections.

It is this interspersal that distinguishes London from New York or even Paris. Geographic distances between social classes are much shorter in London. In London it is uncommon for massive swaths of territory to belong to a single social class (as with some counties in New York) or for whole communities to disappear practically overnight (as with some Parisian arrondissements). Within London's wealthiest boroughs, such as Kensington-Chelsea, pockets of poverty are visible. Westminster, which is also wealthy, contains a substantial working class. The converse is true for poor boroughs. In Islington, middle-class professionals have settled among Irish working classes. Within Southwark a similar settlement of young professionals has taken place amid the families of unemployed dockworkers.

Class interspersal in much of London does not mean class interspersal in all of London. London retains the social residue of the industrial era. The working class still occupies the streets and the pubs of east and south London (Tower Hamlets, Newham, Lambeth, and Southwark). But, after all is said and done, London is not as starkly separated by class habitat as New York or Paris. Thus far, London has been less upset by post-industrial change than its sister cities. And because the class fabric of the industrial era is still intact, neighborhood and family ties are more vital.

We can better appreciate this idea of continuity amid limited change by consulting the statistics. Table 6.2 presents data for the years 1971 and 1981 on the percentage distribution of occupations in Greater London. Looking across the table at the first category, white-collar workers (professionals, employers, managers), note the relatively modest changes that have occurred in each of London's parts. Central London augmented this post-industrial class by less than 3 points; Inner London and Outer London rose in this category even more gradually. Compared to New York or Paris, these gains were quite modest.[33]

The category of other nonmanual remains nearly stable. Central London actually incurs a decrease. Again this compares vividly with New York and Paris, where white-collar workers are dramatically on the rise. Furthermore, though the percentages of white-collar workers

Table 6.2.   Employment by Occupation in Central, Inner, Outer, and Greater London: 1971 and 1981 (by place of residence; in percentages unless otherwise indicated)

Occupation	Central London 1971	Central London 1981	Inner London 1971	Inner London 1981	Outer London 1971	Outer London 1981	Greater London 1971	Greater London 1981
Professionals, employers, managers	21.0	22.8	11.9	14.5	16.4	18.6	14.5	17.1
Other nonmanual	38.4	36.4	34.5	34.5	38.1	38.6	36.6	37.1
Skilled manual	12.2	11.8	21.4	18.4	22.7	20.3	22.2	19.6
Semi-skilled	14.9	17.0	18.1	18.6	14.8	14.2	16.2	15.8
Unskilled	5.9	5.4	9.1	7.4	5.1	4.4	6.8	5.5
Other	7.6	6.6	5.0	6.6	2.9	3.9	3.7	4.9
Total Employed (in thousands)								
1971	371.6		1614.8		2225.3		3840.1	
1981	258.9		1268.7		2102.2		2270.8	
% Change								
1971-1981	−30%		−21%		−6%		−12%	

Source: Compiled and adapted from *YP 67 ECONDAT* (London: Greater London Council, 1984), Tables 26 and 27, pp. 66 and 67.

are higher in Central London than in Inner and Outer London, the differences between them are not terribly dramatic. Certainly in London the discrepancies between habitats for different social classes do not match the imbalances that are so acute in post-industrial New York.

The next three columns (skilled manual, semi-skilled, and unskilled) represent a broad category of blue-collar workers. Note that the percentages of skilled and unskilled workers shift downward in all parts of London. Still, this is not true for all blue-collar workers. Semi-skilled personnel either rise or remain nearly stable. Why semi-skilled workers move against the trend of blue-collar decline is not entirely clear. One possible explanation is that they have found jobs in maintenance, transport, or communication. Whatever work these individuals have found, it is probably close to Central London. This is where these workers live and it is characteristic of London that its central boroughs can still accommodate blue-collar households.

The figures show that London's residential population has undergone a shift in the last decade. A growing majority of the population has moved toward white-collar occupations. But this transformation is neither complete nor overwhelming. Much of Inner London's population is still blue collar. Blue-collar workers also constitute a significant minority in Outer London.

Like New York and Paris, London is a multi-ethnic and multi-racial city. The largest ethnic groups come from the New Commonwealth and Pakistan (designated NCWP by British census takers). These countries include India, Pakistan, Bangladesh, and smaller nations in the Caribbean and Far East. Still another category of immigrant is drawn from what British census takers call the Rest of the World (ROW). This includes a panoply of nationalities, mostly from Spain, Poland, Greece, and parts of the Middle East. The Irish are another major group and for historical reasons are separately classified.[34]

By the 1980s, NCWP households constituted 15 percent of Greater London's population; those from the ROW held 6 percent; and the Irish made up 5 percent. All told, this ethnic mélange amounted to 1.6 million people.[35]

Of this ethnic population, Central London has the highest proportion (39 percent), followed by Inner London (34 percent) and Outer London (26 percent). Although the allocations are not perfectly even, the ethnic population is reasonably well spread throughout.[36] There are also clumps of ethnic settlement in boroughs like Islington (Irish), Brent (NCWP), and Kensington-Chelsea (ROW). All told, the segregation is not rigidly fixed or anything like New York's neighborhoods. Relatively speaking, London has managed its ethnic settlement in much the same way that it has handled class settlement, by interspersing ethnic groups among its various parts.

Why is it that London has been able to intersperse social and ethnic groups? Truncated post-industrialism and the ensuing slow pace of social change are partial explanations. Other public policies have also been effective. The availability of public housing has been an important instrument in fostering social equity.

Of the three cities, London has the strongest tradition in providing public housing. Roughly 31 percent of Greater London's housing stock is owned by the public sector. By far, the public sector has been the catalyst for new housing.[37] Between 1972 and 1983 two-thirds of all housing starts were carried out by the GLC and the boroughs.[38]

Again, the allocation of public housing among London's parts is not perfect, but neither is it lopsided. By the early 1980s the distribution stood at 29 percent for Central London, 43 percent for Inner London, and 23 percent for Outer London.

Public housing is a commodity that is highly valued and sought after. In most cases the dwellings are low density, attractively built, and fronted by neat gardens. The rent is inexpensive and the amenities are decent. Unlike New York, there is no stigma attached to living in "council housing." Often it is difficult to obtain. Applicants who are longtime borough residents are given preference.

Limited as these conditions may be, public housing has been an important instrument of social policy. Frequently a source of controversy between Tories and Socialists, its resilience had withstood the test of over half a century. Today, Thatcher has put this tradition under radical attack.

Land and Office Towers

The period immediately following Abercrombie's and Robson's initiatives was a good one for London. The outward movement of factories and population seemed to do little damage. On the contrary, the 1950s and 1960s were boom years, especially for the CBD. The skyline of Central London began to change rapidly as developers poured money into renovations and new construction. An aura of "property boom" hung in the air as speculators bought land in the City, Westminster, and Kensington and Chelsea.

The property boom hinged on the freedom to build. Oliver Marriott traces the "starting gun" of land speculation to 1954, when the

Conservative government announced that building licenses would be "issued freely in nearly all areas."[39] Thus began an era when brazen men became quick millionaires. Property tycoons like Charles Clore and Joseph Cotton made fortunes by getting in early and holding their property until the price of land skyrocketed. Others took advantage of loose tax laws and zoning codes that permitted them to build and then sell or rent at enormous profit. Overnight, plots of land in the City increased by more than 70 percent.[40]

Prosperity permeated the realty markets of London and there seemed no end to it. Between the end of World War II and 1964 a total of 37 million square feet of office space had been built in Greater London. This gave London more than three times as much office space as Birmingham, Manchester, Liverpool, Glasgow, and Edinburgh combined. Permissions for still another 25 million square feet were already through the planning agencies.[41] Along with the construction boom, jobs were flocking into the CBD.

During the 1960s London was moving headlong toward a post-industrial order, or so it seemed. From the viewpoint of planners and policy makers, this was worrisome. Too much was happening too quickly, too much was being constructed in the CBD, and too much was being concentrated in one corner of Great Britain. If Abercrombie's vision of stability and balance was to be upheld, decisive action would need to be taken.

Since the end of World War II the government had pursued a policy of industrial decentralization and had imposed restrictions on the building of factories in the London region. Any manufacturer wishing to build facilities in excess of 10,000 square feet had to obtain an Industrial Development Certificate (IDC) from the central government. Apparently these restrictions were having little impact. A Labour Party spokesman was so upset with what expansion was doing to the London region that he declared, "we should now put a fence around all these conurbations and put up a sign saying, Stop! No further industries must come here."[42] A regional plan of the period issued a warning:

> We are all proud of London's position not only as our capital but as a unique international centre for commerce and finance, as a worldwide tourist attraction, and as a center for the arts, education, religion and science. It is of very great importance for the nation's prosperity that it should continue to be so. Our plans for the future must enable London to work as efficiently as possible.
>
> To this end the growth of London must be contained. Firm con-

trols must be exercised to relieve traffic congestion, to reduce the difficulties and excessive costs of business firms, and to make life as pleasureable as possible for the individual Londoner. . . . Continued efforts must be made to prevent unnecessary concentration of activities in London, particularly in the Central Area.[43]

By the mid-1960s sterner measures were invoked by the central government. For prospective factories, the limits on IDCs were tightened to include any facility over 1,000 square feet. For prospective office towers, Office Development Permits (ODPs) were required for any building that exceeded 10,000 square feet. IDCs and ODPs were issued by the central government's Board of Trade. To win a permit, said the president of the Board, an applicant would have to show that the project was "essential to the public interest. . . . Mere inconvenience or extra cost" to the businessman was not enough.[44]

Should these obstacles be insufficient, the GLC or the borough was in a position to deny construction permits. Soon the central government did away with any illusions builders might entertain about special projects. Upon coming to national power in 1964, Labour adopted the "Brown Office Ban." This put a virtual moratorium on any further construction of office towers in Central London.

For those offices that were already established, the government created the Location of Office Bureaus (LOB), which by gentle persuasion sought to move white-collar facilities out of Central London. Surprisingly, volunteerism had its impact: 116 firms and more than 12,000 office jobs left for other parts as a result of LOB efforts.[45]

Thus, ten years after the "starting gun" fired, its sound was muffled. IDCs, ODPs, the "Brown Ban," and the LOB had brought the redevelopment of Central London to a near halt. Just as the construction boom had spurred jobs, so its demise resulted in reduced employment. In the years prior to controls (1959-1963), Greater London held in the range of 4.6 million jobs and the employment curve skewed slightly upward. During the period of controls (1964-1973), the curve skewed downward, especially after 1968 when construction projects were no longer in "the pipeline" because of previous permissions. By 1974, Greater London's jobs were down to the mid 3 million mark, a loss of almost 17 percent in under a decade.[46] Not all of this decline should be attributed to the halt of office construction. But there is no doubt that controls hurt. One study maintains that controls heightened annual job loss by twentyfold.[47]

We can trace the effect of controls on office development. Figure 6.3 covers the late 1960s through the mid-1970s. We consider the years through 1973 as the period when controls were operational. Soon afterward controls were relinquished, and the pipeline began to work again. Observe, during the 1960s, the low trajectory of London's total office development. This was followed by some erratic years. Only from 1974 on did construction turn upward and not in all parts of the metropolis. Normally, corporations count on Central London for 60 percent of their stock of office space.[48] In the minds of business executives, the CBD is London's great attraction. And yet for many of these years, it was blocked off.

Central London's recuperation, however, was never quite complete—at least as one plots long-term projections. Through the 1980s office development went on a roller coaster. For a time it would veer sharply upward only to plummet a short time later. Figure 6.4 shows this pattern for the 1980s.

This does not deny Central London's place as a primary office producer. The point is that London's performance has been uneven and unsure.[49] It has not matched the enormous dynamism of New York and has missed the creativity of Paris. Policy makers either failed to build on the attractions of Central London or could not develop a fruitful alternative. As we shall see in the following chapter, this was not for want of trying. Efforts were made to establish special zones that would concentrate commerce. Still other zones, called "strategic cen-

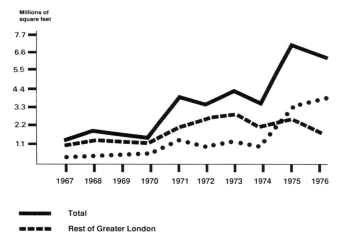

Fig. 6.3. Office Construction in Greater London and the London CBD: 1967-1976. Source: Adapted from L. Weatheritt and O. N. John, *Office Development and Employment in Greater London, 1967-1976*, Greater London Council Research Memorandum 556 (London, 1979), p. 15.

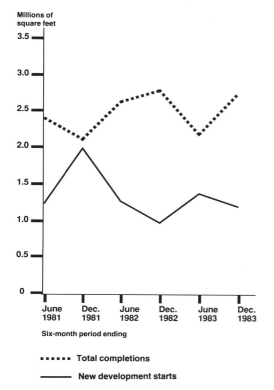

Fig. 6.4. Office Development in Central London: 1981-1984. Source: Adapted from *Central London Offices Research* (London: JLW-CLOR, Research Library, 1983), Figure 1.

ters," were established in boroughs throughout London to decentralize other types of commerce. But these efforts were more a reflection of tensions in the system than clear pathways toward post-industrialism.

Significance

Like New York and Paris, London has experienced a post-industrial transformation during the last quarter century. Unlike its sister cities, London's transformation has been incomplete. Office employment declined in absolute numbers when it should have risen to fill the vacuum left by departing manufacture. High unemployment plagued all parts of Greater London.

No doubt the crises of the British economy limited London's capacity to respond to the challenge of post-industrialism. As mentioned in Chapter 1, we cannot discount the importance of national factors and

195

the parameters set by the state. Nonetheless, London is not helpless. Indeed, as the seat of the British nation, London enjoys great advantages in attracting employment and capital. As a world city it commands international attention in trade, finance, and politics.

During the heady days of the 1960s, London profited from this prominence. It also chose to restrain business expansion in the interests of better ecology and a more humane city. Industrial decentralization and controls on office development were undertaken to realize these objectives. Other policies like density controls, the expansion of green space, and public housing also contributed to these aspirations. The salutary consequences can be seen in a reasonably well balanced metropolis that intersperses social classes throughout Center, Inner, and Outer London. At the same time, these policies were laden with political tensions and economic contradictions.

CHAPTER 7

London: Geoplanning, Geopolitics, and Liberal Corporatism

All day I loafed in the streets, east as far as Wapping, west as far as White-chapel. It was queer after Paris. Everything was so much cleaner and quieter and drearier. One missed the scream of the trams, and the noisy festering life of the back streets, and the armed men clattering through the squares. The crowds were better dressed and the faces comelier and milder and more alike, without the fierce individuality and malice of the French. . . . Knots of men stood on all corners, slightly underfed, but kept going by the tea and two slices which the Londoner swallows every two hours. One seemed to breathe a less feverish air than in Paris. It was the land of the tea urn and Labour Exchange, as Paris is the land of the bistro and the sweatshop.—George Orwell, *Down and Out in Paris and London*

W E HAVE SEEN how London has developed politically and demo-graphically since the 1960s. Its search for identity led to the creation of a Green Belt; its effort to rationalize planning brought about three-tier government; and its measures to control growth have slowed down its economy.

What have been the contemporary responses to these events? The responses have been made by the boroughs, have involved policies set by the GLC, and have brought in the central government. Examining the cases of Motorways, Covent Garden, and the Docklands will aid our investigation of how planning interacts with liberal corporatism.

Geoplanning: The Strategy and Ambivalence of Development

As the troublesome results of earlier policies became apparent, Londoners began to turn in another direction and to seek other solutions. Critics in both political parties blamed industrial decentralization and controls on development for London's losses. In a rash of reversals beginning in the late 1970s, the government lifted restrictions. The LOB, which had exuberantly helped white-collar firms find offices elsewhere, was summarily abolished. IDCs and ODPs, which were both real and psychological barriers to developers, were also eliminated. For the first time in decades London was allowed to advertise vacant industrial space.

For its part, the GLC began to take action in order to stem the outflow of jobs, industry, and population. The GLC's actions were essentially defensive and designed to reduce the competition from localities in the surrounding region. In earlier years London had followed a policy of reducing its population by building housing within or beyond the Green Belt. Now that policy was revoked, and there would be no further agreements with townships to invest in housing estates.

Believing that London's losses were tied to gains in the rest of the region, the GLC lobbied the surrounding localities to restrain their own industrial growth. Some proposals were adopted in strategic reports issued during the 1970s. These reports called attention to London's mounting difficulties and suggested that development be concentrated in designated centers. The integrity of the Green Belt was to be maintained and development would not be allowed to run rampantly through the OMA, endangering the anticipated recovery of the urban core. Still, the results were not encouraging. As difficulties continued through the 1980s, promises to restrain development rang hollow. In frustration the GLC adopted an addendum to the Greater London Development Plan (GLDP) that asserted that the Council was:

> acutely aware of the potential damage to the objectives for Inner London which could result from the relaxation of regional restraint. . . . Without such restraint there is an increasing probability that the loss of manufacturing jobs in Inner London will be followed by an accelerated loss of service sector jobs and that the economic base of London will be irreparably undermined. The Council looks to structure and local plans in the region to resist erosion of the Green Belt, about 90 percent of which lies outside Greater London, and to restrain developments which might be detrimental to policies aimed at improving economic, social and employment prospects in London.[1]

No doubt the GLC was anxious to change its fortunes by stimulating industrial growth and by halting further losses in population. To do this it was ready to put the brakes on the legacy of Abercrombie. At the same time there were enduring values that Abercrombie had provided and that the GLC was not willing to change. The Green Belt was obviously one of these, and though it had always been regarded as a perimeter by which London could achieve cohesion, it could now be held as a shield against industrial piracy.

Above all, the GLC supported the value of urban civility, of a London that was humane and that cared for the quality of its life. Cosmopolitan and dynamic as London might be, it also needed to be eminently conservationist. So much the better if an energetic and growing metropolis could accommodate these values, and through the 1980s a Labour-led GLC endeavored to reconcile these difficult objectives. Frequently these objectives were pursued with startling naïveté, as when one Labour politician exclaimed, "It's not office jobs that we object to, it's construction of those damned office towers that are so lamentable." Over the years London's Labour Party chose low-cost public housing over industrial development and campaigned under the banner of "Homes before Jobs." Not until the jobless rates of the 1980s revealed that families could not afford the rents did some Labourites shift their emphasis.

Despite these mistakes, Labour believed it had learned much from the harsh recession of the 1970s. It also believed it could enjoy the fruits of post-industrial expansion without raking up the soil of London's residential communities. Its objectives for the 1980s can be summed up in the idea of controlled post-industrial expansion. To do this, the GLC distinguished between a Central Activities Zone (CAZ), which is supposed to absorb major post-industrial growth; twenty-eight "strategic centers," which are dispersed through Greater London as foci for smaller post-industrial expansion; and Community Areas, which are safeguarded for residents. The strategic centers are supposed to provide balance between a strong core (CAZ) and prosperous peripheries (Community Areas). Figure 7.1 outlines the broad contours of the Central Activities Zone–Community Area plan. Also designated are the affected Inner London boroughs, the CBD, and major landmarks.

Observe that the CAZ constitutes only a part of the CBD. This sliver of land borders on or contains areas of international and national repute such as Piccadilly Circus, Trafalgar Square, Charing Cross, and the City. Major commercial stretches are also within it such as Victoria Street, the Strand, Holborn, and Liverpool Street. The CAZ has been designed as a compact and efficient core at the heart of Central London that will accommodate activities appropriate to its role as an international center. It is London's zone for tourism, entertainment, high finance, fashion, and office development.

In a roughly sketched ring around the CAZ are the Community Areas, encompassing portions of Inner London. These areas are reserved for urban and residential conservation. Although boroughs within the Community Area contain at least one strategic center for commercial development, the GLC was wary about overheating them with investment. Located around Central London, the Community Areas are predominantly working class and vulnerable to gentrification and commercial spread. The GLC was especially careful about con-

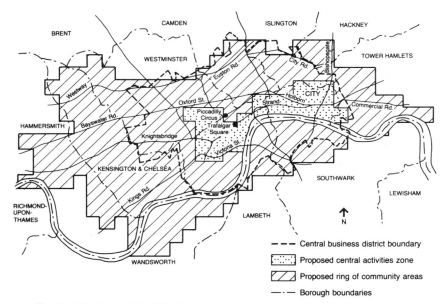

Fig. 7.1. The Central Activities Zone and Community Area Plan: 1984. Source: Greater London Council.

serving the indigenous quality of these boroughs and stated that it took a "restrictive view toward granting permissions for commercial development."[2]

The Community Areas have been likened, in fact, to an urban green belt into which only limited amounts of post-industrial expansion can seep. The rest of this land is to be reserved for the people and guarded against investment pressure. Thus the same conception that compartmentalized Greater London from the OMA was applied to Central London vis-à-vis the inner boroughs. And the GLC was ready to take the necessary steps in order to protect the integrity of its constituent communities. As the GLC explained in a major document:

> there has been a growing awareness of the problem experienced by communities in and around . . . Central London resulting from pressure for commercial development. The concept of Community Areas has the specific objective of protecting and assisting deprived and declining areas whose problems are made worse by past, current or prospective commercial development.

Further on, the GLC document states:

Greatly inflated land values and, in certain cases, land hoarding have made it difficult for the local authorities [i.e. the boroughs] to intervene on behalf of local communities of those areas. Analysis shows that, notwithstanding the policies in local plans to resist commercial development pressures, extensive commercial development has taken place and further strong pressures continue. The local authorities [i.e. the boroughs] are not providing, and in some cases are unable to provide, the resources necessary to deal with the social problems of these areas, . . .[3]

In short, where the boroughs could not act, the GLC was ready to safeguard the physical and social fabric of Inner London. On paper the CAZ–Community Area plan outlines a strategy for introducing post-industrial growth and containing it. The GLC hoped that it might profit from the increases in jobs and revenue that came with growth while it kept London's communities (and its constituents) intact.

The reality of controlling post-industrial development is more problematic. For one, formal rules and regulations can be fragile mechanisms for coping with human behavior. They cannot always be enforced with accuracy, and they do not always fulfill the intent of their makers. Private firms have found any number of ways to sidestep rules. Nor can the designation of a Community Area relieve a neighborhood from the very significant pressure that comes from gentrification. Gentrifying neighborhoods slip away from regulation by gradual changes in housing value (retain the old façade, gut the interior, and jack up the price) or by shifts in functional use (from butchers to boutiques). Boroughs in the Community Area like Kensington-Chelsea, Islington, and Southwark are already in the midst of transformation. The GLC may have been able to keep the physical container intact, but its contents will be dramatically altered.

Second, controlled post-industrial expansion was bound to be resented by localities in the outlying region. While the second ring was asked to restrain development, Greater London was trying to channel it into a CAZ and into twenty-eight strategic centers. What possible advantage could the second ring gain in allowing London to select high-paying, non-nuisance firms, while it accommodated the slough in designated centers? Adding to the difficulty is that nondesignated townships were expected to restrain development in the interests of preserving a Green Belt cherished by Londoners.

Finally, what made the GLC strategy so problematic was the conflict that came from intergovernmental dispute. Conflict between boroughs and the GLC was nothing new, and some boroughs resented a heavy-handed GLC preaching to them about "not providing . . . the resources" needed to protect their residents. And other boroughs, particularly in Outer London, disagreed with GLC strategy and claimed it was an intrusion on local prerogative.

The toughest conflict arose from policy differences between central government and the GLC. Under Thatcher, the Conservatives have continued to press for growth in the OMA and the rest of the region. The Secretary of the Environment refused to allow statutory authority for the GLC's new plan and hampered its implementation. The GLC returned the favor by attacking the central government for failing to halt industrial piracy.

What lies behind these differences is an ideological conflict over land use. More precisely, GLC planning stemmed from a Socialist orientation that wanted to control growth, preserve existing communities, and restore London's lost manufacture. By contrast, the Tories favor aggressive expansion, see neighborhood change as inevitable, and are convinced that old industry is forever gone. It is one of those ironies of British politics that places Socialist Labour in the fold of conservation while Conservatives favor radical physical change.

Geopolitics: Liberal Corporatism and Urban Space

London differs from New York and Paris in both its organization of government and its manner of dealing with interest groups. In New York, government is not so much tiered as it is haphazardly organized. Overlapping jurisdictions and quid pro quo arrangements are the hallmarks of New York politics. Though interest groups are endemic to New York, they operate from outside decision-making circles by trying to make their mark upon them. Like hit-and-run guerrillas, interest groups concentrate their firepower on small targets for short periods of time. When a decision is finally resolved they retire until it is time for the next campaign. New York politics is free-flowing, its interest groups are self-generating, and, by European standards, its processes are sloppy.

Parisian decision makers are better shielded from interest groups. Decision making is more centralized and its objectives have a well-defined purpose. In France, public power is concentrated in the ministries, the office of the Mayor, and the prefects. This elite is buttressed by hautes fonctionnaires who then interact with interest groups. Parisian interest groups are more like a reserve army, called up for action when the decision is ready for additional action.

Nothing so vividly marks London as the role played by different and contending tiers of government. These tiers are in the hands of different politicians and technocrats, who work with different interest groups. Central government, the GLC, and the boroughs often locked horns on crucial issues, and the central government and the boroughs still do. If it wishes, the central government can override the local opposition with impunity, but it rarely does.[4] Restraint, consultation, and fair hearings typify the political process, and this provided the GLC as well as the boroughs with considerable leeway. Moreover, on rare occasions the central government may itself be divided and this gives the localities additional leverage.

Unlike New York's guerrilla tacticians or Paris's reserve army, London's interest groups are more like the standing infantry. They function with a great deal of continuity and are well integrated into the GLC or the boroughs. These governments even fund interest groups (called voluntary associations) to better enable them to carry out their tasks. Interest groups often receive free space, supplies are furnished to them, and their staffs are put on the public payroll. The public even provides for special elections so that interest groups can be better constituted to serve government. Thus a special type of organization, called a Forum, is created out of specific constituencies within a community. Special delegations within a Forum are elected to represent landlords, tenants, shopkeepers, professionals, or any other stratum of the population.

Furthermore, once they are organized, interest groups take to the partisan battlefield. It is not unusual for one tier of the government to support an interest group so it can work against another tier. The Labour-led GLC, for instance, supported feminists who lobbied for policies staunchly opposed by the central government.

There is, in London, a syndrome not unlike that experienced by American cities in the 1960s. At that time Community Action Agencies were elected out of urban neighborhoods to lobby on behalf of the poor. In America the experiment was soon curtailed and later eliminated. In Britain it has a long-standing (and less volatile) tradition. One can see storefronts in Inner London occupied by community activists who organize the citizenry and provide information.

All this is done with characteristic order and propriety. Indeed, there are decisional mechanisms for focusing democratic participation and for bringing controversies to a head. Two mechanisms that can be particularly important to planning are put into effect by the central government: commission hearings and public inquiries. Royal Commissions are carefully selected to include persons of prestige who represent a range of viewpoints. They are given a specific task, are responsible for carrying out a thorough investigation, and are expected to deliver a set of workable recommendations. Unlike the typical American investigative commission, whose findings make good stepstools for short librarians, a commission's findings are taken quite seriously. They are frequently enacted into legislation or made a part of government policy.

Public inquiries are also important devices for channeling citizen participation and should not be confused with American legislative hearings. American hearings are relatively loose and conducted by partisans, who hear testimony and ask questions of witnesses. In Britain public inquiries are formal affairs. They are presided over by a single inspector, appointed by the central government. Barristers represent opposing sides, witnesses submit "proofs of evidence," and they are subject to cross-examination. Afterward the inspector submits a formal report to the head of the relevant ministry, who ultimately decides the matter.

Decision making in London gives government a high profile. The process is highly structured, and there are precise roles carried out by each political tier as well as by each participant. Unlike France, the structure is less monolithic; British traditions soften the power of technocratic elites. Nor is the structure as permeable or as saturated with the possibility of judicial blockage as in New York. The British system can be likened to a series of channels spiralling gradually upward. There are ebbs and flows between the contestants as they move through these channels, but decisive action is eventually taken. On critical issues final actions are taken at the highest level, which is the central government.

Contentions among the three tiers of London's political system and the interest groups that are incorporated into these tiers are the warp and woof of London's politics. One might surmise that in the post-abolition era, the GLC would disappear to make the picture less complicated. Quite the contrary, since abolition a number of "GLCs-in exile" have sprung up to intensify the struggle.[5]

In 1983, the Labour boroughs formed the Association of London Authorities (ALA) in order to develop common policies and work together in battling the central government. The central government had refused to recognize the ALA as anything but a partisan pressure group. But the ALA went to court and won the right to be consulted as an association of local authorities. This provided a great boost for the collective influence of Inner London boroughs, and the ALA now funds some of the same interest groups that were supported by the GLC. One new organization that works as an arm of the ALA is the London Strategic Planning Unit (LSPU). With a staff of three hundred, the LSPU has gone on to pursue the same planning issues that occupied Ken Livingstone's GLC (public housing, green space, women's rights). Adding to this, the statutory body created to fill one GLC void, the London Planning Advisory Committee (LPAC), has begun to turn its wheels. LPAC now takes many of the GLC's principles as starting points to render strategic advice. Among the ideas it has chosen as guideposts are the CAZ and Community Areas Plan. It remains to be seen just how far these ideas will be taken, but LPAC is not likely to remain out of the clutches of partisans. It already interacts with interest groups and GLCs-in-exile. After the dust of abolition settles, Labour will try to use LPAC against Thatcher, while the Tories fend off the attack and the Alliance Party tries to become a balancer.

In a word, there are continuing forces that propel London politics. Institutions like the GLC gave expression to those forces. The vehicles for that expression may have changed with abolition, but they have not disappeared.

The Geopolitics of Motorways, Covent Garden, and the Docklands

The politics of land use in Greater London comes closest to a model of liberal corporatism. The following propositions characterize political struggles and serve as a guide for case studies.

➤ Three-tier government sets the structure and the process of London politics. Conflicts are played out in a number of permutations between the central government, formerly the GLC (and more recently the "GLCs-in-exile," which are included under the rubric GLC throughout this discussion), and the boroughs. It is not easy to predict how alliances between tiers will be established. In Motorways, the GLC allied with the central government against the boroughs. In Covent Garden, the central government sided with the boroughs against the GLC. In the Docklands, the GLC and the boroughs stood together in opposition to the central government.

➤ Although common party ties between tiers of government do not always bring agreement, these ties do count. Common party identity promotes cooperation; partisan difference promotes conflict. Political parties are paramount in the system and typically separate one decision maker from another. Politicians take their cues from the political party and this frames the debate.

➤ Political parties are disciplined instruments of power. Unlike New York, partisan contests in London are conducted almost entirely within a party's internal organization. There are no party primaries to open up contests to an outside public and no governmental referenda, which make issues vulnerable to interest group pressure. The upshot

205

is that as interest groups seek to influence policy, they have little choice but to become partisan. Interest groups may start out spontaneously. They may gather in local pubs or meeting halls, but sooner or later they are brought to the political parties.

➤ Political parties are not the only mechanisms that absorb popular participation. The GLC and the boroughs also serve as focal points for interest groups. Early in the formulation of issues, popular expression is converted into some kind of organizational expression. The GLC or the borough councils may pick up an issue and convert it into a formal debate between governmental tiers. Auxiliary bodies (Forums, inter-borough committees) work in concert with the GLC or the boroughs and are capable of expropriating interest group demands.

➤ The political process is orderly and also polarized. Lines between Conservatives and Labourites are sharp and, as time passes, appear to be growing sharper. Partisan outlooks on urban development are worlds apart. Tories stress free markets, private property, and an enthusiasm for post-industrial expansion. Socialists place a stronger emphasis on public facilities, collective ownership, and the retention of manufacturing jobs.

➤ Ideology notwithstanding, the major political parties rely on government and on its politicians and technocrats to initiate development. London's Conservatives take the "free market" just so far and support a strong though limited government. Conservatives endorse government as a catalyzer for private initiative. Labour sees the public sector with more embracing ends—as an employer, a housing provider, and so forth.

➤ A key feature of London's political parties, and of government at all tiers, is their ability to coopt the opposition. This occurred in the case of Covent Garden. Shortly after a public inquiry was held, part of the opposition was organized to work with politicians and technocrats on the GLC. Cooptation also occurred in the Docklands when some Labour politicians from the boroughs collaborated with an organ of the central government.

➤ Another feature of the London system is that it makes it incumbent upon challengers to assume responsibilities rather than remain as outside critics. The effect is first to bring diffuse challengers into a partisan organization. Should the opposition prove strong, it is next incorporated into a decision-making channel. This happened in Motorways, where citizens first organized into pressure groups (absorbed by the boroughs), later formed an independent political party, and still later were amalgamated into Labour and the GLC.

➤ Orderly as these procedures may appear on paper, the system is vulnerable to ebbs and flows, affirmation and reversal. Decisions can change midstream. Though governmental authority is definitive, it is not immutable. All three cases were characterized by decisional change. In Motorways the idea was slowly truncated and then abandoned; in Covent Garden radical plans were whittled away to the point where they had to be altogether scrapped; in the Docklands, the original plans and the organization for carrying them through were eliminated.

➤ The ease of decisional reversal is partly due to London's three-tier politics. Appeals can be made to different layers of authority and decisions can be waited out until an electoral contest brings in the "right" government. These strategies of reversal were used in all three cases. Opponents of Motorways launched a strong campaign within the boroughs, at the GLC, and with the central government, but they finally waited until an election brought the "right" party into power. In Covent Garden and the Docklands, interest groups worked with different tiers of government, used the public inquiry, and waited for a favorable turn of government.

➤ Last, we can observe that the absorption and cooptation of interest groups can work both ways. Outside participants are not only affected by the political process, but they also manage to have an effect on it. Decisions were reversed and projects were changed because organized interests became an integral part of the decision-making structure. This occurred in Motorways and Covent Garden. Outside participation is also likely to modify the course of development in the Docklands.

Motorways   Between 1965 and 1973 the GLC initiated a massive program to build concentric motorways or "ring roads" through sections of Central, Inner, and Outer London. Though the idea was paraded as a brand new invention, it had its origins in Abercrombie's proposals of the 1940s. Abercrombie envisioned London as an agglomeration of small villages and communities. He often used the metaphor of a living organism to describe London and pictured it as a hierarchy of cells that needed to be protected and preserved. For him highways were not a menace to urban living, but a way to canalize traffic around London's living cells, free the streets from intrusive automobiles, and provide its organic composition with definition and purpose. Motorways were to the city what blood vessels were to the human body; they functioned as a circulatory system that nourished its individual parts. The trick was to permit circulation without congestion and without upsetting cell life. Abercrombie's terminology followed its logical functions. Motorways would function as bypasses around communities; they would act as pressure valves to relieve congestion; and they would serve as defensive barriers to prevent unwanted growth.

What emerged from this abstract vision was a series of ring-cross motorways throughout London and the region beyond. Five ringed motorways were set in concentric circles. The smallest began at the very center of London, and like ripples in a pond, each ring road circled farther out into the countryside. These motorways were connected by cross roads so that automobiles could switch from one ring thoroughfare to another. The idea was that outer ring roads would "pull" faster, long-journey traffic around London's perimeter and the inner motorways would "push" slower, short-journey traffic around different stops in Inner London.

Little more than twenty years later Abercrombie's scheme emerged once more, albeit in modified form. London, it was argued, was suffocating with traffic. In just six years peak-hour traffic in Central London had fallen from an average of 11 to 8 miles per hour. One official body warned that "unless radical action [is] taken traffic will come to a standstill in the Central Area."[6]

No sooner had the GLC come into operation than it began to take the radical course suggested. The plans were drawn up by an elite of civil servants at County Hall. Both the major political parties were for it. The public, it was believed, would rally behind it. Better than all these reasons, the plan was bold and would show just what the GLC could do.

With the blessings of the central government, County Hall churned out plans for the most expensive single project ever undertaken during a time of peace in Great Britain. Three major ring roads connected by cross roads would circle in broadening paths around Greater London and part of the OMA. Ringway 1 was thirty-five miles long and eight lanes wide. It formed a rough rectangle four to six miles from Central London—hence it was called the Motorway Box. Ringway 2 ran for more than fifty miles through parts of Inner and Outer London and held eight lanes of traffic for most of its route. Ringway 3 orbited for more than one hundred miles along the boundary of Greater London and the OMA, dodging in and out of the metropolis. Hundreds of miles of cross routes connected the ringways to each other, for easy switching either to "push" traffic through Inner London or to "pull" it around the periphery. In its full conception, the Ringway plan bore a remarkable resemblance to Abercrombie's earlier proposals, though few planners cared to point that out.

Figure 7.2 shows a map of the Ringway plan as it was presented in 1967. All told, the ringways and cross routes would cost £200 million. The ringways alone would consume more than 6,000 acres of land. At least 20,000 houses would be razed and an estimated 100,000 people would have to move. Like a sharp blade, the Motorways would make strategic cuts through the fabric of Greater London, so that automobiles could hurry along their new paths. London might be the last great city to have freeways, but once built, the British would have the best of them.

At the time American planning had an imposing presence. Many British planners had been to schools in the United States and others were persuaded by the success of Los Angeles. A prosperous world economy reinforced the optimism generated by North America. Projections told London's planners that all of Europe was in a period of boundless growth; that more people would be traveling more often; that the British economy would boom; and that more people would be purchasing automobiles. Indeed, given the projections, planners felt that the ringways they were proposing might not even be sufficient to

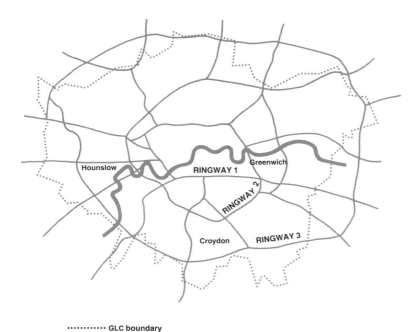

············ **GLC boundary**

Fig. 7.2. The Ringway Plan. Source: Adapted from Greater London Council.

hold London's burgeoning population. As one originator of the scheme reflected

> our training taught us about traffic forecasting on the back of the American experience. At peak time 33,000 vehicles took to a single roadway. Now normally one lane of traffic passes 1,500 vehicles per hour. . . . Just divide 1,500 by 33,000 and that gives you more than 20 lanes of traffic.
>
> In today's terms that sounds preposterous, but that was what the methodologies told us. It's rather like a mathematical sum when you add a + b + c and it gives you d, nobody can deny the results. All one can say is, good heavens this contradicts my human experience.[7]

GLC planners mixed intuition with empirical evidence and came up with a seemingly modest eight-lane highway. They then persuaded politicians (members) on the GLC to adopt the plan. Why it was that veteran politicians would be persuaded that Motorways was politically viable is still a mystery. But one planner offered the following explanation.

> Members were just not well informed about transportation and about a great many things. They were amateurish about local government. . . . If professionals were going along with it, members were to some extent persuaded on their argument.[8]

Planners of the GLC also carried their success to the central government. After thrashing out the details of the plan, the Ministry of Transport (MOT) agreed to take responsibility for Ringways 2 and 3. The GLC's primary task was to build the Motorway Box. Other organizations joined the GLC and MOT. The Royal Automobile Club and the British Road Haulers lent substantial support, as did the London Chamber of Commerce and the business community.

Others felt differently about Motorways. As the scheme unfolded, the opposition began to mount. Nearly a hundred anti-Motorways groups were formed, especially in the affected neighborhoods. Citizens held protest rallies and walking marathons to dramatize the issue. Throughout Inner London, "action groups" were formed in the parks, pubs, and people's apartments.

At first the opposition was fragmented, spontaneous, and free-wheeling. Motorways looked like a contest between supporters organized along corporatist lines (GLC, MOT, Labour and Conservative parties, motorist organizations, truckers, and business) versus a pluralist opposition (ad hoc groups, neighborhood groups) that had little experience with power.

But as anti–Motorways groups built up a head of steam, the movement became both more conventional and better attuned to orthodox politics. The first step toward convention involved the creation of two London-wide umbrella groups, the London Motorways Action Group (LMAG) and the London Amenity and Transport Association (LAMTA). Both LMAG and LAMTA were still militant and apart from the establishment. They were, however, the seedlings of better organization, and together they issued convincing rejoinders to the case for Motorways. Under the vigorous leadership of Michael Thomson of the London School of Economics, LAMTA gathered mounds of information against the highways.

The next step for anti–Motorways groups involved the formation of a single-issue political party called Homes Before Roads. This party mounted an extraordinary and continuous campaign against the ringways. In the GLC election of 1970, Homes Before Roads fielded eighty-five candidates and garnered 80,000 votes (the fourth highest after Labour, Conservative, and Liberal parties).[9]

Still another step was taken at the borough level. As the movement matured, the action shifted from street parades to local councils. Homes Before Roads was especially active within the town halls of Inner London. Borough councils voted resolutions against Motorways and brought their objections to both the GLC and the central government. The London Boroughs Association also began to lobby the GLC in opposition to the plan. Relying on the tactic of divide and conquer, the GLC declined to negotiate with the Boroughs Association. Better to deal with one borough at a time than face their collective hostility.

The boroughs continued to press their case. Inner boroughs like Camden, Lewisham, Tower Hamlets, and Kensington-Chelsea were especially fervent about stopping Motorways. As Labour began to back-pedal on its earlier support, the blame fell on the Conservatives. Tory councillors in Hampstead, Battersea, and St. Pancras took a thrashing and eventually promised to break with their own party in opposing Motorways.

Before long LMAG, LAMTA, and Homes Before Roads became adjuncts to either the borough councils or to the Labour Party. The leadership of LMAG fell to Douglas Jay, who was a former Labour Member of Parliament and Minister. Anti–Motorways activists participated in the work of borough councils by drawing up arguments against the plan. They also ran for office under the Labour banner. By 1972 Labour was ready to drop almost the entire scheme and its leader, Sir Reginald Goodwin, asserted that his party pledges itself to abandon the disastrous plans to build two motorways which threaten the environment of Central London. . . . We call on the GLC not to enter into any contracts which would authorize the commencement of work on any further motorway construction . . . so that Londoners can give their verdict on this urban madness.[10]

Goodwin's counterpart in the Conservative Party, Sir Desmond Plummer, was more sanguine about the prospects for Motorways. He interpreted his party's sweep of the 1970 GLC election as a mandate for radical highway planning. Plummer believed that without new auto routes, London was lost. "Look, London needs purpose-built motorways," he told a reporter. "Other cities have them. London must have them. The future prosperity of the metropolis depends on it. Otherwise people will just leave and the place will begin to die."[11]

Before the issue could be fought out in another GLC election, the central government also had a chance to deal with it. By 1970 the Conservatives had taken over Whitehall. Coincidentally, the entire Greater London Development Plan was scheduled for review by a panel of inquiry. The panel took its name after the prominent barrister who headed it, Frank Layfield, and began its deliberations amid great tension. As it turned out, the Layfield Panel lasted for two years and Motorways received the lion's share of attention. Nearly 30,000 objections were filed, 75 percent of which dealt with the ringways.

The inquiry did provide the opposition with a public platform and a chance to embarrass Motorways supporters. It also gave the opposition an opportunity to coalesce. Twelve boroughs plus the City came out against Motorways. But despite the pressure, the Conservative GLC held firm. It was butressed at Whitehall by the MOT, which communicated to Conservative leaders its intent to stand by the plan.[12]

The Layfield Panel issued its report in 1972. One year later that report was endorsed by the Secretary of State for the Environment, Geoffrey Rippon, but the verdict was hedged with qualifications. Boiled down, it told the GLC that a much scaled-down version of Motorways ought to be built. Both Layfield and Rippon were convinced that London was choked with traffic and that a Motorway Box was the only way to unsnarl the metropolis. Many of the other routes, they suggested, should be scrapped.

The tepid endorsements and reductions took their psychological toll. The outpouring of mass criticism, the opposition from the boroughs, and a new anti-Motorways plank in Labour's manifesto were signs that the plan might be defeated.

As the GLC elections of 1973 approached, the Conservative Party held on. Plummer still believed that Motorways could be salvaged and continued its promotion. In the campaign he claimed that "only with Ringways can we get the environmental improvements to Central London which we all want to see."[13] Other Conservatives were less comfortable with the idea. To them, Layfield, Rippon and the central government looked more like angels of death than political saviors.

The election results told the tale. For the first time in six years, Labour swept the GLC. It carried 58 seats against 32 for the Conservatives and 2 for the Liberals.[14] Reginald Goodwin promptly fulfilled his earlier promise and directed GLC planners to cease all work on the ringways. He also poured salt on Motorways' wounds by appointing Michael Thomson of LAMTA as the GLC's transport consultant.

Ultimately the Labour Party found itself retracting the very proposals it had promoted years before. Given the mood, there was very little that the central government or MOT wanted to do. They might tell the GLC that London needed better transportation, but they were reluctant to furnish the remedies. Motorways was said to have died from a Parkinsonian affliction—negation by delay. A hapless Desmond Plummer put his own epitaph on the plan when he said, "We seem to have lost our will to do anything positive in London any more."[15]

Covent Garden   To most Americans the image of Covent Garden conjures up a scene in "My Fair Lady." It is a picture of open street markets with waifs selling flowers at busy intersections. It is a community ribboned by dark, twisting streets, littered with fruit crates, and congested with wheelbarrows. Its sound is the din of market trading and hauling, interrupted by funny-looking men with flat caps who muffle their vowels and drop their word endings. Tenements and warehouses spew their cargo onto sidewalk aprons so narrow that the gutters must be used for pedestrian traffic.

The old Covent Garden was a jumble of activity. Though dominated by its fruit, vegetable, and flower markets, it was not defined by them. Twenty years ago a walk through the area took one past printers, booksellers, barrowmakers, ironmongers, glassblowers, grocers, suppliers, pubs, restaurants, and blocks of residential flats. It was even a site for theaters and the Royal Opera House.

The great diversity of Covent Garden left it unkempt and unregulated. It was alive 24 hours a day and had been so for centuries. Its historic roots were rich and strong. Nell Gwynn sold oranges on its streets. Dryden was beaten up by thugs there. Dickens, Thackeray, and Langtree held court at its most famous restaurant. At one time or another endless numbers of luminaries came to Covent Garden. Among them were literary figures like Pope, Boswell, Swift, Defoe, and Voltaire; or men of politics like Walpole, Disraeli, and Louis Napoleon.[16]

Behind the romance and funky charm there was a real community of people whose lives and livelihoods depended on Covent Garden. For most of this century, over four thousand souls lived in its rooms and flats. Many of them were working-class people who saw the area as an ancestral home. Families had lived there for generations. Forty-three percent of its residents had been in the area longer than twenty years. People who used its streets knew each other. One-third of those who lived in Covent Garden also had relatives living there.[17] For them Covent Garden was a familiar community; some called it the last working-class bastion of Central London.

Others saw it as less of a bastion and more of an eyesore. For them its ramshackle buildings, cold-water flats, and families living without kitchen or toilet facilities were a bad vestige of another era. For them Covent Garden was a slum that deprived its residents of a decent life and deprived Central London of progress.

Change seemed inevitable when, in 1962, the market and adjoining properties were sold to a public authority and put under the planning aegis of the GLC. Two years later it was announced that the market would be moved to Nine Elms on the south bank of the Thames. The planners of the GLC wasted no time in readying Covent Garden for a complete redoing. Approximately 96 acres were prepared for designation as a Comprehensive Development Area, or CDA. This would give planners the power to acquire property by eminent domain and establish zoning regulations.

Although the usual elite of GLC civil servants took charge of the details, a political mechanism was set up to approve strategic decisions and act as a legal representative. Initially, this was a Consortium of equal partners. It included the GLC, which exercised its right as a strategic authority for vital redevelopment, and two boroughs, Camden and Westminster, which shared the territorial boundaries of Covent Garden.

With site assembly in the hands of GLC staff, the Consortium began contacting key organizations. The most important of these were property developers and investors. By 1969 the Consortium was negotiating with Prudential Assurance, Bernard Sulley Investment Trust, the Bovis Group, and other powerful enterprises. When the carving was complete, large pieces of Covent Garden and its periphery were put up for redevelopment.[18] A map could be laid out of Covent Garden's rough rectangle. On its sides blocks of territory were parceled out as office towers, hotels, and residential high rises.

Redeveloping 96 acres in the center of London is no easy political affair, and it soon became apparent that the Consortium was too cumbersome. The borough of Camden had been pressing for public housing, Westminster was opposed, and the GLC wanted to get on with the project. Other writers have commented that the Consortium was "too slow" and that the GLC sought "a free hand to make quick and important decisions." Moreover, "large developers like to deal with one authority and not three."[19] So the GLC replaced the Consortium with a Joint Committee it could control, consisting of ten GLC members, three Westminster representatives, and two Camden representatives. In any combination of votes the Conservatives were assured of a majority. Above all, it was a useful political device. With it GLC Conservatives could orchestrate the interests of the boroughs, the property developers, and the affected publics.

The planning of Covent Garden would have to be imaginative to satisfy all interests; and it was. The earliest plan called for 55 of the area's 90-odd acres to be redeveloped. Evidently the GLC was still intrigued by orbital highways. At their first opportunity, the planners designed underground roads along the outer periphery of Covent Garden. These were to connect to another major route (the Strand).

The chaos of the community would be eliminated. In its place were "spines" of development. To the south, closer to the Strand, there was to be an entertainment area with theaters, hotels, an international conference center, offices, and some residences. The southern spine was more residential, although it too would contain hotels, shops, and office buildings. Running between the two spines was a "line of character" that featured preserved buildings along with some newer additions. The "line of character" was supposed "to assimilate the new to the old" and integrate the traditions of the community to its new uses.

Figures 7.3, 7.4 and 7.5 provide a glimpse of the scheme. Figure 7.3 shows an overview of Covent Garden along with road and open space proposals. Figure 7.4 shows the North Spine, which remakes the residential community. Figure 7.5 shows the South Spine and its impact upon historic landmarks. These plans represent GLC thinking during 1971 and 1972.

The professionals of the GLC were proud of their work and inspired by the best research of the day. Wanting to learn from past mistakes, they read Lewis Mumford, Jane Jacobs, Kevin Lynch, and others. They prepared themselves with "character studies" of the area and

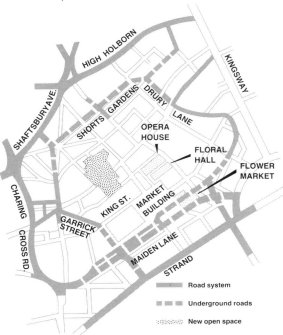

Fig. 7.3. Convent Garden: Landmarks, Road, and Open Space Proposals.
Source: Adapted from *Evening Standard*, November 14, 1972.

conceptualized their planning with Lynch-like terminology. "Districts" would define subsections of Covent Garden; "edges" would mark off different communities; "nodes" would serve as gathering places or visual references; and "pedways following lines of desire" would accommodate pedestrians.[20]

Figures 7.3, 7.4, and 7.5 outline what GLC staff believed was a humanized environment. Following Abercrombie's reasoning, the road system allows for pedestrian use of the streets, and part of it is underground. In concert with Mumford's monumental studies, there is ample room for open and public spaces. Along with Jacobs's admonitions there are opportunities for "mixed uses" (hotels, shops, residences, community centers, offices) to promote interaction and enliven Covent Garden. Planners also pointed out that the introduction of new business was a realistic way to support public amenities. They reasoned that lucrative enterprises could make up for "low return uses" like open space and community centers. Thus strategic planning, when cleverly applied, could satisfy all interested parties.

Not everyone was pleased with the outcome, especially the people

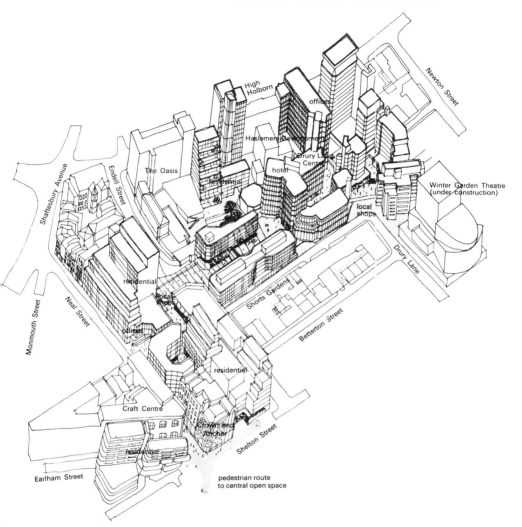

Fig. 7.4. Covent Garden: The Proposed North Spine. Source: *Covent Garden: The Next Step*, Covent Garden Joint Development Committee, Greater London Council, 1971. Reproduced with permission from the London Residuary Body, successors to the GLC.

of Covent Garden. As the plans came out of County Hall there was disquiet, then open anger; and it was easy to see why. With the stroke of the planner's pen and the words of the politicians, the community was being wiped away. Promises of new housing were in vain, when 60 percent of existing dwellings were threatened with destruction and

217

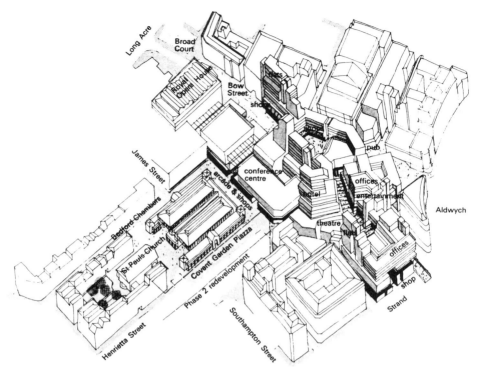

Fig. 7.5. Covent Garden: The Proposed South Spine. Source: *Covent Garden: The Next Step*, Covent Garden Joint Development Committee, Greater London Council, 1971. Reproduced with permission from the London Residuary Body, successors to the GLC.

there were few places to relocate. The prospect of resettlement counted for little, when most residents were paying less than £10 per week for rented flats and could afford no more. "Pedways" made no sense when most people already had the use of familiar streets and shops. New roadways were a menace to community life, because they would destroy some of the oldest establishments in Covent Garden. Even the best schemes to speed automobile traffic had no relevance to people who did not own automobiles.

Local people knew very well that their community was about to be turned over to outsiders, and they mobilized for action. It was a mobilization that sprang from the grass roots of Covent Garden. Residents, workers, street people, and students who lived in the area banded together and formed the Covent Garden Community Association (CGCA). Like the anti-Motorways groups, the CGCA was organized spontaneously as a result of a threat to the existing environment. Also like the anti-Motorways groups, the CGCA knew how to publicize their plight and win support. Street festivals and parties were organized to spark community spirit. Community meetings were held to discuss the GLC's plans and rally the opposition. A community newspaper was started to alert residents. Even finances were raised from local sources. A benefit performance of *Godspell* was staged by friendly actors, with the proceeds going to the CGCA.

By all accounts the CGCA was a fiery and effective pressure group. Its cause was clear—stop the GLC and bring back industrial jobs to Covent Garden. Its constituency was solid—the rock-ribbed blue-collar workers of Covent Garden. Its style was radical—protest, resist compromise, do not trust the establishment. It succeeded in bringing the case of Covent Garden to the British public and it embarrassed public officials with its skill and thoroughness. Also, like many of the groups in the Motorways case, the CGCA's thrust became harnessed to organizational politics.

The first channel for this conversion was the public inquiry. If the GLC was to proceed with Covent Garden, it needed to have it declared a Comprehensive Development Area (CDA) and go through the steps of a public inquiry. The inquiry was begun in the summer of 1971 and lasted for forty-two days. Testimony by witnesses, cross-examination by hired barristers, proofs of evidence, and other trappings dominated the procedure. Much of the testimony went to the very heart of what Covent Garden meant to its people. It was a testimony that told planners they had missed the point about Covent Garden and that mocked their good intentions. As one witness said:

> Not only is the street the place where the local pubs are, the local shop keeper, but it is also the channel of local information. . . . It was . . . of some distress and concern to me to see this structure vitiated into . . . "pedways following lines of desire." What is proposed is a series of urban foot roads carrying foot traffic along paths conditioned by the most minimal of activities—movement to and from work and to and from the lunch time café. . . . Streets are for milling around in, hearing what's happening to family and friends, chatting about whatever interests people at any moment, in short of conveying a sense of belonging inherent in local culture. It is *not* the speedway, motorway, freeway by which the pedestrian hurries through a "productive" life toward a premature coronary.[21]

Other arguments were not about the people of Covent Garden, but about what to do with the land. These issues were fought between the GLC, acting as guardian of intelligent, progressive planning, and the CGCA, which took up the cudgels against greedy developers. After the proceedings, recommendations were made by the presiding inspector and Covent Garden awaited the final verdict that would come from the Secretary of the Environment. Once again the Secretary giving the verdict was Geoffrey Rippon.

Two years later, Rippon was ready. CDA powers were indeed granted, but with so many qualifications the GLC could hardly recognize the victory. The new roadways were rejected as "having a damaging effect on the environment." Plans for additional hotel space and shopping centers were turned down. The GLC was told to reduce the scale of its plan and emphasize rehabilitation of the urban fabric. To underline this point, Rippon placed an additional 250 buildings to a list of a mere 80 protected sites that had been designated by the GLC.[22]

As a Conservative, Rippon did not want to undo his fellow Conservatives still in control of the GLC, yet he wanted to uphold the mantle of urban conservation. So he struck upon the solution of granting CDA powers, constraining them with conservationist qualifications, and for good measure, mandating some kind of public participation. Rippon's statement read:

> What I want to see is neither . . . a wonderland of concrete, glass and sunken roads nor an area . . . preserved for the benefit of tourists and visitors as an historic memorial. . . . The thing to realize is that public participation is not something to be stuck on afterwards. It is part of the process and the form it takes will depend upon the decision.[23]

Rippon was telling his Conservative friends to build if they must, but to go easy on the environment and to court public approval as they went along. The mode of participation was up to the GLC, and it wasted little time in organizing that participation.

By June 1974, the GLC already had its citizen organization selected through formal elections. The representative body, known as the Forum, was quintessentially corporatist. Covent Garden was not to be treated as an electoral whole, but as a community with distinct vertical divisions or organizations. Each division was defined by its economic stake. There were categories and subcategories for landowners and land occupiers, for commercial organizations that traded in merchandise, and for those that serviced the community. Each category was entitled to its own representation, which was allocated among thirty members in the following way:

➤ 9 Residents: 2 council tenants; 1 housing tenant; 6 others

➤ 9 Businesses: 3 shops, retailers, wholesalers; 5 offices and professional practices; 1 restaurateur

➤ 9 Services: 4 theaters; 2 crafts; 3 welfare, hospital, religious organizations

➤ 3 Property Owners: landlords, developers, shop owners

What had once been an opposition was suddenly converted into a collaborative organization with special access to decision makers. The Forum joined in special working parties with GLC staff, members of the Forum attended all meetings of the Covent Garden Joint Committee, and the Forum was allowed to make separate comments on planning applications for Covent Garden. The Forum received a modest budget to maintain a director and was allowed to use GLC-owned space free of charge.

The GLC was proud of this enlightened and orderly form of participation. Both politicians and planners saw the Forum as a broad-based organization that reflected the complexities of the community. They pointed out that although the Forum contained people who were "extremely right wing," it also included communists, and on the whole it offered a "composite picture" of Covent Garden.[24]

In addition, the Forum's pattern of organization was well suited to the GLC's own structure. Leaders on both the GLC and the Forum understood that if their divergent interests were to arrive at a common solution, those interests must be broken down, deciphered, and then reconciled. The best way to do this was to organize the participants along functional lines. The idea was to plug the interests to be served into the tasks to be carried out. The interaction between the Forum and the GLC amounted to a sociopolitical division of labor. As one leading participant put it:

> The reason we got on so well with the Forum was that our organizations really matched. The Forum was bureaucratic. Being two bureaucracies you sort of lock into one another. You get good concentration of like-minded people and a close continuous consultation.[25]

Activists on the CGCA felt very differently. For them the Forum was little more than a ploy to defang the opposition. As they saw it, the Forum's collection of organizations forced it to negotiate internally rather than stand up to the GLC. For CGCA dissidents this translated into a dilution of Covent Garden's capacity to oppose. The GLC could easily play one Forum division off against another. Moreover, the dissidents argued that the Forum's new legitimacy made it less prone to contest

GLC policy and more vulnerable to getting lost in the technicalities of densities and specific uses.

Participation of the Forum was especially frustrating for CGCA radicals. After a short period of collaboration, the CGCA forbade members of its executive committee from running in Forum elections. To the CGCA, the Forum's multiple constituencies were the neighborhood's "users" (landlords, professionals, businessmen) and not its "people" (blue-collar workers and long-time residents). The Forum represented a privileged bourgeoisie of the powerful and of those who possessed the resources and inclination to work with the power structure. The sense of wrongdoing was acutely felt by one CGCA leader as he exclaimed:

> Look, I don't give a cow's tit about your kind of democracy. The property developers and the traders have ample representation. The people who really live here have no one to speak for them.[26]

The feeling of having to battle against the odds heightened the CGCA fight against the GLC. The CGCA continued to work from outside the channels of authority and protested the Forum's alliance with the GLC. These tactics achieved some results in getting a few benefits for its blue-collar constituency (a recreation hall, a pub, promises of better housing). But the Forum was clearly at the helm of community participation. It was the legitimate speaker for the community and it took the credit (or blame) for what was to become of it.

In the end, preservation and restoration won out over radical reconstruction. Covent Garden's conservation reflected both the fondest wishes and deepest fears of its community. On the plus side the urban fabric was safeguarded—buildings were renovated, the central market was saved, theaters and streets were kept intact. So too was most of the old community kept alive. Legally, the GLC had been converted to the position that its "main objective [was] to ensure that numerically the resident population [was] safeguarded and increased."[27] Toward this end, the GLC provided housing guarantees and took steps to ensure that enough public or nonprofit housing would be furnished.

On the other hand, Covent Garden will never be the same. Though displacement has been avoided, it has not stopped gentrification. New classes have occupied one of the most chic locales in Central London. A whole new social structure has been interspersed with the old. Some of the old shops have been replaced by fancy wine bars, patisseries, and art galleries. The market building has been converted into a glass-covered enclosure for boutiques and restaurants. By day the streets are filled and by night the theaters draw crowds from all over London.

No doubt Covent Garden has kept its scale. It neither overwhelms nor intimidates, and this has made it all the more attractive to outsiders. Covent Garden also tells us that community preservation may not just be preservation for the community.[28]

The Docklands The land on the eastern side of the Thames contains the London Docklands. It stretches for eight square miles and cuts through Inner London. Two hundred years ago most of this land along the river's edge was green and not far from farmlands. But the industrial revolution changed it. The great docks arose—Surrey, Milbank, St. Katherine's, London, and East India—to gobble up the world's produce and disperse it to Europe. The rest of the land, to the north, was also changed, becoming a home and workplace for the working classes of Great Britain and immigrants from Eastern Europe. Whitechapel, Wapping, Stepney, and Bethnal Green were the old East End that epitomized cockney London. They were the places that furnished cheap labor for the sweatshops manufacturing clothing, for the factories making furniture, and for the breweries fermenting bitter and lager.

By the turn of the century, the area that is now Tower Hamlets held over 600,000 people. Today that population has dropped to 142,000 and it has the highest unemployment rate in London.[29] Most of the industry has left and the social indicators are bleak. Per capita income is among the lowest in London, educational levels are disappointing, and the area has one of the highest death rates in the region. Tower Hamlets' high mortality is largely due to the number of old-age pensioners who live there as well as the large number of vagrants who walk its streets. Quite a stir was caused in the GLC when a Tory member referred to the borough as the "squatter capital of the universe."[30]

Just as dramatically as the docks arose, they now are disappearing. East India Dock closed in 1967, St. Katherine's and the London Docks shut in 1969, and work stopped at the Surrey Docks in 1970. West India and Millwall Docks ceased their operations in 1980. Most of the business has gone down the Thames to Tilberry, which can accommodate larger ships and has automated its loading. The Royal Docks still do a trickle of business, though it is doubtful how long they will remain open. To walk through the Docklands in 1984 was to witness an industrial graveyard. Pilings that once sustained heavy cargo had rotted, piers were broken, warehouses looked as if they were about to crumble. Access to the Docklands was not easy. As a gesture of aesthetic mercy, routes into the area became impassable.

The other side of the story is that the Docklands is an area of immense potential. Miles of empty riverfront land lie just a few kilometers from the heart of London. The opportunities for redevelopment seem limitless. Even the British bureaucracy, which trades on issuing monotonously guarded reams of paper, has been able to wax enthusiastic over the possibilities. Sounding more like a tabloid than a state document, a White Paper on the Docklands proclaimed that it was "the biggest thing in London since the Great Fire of 1666—the biggest in Europe—*a tabula rasa* (once the clearing and filling is done) of 5,500 acres."[31] In an editorial on the subject the *Times* of London insisted that hopes for the Docklands beckoned for the creative genius of a Baron Haussmann.[32]

Figure 7.6 presents a map of the Docklands as the River Thames wends its way toward the City. Located on the map are the Surrey, India, Millwall, and Royal Docks. Just below Millwall Docks is the Isle of Dogs, which is a prime site for redevelopment. As indicated on Figure 7.6, the docks can be found in the five boroughs of Tower Hamlets, Newham, Southwark, Lewisham, and Greenwich. In 1973 the Secretary of the Environment allowed the boroughs to form a Docklands Joint Committee (DJC) which began operations the following year. Its task was to work collectively in planning the redevelopment of the Docklands.

The DJC was a loose corporatist body that amalgamated the interests of different organizations. Its members were drawn from the five bor-

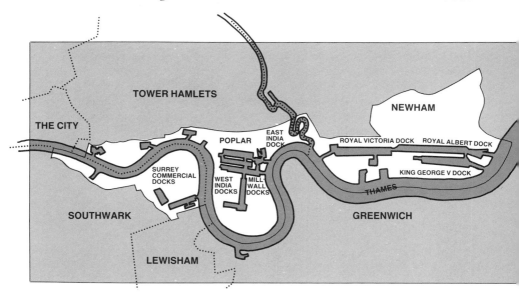

Fig. 7.6. The London Docklands

oughs, the GLC, nominees from the central government, and umbrella organizations from trade unions, trades councils, employers' federations, and local groups. The Docklands also had a Forum, similar to Covent Garden's, which was elected from the area. The Forum too participated in the DJC.

Over the years the composition of the DJC varied, but its last form held twenty-four members; eight of whom were drawn from the five boroughs, eight from the GLC, and eight nominees from Whitehall and organizations within the Docklands.[33] It was then a multipartite organization holding representatives from three tiers of government, trade unions, business, and community residents. The division of power split into thirds so that the organization was vertically segmented around 1980 as

➤ Five Boroughs (8): Tower Hamlets, Newham, Southwark, Lewisham, Greenwich

➤ Greater London Council (8): Members drawn primarily from Docklands area

➤ Nominees from Whitehall and local organizations (8); business, trade unions, the Forum (community action groups, council and other tenants, property owners)

From the vantage of democratic participation, the DJC was an enviable political instrument. It incorporated a large number of organizations and needed to muster a majority consensus before it could act. Like the Consortium at Covent Garden, the GLC and the boroughs played leading roles. Because the GLC and the boroughs were strongly Labour, the DJC could count on a common ideological orientation to achieve consensus. As such it was able to produce plans that emphasized the retention and well-being of the existing communities. A London Docklands Strategic Plan (LDSP) was adopted that emphasized housing, gardens, open space, and transportation for the affected communities. The LDSP also contained a major component for industrial development, based on the hopeful prognosis that industry could be attracted.[34]

However, from the vantage of decisive executive action, the DJC was problem-ridden. Boroughs were more tied to their individual constituents than to a common cause for the Docklands. The GLC had a different approach to the land and wanted to develop the Docklands in accordance with its own strategic plan. It often clashed with the DJC over differences of priority in developing the area. Critics also charged that the DJC was a debating club, taken up with political quibbling.

In fact, the DJC was hamstrung by the singular concerns of its constituent organizations. Pressure from the trade unions led the DJC down the trail of focusing on blue-collar jobs rather than office employment. Pressure from local industries caused it to worry more about the survival of foundering firms than the attraction of new ones. Pressure from tenant organizations prompted the DJC to plan for more public housing, even though it lacked the resources to build.

After six years of operation, the DJC found itself woefully short on its early promises. On employment the LDSP had projected that 10,000 to 12,000 new jobs would be created by 1982; only 800 additional jobs were started while over 8,000 jobs were lost in the intervening years. In housing, the LDSP set a target for the construction of 6,000 new dwellings by 1982; only 2,200 were built or under construction. What bothered the Tories most about housing in the Docklands was that the majority of flats were public housing, usually owned by the boroughs. In Tower Hamlets more than 97 percent of the housing was publically owned.[35]

The DJC countered that few borough residents could afford to buy private homes and that renting private flats was just as prohibitive. If borough residents were to live in the Docklands, the councils would have to build housing for them. It also asserted that a huge part of its time was consumed with land acquisition, drainage, road repair, and infrastructure. In addition, Labourites felt that Tories were annoyed with the DJC approach, which stressed community needs rather than economic vitality. Once in power the Tories were determined to ignore the LDSP, regardless of performance.[36]

On at least that count the Socialists were correct. By 1981 the Thatcher Government had had enough of the DJC and dissolved it. An appeal was made to the House of Lords, but after it heard the issue, the government was upheld. In place of the DJC, the Secretary of the Environment established the London Docklands Development Corporation (LDDC). Once the Docklands was put under the LDDC, the area covered just three critical boroughs—Southwark, Newham, and Tower Hamlets.

Curiously, the LDDC draws much of its inspiration from the United States. It is a public development corporation, capable of acquiring land, investing in it with infrastructure and services, and putting it up for sale or lease. It is run by a board of directors and organized so that it can deal rapidly in the marketplace. The LDDC has powers that were never enjoyed by the DJC. It has an almost unlimited right to acquire land and is subvended by a hefty government grant. Given this support, the Tory government expected that the LDDC would behave like its American forebears, boldly developing the land, quickly selling it off, and buoying the area with post-industrial investment.

The LDDC has fulfilled those expectations. It has built an impressive infrastructure and brought private development onto the finest waterfront property in London. The Docklands is developing so rapidly cartographers can hardly keep up with the pace. New streets, roads, squares, parks, and commercial and residential facilities are springing up. Land prices have skyrocketed. In 1987, a one-bedroom apartment in one of the finer sites was selling for about $200,000.

This has irked Labour critics, who see the Docklands going to outsiders. Just as troublesome is the fact that the LDDC has sought white-collar and high-technology business. The LDDC claims to have already attracted 8,000 jobs and forecasts a tenfold increase in the next decade.[37] To the LDDC this objective makes sense, because outsiders and new jobs will change the face of the area. To Socialists in the boroughs, this is an abuse of a public trust and a threat to the existing community.

Especially nettling the boroughs is the LDDC's mood of militant capitalism. The corporation prides itself in having created one of Britain's first "urban enterprise zones" on a forlorn site called the Isle of Dogs. The guiding principle of the zone is that red tape, restrictions, and taxation have killed incentive. Hence, businesses that set up there are excused from most of these encumbrances. All they need do is produce and let the market flower. Mostly within the zone is planned a huge office complex on a site called Canary Wharf. Three giant office towers, devoted to international banking and financial services, will stand out along the Thames, and these are supposed to be the nucleus for the construction of still more mid rise buildings. Along with other portions of the Docklands, Canary Wharf will be connected by a light rail system to Central London. If successful, Canary Wharf could become London's second "City," a fitting rival to Wall Street, the Bourse, the World Trade Center, and La Défense. Significantly, the leading developer is a North American–based firm.

Great Britain, however, is not the United States, and the LDDC has had to deal with London's political realities. The most compelling realities are the boroughs, upon whose turf the LDDC has poached. The boroughs still smart over the corporation's role in the Docklands and they are anxious to regain their rightful place. They still have some leverage over the LDDC; by statute it is obliged to consult with the boroughs and encourage popular participation.[39]

Such obligations have brought the LDDC into the thicket of local politics. Politicians from Southwark, Newham, and Tower Hamlets have sat on the LDDC board. The LDDC also maintains a liaison with some borough council members and appointed a popular Labourite as its Vice President. It even curries favor with community groups by giving them financial support and it publishes a community newsletter.

But the opposition is unassuaged. In the wake of DJC's demise, the boroughs have continued to fight. A number of counterorganizations, first supported by the GLC and now supported by a consortium of localities, have sprung up to press the populist cause. A Docklands Forum represents organized interests in the area and regularly asks to be consulted. Community action groups demonstrate, hold mock funerals, and testify at hearings. A Docklands Development Committee issues reports and publishes a newsletter.[40]

The local rallying cry is, "Don't join up with the Vichy Regime. Resist the LDDC, because in the long run, we can beat them." Two boroughs (Southwark and Newham) have refused to send liaison officers or furnish vital information to the LDDC. Those politicians who do cooperate are held in disfavor.

The borough strategy is to conduct business as usual, draw up structure plans for the Docklands, and put the onus on the LDDC for having violated those plans. In short, the boroughs believe they can win by behaving as if they are the sole legitimate authorities for the area. They would let the central government bear the brunt for undoing them.

It is a risky gamble. In the borough of Southwark, just one day before its structure plan was to take effect, the central government "called in the plan." For the first time in Greater London's history, a plan formally adopted by a borough council was deemed unacceptable. A public inquiry and a judgment by the Secretary of State for the Environment were required to settle the matter.

In the fall of 1984 an inspector from the central government came to Southwark to review the called-in plan. It was a hearing that pitted Southwark against the LDDC, and the inspector left little doubt about whom he favored. Southwark, he wrote, was "inward and backward-looking."[41] Its plan was "dogmatic and very immoderate" and too heavily reliant on public finance and "controlled investment to implement . . . key proposals."[42]

Mostly, the inspector criticized the "appalling state of relations between the LDDC and the [borough] councils."[43] He blamed Southwark for "turning its back" on the corporation and showing "open hostility" toward it.[44] He urged that the borough follow the government's wishes and work with the LDDC. The bridge between the adversaries, he suggested, might be a mixed community with half the Docklands devoted to private-home ownership.

Southwark takes a dim view of what it regards as central authoritarianism (the LDDC, the inspector, and the ministries). Its struggle was supported by the GLC and is now backed by a number of "GLCs-in-exile" such as the Association of London Authorities. In the boroughs one sees the slogan "Docklands Fights Back"; murals are painted that depict children marching against the LDDC; and graffiti is scratched on walls exhorting "Homes for Rent: Not for Sale."

Much the same feeling is reflected in neighboring Newham. There too, the borough council has continued with its structure plan and ignored the LDDC. They too expect a public inquiry on the matter.

Docklands politics, like London politics, is a waiting game. Controversial decisions are pushed from one organizational ladder to another—waiting for some ultimate authority to decide. Referring to the Southwark experience, a sign in its town hall reads:

> 30,000 hours of consultation and 1,000 community groups went into making this plan. And it was all stopped by one man on January 28, 1986.

The opposition may well have to wait five years before another election provides the opportunity to change the central government, the man, or more important, the woman.

Summary Analysis

London's politics of land use flows through established organizations. Citizen groups may sprout at the grass-roots level, but they are most often transplanted into one or another of these organizations.

This quality of incorporation is the bedrock of corporatist politics. In nearly every case, one group after another was made part of a government or quasi-government organization. In the Motorways case, separate interest groups and a single-issue party were incorporated into either the Labour Party, the boroughs, or the GLC. In Covent Garden, a zesty and spontaneous movement was incorporated into a Forum that then structured participation along vertical socioeconomic categories. In the Docklands, interest groups were segmented along functional lines (politicians, businessmen, trade unionists, tenants, and landlords) and then incorporated into an interborough committee.

The absorption of small groups into larger organizations leaves little room for autonomy. In only one instance did a significant interest group (the Covent Garden Community Association) continue to stand outside the political system. Maverick groups are few and far between, and their insistence on autonomy frequently leads to a diminution of their influence.

Thorough as political incorporation may be, it is not embedded in a unified political order. London's politics is compartmentalized between contending political bases in the town halls (boroughs), County Hall (GLC or "GLCs-in-exile"), and Whitehall (central government).[45]

Compartmentalization allows different contestants to avail themselves of political opportunities. We have observed how, in the Motorways case, groups fought the GLC/MOT plan through the boroughs. They later unhinged the plan by moving into the Labour Party and relied on Labour to win control of County Hall. In Covent Garden, groups became part of a Consortium of two boroughs and the GLC. When the Consortium was abolished, group participation was linked directly to County Hall. In the Docklands, three town halls, in alliance with County Hall, fought against Whitehall.

London's land-use politics differs from either of its sister cities. London shares the Parisian penchant for organization, but it does not integrate its political elite. Though London shares New York's disposition toward open conflict, its conflicts are not open-ended. London's politics resembles a kind of monopolistic competition. Its contenders are legitimized by government and its contentions are controlled.

This quality of control is assisted by a high degree of decisional resolution. Final decisions are made at fixed points in the system (an election, a GLC resolution, a panel of inquiry, ministerial or parliamentary determination). Political tensions are registered at these junctures, often heightening the drama of a decision. That drama is played out between contestants trying to alter the built environment and those who want to conserve it.

Through the 1960s and 1970s, those charged with final decisions were cautious about radical change. In the Motorways case, a Conservative central government refrained from pushing a Motorway Box, even though it was explicitly committed to do so. In Covent Garden, a Conservative Secretary of the Environment opted for preservation, even though local Conservatives wanted full-scale redevelopment.

The sources of this restraint have long been embedded in the cultural dynamics of London and consist of a respect for gradual rather than quick change, as well as a disinclination to rip up viable communities. Both these factors are writ large through the institutions and the practices of the Greater London Metropolis. They can be recognized in everyday conversations with citizens. They can be heard as people couple the word "gradualism" with the belief that it is "the English way." This can be spotted in the well-worn phrase that "a man's home is his castle."[46]

Still another factor encouraging restraint lies in the organizational pressures that emanate from liberal corporatism. That is, the very absorption and ensuing legitimacy of competing organizations has been a chief source of the system's inertia. Both within and between tiers of government, organizations can stall a decision and generate the seeds of defeat. Negation by delay not only killed Motorways, but it negated parts of the plan for Covent Garden.

Negation by delay is no stranger to politics. Political scientists have described American pluralism in similar terms.[47] In liberal corporatism it works differently because the groups are legitimized and remain within the system.[48] They become an integral part of the process, thereby making resistance more formidable. In pluralism, groups stand outside the system. Their influence is unstable, their fortunes whimsical, and their outcomes ambiguous. This is why decisions seem endless in New York. It remains the only city where two cases (Lincoln West and Westway) have been resurrected in another form. In New York groups remain apart from the system and refuse to believe they have lost.

A quick comparison between Westway and Motorways shows the differences between systems. In Westway the opposition was always inchoate and fragmented. From the start they were in battle against the government. Even as Westway went down to defeat, Marcy Benstock stood as a victor against the politicians, never joining them. In Motorways, fragmented groups were first unified and then brought into more sophisticated organs of public policy. Their triumph was heralded as one of their leaders, Michael Thomson, went to work for the GLC. For Londoners, incorporation into organization politics is commensurate with success.

As London moves toward the 1990s, traditional restraints have weakened. Right-wing conservatives and the militant Left have strained liberal corporatism. Partisan commitments are increasingly hardened and less given to mutual understanding. The abolition of the GLC is regarded as a sweepingly arbitrary action. GLCs-in-exile allow Inner London boroughs to resist and fight on.

The next decade could see a polarized politics meshing with radical land-use decisions to change the nature of liberal corporatism. The Docklands could be the testing ground for such a transition. Should a white-collar urban enterprise zone and office towers arise amid massive joblessness, central and local authorities would be brought to a new crisis. A takeover of the Docklands by outsiders living in luxury housing could bring forth new war cries against them. The old trialogue between politically contending organizations would be replaced by outright defiance. The old spirit of compromise could crumble under the weight of noncooperation.

Fig. 7.7 (*above*). Inside Old Covent Garden. © Ena Bodin, Photographer

Fig. 7.8 (*at right, top*). Old Covent Garden Yard. © Ena Bodin, Photographer

Fig. 7.9 (*at right, below*). Inside New Covent Garden. Photo/H. V. Savitch

Fig. 7.10. Store: Old Covent Garden. Photo/Clive Boursnell

Fig. 7.11. Same Store: New Covent Garden. Photo/Clive Boursnell

Fig. 7.12. The Docklands with Tower Bridge in Foreground. Photo/London
Docklands Development Corporation

Fig. 7.13. Dilapidated Docklands. Photo/London
Docklands Development Corporation

Fig. 7.14. Construction in the Docklands.
Photo/London Docklands Development Corporation

Power Structures

It may turn out that each city is unique and no useful generalization can be made using the city as the unit of analysis. Or the city may really be the most useful microcosm of the political system in which all essential processes, structures and relationships can be found. The professional conclusion probably lies somewhere between. We will not know without systematic comparative study.—Robert Salisbury, "Urban Politics: The New Convergence of Power"

IN THE 1950s Harold Lasswell published his classic study on power, *Politics: Who Gets What, When, How.* The book dealt with the behavior of political elites and it changed the future of political science.[1] This chapter takes liberty with Lasswell's snappy title by asking, "who *does* what, when, how?"

The question of "when" great decisions were made in New York, Paris, and London has already been answered. Post-industrial transformation occurred in those cities from the early 1960s through the 1980s. In New York, critical decisions were made in 1976, 1980, 1982 and 1984; in Paris they were taken in 1968-1969, 1973, and 1978; in London the high points of decision occurred in 1967, 1972-1973, and 1981.

If we are to take Lasswell's aphorism seriously, there still remains the question of "what" the political process is about in these cities, "who" runs the process, and "how" decisions about the built environment are brought about. We respond by examining the power structures that predominate in New York, Paris, and London. More precisely, the typologies of pluralism, elitism, and corporatism may be put to the test of our case studies. "What" do power structures look like in New York, Paris, and London? What can be said about them after they are compared? Is the face of urban power made from its politicians, from its technocrats, from interest groups, from the wealthy and the well born? Alternatively, are there many faces to urban power, with each containing different features and a different genealogy?

The "who" of power is a matter of looking at the purveyors of power. Who exercises power and whose perspectives are involved in the making of decisions?

The last of Lasswell's questions concerns the "how" of politics. For Lasswell as for us, how politics is run concerns methods of influence.

238

When applied to the making of the built environment, this turns on the question of the political techniques used to bring about physical change. In answering the "how" questions, we return to the builders of New York, Paris, and London. Robert Moses, Paul Delouvrier, Patrick Abercrombie, and William Robson are seen as great urban impresarios, and we may inquire whether the study of these builders reveals anything about the environments from which they sprang.

Comparing Case Studies

In our nine case studies in New York, Paris, and London, New York came closest to a corporatist-pluralist hybrid, Paris most resembled mobilizing corporatism, and London best conformed to a typology of liberal corporatism. These typologies can be systematically compared to the case studies by isolating three stages of the decision-making process. These stages are (1) initiation, which concentrates on who originated and moved a decision through the political process; (2) consideration, which focuses on the process and outcome of the debate over a decision; and (3) implementation, which emphasizes who carried out a decision and how a newly built environment was created.[2]

When compared, the cases should reveal a pattern of behavior or a result that bears upon one or another typology. During the initiation stage, pluralist behavior would be characterized by numerous private businesses or groups moving the action, elitism would show a cohesive upper class ordering the action, and corporatism would put the initial action in the hands of a political or technocratic elite.

The stage of consideration would generate other differences. Pluralism would be ridden with conflict and end in either substantial compromise, defeat, or stalemate. Elitism would be characterized by class dominance and result in decisions left largely intact. Corporatism would feature collaboration between well-organized interests, which could result in decisions either left intact or compromised by a political-technocratic elite working in conjunction with organized interests.

The final stage of implementation should also sharpen the differences between possible outcomes. Pluralism would leave the execution of projects mainly to the private sector. Public interference would be limited and usually indirect. Typical instances of the public role might encompass making zoning ordinances, ensuring public safety, and guarding against public nuisances. Under pluralism one would expect an even-handed government to sometimes hinder or sometimes help private parties. These might include steep real estate taxes in congested areas or tax abatements in sections that needed further development. Elitism would also leave the execution of decisions to the private sector, except that public policy would be put entirely at its service. Under elitism one would expect unbridled private development and a persistent pattern of favoritism granted to investors. These might include extensive zoning variances, tax abatements, and a slackening of building controls. Corporatism would carry out projects in an altogether different manner. Most decidedly, the public sphere would be dominant and retain control, but private interests would also be accorded a significant role. One would expect the connection between public and private spheres to be marked by the delegation of authority to quasi-public bodies or organized institutions. As one writer on corporatism has suggested, "one of its most prominent features is a set of statutory institutions to accommodate indirect contacts between government officials and representatives of authorized interest groups."[3] Examples of such delegations of authority might range from the participation of investment bankers in mixed corporations to tenant representation on boards that determine housing priorities.

Political traits for each of the typologies are summarized and attributed to decision making in Table 8.1. Organized by case study, the outcomes for each trait are set out in Table 8.2. The first thing to be noted is that the fit between the case studies and the expected typological outcomes is not perfect. Boundaries between different typologies

Table 8.1. Political Traits in Elitism, Pluralism, and Corporatism

Decisional Stage	Elitism	Pluralism	Corporatism
INITIATION			
taken by	cohesive upper class	private groups	political or technocratic elite
CONSIDERATION			
process	dominance	conflict	collaboration
outcome	decisions are left intact	decisions are compromised, stalemated, or defeated	decisions are left intact or compromised
IMPLEMENTATION			
who	private	private	public
	unlimited prerogatives to develop land given to a unique class	limited prerogatives to develop land won by competitive groups	delegated and continually controlled prerogatives allocated to select organizations

Table 8.2. Nine Cases: Behavior and Outcomes in New York, Paris, and London

		New York		Paris		London
INITIATION taken by	LW	private groups	LH	pol.-tech. elite	Motor	pol.-tech. elite
	TS	pol.-tech. elite	LD	pol.-tech. elite	CG	pol.-tech. elite
	West	pol.-tech. elite	SSE	pol.-tech. elite	Dock	pol.-tech. elite
CONSIDERATION process outcome	LW	conflict-collaboration compromise	LH	conflict/collaboration intact	Motor	conflict defeat
	TS	conflict/collaboration intact	LS	collaboration intact	CG	conflict/collaboration compromise
	West	conflict defeat	SSE	collaboration intact	Dock	conflict intact
IMPLEMENTATION who how	LW	private ltd. prerogative	LH	public delegated	Motor	not applicable
	TS	public/private delegated	LD	public delegated	CG	public delegated
	West	not applicable	SSE	public delegated	Dock	public delegated

Key to case studies:
New York: LW—Lincoln West; TS—Times Square; West—Westway
Paris: LH—Les Halles; LD—La Défense; SSE-Secteur Seine Sud-Est
London: Motor—Motorways; CG—Covent Garden; Dock—Docklands

are porous and characteristics of one system may seep into another. As Table 8.2 indicates, London is most porous in its mixture of corporatist and pluralist typologies. During consideration, all of the cases manifested signs of conflict and one case (Motorways) resulted in the defeat of a decision initiated by politicians and technocrats. In New York, pluralist-corporatist boundaries are porous throughout all stages. This is to be expected, given its characterization as a hybrid system.

Having observed some mixing of typologies, the next thing to be said is that the generalizations do hold up. In each city the preponderance of outcomes conforms to hybrid or to corporatist typologies. New York shows a consistent pattern of alternation and mixing between pluralism and corporatism. Decisions were either initiated by private groups, political-technocratic elites, or a combination of both.

The consideration stage was characterized by conflict. This usually meant that groups would do battle over zoning changes or high rise construction, but the fighting was often replaced by collaboration (Lincoln West, Times Square). The implementation of decisions showed a similar splitting of pluralist-corporatist features. This was particularly evident in Times Square, where a public authority took charge of the project and delegated certain prerogatives to private investors. A part of the profits made by private investors will be shared with the city. In all the New York cases private investors were accorded privileges, but these were limited and guided by the public sector.

Paris showed the strongest adherence to corporatist patterns. Only in Les Halles did open and popular protest arise, and that insurrection was tamed by coopting the most active leaders. The others were tempered by a political-technocratic elite that initiated development, collaborated with designated organizations, and delegated limited privileges to them.

London, too, showed conflict during consideration, but other stages conformed to the corporatist model. Popular protest became effective only when channeled into organizational forms that were joined to a competing political elite. Motorways was blocked when an opposition party decided to drop it. In Covent Garden, much of the opposition was placed in a statutory body (the Forum). In the Docklands, conflict was limited between different statutory bodies (the boroughs, the central government, and the London Docklands Development Corporation).

In comparison with pluralism and corporatism, there is little in the case studies to warrant an elitist interpretation. In no case did a cohesive upper class initiate a decision; in no case was that class dominant when decisions were considered; and in no case was a cohesive upper class allowed to implement decisions with unlimited prerogative.

In some decisions there were signs of an elitist impetus, but these were met by the countervaillance of other powers. In New York's Lincoln West, a wealthy businessman and foreign investors won the endorsement of City Hall and appeared to be sailing on an easy course. Soon afterward, the community board and local politicians protested. The resulting compromise entailed a costly package of public amenities that had to be defrayed by the developers.

Another hint of elitism occurred in Covent Garden, when GLC planners contacted leading businessmen and talked about parceling out pieces of territory for development. When finally presented, however, the original plan was a complicated document that accommodated a variety of interests, including those of business, labor, and ecology. Furthermore, the original plan for Covent Garden was substantially compromised. Although the results were also a boon for the middle class, it can hardly be argued that the new Covent Garden has been put at the service of a private elite.

The outcome that most invalidates the elitist typology is the prominent and, in most cases, dominant role of a political/technocratic elite. Although that role differs from city to city, it points up the importance of a public sector that can act on its own behalf and function as an agent of change.[4]

In New York technocrats brought issues to the attention of politicians, who then took command. In Paris technocrats joined politicians in a rough de facto partnership. London too followed a pattern of a techno-political partnership, but that partnership often tilted toward the expertise of technocrats, and politicians were left to approve their decisions.

A surprising eight out of nine cases show that politicians and/or technocrats were the primary movers. In New York the technocrats formulated a plan and, soon afterward, the politicians recruited investors and interest groups. Times Square and Westway are both illustrative of this process. In Times Square, the Governor and the Mayor worked mightily to steer their way between competing developers and pool investment dollars. In the case of Westway, technocrats and politicians took up the cudgels for a super highway and were joined by a coalition of business and labor.

In Paris and London, development was always within the grip of a political-technocratic elite. Not until plans were well under way did that elite begin to solicit the involvement of outside groups. This pattern is particularly true for Paris, where so much of the land was already in public ownership (Les Halles and Secteur Seine Sud-Est) or could be expropriated (La Défense and parts of Les Halles).

Considerable advantages accrue to politicians and technocrats when government is the landlord. They can work up plans, set parameters for development, and establish a strong posture before dealing with outside groups. Technocrats were especially salient in La Défense and Secteur Seine Sud-Est, where they almost single-handedly imposed conditions for development. In Les Halles, not only were the technocrats instrumental in putting together a radical plan, but they recruited the capital (both private and public) to construct a new environment.

London's technocrats are both stronger and weaker than their Parisian counterparts. Their strength derives from the absence of a politically elected chief executive. London has no real mayor who can pull the metropolis together. Instead, executive leadership is spread throughout the majority party (Leader, Whips) and in various committees of the GLC (or GLCs-in-exile) and the boroughs.

Vis-à-vis the politicians, the technocrats enjoy considerable freedom. As full-time professionals, they command points of administrative access and run the machinery of government. With their expertise and tact, they are able to win the support of the majority party. As professionals, too, they are able to keep pressure groups at a safe distance and make sure their plans are kept free from outside intrusion.

At the same time, London's technocrats are made weaker by the multiple tiers of government that punctuate decision making. These tiers allow contending organizations (political parties, interest groups, forums) to block the aspirations of technocrats and their political allies. The upshot is that in the short term the political-technocratic elite strikes a powerful pose. Over the longer term, however, they stumble over one or another tier. Motorways and Covent Garden illustrate a dynamic that allowed politicians and technocrats to prepare pieces of London for radical surgery, only to have the patient plucked away before the operation could take place.

This explains how London's liberal corporatism differs from that which prevails in Paris. London's system has built countervailing organizations into the different stages of decision making. These organizations are widespread and rely on separate bases of power (boroughs, GLC, central government) to press their case. In Paris the system is formally centralized, and organizations are less prone to use different levels of government against one another. But apart from that, elites at all levels of French government share a common professionalism and are more likely to bargain among themselves.[5] This is especially true for the Mayor of Paris and his entourage, who occupy a special place in the nation's political hierarchy. When there were differences between Mayor Chirac and President Giscard d'Estaing over Les Halles, or between Mayor Chirac and President Mitterrand over Secteur Seine Sud-Est, those differences were settled directly.

The political collaboration between the French state and La Ville de Paris extends into the professional realm. A high-level planner related how, when Chirac was only Mayor, he could reach any of the Socialist Ministers and obtain their cooperation. The placement of the Finance Ministry in Secteur Seine Sud-Est was done at the personal behest of a Gaullist Mayor to a Socialist President.[6]

There are common elements in the political composure of New York, Paris, and London. All three cities rely on a combination of politicians and technocrats to initiate development. All three cities accommodate interest groups (labor unions, bankers, developers, community and tenant associations).

Common as these features may be to the body politic of the three cities, they mix and manifest themselves in very different ways. In New York, interest groups enter decision making at an early phase of initiation and work closely with the political-technocratic elite. Boundaries between public and private spheres are hazy and politicians are vulnerable to outside pressure.

In Paris, the political-technocratic elite is able to maintain a distance from pressure groups. From the outset, French politicians and technocrats are able to take command and proceed with confidence that their projects will be funded. Only during the latter phase of consideration and during implementation do interest groups play an important role.

In London, politicians and technocrats take quick charge and interest groups are rarely aware of their initiatives. Only after elaborate plans have been published is the opposition triggered into action. The triggering of outside groups usually occurs during the stage of consideration. It is at this point of decision making that interest groups turn to other levers of power and blunt the influence of politicians and technocrats.

Politicians, Technocrats, and Decisions

New York's environment for decision making is laden with interest groups. The environment is rich in ideas and amenable to a multitude of initiatives. Politicians and technocrats are inundated with any number of sources that have the potential to change the urban fabric. The community boards registering citizen dissent, businessmen seeking opportunities for profit, labor unions seeking work for their members, the press trying to hold public attention with banner headlines—all of these encourage political initiatives.

Leading politicians are either pelted with opportunities or sometimes push their own pet projects. Contrary to the picture painted in much of the pluralist literature, New York politicians are not coy, noncommittal, reactive.[7] They are, in fact, proactive about development because development means jobs, higher tax revenues, and adrenalin for the commercial life of the city.

Most issues swirl around politicians and planners. The politician and high-level technocrat can be likened to political entrepreneurs, choosing from an emporium of opportunities. If they choose correctly, they can bolster their images as well as their careers. Should they make too

245

many mistakes, they can be stuck with a "white elephant" and held up to public ridicule. Westway and Times Square reveal the hazards as well as the opportunities of political entrepreneurship.

The Parisian context is much different. Lines of innovation are straight, smooth, and more predictable. This is partly due to the fact that Paris encompasses a much smaller terrain than either New York or London. Space for development is limited and this makes for a clearer set of opportunities. More than political geography, political culture shapes the planning context. Though the word "technocrat" has begun to sour, the French technocrat is still an important and respected figure. To be a haute fonctionnaire is to occupy an important place in decision making. Many of the hautes fonctionnaires go through the Ecole National d'Administration (ENA) and learn the same values, approaches, and techniques for dealing with problems. They even adopt common mannerisms and accepted forms of pronunciation. To be an Enarque (graduate of the ENA) is to be assured of an elite position within the ranks of technocrats.

It turns out that in France, politicians and especially technocrats like to put things in a neat and ranked order. Disorder is the bane of planners and little can be accomplished or settled with a sloppy agenda. Projects are typically generated with an eye to coordinating different pieces of development and aligning them along a common axis. Much of Paris is built along this principle, so that major boulevards are frequently broken by a common plaza that serves as a reference point for the local environment.[8]

There is a certain analogy between the structure of the built environment and the structure of decision making. Enarques are the reference point for the planning hierarchy. They are joined by leading politicians (sometimes themselves Enarques who have chosen a different career path). From this common command post, the directives flow to the planners, architects, and researchers who carry out the professional work. Directives also seep downward to the city councillors and other politicians in the local arrondissements.

The analogy does have its limits. Directives are not made in a single-step flow or in a straight line of military commands. Technocrats at the lower levels are able to influence their superiors merely by shaping the information. Politicians at the grass roots do respond to what the leaders have determined and are likely to modify priorities. But as much as directives can be concentrated in a democratic and open society, they do in fact originate at the top and take root at the bottom. That formulation at the top involves the setting of major priorities, ordering them into preferences, and coordinating them between the state and La Ville de Paris. Les Halles, La Défense, and Secteur Seine Sud-Est show how political-technocratic elites cohere in order to bring about sharp changes.

London does not so much join its political-technocratic elite as it does distinguish between them through a formal division of labor. Careful distinctions are made between the roles of politicians (members) and those of technocrats (officers).[9] Although those distinctions are formally followed in New York and Paris, they count for much more in London. British tradition and the habits of the civil service have always emphasized the importance of a neutral bureaucracy, ready to carry out orders without regard to partisan preference. New Yorkers and Parisians have fewer illusions about the purity of technocrats. In New York, the tradition of a "spoils system" has shattered any pretense about nonpartisan technocrats.[10] In Paris, heads of government freely change prefects each time there is a political shift. Moreover, in New York and Paris, technocrats became embroiled in politics because there was little alternative. In New York the fading influence of the political party no longer shielded the bureaucracy from political responsibility. In Paris, the shakiness of the Third and Fourth Republics forced the bureaucracy to provide governmental continuity.

Not having experienced party disintegration or governmental instability, London's technocrats enjoy a strong professionalism. Not only do the traditions of the British culture bespeak the virtues of nonpartisan technocrats, but daily work habits give force to the segregation of planners from politicians. Most politicians in London have full-time jobs in industry or in business. The technocrats give their full time to government, and they use their knowledge to influence the earliest stages of decision making. After plans have jelled, planners tactfully enlist the support of politicians. Motorways is a good example of how London's technocrats work. The project was entirely initiated by planners. Straight-line projections of auto traffic told planners that London needed to be saved from slow strangulation. They promoted a ringway system that purported to preserve London's neighborhoods. Swayed by the evidence, politicians eagerly gave their support to ringways. Covent Garden was also in the hands of planners, who promoted a scheme they believed would safeguard Central London. Again, the politicians joined them. The development of the Docklands was first taken up by a consortium of planners from five boroughs. Politicians gave the planners free reign, until the central government interceded.

Within the three cities, the interactions between the political-technocratic elite are different. At one end of the spectrum is New York, where politicians take early cues from planners but soon occupy the most visible roles. At the other end is London, where planners begin the process of strategic planning and continue to play a visible role. In between is the Parisian model, where politicians and technocrats coalesce at the very beginning, work up a common scheme, and both remain visible throughout the process.

Who Does What and How

Questions about the "what," "who," and "how" of power can be translated into an investigation of the *form, content,* and *operations* of power. Form pursues the "what" question by investigating the basic shape of decision making. Form analyzes the relationship among formal decision makers as well as the role of outside groups in the process. Content examines the "who" question by identifying the decision makers, their status, their values, and their perception of the "public interest." Operation analyzes the "how" question by focusing on the style and techniques of influence. Operation speaks to how decisions are politically executed.

The Form of Power

New York's power structure is spherical in shape, with major participants orbiting around the political/technocratic elite (the Mayor, the Governor, the heads of City Planning, and ad hoc collaborators who are drawn from other political ranks).[11] Interest groups, community boards, the press, and politicians are loosely interspersed throughout the sphere. In Paris the form is pyramidal. Top politicians and technocrats are at the apex. On subsequent strata of the pyramid are other levels of the political-technocratic elite. At the base of the pyramid are the directors of various enterprises for public development and the interest groups. In London the form resembles a series of channels. Each channel holds its own political-technocratic elite. We should also recall that in London interest groups are formally incorporated into organizations that have access to different channels of government. These interest groups are frequently supported by different tiers of government and have been used by one tier or another to work against a development project. Figure 8.1 portrays the form of power in each of the three cities.

The spherical configuration of power in New York conveys the notion of free-floating actors circulating around a core of top politicians and high-level technocrats. Outside the core, political coalitions are generally fluid. Within the core, alliances are more stable. In contrast to other policy arenas, land-use decisions are undertaken by a cohesive political elite.[12] New York's mayors and governors collaborated on

Westway (Lindsay, Beame, Koch and Rockefeller, Carey, Cuomo) as they did on Times Square (Koch and Cuomo). Most of the Borough Presidents gave the top leadership their tacit, if not their open, support. The Mayor's office was also the leading force in securing approval for Lincoln West. Again the core held and the Board of Estimate cooperated.

Although the core was stable, it needed to interact with other interests. This interaction occurred shortly after top leaders decided to support the projects. It also meant these projects would be modified by the individuals, groups, and institutions that were consulted. In Westway and Times Square, the Mayor(s) and the Governor(s) were in constant communication with labor, business, the developers, the press, and the relevant community boards. In Lincoln West, the Mayor and Deputy Mayor worked with developers and the community boards to shape planning. If Westway II and Lincoln West II are going to be built, they will require a similar kind of intercession.

The pyramidal configuration of Paris tells much of its own story. Elites in the central and/or local governments put the decisions together, leaving little room for outside competition. Unlike New York, there is little or no solicitation of outside support before plans are fully conceived. Even then, the political-technocratic elite does not seek support or try to win over interest groups. Rather, they follow formal procedures and submit their plans to the appropriate legislative body. The elite pushes for speedy ratification and does not lobby private groups. In Les Halles, the Prefect and technocrats from the Parisian Planning Service drew up the plans that were eventually approved by the City Council.[13] In La Défense, the Prefect acted again, and after consultation with local mayors, those plans were approved by the central government. In Secteur Seine Sud-Est, technocrats and Mayor Chirac drew up a plan and managed its ratification with relatively little difficulty.

As the Parisian pyramid illustrates, most of the interaction with interest groups occurs after projects are in the hands of the development directors—or during the stage of implementation. At that point, interaction also jumps upward to the political-technocratic elite. By then, however, the basic contours for the new environment are already set. Interest groups can negotiate rental agreements, architectural modifications, and other details of a project. But they are hardly in a position to shape its principal design.

London's channels of power show three governmental tiers arranged in a slightly descending horizontal order. Power is distributed into each of the tiers along what is supposed to be clear-cut functional lines.

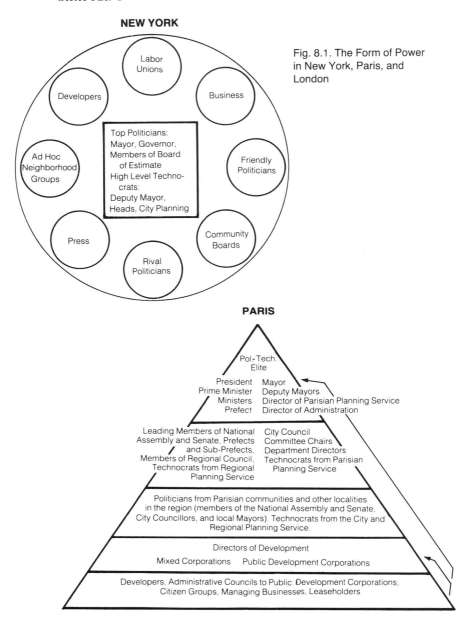

NEW YORK

Labor Unions

Developers

Business

Ad Hoc Neighborhood Groups

Top Politicians:
Mayor, Governor,
Members of Board
of Estimate
High Level Techno-
crats:
Deputy Mayor,
Heads, City Planning

Friendly Politicians

Press

Rival Politicians

Community Boards

Fig. 8.1. The Form of Power in New York, Paris, and London

PARIS

Pol-Tech. Elite

President   Mayor
Prime Minister   Deputy Mayors
    Ministers   Director of Parisian Planning Service
     Prefect   Director of Administration

Leading Members of National   City Council
Assembly and Senate, Prefects   Committee Chairs
    and Sub-Prefects,   Department Directors
Members of Regional Council,   Technocrats from Parisian
Technocrats from Regional   Planning Service
Planning Service

Politicians from Parisian communities and other localities
in the region (members of the National Assembly and Senate,
City Councillors, and local Mayors). Technocrats from the City and
Regional Planning Service.

Directors of Development

Mixed Corporations   Public Development Corporations

Developers, Administrative Councils to Public Development Corporations,
Citizen Groups, Managing Businesses, Leaseholders

LONDON

Central Government	
Ministers & Members	

Ministries:
  Environment
  Trade and Industry
Parliamentary Committees:
  Urban Affairs
  Environment
Royal Commissions
Panels of Inquiry
	Inspectors
	Directors and Officers:
	  Environment
	  Housing
	  Transport

GLC-Sponsored Organizations

Greater London Council	
Members	Officers

Leader, Whips,
Committees and
Committee Chairs:
  Planning
  Environment
  Housing and Transport
	Chief Executive
	Directors:
	  Strategic Planning
	  Environment
	  Housing and Transport

Forums

The Boroughs	
Members	Officers

Leader, Whips, and
Committee Chairs:
  Planning
  Environment
  Housing and Transport
	Town Clerk
	Directors:
	  Environment
	  Housing and Transport

London Docklands Development Corporation

Docklands Development Committee

In practice the lines are less clear, and conflicts between different tiers have caused ambivalence about power and its proper exercise.

The ambivalence toward power has manifested itself in a number of ways. One is that the GLC and the central government gave lip service to sharing power with the boroughs, but grew impatient when the desired results were not forthcoming. Thus, the early planning of Covent Garden was carried out by the GLC, which agreed to share power with two boroughs under a Consortium. When that venture became too complicated, GLC leaders began to worry. They realized that the last thing they wanted was a grueling and embarrassing debate between themselves and the boroughs. Their response was to abolish the Consortium and replace it with a GLC-controlled mechanism. The head of the GLC's planning team on Covent Garden explained the move as a political sleight of hand. "It was Big Brother GLC," he admitted, "saying we want to do it; we don't think the boroughs and ourselves can do it [together]."[14]

Similar impatience with the boroughs was evident in the Docklands. The project was initially in the hands of a five-borough consortium, only this time it was the central government that became impatient. The consortium was abolished and replaced by a development corporation more to the liking of Conservatives at Whitehall.

A second source of ambivalence comes from the difficulty of dealing openly with the issue of direct public participation. The British take pride in grass-roots democracy and would like to respect popular sentiment. But political principles have clashed with economic pressures for development. Those in command have been put in the contradictory position of initially sponsoring popular participation, only to deny its conclusions.

In Covent Garden, officers of the GLC first solicited public opinion, but when it turned out to be negative, they misrepresented that opinion before an official tribunal. The Deputy Chief of the Covent Garden Planning Team was fired because he sided with the community against the GLC plan.[15]

In Motorways, the GLC was taken aback by citizen opposition to its plan. Both politicians and technocrats tried to write off criticism as belonging to a minority of naysayers, until a GLC election revealed the strength of the opposition.

What then can be concluded about power holders and about those same power holders vis-à-vis outside groups? Evidently, different forms of power prevail in each city. New York is led by a mayor surrounded by a core of actors and a fluid group of outside participants. Interest groups are openly accommodated early in the process. Paris is led exclusively by politicians and technocrats, representing the state and the city. Interest groups do not play a significant role in the making of essential decisions, and French officials have not been bashful about dismissing them as intrusions into the general interest.

In London, power is segmented between politicians and technocrats in different tiers of government. Although the divisions of power are set out in theory, the facts reveal a good deal of ambiguity in practice. Moreover, there is no single focal point for decision making. Leadership often falls into limbo with no single politician able to pull the different tiers together. What remains are strata of politicians and technocrats at each tier, trying to cope with interest groups, without substantial coordination at the top.

As discussed in Chapters 6 and 7, the abolition of the GLC has not yet eliminated old political patterns. Segmentation between politicians and technocrats continues at all levels of government. GLCs-in-exile have already begun to fill the void left by abolition and now represent the collective interests of most Inner London boroughs. Instead of the GLC, interest groups now find sustenance from the Association of London Authorities, the London Strategic Planning Unit, and the Inner London Educational Authority. Where formerly one GLC sufficed, now several GLCs-in-exile function as a shadow tier of government (for further discussion, see Chapter 10).

This exacerbates the countervaillance of power within the system, putting politicians and technocrats in a confusing and awkward position. London's political-technocratic elite can neither easily manage contacts with interest groups (as in New York) nor keep groups at arm's length (as in Paris). The result is embarrassment, contradiction, and the frequent reversal of decisions.

The Content of Power

Most mayors of New York City and, to a lesser extent, governors of New York State are professional politicians. That is, they have spent most of their adult lives seeking and occupying political office. Mayor Ed Koch was a Congressman and city councilman for eleven years before gaining the mayoralty in 1977. Governor Hugh Carey spent fifteen years in Congress before he became Governor of New York State in 1974. Never having held public office before coming to Albany, Mario Cuomo is an exceptional figure. Gaining high office in New York requires political apprenticeship. Politicians are not usually drawn from the ranks of corporations or developers. Their social backgrounds vary and their experience is multifaceted. Most of them spend their lives working with community groups, business, labor, the press, and other politicians. Their experience and outlook bespeak their profession as bargainers, brokers, and spokesmen for a variegated public.

These then are the internal values of New York's politicians, the influence *within* them. What about the external pressures and the influence *upon* them? No longer are top politicians selected by party leaders; more often they earn nomination by running in primary elections. This opens up the system to interest groups. And it is a fact that realtors, developers, and businessmen contribute heavily to mayoral campaigns. Well-connected lawyers are hired to lobby on behalf of these interests. But it is also the case that labor and community groups are active and powerful in New York. Mario Cuomo was above all a candidate of organized labor. Other governors and mayors have won office by building a coalition among business, labor and community groups. A favorable press has always been an important component of victory. To be sure, developers and banks have influence over those who make decisions—and that influence is substantial and dispropor-tionate—but it is also shared with a host of other groups and organi-zations.[16] In New York, the politicians believe they represent the "public interest" when they piece together a compromise between dif-ferent groups. The "public interest" is constructed out of the day-to-day reality of working with outside groups. Its construction is induc-tive, incremental, and pragmatic.[17]

Paris presents a contrasting picture. As noted, Parisian decision makers are a class unto themselves. Their apprenticeship is a product of formal training and short-term internships taken under the super-vision of senior officials. The sense of a public service élan is reinforced by the fact that leading politicians are almost always full-time career-ists. Structural conditions within French local government encourage this by allowing mayors to nominate elected city councillors as their deputies. In Paris a number of Deputy Mayors are regularly chosen from within the City Council. In 1986 twenty-seven city councillors served, in varying degrees of importance, as Deputy Mayors to Jacques Chirac. The system permits a bridging of function and contact between city councillors and the Parisian executive. The Deputy May-ors are put in charge of specialized functions (budget, transport, urban development) and become extensions of mayoral authority.

From 1976 to 1988 bridges were extended between Paris and the French state by virtue of Chirac's personal clout, his position as Prime Minister, or his position as Mayor of France's most important city. During this time it was common for Deputy Mayors and chief plan-ners to meet with ministers and members of the National Assembly.

The French also permit politicians to hold more than one office at a time (*cumul des mandats*). This can be done at multiple levels of govern-ment so that the system is knit together by innumerable threads of communication.[18] Thus mayors or city councillors may, at the same time, hold seats in a municipality and in the National Assembly or Senate. The cumul des mandats became especially significant for Pa-risian Gaullists when they won the 1986 national elections. Not only was the Mayor of Paris also Prime Minister, but a number of Deputy Mayors held seats in the nation's legislature.

All in all, French politicians and technocrats are well deserving of their description as an "elite." By selection, training, interaction, and élan they constitute an extraordinary stratum of leadership.

It is not surprising that this elite would develop a special conception of the "public interest." The idea begins as an abstract principle and takes on meaning as young politicians and technocrats work at their métier. This meaning is also shaped by a political or social philosophy. Individuals can be identified as belonging to the Left, the Center, the Right, or as planner-technocrats. Philosophy shapes behavior and approach. The "public interest" is constructed out of deductive, wholistic principles that are then applied to problem solving.

This approach is extended into basic attitudes. Politicians and technocrats believe they are the holders of the public domain and entrusted with its proper representation. The idea of making policy around the wishes of interest groups or a narrow segment of the public strikes them as bizarre. When a leading planner was asked why there was so little consultation with the community around Les Halles, an incredulous look came across his face, his voice took on a tone of astonishment, and his reply was resolute: "Why sir, that is complete idiocy. It's truly idiotic to think that one could build Paris around the wishes of neighborhood people. Don't you see Paris is for everyone, not just for the Parisians, and certainly not just for the neighborhood associations. It is for France. Paris is for the world."[19]

The planner continued and this time turned the question around as he asked, "Would one ever try to build New York or London around the wishes of the neighborhoods?" The rather surprising response to him was, yes—sometimes. Yet the fact that the question could be posed by a French planner as rhetorical is indicative of his approach toward the issue.

In London the content of power is more complicated. Like their Parisian counterparts, local politicians orient their values along party affiliations. Class is an important reference for deciding issues. Labour members tend to side with poorer, nonpropertied residents; Conservatives are apt to sympathize with business and property owners. When it comes to building office towers and high-density commercial centers, it is the Tories who push for development and the Socialists who favor conservation.

Unlike the Parisians, London's leadership is unpaid and part time. When they serve, they do so with great personal sacrifice. Regular members have even less time to devote to politics than do party leaders and chairmen. Most politicians function in the shadows of power rather than as its substance. Elkin sums it up in a quote from a veteran politician:

"There tend to be only a few members who can spend the time required to be Leader or Chairman. Most ordinary members give only two or three hours a week. They tend to be passengers frankly. They have confidence in people who have gone into the problem and who have the time, unless they see something outrageous and then they get upset."[20]

Hard-working as the leading politicians may be, they are still amateurs. Politics is neither their livelihood nor their usual preoccupation.

Covent Garden was particularly susceptible to a clash between amateurs who fought the battle on ideological lines. It was a struggle between militant Socialists who wanted to keep the old community intact and ardent capitalists who wanted to rush into post-industrial transformation. The Socialists came out of a cadre of young community activists. The capitalists were largely represented on GLC and borough committees. Early in the project, Conservatives wanted to deliver land into the hands of property developers. One committee chairman suggested that the GLC assemble land and turn it over to developers. His idea was to lease six chunks of terrain to separate investors, each being obliged to commit a stipulated amount of money for development.[21]

The enthusiasm for full-scale development was matched by a decided enmity toward the existing community. Given the Conservative's urgent pleas for radical reconstruction, it was not surprising that they would look askance at community participation. But they dared not say that aloud. Instead they spoke in whispers and a Conservative member wrote a letter to the Chief Planning Officer telling him to "back-pedal" on the idea of local consultation. He explained that pressure groups "lead to a lot more trouble than they are worth."[22]

Although these suggestions reveal the strongest pro-development attitudes, none of them ever took hold. As described in Chapter 7, the opposition was steadfast and central authorities were sympathetic to the cause of conservation.

The attitude and perspective of British planners explain why development projects are initially so bold. London's technocrats are a breed apart from their political overseers. Their beliefs are clear-cut and their conceptions are often sweeping. Theirs is an ideology born from the experience of World War II, when Nazi bombs laid waste to London, Coventry, and Bristol. Postwar recovery taught them to treat city building as a problem in radical reconstruction. The aim of British planning was to "sweep . . . it all away in one operation."[23] Ruin and obsolescence were the diseases—radical reconstruction and orderliness were the remedies.

It was no wonder that the first thing London planners wanted to do for Covent Garden was make it a "comprehensive development area." After that, they laid out plans to bring order into the community. As one member of the Planning Team said, "Houses will no longer be spotted around, . . . shopping will be put together instead of being patched around."[24]

The same ideology dominated the idea for Motorways. Automobiles and people simply could not mix. Areas need to be segregated according to use. An ordering of the process required that a hierarchy of uses be established, so that different ringways served different purposes and different people.[25] London would have to be catapulted from its obsolescence by the greatest metropolitan auto routes in Europe— maybe in the world.

The irony is that it was the technocrats and not the politicians who led the way on Covent Garden and on Motorways. Conviction led the technocrats to convince the politicians. Like all ideologues, the planners also believed that those citizens who were not already convinced would soon be persuaded. Believing they were acting in the "public interest," the planners thought the public would naturally follow.

As guardians of the "public interest" and as devoted professionals, London's planners are like their Parisian cousins. The difference is that there is a fault line that separates the politicians from the technocrats. Politicians may cross that line and follow technocratic advice, but they do so with some trepidation. And when the political system begins to quake—when the tiers of government move in opposite directions— that fault line turns into a chasm. Politicians are embarrassed by their defeat, the judgments of technocrats are held in doubt, and the entire system is held in question by its critics.

The Operations of Power

The history, structure, and dynamics of each city have contributed to the making of different kinds of political operations. In New York the operation of power can be described as political entrepreneurship, in Paris it is executive directed, and in London it is organizational response and counter-response.[26]

Political entrepreneurship depends upon coalition building as its *modus operandi*. In New York, it has centered around one or two dominant personalities who by dint of character and skill, have been able to patch together agreements. Entrepreneurship draws much of its style from the tradition of "boss" politics that typified American cities when they were the bastions of heavy industry and ethnic politics. Industrial cities bred a style in which political bosses traded ambiguous favors ("do it for me and I'll owe you one"). Their post-industrial successors have stressed the cooler politics of interest accommodation ("here's how we can cut up the pie").

Nonetheless, the success of political entrepreneurship still rests on the energy of personality. Charisma is important, bargaining is a primary tool, and making the big deal is the main objective. Because of this, the planning agenda tends to be short term and to focus on decisions that are made one at a time. The term given to this is "disjointed incrementalism." Briefly paraphrased, it means that decisions are made through sequences of small cumulative steps.[27]

The decisional calculus of political entrepreneurship is based on the self-interest of the participants.[28] Developers intend to earn a profit, labor unionists want to work, residents hope to safeguard their neighborhood, and minor politicians want to defend their constituency. Political entrepreneurs must construct a happy solution for a majority of these interests. And they must do it not as neutral brokers but as partisan catalysts. They may negotiate, cajole, and sometimes broker between parties, but above all they must push and encourage. As such, political entrepreneurs throw political capital into a venture and become risk takers. These risks bring dramatic victories and equally dramatic defeats.

Times Square and Westway furnish examples of both the success and the failure of political entrepreneurship. For years top politicians labored, without result, to reconstruct Times Square. In 1980 Governor Cuomo and Mayor Koch hit upon a promising formula. Every decision tested the strength of that formula and both leaders built a common coalition. At the Board of Estimate, Koch and Cuomo triumphantly grabbed the prize.

Westway was a protracted conflict where coalitions won and then, surprisingly, lost. For a while it looked like Koch and Cuomo would gain this prize as well. To these leaders' consternation, the courts questioned Westway, and other sources of support unexpectedly caved in. The words of Yogi Berra hold as true for New York's politics as they do for its baseball. When his team fell hopelessly behind, Berra wryly observed, "It ain't over till it's over."

In Paris, executive direction begins with a set of prescriptions, followed by consensus building. The prescriptions and the consensus are hammered out within the political-technocratic elite.

Before a prescription is adapted, there must be an inspection of alternate planning rationales. One planner's rationale may differ from another's. Infighting at the top is not uncommon. Victory by a technocrat means more political influence. Defeat means loss of status and

influence. Different technocrats may solicit different political sponsors. Those who emerge with a well-forged alliance and with top politicians at their sides will prevail.

In Paris a top technocrat can stake his future on a single crucial decision. Its rejection can lead to a resignation and to a discreet change in
professional position. When the top Parisian planner promoted an idea
for Secteur Seine Sud-Est that turned sour, he eventually shifted to a
less conspicuous post. It may also be important to carry out the correct
party affiliation. By the reasoning of the system, partisan affiliation
shapes a planner's approach to a problem. The wrong approach can
also lead to a change of assignment.

Given the pyramidal form of decision making, an alliance between
technocrats and politicians is a necessity. Such allliances are steeped in
the nineteenth-century tradition of Haussmann, who joined the formal
authority of the prefecture with the emperorship of Napoleon III. Under that combination, Haussman built Paris as the commercial seat for
heavy industry.[29] The operations of post-industrial Paris are, however,
more complicated. Eight prefects now partake of the power that once
belonged to one. Political power is also distributed somewhat more
broadly to democratically accountable officials.

Nonetheless, it is at the top where technocrats win or lose, and
where prefects or other technocrats must have their plans ratified. The
"top" is usually defined by a conjuncture of authority between the state
and La Ville de Paris. Even though a project may be identified as belonging to the state, there is consultation and usually collaboration.
When asked what would occur if the state proceeded to build in Paris
without consultation, a Deputy Mayor responded, "Why that would
mean war. It would be a war which nobody could really win."[30]

Once political agreement is reached (by no means a certainty), decisions become more a problem of accurate transmission than of further debate. Modifications can be made at lower levels, but these are
generally minor and unlikely to disrupt the thrust of change. It is this
centralization of decision making that gives operations on the built environment their quality of executive direction. In post-industrial Paris,
decision making is usually collective. Hardly ever will the decision
maker be just one person. At times it may consist of two individuals,
and more frequently it will hinge on several officials (e.g., President
and Prefect, Mayor and Director of Planning).

Executive direction is often masked—perhaps mystified—by the
widespread belief that the adoption of a single plan is the only rational
way to proceed. The operations of power are perceived as ruled by a
higher order of thinking. In fact there is a phrase in French planning

259

parlance that justifies the inevitability of decisions. It is called "the dictatorship of sound ideas."[31]

The decisional calculus of executive direction is the supremacy of the rational idea. Once the idea occupies its political place, it is carried out. The idea moves through the rest of the system and organizational interests are then plugged into it. Developers, tenants, business, and local authorities are accommodated within the framework of the idea. This is how La Défense was brought into being. Building capacity, height, and density were not arrived at by ongoing negotiations with clients, but decided years before at the desks of high-level technocrats. And this is how Secteur Seine Sud-Est is currently being built. Teams of planners are already laying out the dimensions of the land, piece by piece, in accord with a general plan laid out in 1973. In Paris the planning agenda tends to be long term.[32]

In London organizational response and counter-response is dictated by one governmental tier producing plans and another responding to those plans. In contrast to New York and Paris, the role of a preeminent personality is much diminished, if not entirely absent. Much of the work is done by separate committees, commissions, consortia, or joint working parties of technocrats and politicians. Often committee members are not even drawn from the borough affected by a new plan. Their stakes in a development are tied neither to their constituency nor to their reelection. The politician's role is neither that of an entrepreneur nor of a director, but rather to work as part of a larger team and deliberate in a larger process. Above all, the average member is a team deliberator who rarely abandons fellow partisans.

London's system is depersonalized and the responses are more or less automatic. One tier of government acts and expects that its decisions will be ratified, modified, or rejected. Most policy is broken into pieces so that the boroughs, the GLC or GLCs-in-exile, and the central government can take charge of pieces while trying to make sense of the whole. This places a premium on cooperation and coordination.

There is tradition to sustain this approach. The boroughs—or what is equivalent to neighborhood government—have always enjoyed a certain amount of independence. As London grew, the old London County Council entered into relationships with outlying counties.[33] And as London became Greater London, the relationship between the sum of the parts and the whole became more sophisticated. A set of mechanisms grew up to adjust those relationships and Londoners became accustomed to following established procedures.

The traditions also held that each tier, and each organization connected to that tier, had its own constituency and its own priorities. The work of each tier depended upon its own popular base, and organizational routines were adapted to meet its needs. Boroughs would approach a problem, say, as it impacted upon the availability of cheap local housing. The GLC would approach the same problem as a way of boosting the attraction of Central London. The central government would either arbitrate between the tiers or make its own decisions.

The planning agenda reflected these differences. It began as a long-term proposition (by the GLC) but was modified by short-term concerns as it passed through different hands.

London's decisional calculus, then, is shaped by the routines of its different governments. Outside groups are able to plug into those routines and become cogs in the machinery. The most used cog is the Forum. In Covent Garden, the Forum helped resolve technical questions. In the development of the Docklands, the Forum (among other organizations) helped make basic policy. Indeed, for the Docklands, the organization of outside groups into the apparatus was enough to bring about the accusation that decision making was paralyzed by special interests.

In London decisions are made in several ways. From simplest to most complex, first is by a willing compliance of the localities to central government initiatives (as in the Green Belt); second is by dictate of the central government (the Docklands); and third, more subtly, by compromise among the tiers (Covent Garden). Decisions are unmade by organizations taking hold of a crucial tier. In Covent Garden, outside groups worked to win the support of the boroughs and the central government. In Motorways, both the boroughs and various organizations reversed the decision by winning the GLC.

A Note on Moses, Delouvrier, Abercrombie, and Robson

Most political systems are characterized by change and continuity. The changing aspects of a metropolis can be seen in its built environment or in the personalities who hold office. Thus urban development may sometimes take on a frantic pace and at other times slow to a crawl. Eventually top politicians and great builders are replaced. By the same token, continuity can be found in the relative constancy of political structures and in the political culture of a people. If a great builder is to have an impact, that builder must manage those structures and work within the context of a political culture. These factors continue to shape the styles and operations of great urban builders.

The builders of New York, Paris, and London shared one major characteristic. They emerged at a critical time and built their cities for a post-industrial order. Apart from that, their style and methods of operation were very different and reflect the political and cultural exigencies of the cities in which they worked. Robert Moses was a political entrepreneur. Paul Delouvrier became an executive director. Patrick Abercrombie and William Robson were thinkers whose ideas percolated through the organizational responses of government.

Moses was a man who inched his way to power through the favors of Governor Alfred E. Smith.[34] Smith was a former Tammany politician—a political boss—whose streetcorner slang won the affection of New Yorkers. Through Smith, Moses built his reputation as a pioneer in planning. Moses called himself a "reformed reformer,"[35] meaning that he knew enough to recognize the need for change and was cynical enough to accomplish it.

Moses grew into somebody very different from his patron; he was no ordinary street boss and he despised Tammany. His clientele included banks, labor unions, contractors, bond underwriters, and hundreds of other benefactors. Moses gave private interests a stake in parks, bridges, and highways. Public works made the money flow; it gave big financial houses something to insure, engineers something to design, and laborers something to build. It also gave Moses his *raison d'être*, for he was the one who negotiated the plans and awarded the plums. Contracts for work were a form of patronage. Patronage created dependencies, and dependencies meant that Moses could bring his power to bear. Moses walked a tightrope between public and private interests. His balancing rods were his clients, the press, and a cheering public.[36]

Compare this with Paul Delouvrier. This great builder began his career out of the French *grands corps* and worked as a high-level technocrat for Jean Monnet, who planned the postwar recovery of France. When General de Gaulle summoned him to Paris, Delouvrier switched technocratic roles.

De Gaulle's early words to Delouvrier were instructive of how things would work. "I want everything put in order," exclaimed the General, "You have my trust and my authority."[37]

These were fairly vague words, but they could also be compelling. Delouvrier's first reaction was to consult history. He borrowed a copy of Haussmann's memoirs and learned that the great Prefect had seventeen years to do his work and that he was supported during all those years by Napoleon III. How was Delouvrier, a novice to Parisian planning, going to make his mark in a fraction of the time?[38]

Delouvrier determined that the key to power lay in working directly with the Prime Minister. In a pinch he could always call upon de Gaulle's promise, but Delouvrier's success would lie in painstaking preparation. He therefore set to work by keeping a staff of just four professionals. Together they would make the diagnosis and prescribe the remedies. Discussion of these plans gave Delouvrier direct access to key ministers. It also provided him with a much needed alliance that actively directed post-industrial change.

Still a third model can be seen in the personages of Sir Patrick Abercrombie and William Robson. Both were intellectuals rather than operatives. Abercrombie was an architect of great distinction. His work was accomplished through committees, issued as reports, and finally adopted by governmental bodies of one sort or another.[39]

Robson was a professor at the University of London. His work was not put on the drawing boards but on the pages of scholarly books.[40] When London became ripe for political reorganization, Robson organized a group of scholars who gave legitimacy to the cause. Their testimony before the Herbert Commission turned out to be decisive.[41]

The implementation of Abercrombie's and Robson's work took place at a distance from the personalities themselves. Both men worked apart from one another. Once their ideas were digested, they would make their imprint on London's environment. But it was an imprint that was passed through the hoppers of government and was processed like any other innovation. The segmented nature and organizational routines of London took hold. The makers of the idea were divorced from its realization.

The approach that each builder took is also reflective of each system. Robert Moses was not as much a long-term strategist as he was a short-term tactician. He always admonished planners to search for "limited and realizable objectives."[42] Moses showed contempt for "long-haired planners" and delighted in taking part in "the sweat and mud of battle."[43]

Delouvrier was quite the opposite. Though a man of action, he approached planning as a long-term strategist. "From the start," Delouvrier confided, "I needed a philosophy and I found it."[44] La Ville de Paris had to be conceived in relation to its parts. Subcenters must be tied to it.

Abercrombie and Robson were conceptualizers. They laid out the skeletal structure and waited for others to add the flesh. Abercrombie would speak in metaphor of London as a "living and organic structure" whose parts were suffering from "overgrowth and decay."[45] Robson was a Fabian Socialist and a democrat. He wanted a functional ordering of government to fulfill those principles.[46]

Uncanny as it may seem, the professional biographies of these men are microcosms of their environment. Moses, the political entrepreneur, brokered his way to power and worked at the seams of the public sphere and outside interests. To do this successfully, he had to be "pragmatic" and pursue a short-term strategy.[47] Delouvrier, the executive director, was a creature of the state who could command its sub-organizations into compliance. His most pressing task was to implement the grand strategy. Abercrombie and Robson acted within a set of organizational responses. After their role was played, their jobs were done.

To RECAPITULATE, we make the following propositions about power in three cities. In New York the structure is a pluralist-corporatist hybrid, the form is spherical, and the content consists of top politicians leading the actions of technocrats or interest groups. The operation is governed by political entrepreneurs. In Paris the structure is mobilizing corporatist, the form is pyramidal, the content includes a political-technocratic elite orchestrating the action. The operation is run by executive directors. In London the structure is liberal corporatist and planning flows through a series of governmental channels. The content of power is segmented between politicians and technocrats who work within governmental channels. The operation takes place between those channels as responses and counter-responses.

In the next chapter these dimensions of power are treated under the single concept of political combination. Since each city holds a different political combination, how does it shape planning strategy? We shall see that much as political combinations differ, in New York, Paris, and London so, too, does planning.

CHAPTER 9

Political Combinations and Planning

*God and his reason commanded [man] to subdue the earth . . . and lay out
something upon it that was his own, ... He that in obedience to this command of God subdued, tilled, and sowed any part of it, thereby annexed to it
something that was his property, which another had no title to, nor could without injury take from him.*—John Locke (1690)

Property is theft.—Pierre Joseph Proudhon (1840)

Property is a system of authority established by government.
—Charles Lindblom (1977)

Political Combinations

POLITICAL institutions and practices do not generally take root in
unfamiliar soil. More often they are a product of history, culture,
and economic necessity. Trying to establish the genesis of a city's institutions and practices is like trying to trace the first wave in an ocean
of complexity. History, culture, and economics mix in many skeins
and relationships. Form follows function, but sometimes function is
changed by the form of decision making. How a decision is made will
bear upon what will be made.

The idea is an old one. Its beginnings can be traced to Aristotle's
Politics, its praxis can be found in Madison's *Federalist Papers*, and its
revision can be read in Schattschneider's *Semisovereign People*.[1] The
very form of the system provides some actors with strategic position.
Strategic position allows those same actors to shape the agenda and
influence its outcomes.[2]

In New York, Paris, and London, the major actors were the politicians, the technocrats, and the interest groups. Those actors were
combined by both the form and the functions of the political apparatus. That mixture yielded different combinations of power within each
city, and it was a particular combination of power that brought a perspective to planning and to the marketplace. Thus although the first
wave in the ocean may not be identifiable, the last ones to wash ashore
can be spotted. They run from the interests of the actors, to the combinations of power formed by those interests, to the perspectives taken
by that combination, and finally to the decision itself.

Consider the politician's role. It is in the interests of politicians to satisfy their constituents and deliver something for their city. That "something" may vary from place to place. In New York it may mean more jobs and economic stimulation. In Paris it may be a great public attraction for culture and commerce. In London it may be the preservation of open space and a humanistic environment. Whatever that "something" may be, politicians need to look good before their constituencies. In order to sit and decide, they must continue to stand up for issues and run for office.

What about the technocrat's interest in planning? Technocrats often want control, rationality, and a comprehensive scheme. Their inclination is to make the parts fit, and they want to present that "fit" in a professional manner so they can impress the politicians and the public. There are differences between European and American technocrats. European planners are more accustomed to power and status. Their values are more elitist and they are more commonly regarded as high-status professionals. Although American planners have doubts about their professional image, they do hold to a strong credo. Study after study points up the high value American planners give to rational comprehensiveness.[3] The technocratic perspective is usually long term, and it strives for completeness.

Interest groups have a different interest in planning. They are almost by definition "parochial." Their intersts are limited to the situation, to the immediacies of the question, and to a piecemeal approach to the environment. This is as true for neighborhood associations as it is for business people. Community groups want to protect low-density environments and guard against outside intrusion—regardless of the cost to the local economy. Developers want to build—the more profitable the better and in Manhattan this means the higher the better. They would pack the city landscape with a blind eye toward the environment.[4]

How these interests are put together explains a good deal about the politics of each city—and ultimately about the choices that are available. We have seen that New York's top politicians brought interest groups into the decisional process at an early stage. By experience, reason, and instinct Mayor Koch and Governor Cuomo knew that they first needed to work out the issues with the interest groups. Only after the broad contours of a project were agreed upon could they contend with procedure and the city's political institutions. Koch and Cuomo were responding to the strongest points in the system by putting their own executive powers in league with the power of interest groups. New York is a city where executive powers are formidable, legislative structures are weak,[5] and interest groups are strong.

In Paris, interest groups were consulted only at the later stage of decision making. This was logical for political elites, since they were the ones who had the power and they knew it. Paris is a city where political leadership is strong and supported by an equally powerful technocratic class. Further down the line, the political institutions are tangible and authoritative. This is particularly true of the bureaucracy, which holds a good deal of discretionary power. Interest groups may be well organized (unions, employer associations, community associations) but are not influential on planning issues.[6]

In London, interest groups enter the decisional process somewhere at mid-stage. Leadership at the top is overburdened and diffuse. Technocrats at the GLC and the boroughs have been mainstays of the system; it is at these middle and lower levels where procedure and structure are firm. And it is precisely at those levels where interest groups have found refuge and support. For their part, interest groups are well organized and active at the grass roots (ward and borough) of the system.[7] London is a metropolis where the pulling power of top politicians is weak, but where the deliberative capacity of legislatures at the middle is strong.

In comparing the major players with the interest-group entry point into the decision-making process, we get the combinations shown in Table 9.1. If the interests of the players are linked to their position within each city, the pattern is evident. In New York, interest groups are divided, though numerous and active. They interact with strong political executives from the earliest stages of decision making—when

Table 9.1. Political Combinations and Interest Group Entry Points in New York, Paris, and London

	New York	Paris	London
Top political executives (strong–moderate–weak)	strong	strong	weak
Middle levels: legislators, bureaucrats (strong–moderate–weak)	weak	strong	strong
Interest group composition (organized–divided) (active–inactive)	divided/active	organized/inactive	organized/active
Interest group entry point into decisional process (early–middle–late)	early	late	middle

alternatives are formulated and priorities are decided. Welling out of this combination are pressures to adjust the disparate interests (the larger city, the developers, the community groups). Planning becomes piecemeal rather than comprehensive and focuses on short-term pay-offs rather than long-term visions.

In Paris, interest groups are organized though inactive. They are relegated to the later stages of a decision and at all levels must deal with strong politicians, technocrats, and bureaucrats. The result is predictable. Working closely with technocrats, politicians address their constituency as they see it—that is, in its larger mass. Populations are conceived not in groups but in statistical trends and projections. Planning is comprehensive, territories are given a function, and priorities are ranked. The scope of planning is broad and the goals are strictly fixed.

In London, top local political executives are weak. Technocrats take initial charge of decisions. However, they do not hold the final word. Interest groups are both organized and active. They enter the process at the middle levels of government and at the middle stage of decisions. Interest groups have clout, but it is a clout that is tied to governmental bodies and partisan causes. The outcome is seesaw planning. Planning begins with an underlying conception of the whole and of mass populations. That effort soon falls apart and comprehensive plans are whittled down to accommodate different pieces of the whole.

Over the years, London technocrats have adjusted their thoughts to meet local objections. As might be anticipated, they have adopted a strategy of trying to reconcile the ideals of planning to political exigency. The result is a curious blend of strategies that at first appear to be sweeping and bold. On closer inspection, the plans turn out to be cautious steps taken along the path Abercrombie charted four decades ago.

Before going on to analyze planning approaches, it is useful to consider another dimension of the process, the question of how political combinations face their local marketplaces.

Political Combinations and the Marketplace

As "free enterprise" economies, all three cities are ensconced in one or another marketplace.[8] It is the marketplace that plays an important role in the valuation and allocation of land. And it is the marketplace that lures or discourages private investors. Nonetheless, capitalism has many faces and these change with time, place, and circumstance.

The key to understanding planning is the degree to which political combinations control marketplaces. The instruments by which that control is accomplished are (1) public investment, (2) taxation, and (3) strategic or land-use planning. These instruments are used in all three cities, though applied in different ways and with varying degrees of boldness.

New York City works in close conjunction with the marketplace. It seeks neither to change it through direct intervention nor to challenge it with public alternatives. The New York approach builds upon the strengths of the market and sweetens it with publicly induced opportunities. It seeks to expand growth in an already vital CBD and nudge it into adjacent localities.

The market is approached from its flanks and the means of affecting it are largely "positive." Public investments are offered to entice ("leverage") private capital. Tax abatements are used to lure investors into unsure terrain. An already tolerant zoning code is made still more liberal by allowing for taller buildings.

Paris challenges its marketplace by sometimes taking control of it and at other times closely regulating it. The French approach is unhesitatingly direct and can sometimes mean a frontal assault on the marketplace, usurping it. Alternatively, it may entail a less drastic combination of public-private partnerships that moderate the impact of market forces. We have seen how ZADS, ZACS, and mixed corporations have respectively worked to freeze the price of land, invest it with a heavy infrastructure, and shape its development.

Still another way to appreciate how Paris treats the marketplace is to recognize how substitute markets are created by the imposition of public authority.[9] In this instance, it is the public sector that functions as entrepreneur within its own created market. Commodities are then sold to private buyers. In America, it is the government that acts as consumer for products produced by private contractors. In Paris, it is often the government that produces commodities and private parties that consume it.[10] New towns, La Défense, low-cost housing, and Les Halles are just a few examples of publicly created markets where products are put out for sale, lease, rental, and general use.

London's approach to the marketplace has checkered between Socialist interventionism and Tory laissez fairism. This checkering has both territorial and temporal aspects. The territorial pattern is reflected among the boroughs that vote for either the Conservative or the Labour Party. Most inner boroughs have consistently favored Labour, while the majority of outer boroughs have chosen Conservative majorities. The GLC reflected this split in temporal swings of the vote. Between 1964 and 1984, Conservative and Labour majorities held sway over the GLC for equal periods of time (eleven years each). This occurred in fairly regular alternations of power.[11] In recent years, the

Labour Party controlled the GLC. These alternations in partisan control do not always coincide with partisan control of the Central Government. Since 1979, Conservatives have been in charge at Whitehall.

London's partisan and ideological checkering is most easily expressed in the built environment. The different approaches to market forces live a quarrelsome coexistence. The inner boroughs usurp the market with public housing; outer boroughs seek to free up market forces with private ownership. The GLC switched back and forth, buying housing then selling it off, only to buy it up again and later to reverse the process.

Depending upon who controls what terrain, a given approach will dominate. When five inner boroughs controlled the Docklands, they pushed for public development. Public housing, borough-owned factories and open space were emphasized. Once a Conservative central government took over, there was a decided change. Land was sold off to private developers, the number of public housing units was sharply curtailed and the search was on to find ways to make the Docklands attractive to private investors.[12] Taxes were reduced, zoning requirements were relaxed, and investors were told that sections would be turned into a "free enterprise zone."

London, then, is a patchwork quilt that holds elements of both the New York and Parisian approaches to market forces. But it is an incongruous blend that does not easily harmonize. As we shall see, the Labour Party has been very guarded and its strategy is largely defensive. The Tories have taken up the cudgels for "free enterprise," and Thatcher will push even harder in the coming years (see Chapter 10).

Market Control: Political Combinations in Ideological Context

Ideology expresses an attitude about the marketplace. Conservatives stake their claims on the protection of freedom; Socialists and American liberals pursue the cause of equality. Are these arguments converted into real policies or are they political fodder? The question is complicated and cannot be answered with a simple yes or no. To find an answer, each city may be put through a brief test. This test compares ideology, as it is shown in voting behavior, with policy response, as it is revealed in planning trends. We begin with London.

The ideological segmentation between Inner and Outer London is shown in Figure 9.1, which portrays political control in London's thirty-two boroughs. The boroughs divide into fifteen held by Labour, eleven with Conservative majorities, three held by the Alliance, and three that are hung. Note the spatial distribution of this political

Fig. 9.1. London's Vote for Borough Councils: 1986.
Source: Greater London Council.

contest. Inner London is predominantly Labour. In Outer London the boroughs more evenly checker their vote among Conservatives, Labour and Alliance parties, or are hung.

No doubt ideological divisions are important in how a city handles the marketplace. They predispose the political-technocratic elite toward market intervention or laissez fairism and toward the acceptance or rejection of interest groups. But in and of itself, ideology is insufficient for determining market strategies. In London ideological divisions are reinforced by a segmentation of power that has given each ideological stratum its due. Ideology is lodged within tiers of government that, in turn, generate a system of checkered responses. The key to understanding is not in ideology alone, but in how ideology interacts with political combinations.

Paris provides a good contrast to London. The French have a reputation for ideological politics and cleavages run deep in the rhetoric of

271

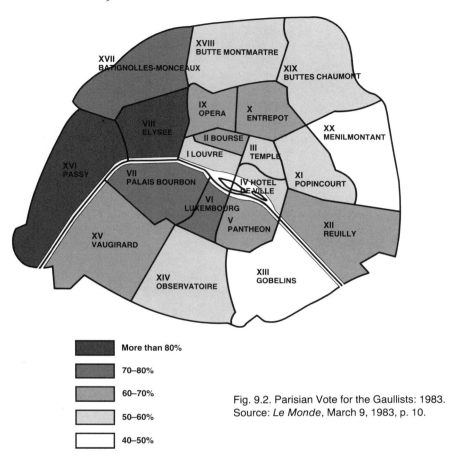

Fig. 9.2. Parisian Vote for the Gaullists: 1983.
Source: *Le Monde*, March 9, 1983, p. 10.

the nation. But urban practice modifies the image. Ideology is managed by pragmatic arrangements among politicians and by the work of the political-technocratic elite at all levels of government.

In its ideological complexion, Paris has more and more turned toward the Right. In 1983 the city voted overwhelmingly for the Gaullist party, which by most standards is considered to be "conservative." Under Chirac the Gaullists have campaigned for less government intervention, lower taxes, and a freer economy. The power of the Gaullists within Paris is shown in Figure 9.2, a political representation of the municipal vote in twenty arrondissements during 1983.

Only two arrondissements (the Thirteenth and the Twentieth) gave less than 50 percent of their vote to the Gaullists. Similar to Inner London, those areas voting for the Left were found on the eastern side of the city. As we look westward, there is a decided shift toward the Right. Two arrondissements on the western edge provided the Right with more than 80 percent of their vote, and most of the others gave it between 60 and 80 percent of the vote.

It should also be noted that between 1981 and 1986 the Socialists controlled the state, and there was an ideological split between Gaullist Paris and Socialist central government. Between 1986 and 1988, the Gaullists held control in both the central government and Paris. Yet despite the previous ideological cleavage and despite the recent dominance of the Right, Paris suffers little of the stalemate or the resistance to state intervention that characterizes London. If anything, government actions are quite bold and statism reigns supreme. Whether it be the Left or the Right, government retains control over the shaping of the built environment. Delouvrier was a Gaullist technocrat, and he accomplished the most thorough revamping of the Parisian region in a hundred years. The replacement of old Les Halles with a different kind of "public market" was achieved under "conservative" regimes. New towns and suburban growth poles were begun under the Gaullists. Secteur Seine Sud-Est is currently being developed under the guidance of Gaullist-Socialist collusion. Paris furnishes an endless list of private markets that have been usurped by the power of the state, regardless of the ideological complexions of government.

Why is this so? The answer is to be found in political combinations that build bridges between partisans and lock out interest groups until plans are well under way. The perspective given to planning and to the marketplace is one that is created by the daily interactions of politicians and technocrats. This does not deny that existing tensions run strong between Gaullists and Socialists. Still, interest groups have little opportunity to give tangible expression to those differences.

As long as those differences are dealt with over the working desks of governing elites, there are means of reconciliation. For one, there are traditions that bind partisans at all levels of French government. What may be distinctly "capitalist" or "Socialist" in some cultures may be bridged by a "French approach" to the marketplace.[13] Those bridges are traversed by planning instruments (ZACs, EPAs) or by political adjustments (*cumul des mandats*) that make it easy for politicians to move between local and national governments.

Second, the ease of intergovernmental movement means that elites concentrate on problems rather than on territorial division. This allows governing elites to coordinate planning and to negotiate across territorial spheres. What belongs to the Gaullists and what belongs to the Socialists can belong to both, it can be split, or it can belong to neither. Compared to Britain, local and national boundaries are open and political currents flow more easily between them.[14]

Last, all this helps blur ideological debate (at least in private) and puts the emphasis on working out an agreed-upon plan. Technocrats are important because the dynamics of the process make them so. Their strategic position is all the more important because they wear the guise of an expert working in the interests of the state. It may be paradoxical that a nation like France, which prides itself on the vitality of political debate, can so easily accommodate itself to quiet arrangements. The cynic might explain that the public arena is for venting grievances, while the private arena is for conducting business. The truth is more complex. Ideology counts, but combinations of power make it adaptable to the necessities of urban development. Or, to change the emphasis, combinations of power inject an altogether different political discourse into planning. It is a discourse that is shielded from public view and is carried out in the shade of a political-technocratic stratum.[15] Because of this, Parisian planning is profoundly different from planning that is conducted amid the rhetoric of ideological debate.

New York both reinforces and clarifies the importance of a combination of power, considered in ideological context. We should be careful, however, about the linkage of ideology to partisanship. In America ideology is less fervent than it is in Europe. Ideological lines are not as sharp and they are blurred by ethnic affiliation, regional differences, and the personality of the candidates themselves.[16]

Yet partisan ideology does provide a cue for how a candidate is *supposed* to deal with the built environment. Democrats are stationed to the left of Republicans. Democrats are supposed to be more interventionist; Republicans stress the free market. Democrats support publicly assisted housing; Republicans oppose it. Democrats stress planning and social equity; Republicans call for lower taxes and free enterprise. Ideological polarity does loom from time to time and can set the tone of public debates.

New York is a solidly Democratic city. The Board of Estimate and City Council are overwhelmingly Democratic, and Republicans have a difficult time winning office.[17] As for the mayoralty, Democrats have usually commanded that office. In the last decade all the city's mayors have run as Democrats. Figure 9.3 shows the strength of the Democratic mayoral candidate in 1985.

As shown, Democrat Ed Koch swept every county in the city, win-

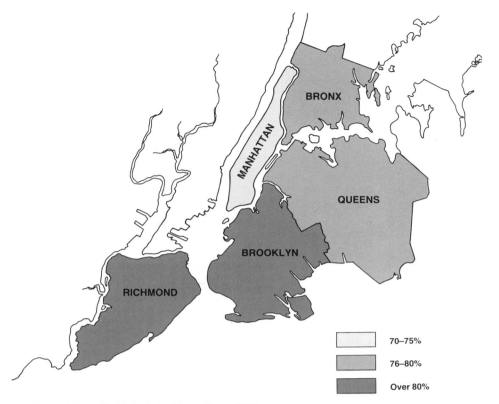

	70–75%
	76–80%
	Over 80%

Fig. 9.3. New York's Vote for Mayor Koch: 1985.
Source: Board of Elections, City of New York.

ning by at least 70 percent. Democrats have now held the governorship of the state for over a decade and handily won the 1986 contest. When it comes to land-use decisions, single-party control is well established within the city. Top politicians within the city and the state have been Democrats and, within the city, middle levels of power are in Democratic hands. Just as Paris has been within the purview of the Gaullists, New York has been within the partisan grasp of the Democrats, and this culminated for both cities in 1986.

Under the circumstances, we would expect partisans to direct the marketplace toward their respective objectives. Parisian Gaullists should give greater freedom to the marketplace and less to planners, and New York Democrats should pursue social equality through more planning intervention.

275

The result, however, does not square with the expectation. Gaullists have increased the directive capacity of technocrats, not only with more discretion but with more public money. Democrats have just about abandoned comprehensive planning and are loathe to use public money to foster equality. For New Yorkers, social equality has been translated into more jobs, and more jobs have been translated into a need to entice private investment. The focus is on an overheated Manhattan and on piece-by-piece planning. Market intervention exists in Democratic New York, but it pales by comparison to rightist Paris.

Most significantly for New York, when intervention occurs, it is tailored to the very narrowest issues. Rarely does intervention go beyond the direct, immediate, and tangible interests that are at stake. Westway was an enormous project and yet its implications for regional development and the future of mass transit were given scant attention. Instead it was managed on a neighborhood-by-neighborhood basis and as an issue of local development. Times Square was treated in similar fashion. It was fraught with implications concerning the overconcentration of resources in the CBD, the overcrowding of mid-Manhattan, and the general problem of uneven employment. And yet it was mostly resolved as an issue of local import.[18]

Are these conspiracies? Far from it. The issues have been publicized and fought in nearly every political arena. The answer is not to be found in plots or in manipulation, but in how power has been combined to resolve the issues. As New York develops piece by piece, so too does it incorporate interests piece by piece. In putting decisions together, top politicians turn to the affected interests. Resolution depends upon interest satisfaction, and the marketplace is nudged just as far as necessary to accommodate those interests, and no farther. This is why positive inducements rather than measures of outright control are so popular in New York. The mentality of interest-group bargaining stresses reciprocity and exchange. The New York approach trades on benefits to groups in exchange for benefits to the city.

The search for open space illustrates how the process works. In an effort to augment open space, New York turned to "bonus zoning," which allowed developers to build higher, should they agree to provide more room at the street level. The perception is that everybody gains (the public with an open sidewalk and the developer with a higher, more profitable building).★

★ That nobody loses through this kind of exchange is, in fact, very doubtful. This approach has caused blocked sunlight, windy streets, congestion, and other hazards. It is an approach that puts a premium on short-term benefits to the detriment of long-term and less tangible advantages.

276

Because Paris and London combine power differently, they are more apt to guide the urban environment. Again, the search for open space exemplifies the difference. In Paris, politicians and technocrats combine to produce new towns, La Défense, and centers of national prestige. The French mentality does not stress reciprocity but command. The Parisian approach rests on collusion between politicians and technocrats who see the city as an object of their work. In London, the boroughs and the central government agreed upon a scheme that focused on the protection of territory. The creation of a Green Belt amounted to a ban on further urbanization. The designation of Community Areas was a form of restrictive legislation that put some boroughs out of bounds for high-powered development and designated other parts of Central London for growth. The English mentality is one of neither reciprocity nor command, but one that makes arrangements among contending government units. For most of this century, London's approach saw the city as belonging to multiple constituencies. More currently, Thatcher's abolition of the GLC is best seen as an attempt to radically change this balance. In effect, abolition is an ideologically motivated step to change the combination of power by eliminating the collective ability of the boroughs to control the marketplace. Should London continue to be left without that collective ability, the boroughs might begin to fend for themselves, ultimately against one another. This would introduce a new dynamic into the system, leaving the boroughs vulnerable to wildcat development.

Planning Strategies

Within a combination of power, the interests that prevail and the market approach adopted make a great deal of difference to planning strategy. A combination's interests infuse planning with values and objectives. A combination's market approach gives it the ability to reshape the environment.

In speaking about planning strategies, I refer to its predominant themes, impetus and inspiration. In elaborating on the planning motif, it must also be recognized that planning is not only a reflection of combinations of power but an adaptation to an environment's physical potential. Combinations of power are the motor force of the planning process while the environment sets the bounds within which the process works.

Planning strategies have differed in each of the cities considered here. New York follows a "Manhattan strategy," Paris pursues an "axes strategy," and, thus far, London has defended a "containment strategy."[19] As the name suggests, the Manhattan strategy concentrates investment and development within a specific part of New York. That area is limited to Manhattan, south of Harlem. It emphasizes intensive development within and just astride the CBD. This intensity is made possible by designating a number of points (Battery Park City, the Convention Center, Midtown, and Times Square) and trying to connect those points with a short chain of continuous development (Westway).

The intensity of the Manhattan strategy imposes spatial limitations on the range of planning. Very little, if any, of the strategy reaches into other counties of the city. Aside from Westway, whose feeder routes would have run from the first ring, the Manhattan strategy is self-contained. Its objective is to draw on existing currents of post-industrial growth and pull it further along. Planners attempt to draw those currents into the western rim of Manhattan.

The Parisian axes are also based on high investment and development. The difference is that they are made along extended points of the built environment that are linearly connected by a heavy transport infrastructure (rail, subway, highway). Rather than being intensive, the Parisian axes are an extensive strategy. Sometimes the axes may draw on the strength of the built-up urban core, but they probe into distant terrain. French new towns and suburban growth poles form a contiguous band that stretches 117 miles across the Ile-de-France. The much smaller axis between La Défense and Secteur Seine Sud-Est forms another contiguous 7.5-mile band through the heart of the urban core.

The Parisian axes are intended to establish whole new waves of development. Untried terrain like La Défense is flooded with a post-industrial infrastructure and connected to other parts of the region. Where Americans accommodate the current, the French push it into a new frontier.

London's containment begins by distinguishing between urban, semi-urban, and nonurban environments. Containment draws concentric or oblong boundaries between designated environments.[20] The idea is to encourage regulated growth within the context of territorial conservation. The Green Belt, the Central Activities Zone (CAZ), the Community Area Plan, and the strategic centers are illustrations of containment strategy.

Rather than intensive or extensive, London's containment is a balanced strategy. Although containment encourages post-industrialism, it resists growth when it is at the expense of the ecological fabric. Containment protects territorial integrity and guides development into areas that are appropriate for a given level of growth. The Green Belt is kept free from industrial intrusion, the CAZ is reserved for high-powered investment, and Community Areas and strategic centers receive measured amounts of commerce. Finally, the Docklands is held out for potential rebirth. All this underscores a concern for proportion, propriety, and gradualism.* Unlike New Yorkers (who accommodate private investment) or Parisians (who push growth with vigorous public intervention), Londoners have emphasized the regulation of urban development.

Containment treats London as if it were a reservoir in need of maintenance. If it falls empty, the response has been to replenish the quantity—perhaps add to its bounty—but within its prescribed limits.

Strategy and System

Planning strategy is an outgrowth of governmental form, political combination, and a combination's ability to control the marketplace. The composition of these factors may work toward comprehensive planning—or they may work for a piecemeal strategy.

The limits of municipal and regional government are a familiar theme in New York. In a recent book on the subject, Danielson and Doig counted nearly 2,200 separate governments within the New York region.[21] Political fragmentation and competitive bidding make regional cooperation difficult, though it is achievable along narrow functional lines. Transportation and highway construction represent such an achievement.

Comprehensive planning requires a much broader system of supports. Zoning, taxation, and spending are just a few policies that need to be undertaken in common for comprehensive planning to succeed. Asking 2,200 governments to do that would be a foreign experience for New York—indeed, it would be strange for most Americans.

Planning can only be as complete as the political apparatus will allow. Since regional government is feeble, a limited spatial strategy makes sense for New York City. After all, why attempt to stretch development past the capacity of government to handle it?[22]

New York City has narrowed its planning vision even beyond these regional constraints. As a municipality, it has the right to plan for postindustrialism within its 319 square miles. And yet it has chosen to con-

---

* This is not to say that London has always resisted aggressive spurts of development. The Barbican, Elephant and Castle Centre Point, Euston, and parts of the City incurred a strong property boom during the 1960s (see Chapter 6). Containment, however, has been able to restrain that level of development in other parts of Greater London. This was especially true for the 1970s and early 1980s.

centrate its attention on less than 22 of those square miles. There was once a time when the city was obliged to publish a master plan. By 1976 the master plan was dropped.

New York gave up on comprehensive planning because facts contradicted aspirations. One of those facts included the ability of interest groups to face off against political elites at an early stage of decision making. The master plan may have presented a colorful collection of maps, good for university lecture halls, but it fell into disuse when pitted against piecemeal pressures.

Another of those facts was the reluctance of political elites to act aggressively against market forces. For a number of reasons, the marketplace is more important in New York than in European cities.[23] By its pure definition, the marketplace is decentralized, spontaneous, and based on individual exchange. It is the very antithesis of the comprehensive ideal, which calls for coordination, predictability, and collective responsibility.

New York's system contains a powerful tension between the objectives of planning and the profits of the marketplace. Developers are always on the prowl for opportunities, and if the planners do not come up with a scheme, sooner or later, private investors will. Westway and Times Square are two cases where planners struggled to come up with a rational scheme in order to prevent "as of right" (i.e., development based on the existing zoning laws) building. Community groups may clamor that planning for a new highway or a new Times Square will ruin adjoining neighborhoods, but without such planning, neighborhoods may be far worse off. The Manhattan CBD furnishes a woeful example of what happens to the environment when "as of right" development is left to run its own course.

The planner must cope, in one way or another, with the marketplace. As a result there are bound to be casualties. Eminent domain is strewn with delay and complication. Public land purchase is hedged by small-scale acquisition. Freezing real estate values is out of the question. Massive spending is difficult.

In order to function, planners pull out the leftover tools of their trade—publicity, persuasion, zoning, and public leverage of private investment. In New York the planner is not the master but the salesman. Like any salesperson, planners must use all the inducements they can muster. Success is measured by what works best, and this is why the Manhattan strategy makes sense. One of America's most notorious criminals, Willie Sutton, furnished a similar logic. When asked why he robbed banks, Sutton dryly answered, "because that is where the money is." In New York, Manhattan is where the opportunities lie.

Paris presents a different relationship between system and strategy. A strong central government and the traditions of the Prefect make comprehensive planning much easier to achieve. Before recent measures toward decentralization, the Prefect could overrule local authorities and take action where mayors had refused or neglected to do so. Prefects could pay debts on behalf of a locality. Prefects imposed their own authority if a mayor could not "assure order, safety . . . and the public salubrity."[24] The so-called *tutelle* (guardianship) of the state ensured a degree of uniformity throughout France.

Over the years the heavy hand of centralism has lightened. Quite often the theory is more stringent than is its observance.[25] As we have seen, bargaining between politicians at different levels of government is common in France, and it would be an exaggeration to picture decision making as a one-way street. But the fact is that traditions carry a good deal of weight. They provide context and a set of norms for politicians and technocrats. The fact is, too, that the state has the capacity to act in the event of noncompliance. This creates an expectation about the need to adjust differences. Local governments expect that a master plan will be produced, and one way or another they know they will follow it.

The form of government allows for the function to be carried out. It not only shapes the perspective of those at the top but creates expectations for those at the bottom.

Both governmental forms and combinations of power also provide the supports for comprehensive planning. The state is an important source of local revenue. It also provides subventions to a regional government whose budget has grown fourfold since the mid-1960s.[26] The region itself has the power to levy taxes and undertake projects. The Ile-de-France is represented by political institutions and stands as a reckoning force. It freely enters into contracts with the state and assimilates the disparate interests of communes, villages, and departments.

The centripetal pulls of the system are formidable. Its resistance to the premature intrusion of interest groups shields planners from what they regard as extraneous. The willingness to pour state and local resources into public projects means that the marketplace can be refashioned. The result is that planning has an altogether different meaning in France than in America. Planning is a long-range process whose objective is to reconcile the parts to the whole. A priori, good planning entails the ability to exact resources from one part of the environment and implant them in another.

The system is so constructed that the approach to planning will be extensive. The axis strategy is simply one technique to accommodate that approach. It is not only large scale, it is long range. In France, the task of the government is to govern. Paris and the region around it are where the government flexes its muscle.

In London the system *has been* the strategy. Above all, containment has been protective. It has protected Greater London by girdling it with a Green Belt. It has protected the boroughs by giving them status as Community Areas. And it protected the GLC by furnishing it with a strategic role.

Containment is perhaps the most "political" of the three strategies. Its thrust is derived neither from economic ambition (the Manhattan strategy) nor from planning command (the axes strategy), but from the distribution of privileges to governmental organizations. As a strategy, containment actually derives from the bargaining positions of London's three-tier government. The boroughs bargain for their share of strategic centers. The GLC fought for jobs by touting the CAZ. As guardian of the nation's capital, the central government puts its imprimatur on Central London.

Containment depends upon a wide consensus among the tiers of government. As long as that consensus holds, its distributive function can work smoothly. Development is balanced among London's parts and made proportionate to London's territory. So too are political considerations balanced among the borough councils and made proportionate to the needs of Greater London and the Central Government. For Londoners, planning is politics. Technocrats are expected to respect citizen participation. Politicians are supposed to represent it. The structure of that participation bears a resemblance to the structure of planning. It is orderly, systematic and incorporates viewpoints at multiple levels of society.

Once that consensus breaks apart, so too does planning. This began between 1984 and 1986, when the Thatcher government refused to go along with London's Socialists and abolished the GLC. Parts of the system now move in opposition to other parts. Instead of accommodation, the tiers argue over the proper course of action. The system is now stalled in resistance and recrimination. Democratic participation and the British sense of fair play are under strain. Unilateral action by the central government is countered by protest from the boroughs or the GLCs-in-exile and then met again by further dictates from the central government. Caught in political controversy, containment is now on trial. Parts of it are in limbo. Some boroughs hold onto the CAZ-Community Area Plan; others are indifferent. GLCs-in-exile promote community conservation, while the central government targets the same communities for growth. Containment is attacked by Conservatives as stultifying and defended by Socialists as a remnant of sanity.

These incidents are puzzling because planning presumes to be a technical rather than a political art. Politicians make choices. Planners propose and implement them. In London the paradox is that the more carefully constructed those technical choices have become, the more politically laden their content.

The Post-Industrial City

There is nothing more difficult to carry out, nor more doubtful of success, nor more dangerous to handle, than to initiate a new order of things.—Niccolò Machiavelli, *The Prince*

Conditions of the Post-Industrial City

JUST BEFORE the turn of the century, Lord Bryce wrote that the "government of cities is one of the conspicuous failures of the United States."[1] Bryce complained that political office in American cities was little more than a residue for service to the party. Once in office the politician was reduced to a string puller for the "getting and keeping of places."[2]

During the same period, a New York–based magazine, advising its readership on the best political traits, suggested that politics was fitting for "neither businessmen, professional men nor college professors."[3] Among the qualities desired, the magazine argued that the politician "must always seem to follow rather than to lead."[4]

European politicians were more actively engaged in the substance of policy, but much of their concern centered on security. In France, Paris was closely watched as "a fortress of sedition."[5] Even Great Britain's political elite was obsessed with urban security. In 1883 William Gladstone declared that the control of the police was the most important of all municipal functions and should be so for London.[6]

The political elite of the industrial city viewed its growth from a distance. In America, politicians partook of the industrial harvest with boodle and patronage. In Europe they increased their surveillance of a restless mass and built "anti-riot streets."[7]

Above all the industrial city was a "private city," built by the invisible hand of unregulated capitalism.[8] Generally speaking, industrialists and politicians carried out their businesses separately. Factories sprang up with little help from the state. Government provided some accommodation for that growth (streets, ports), but its interventions were minimal. Politics and the economy were separate and apart. Planning for a new industrial order was rare. When planning existed at all, it was sporadic and carried out without consciousness of economic design.

It was this quality of "privatism" that furnished the city with its political quality. In America, the municipality responded with machine politics—or in Norton Long's fitting words, by reducing "the politician to the role of registerer of pressure rather than responsible governor of a local political economy."[9] In Europe, royal families treated the city as a monument to kingly glory. Politics revolved around the awarding of architectural commissions and public works contracts.[10]

The rise of post-industrialism changed urban politics, both in America and abroad. Political brokerage and monumentalism could no longer suffice. Energetic and imaginative policy leadership was required. The new politics faced the task of collecting bits and pieces of the social structure in order to build a vastly more complex city. To do this, policy direction would have to replace laissez faire, and collaboration would be a better substitute for unbridled competition. Post-industrialism also required immense investment from the private sector, whose risks would be mitigated by state guarantees.

The political signs pointed toward corporatism. The drift was gradual, in some cases incomplete, and it was not always susceptible to precise measurement. But the signs were unmistakable, and today they pervade the political mood of the post-industrial city.

Adaptation is supposed to be the life-saving resource of human and animal species. The great city, too, is an organic phenomenon capable of adaptation. In order to survive, it must adapt its politics to the post-industrial condition.

One of these conditions is an increased competition between cities as well as between nations. The post-industrial city represents not only itself but the aspirations of its nation. Intranational competition results in advantages for jobs and taxes. International competition entails the higher stakes of world power, prestige, and leadership. Although the unitary governments of Europe can dampen intranational competition by redistributing internal income, they cannot ignore the challenge of international competition. More and more, distinctions are made between military and economic might, and though the post-industrial city can do little to bolster national defense, it epitomizes economic prowess.

The paradox is that the more competition the post-industrial city confronts from the outside, the less competitive it must be on the inside. Great cities can no longer afford a free-wheeling, "build as one might" economy. To compete effectively, the post-industrial city needs to harness its internal resources. Politics becomes both the instrument and the exemplar of this effort. In the more pluralistically laden city (New York), a politics of concertation begins to emerge.[11]

285

Concertation is the first step in organizing formerly competitive groups by inducing them to bargain cooperatively. It gives some groups privileged access and it institutionalizes consultation between these groups and the political-technocratic elite. In New York this collaboration is still in the process of bringing a pluralist society closer to corporatism.

In those environments where the traditions of pluralism are less rooted (Paris and London), the state can more easily fashion the response. In France an already formidable state apparatus developed planning techniques to usher in the transformation. The machinery simply concerted local governments and invited organizations from the private sector to join it. In Great Britain a competent technocratic class also introduced sophisticated planning and development. Concertation of local governments and interest groups is a thornier problem whose success rests upon political consensus and the impact of Tory rule into the 1990s.

Another condition of post-industrialism is the complexity of building a brand new physical environment. Streets, highways, rail terminals, airports, office towers, shopping malls, parks, theaters, museums, houses, hospitals, universities, and research centers need to be constructed with an eye toward the demographics of the twenty-first century. Construction itself is straightforward and a matter of technical mastery. The challenge is to accomplish this smoothly while synchronizing an enormous number of transactions. Facilities need to be coordinated, finances need to be secured, and a whole new system of laws needs to be worked out. There emerges a labyrinth of negotiations between buyers and sellers, landlords and tenants, and those about to take possession and those about to be dispossessed.

Whether they want it or not, politicians are handed the consuming task of making it all work. A multitude of interests must be brought together and satisfied. No longer can the singular role of neutral intermediary be sufficient. To make it happen, politicians and technocrats assume responsibility. Whether it be Times Square, La Défense, or the Docklands, government has underwritten the investment, acquired the land, made it attractive to investors, and taken care of the dispossessed. The details of each project may vary, but the functions of the political-technocratic elite are remarkably similar.

Still a third condition of the post-industrial city has been the rise of assurer government.[12] Politics no longer ends after the ribbon-cutting ceremonies. It continues to insure all parties against the risks of change. Investors are given long-term leases with options to buy, tenants are promised priority housing with moderate rents, citizens are provided with open spaces and amenities. The single institution to which the disgruntled turn is government. Politicians become responsible for the business failures, the destruction of community, and the personal dislocations that ensue from the new environment. Despite neoconservative efforts to reduce government, post-industrialism entices its expansion. Issues that at first glance appear resolvable become pregnant with further issues. Involvement begets further involvement and obligations multiply. New York's Westway was not just a highway but a massive real estate project. Whatever is built in place of Westway will require a continuing set of commitments in public leases, park maintenance, and pollution controls. In Paris, the Secteur Seine Sud-Est will keep politicians and technocrats busy through the end of the century, and after that, the city will retain title to the new projects. London's Covent Garden still has citizen organizations that make demands and a government-supported planning team that acts upon them.

Moreover, the obligations put before politicians are often contradictory. New Yorkers may delight over higher values for their property, yet they also want their neighborhood left intact. Parisians want the benefit of an expanded economy but lament the ruination of the skyline. Londoners moan about automobiles congesting local streets while they refuse to build highways. In all three cities jobs are a major issue, and not only the national government is held responsible. Urban political leaders often stake their record on the economic issue. "The main job of government," said Ed Koch just after his inauguration, "is to create a climate in which private business can expand in the city to provide jobs and profit."[13] From his early days as Mayor of Paris, Jacques Chirac interpreted his mandate broadly and pressed for business growth. "The provinces have grown and so have the new towns," declared Chirac, "while Paris sees its own employment wasting away."[14] London's Labour Party leader, Ken Livingstone, has put the cause of full employment into a larger campaign against classism, racism, and sexism. His strongest denunciations are reserved for the privileged, whom he calls "vandals in ermine."[15]

Whatever formula urban politicians have adopted, they must engage the social and economic system. Passive politics and the politician as "caretaker" are obsolete.[16] Post-industrial politicians must exercise power on their own and must harness it to public purpose. Those purposes involve a certain amount of planning. It can be short-term, piecemeal planning or it can resemble a long-term comprehensive strategy. But once an already built environment is given the challenge of post-industrial change, planning is inevitable. The thrust for change and the planning that ensues from it help generate the policy outputs of the post-industrial city.

Policy Outputs of the Post-Industrial City

Most interpretations of urban decision making focus on conflict and clashes of interest between participants. Conflict is, of course, embedded in all change, and some scholars conclude that conflict is almost invariably resolved on behalf of the economically powerful.[17] Clarence Stone, for example, observes that "governments are drawn by the nature of underlying economic and revenue producing conditions to serve [business] interests."[18] Stone adds that "situational dependencies"[19] confer advantages to the upper strata at the expense of those at the bottom.

To be sure, disagreement, struggle, and conflict are endemic to society. These elements are the fodder of politics. But the settling of the dust also shows that a good deal of collaboration and mutual accommodation takes place. Without this, post-industrial transformation would not be possible. And when that collaboration does falter, the society becomes stuck in stagnation.

Situational dependencies certainly exist. Business classes do enjoy positions as revenue producers, and by virtue of that can be more powerful than others. But they are not always more powerful than others. Their position as revenue producers is not always a monopoly, nor is it unregulated. Government is not in business hands and it is just as certainly not helpless. Situational dependencies can just as easily be converted into situational interdependencies. Business relies on government, just as surely as government relies on business. Labor and the citizenry find their actions linked to those of politicians and businessmen.

Moreover, we cannot assume that a gain for the business class results in an automatic loss for nonbusiness classes. Alternatively, we cannot assume that beating the business interests means that labor, the community, or the urban citizenry will reap the rewards.

Our own lessons from New York, Paris, and London reject black-and-white categorization. These lessons show that policy outputs cannot be regarded as a zero-sum game. There are few sharp demarcations between winners and losers. The stakes of post-industrialism do not fall exclusively on one side of the social fence or on the other. On the contrary, costs and benefits fall in varying proportions upon varying classes, groups, and organizations. Sometimes half the residents of a community will benefit from an action while the other half loses. One class of business may reap profits while another class of business stumbles into bankruptcy. Entire communities can rise or fall with the tides of post-industrial change, affecting landlords and tenants alike.

To take another tack on this issue, some of the contemporary literature on the politics of land development interprets policy outcomes as derived from "prevailing coalitions" that join top politicians with business interests.[20] Commonly, a conflict erupts between this coalition, trying to develop land, and popular neighborhood groups, seeking to protect the environment. While this is a simple scenario, its interpretation can differ depending upon how one looks at the conflict and weighs its stakes.

Again, our own lessons show that coalitions between politicians and private interest groups can be fleeting. Politicians and technocrats form a closer bond with each other than with outside groups and are more likely to constitute a stable governmental elite. Interest groups of many and differing stripes may coalesce with that elite, but they are as apt to move out of it as into it. The elite is likely to maneuver between different groups or even to subordinate private groups to its priorities. What looks like a prevailing coalition at one moment and in one case can become a shifting or a completely changed coalition when viewed over a longer period of time and over many cases. More significantly, the scenario of top politicians and business working against popular bases in the neighborhoods dichotomizes the contest to the exclusion of other parties. Top politicians are elected from at-large constituencies; technocrats must account for the broad implications of their plan. Perforce, their choices are founded upon a complexity of different interests. For a neighborhood, development may very well be a threat to a valued way of life, but for the rest of the city it may be a chance to create a new industry, enhance city services, or "clean up" an area.

The fact of the matter is that there are few absolutes that can be stated about policy outcomes. More fittingly, there are degrees of advantage and disadvantage that can accrue. In any single outcome there are pluses (better housing for residents, more jobs for workers) and minuses (breakup of community, environmental hazards). Nor can much be said about an outcome without qualification. The absoluteness of evaluation can lead us into the thicket of making extreme value judgments (did the community truly profit by blocking development?) or into the foxhole of one or another contestant (neighborhood interests versus the city at large). Under conditions of post-industrialism and corporatism, policy outputs will emphasize the collaborative potential of the social structure. These conditions will encourage the interdependence of vital actors. Politicians, technocrats, investors, laborers, and residents will find themselves sharing the same roof. The resulting policies are best conceived as a trade-off among different options—or, in Peter Blau's conception, as a system of exchange where certain goods are bartered for others in the interests of satisfying certain ends.[21]

The Goodies Are Divisible

In earlier chapters we discussed the economic transformation brought by post-industrialism. Here we take a comparative look at the outputs of that transformation. In New York, the urban core of Manhattan bristles with jobs, office construction, and neighborhood renovation. Office rents are at an all-time high; vacancy rates are low. As the middle class rushes to the urban core, the squeeze on available apartments tightens. From all indications it appears that this new class can pay the costs of Midtown living. Manhattan not only holds the highest per capita income within the city, it also skims the high salary earners. According to the last census, Manhattan held nearly four times the number of households earning at least $50,000 than its sister counties.[22]

The urban core of Paris has also prospered. Once a city known for its proletarian vitality, its street people, and its slovenly charm, Paris is now varnished with the lacquer of propriety. Of the city's twenty arrondissements, only a handful are exclusively working class. The number of middle- and upper middle-class households has risen consistently since the 1960s, and the commercial and cultural fabric has responded to the new demand.

Notwithstanding the parallels to Manhattan, the pace and content of the Parisian embourgeoisement are different. Paris is still very much a mixed city. Class settlement is not as lopsided as in New York and urban living is still a viable choice for middle-class families. Thus the percentage of residents from the upper strata in Paris is half that of Manhattan (22 percent versus 42 percent).[23] Just as important, Paris is not subject to drastic social swings between itself and the surrounding localities. The 1982 census showed that the percentage of those belonging to the middle class was virtually identical (19 percent) in Paris and in nearby departments.[24] In contrast, Manhattan bounds ahead of its surrounding counties (twice the median income and three times the educational attainment).[25]

Despite the talk about the destruction of London's heritage, the metropolis has withstood the blitz of modern architecture. The Victorian skyline still embraces Central London, and Georgian houses continue to adorn the streets of Kensington.

Parts of Inner London have changed since the 1960s, and some boroughs have experienced both physical rejuvenation and social displacement (Camden and Islington). The upper middle class continues to occupy Central London (Westminster and Kensington-Chelsea). But of the three cities, the urban core of London is the least changed. Upper middle classes constitute a lower percentage of the urban core population (15 percent) than in New York (42 percent) or Paris (22 percent).[26] London does not exhibit the radical social shifting of New York, but neither does it show any tendency toward balancing out long-standing discrepancies.[27]

Differences among the three cities are encapsulated in several basic propositions. New York's fast-driving economy has brought an influx of upper middle classes into its urban core, and this has exacerbated differences with its surrounding counties. Paris pursues a course of growth and change that is more moderate, and its imbalances are less dramatic. Thus far, London has changed the least. Though it may be on the precipice of radical growth, it has yet to see massive social dislocation.

These generalizations are better illustrated by pointing to job growth in the three cities. Jobs translate into economic opportunities for urban residents. On the negative side, new jobs are not always given to members of the existing community and their creation can do violence to the social fabric.

Table 10.1 surveys employment patterns in manufacture since the late 1960s and early 1970s. New York, Paris, and London are examined from the perspective of their urban cores and first and second rings.

Table 10.1. Industrial Employment in New York, Paris, and London (by place of work; in thousands unless otherwise indicated)

	New York (1971-1982)		Paris (1968-1982)		London (1971-1981)	
	number	%	number	%	number	%
Urban Core	−139.4	−31.4	−213.1	−42.0	−157.3	−46.4
First Ring	−201.8	−31.5	−132.2	−21.2	−231.7	−36.3
Second Ring	90.4	13.4	61.3	21.9	−7.6	−10.6
Net Regional Loss or Gain	−250.8		−284.0		−396.6	

Source: Adapted from County Business Patterns: 1971 and 1982 (Washington, D.C.: U.S. Department of Commerce, Bureau of the Census); Annuaire Statistique Sommaire, Avril 1978 et 1982 (Paris: Institut d' Aménagement et d'Urbanisme de la Région d'Ile-de-France, 1982); ECONDAT: 1971 and 1981 (London: Greater London Council), Tables 18 and 19; and Employment by Sector in the OMA: 1971 and 1981 (London: Department of Employment).

The shrinkage of manufacture is a familiar theme for the post-industrial city. Recall, however, that the exodus of factories from the inner city usually resulted in a favorable slough-off for the distant suburbs. This was true for New York and Paris, which despite their losses accommodated in their second rings over 90,000 and 61,000 manufacturing jobs. London remains the exception to this rule; its manufacturing decline was uniform throughout the region. The second ring not only failed to grow but also incurred an absolute toll of more than 7,000 jobs. In addition, the net decline in manufacturing jobs was more severe for the London region than for either New York or Paris.

Although it is difficult to pinpoint the cause of London's extensive manufacturing slowdown, the blame has been attributed to conservationist measures.[28] At the same time conservationist policies have yielded desirable results. Outside the first ring, farming has survived as a way of life and green space has been safeguarded. Spreading suburbs and unsightly shopping malls have been contained. Small villages still exist in their original form. Londoners may have paid a price for ecological balance, but they do enjoy an environment that other metropolises have already brought to ruin.

Note, too, that within the Parisian region a wealthier urban core bore the brunt of manufacturing loss. This is because centralized planning plucked up Parisian factories and brought them into the new towns or the provinces. Meanwhile the pains of decline were eased for the first ring (whose older localities lost relatively fewer factories). Neither New York nor London could make this kind of transformation, which required aggressive centralized intervention and direction. In France whole swaths of industry, people, and villages were changed. The targets included labor unions, shopkeepers, and big or small businesses alike.[29]

Turning to the economic "fill-up" since the 1960s, we observe the outputs of each system. Again, the rewards are divisible, the inequities are variable, and the payoffs are dissimilar.

Table 10.2 isolates post-industrial growth and decline for each city. The format continues to emphasize intra-urban as well as interurban comparisons. Observe the changes that occur as post-industrialism takes root. The urban cores of New York and Paris have held up; London's has faltered. Manhattan's proportionate growth is the most dramatic (16.5 percent), Paris makes a steady gain (6.7 percent), and Inner London loses (−11.6 percent). In New York, the "costs" of failed growth are borne exclusively in the first ring, Paris grows in all rings, and London is the sole metropolis to incur a net loss.

The results give rise to evaluations of policy outputs and the choices

Table 10.2. Post-Industrial Employment in New York, Paris, and London (by place of work; in thousands unless otherwise indicated)

	New York (1971-1982)		Paris (1968-1982)		London (1971-1981)	
	number	%	number	%	number	%
Urban Core	62.4	16.5	90.7	6.7	− 95.5	− 11.6
First Ring	− 12.8	− 10.5	309.9	45.3	66.3	6.0
Second Ring	80.9	81.5	370.4	88.4	19.0	69.7
Net Regional						
Loss or Gain	130.5		771.0		− 10.2	

Source: Adapted from *County Business Patterns: 1971 and 1982* (Washington, D.C.: U.S. Department of Commerce, Bureau of the Census); *Annuaire Statistique Sommaire, Avril 1978 et 1982* (Paris: Institut d'Aménagement et d'Urbanisme de la Région d'Ile-de-France: Paris, France); and *ECONDAT 1971 and 1981* (London: Greater London Council), Tables 18 and 19, and *Employment by Sector in the OMA: 1971 and 1981* (London: Department of Employment). The manner of collecting census data in each of the cities does not allow for precise comparability. But I have been able to ferret out rough indices of post-industrial employment. For New York this consists of the FIRE section (finance, insurance, and real estate). For Paris the sector labeled "tertiary services" has been chosen. For London the relevant sector is "services, distribution, and government."

that stem from them. Obviously the most desirable choice is for all parts of the metropolis to grow—or at least remain stable. Only Paris holds that enviable position, and that too is fraught with difficulties. Given the ostensibly less preferable outcome in New York, we should ask whether halting growth in Manhattan might have benefited the Bronx or any other depleted locality. We cannot say for sure, but it is unlikely that curtailing Manhattan's office towers would have caused developers to search for land in adjoining counties. The probability is that builders would have headed far beyond New York City.[30] Far from Manhattan doing damage, its boom furnished tangible benefits for people in hard-hit first-ring counties. For those who were able to find jobs, Manhattan was a source of livelihood and income. Commuters from the surrounding counties found work in the new occupations that were born of post-industrialism. Although losses in the Bronx or Jersey City might go unreplaced, Manhattan stood as a beacon. Marginal firms that might otherwise pass from the scene stayed on because of proximity to Manhattan. Clerks, secretaries, and technicians who might not be able to afford housing in Manhattan could find decent shelter within a 45-minute train ride to the urban core. As a consequence, property could be kept up and the flame of reinvestment kept alive.

These benefits are apparent in surveying the unemployment tallies in Greater London. London points up the stark dilemmas faced by the post-industrial city when economic priorities clash with social values.

The failure to absorb enough post-industrial business has brought economic hardship to much of the metropolis. There can be little doubt that limitations on construction in Central London have exacerbated the plight of the jobless in Newham and Lambeth.[31] One cannot simply write off the realtors and builders as economic piranhas. They play a role in the vibrancy of the post-industrial city, and when these arch-capitalists are suffocated, so too is the local economy.

The social consequences for London are far more salutary. Mention of these inevitably brings a comparison between London's policy of containment and the Manhattan strategy. New York's approach may produce jobs but at a cost that exacerbates problems in the social ecology (severe social imbalance, neighborhood disruption) and in the physical environment. Just the other way around, London's approach has not produced jobs, but containment has managed to sort out commercial activity with reasonable equity and it has salvaged the social structure. More so than New York and Paris, London enjoys neighborhood stability. It is a metropolis of well-balanced, cohesive neighborhoods. Borough government and identity with a town hall have done much to advance this.[32] The urban core has been protected. For London, there is still little sense of social invasion that is common in most of Manhattan and much of Paris. Piccadilly Circus attracts the tourists, but Chiswick and Hampstead are still for Londoners.

By data and outward account, Paris appears to have struck a happy medium between livable neighborhoods and jobs. On closer inspection, the axis strategy coupled to *étatisme* has wrung its costs. Citizen participation is all the more stifled and pressure groups are suffocated. A technocratic-political elite has arrogated much of the decision making to itself and with telling consequence. Parts of the built environment have been hurriedly constructed with little awareness of how it feels to live or play in the new communities. Paris contains block upon block of high-rise dormitories.[33] The French bureaucracy is well acquainted with how to achieve statistical balance, but it has paid little attention to the realities of daily urban life.

Just outside the Parisian urban core, villages have been replaced by blocks of concrete housing called *les grands ensembles*. Put up by technocrats, they were built with neither restraint nor a sensitive hand. In some places, *les grands ensembles* are nothing less than unbroken lines of mortar, steel, and squares of glass. It is as if a wall of buildings erupted in the middle of nowhere. This was done by an insulated class of officialdom who, when confronted with a housing shortage, did its job.

The Goodies Are Different: Revisiting Times Square,
Les Halles, and Covent Garden

Like flagships of the fleet, Times Square, Les Halles, and Covent Garden are the products of their local command. They also underscore differences in values, priorities, and political control in the three cities.

In background and geography, the sites are remarkably similar. All three have been symbols of urban night life and center-city living. All three have been packed with an economy and society of days long past (markets, movie houses, a working class). All three lagged behind post-industrial change, until they became targets for radical reconstruction. All three sit atop land of enormous value. Even the size of their commercial targets are similar—13 acres in Times Square, 16 acres in Les Halles, 34 acres in Covent Garden.

Yet for all these similarities, the outcomes are just as dissimilar. New York and London are the antipodal points. Times Square will be radically redone along the lines of megastructure planning, for economic growth. Covent Garden has been renovated and largely conserved, with social values in mind.

The scope of each project bespeaks its underlying values. Times Square will be built upon the financial mooring of five post-industrial megastructures. Where there was once airy openness amid bright lights, the area will be shrouded by office towers and a high-rise retail mart. The exchange is governed by economics and finance. New York City will receive millions in public improvements, plus a sizable increase in taxes.[34] The developers will be given the right to build more than twice the allowable limits for height and bulk.

Covent Garden has not been so much redone as it has been refashioned. The old market building has been retained but gutted to accommodate shops and restaurants. New construction has been limited by strict controls on height and bulk. Congestion is kept down by density controls. Over three hundred sites are protected as historic landmarks.[35] Though physical conservation has not kept away the gentry, the old working class has survived. This was accomplished by GLC assurances that any resident threatened with displacement would be guaranteed housing. Other supports include a community social hall, pub, and athletic facility. The exchange is as much for the physical environment as it is for the ecology of the community. London receives a renovated habitat capable of attracting new blood and small-scale business, while the community is protected.

Even more dissimilar are the financial ramifications. Times Square is enormously expensive ($2.4 billion); the cost of Covent Garden is modest ($22.5 million).[36] Times Square is supposed to increase jobs fourfold; Covent Garden struggles to recapture earlier losses. Times Square touts an enormous boost in office space; Covent Garden worries about an invasion of too many offices.[37] Times Square trudges on with scant regard for peripheral hardships.[38] An official study admits that "the project will displace an estimated 410 businesses" and that those most hurt will be firms which are "unable to pay high rents."[39] In contrast, Covent Garden makes every effort to retain a balance between white- and blue-collar industry. The official GLC statement on the matter says that "it will be the normal policy to prevent the change . . . from industrial floorspace to other uses."[40]

Les Halles takes a third road to redevelopment. It combines New York's flair for radical reconstruction with London's temperament for a livable, civilized environment. The new Les Halles may have wiped away the old marketplace, but it does not overshadow its surroundings with megastructures. Most of it is built below the neighborhood skyline, and it contains sizable amounts of open space and parkland. If anything, the French have taken pains to respect architectural scale by digging downward to build a subterranean city. The area's eighteenth-century buildings have been renovated and the streets have been restored.

Still, for Les Halles physical decorum does not mean community protection. Unlike Covent Garden, there were no guarantees of neighborhood housing given to residents and at last count only 27 percent of the old inhabitants remained.[41] Most of these people have been scattered around, with only a few social vestiges remaining. Nor has Les Halles been bashful about ushering in the new era. Its structures are extravagant, its cost substantial ($1 billion).[42] The small factories and workshops that once sprinkled the area have all but disappeared. Today the major attractions of Les Halles consist of a cultural center (Pompidou Center), shopping for a new class of consumers, hotels, and inconspicuously placed offices. The Parisian exchange hinges on economic benefits that are more modest than New York's and social values that are vastly different than London's. Its thrust is to replace Les Halles and build it anew, for the beauty of the environment, the culture of the population, and the prestige of Paris.

Behind the redevelopment of the three sites there are significant differences in logic that express different concerns. Discussions of Times Square are filled with the need to rid the area of crime and its raunchy social life. Property value, taxes, and revenue are also major topics of concern. Covent Garden carries the most humane concerns. Much of its rationale is based on a respect for its history, its social scale, and its people. Les Halles bears the responsibility for cultural uplift and the mission of making Paris the world's premier city. Architectural prominence is another keynote for its redevelopment. Compare, for instance, these quotes on each of the sites in Table 10.3.[43]

In short, New York wanted to alter the built environment radically in order to bring about economic vibrancy. London wanted to conserve the built environment and protect the community in the interests of social salvation. Paris wanted to alter the built environment radically for cultural and aesthetic distinction.

Stating these values was not enough. Political control over capital investment was needed to accomplish differing ends. In New York private investment was channeled, but not so narrowly as to strangle private initiative. Developers needed to be given leeway; the profit motive needed to be sustained. To do this, the public sector kept control over the contours of the project. New York's Urban Development Corporation will hold title to the land for fifteen years and will supervise its redevelopment. For their part, private developers will put up the money and, in the sixteenth year, they can exercise an option to buy some of the land.

Times Square is based on the principle of private capital working under the tutelage of the public sector. Its politics is reflected in a mélange of leases, partial public ownership, concessions, and purchase options. Politicians and technocrats led the way and steered a path between competing private developers. They carefully traded on their power to award contracts in return for the resources of private investors. They also traded on a few crucial corners of Times Square in order to salvage its worn-out mid-blocks (theaters, subway entrances, walkways). Thus while private developers furnished the capital, government focused the application of that capital.

Though developers will pay a hefty price and will assume the risks, they have the opportunity of taking title to a bonanza in the heart of Manhattan. But it is a bonanza that is slated to produce over 20,000 jobs and furnish payments to the city.[44] In New York this is made possible through the powers of government (eminent domain, tax abatement, planning), which act in concert with the resources of private enterprise (initiative, risk, investment).

Neither Covent Garden nor Les Halles has the same kind of relationship with private capital. In Europe, control over capital investment is much more complete. Again, the type of control reflects desired ends. In Covent Garden, where protection and preservation are the keys, government has defrayed the costs of renovation. The public sector is

Table 10.3. Typical Concerns: Three Sites

Times Square

The Times Square redevelopment plan is the last chance of the century to eliminate the blight and social decay that threaten to transform this area from a center of commerce and transportation to a miasmal swamp awash with pimps, peddlers and purveyors of our society's greatest social ills.—*Chairman, N.Y. State Urban Development Corporation*

An estimated 4,000 people work in the project area, an extraordinarily low figure . . . a single fully occupied . . . office building alone would house between 4,000 and 5,000 employees . . . the value of the property is also depressed [which is] the direct consequence of the lack of any substantial new construction. . . .—*Environmental Impact Statement, N.Y. State Urban Development Corporation*

I do strongly feel that of all the things that have taken place since I became involved in this issue 25 years ago, this is the worst that has ever emerged. I think it will mean the destruction of Times Square and we will never see it again.—*Chairman, New York City Landmarks Conservancy*

the landlord for the renovated market building. Assorted small businesses rent space and pay a modest $1.12 million per year.[45]

London's tradition of publicly owned housing also goes a long way toward achieving social goals. In Covent Garden, about 30 percent of dwellings are publicly owned, thus the old community could be sheltered in buildings that did justice to its sense of camaraderie and cohesion.[46] Unlike other places, Covent Garden avoided the disastrous path of stuffing its working class in multistory cubbyholes. Finally, control over capital investment is augmented by the influence of community organizations and by borough government. These organizations often put the brakes on projects that threaten social well-being.

Covent Garden	Les Halles
A major attitude which prevailed . . . was the emphasis placed on the general concept of conservation, not so much in architectural value as in terms of the general character and charm of Covent Garden . . . extensive physical change could be very detrimental to this character.—*Greater London Council, Covent Garden Team*	We must give Paris a new heart with a Latin flavor . . . The Pompidou Center will be [Les Halles'] great bridge that will allow the 20th century to make its mark on Paris.—*Mayor, City of Paris*
There has been little disruptive large or medium-scale office development in Covent Garden . . . the Council is operating a policy of firm restraint . . . special regard will be paid to the environment and the traffic aspects of proposed development. —*Greater London Council, Covent Garden Team*	A little after October of 1978 the Mayor of Paris questioned the colossal architecture for the buildings on the north side of Les Halles. He asked for a new plan which might better integrate the architecture with the surrounding environment and have a greater respect for the urban fabric, the traditional streets, and give particular care to open space.—*Director, Société d'Economie Mixte d'Aménagement des Halles*
What I am not going to do is create a bonanza for the developer and if someone has bought in anticipation of erecting some vast edifice somewhere it is not my fault. —*Secretary for the Environment and Inspector for Covent Garden*	The books about [old] Les Halles are very poetic, yes indeed very poetic. I lived near Les Halles when I was younger and it was a very picturesque place. Like the suks of Bangkok or Hong Kong. But Paris is not Bangkok and finally Les Halles was filthy, unhealthy and difficult to pass through. And at the time no one defended keeping the pavilions. The Prefect, Mr. Doublet, knew they had to be destroyed for the good of all of Paris.—*Chief Planner, City of Paris*

In Les Halles, where dynamic redevelopment is coupled to aesthetic value, investment control is lodged within the public sector. But it is a control insulated from direct popular influence, and it purposely incorporates large business firms into redevelopment. The City of Paris holds title to the land and retains authority over design, construction, and architecture. The mixed corporation manages Les Halles and grants construction rights to select developers. Construction rights are hedged by public plans, with which contractors must agree to comply. The formula allows for a tighter control than is the case for Times Square, yet it also permits greater private incentives than is possible in Covent Garden. Chirac can tell the developers what he wants, because he is not completely dependent upon them for capital investment. Meanwhile those investors who do join the venture are able to pour their own initiative into the framework.[47]

Surely it is within the realm of politics to control development by managing the infusion of investment capital. Arrangements can vary a great deal—from the partnership with large capital in Times Square, to the fragmentation into small capital within Covent Garden, and finally to the subordination of large capital in Les Halles.[48]

Times Square, Les Halles, and Covent Garden are incarnations, *mutatis mutandis*, of the other six cases considered earlier. All sites reflect the political complexion of their habitat. The technicalities of planning cannot be divorced from the exigencies of politics: building cities is an expression of city politics.

Corporatist Politics and Change

Times are changing. Three great cities are still in the process of change, and a new politics continues to evolve. The political change is perhaps less perceptible than the physical transformation, but it is no less profound. Politics made post-industrialism possible, just as politics composed its contours and apportioned its values.

Gone are the days when buccaneers could single-handedly develop tracts of land and shape the city. Gone too are the times when hundreds of separate transactions could surface to mold the landscape gradually. The entrepreneurs can no longer build cities by secretly negotiating with political glad-handers or by paying homage to the royal family.

This is not to say that the corporatist sweep will clear the way for more popular participation or that it will do away with political corruption. Rather than disappear, these problems will take on different qualities. More people may be able to plug into corporatist modes of participation, but the impersonal nature of that participation will increase citizen alienation. Granting recognition to one group will result in the lost influence of another group. As politics becomes more complex, favoritism will be elevated to a grander scale. We can expect that corporatist politics will standardize favor-giving, that contracts will go to organizations with the most political clout, and that less organized groups will be left out. Thus, the inherent structure of corporatism will continue to pose problems.

As Samuel Beer has theorized, this is an age of collectivism.[49] It is an age of mass organization. Whether mass organizations are composed of business, labor, communities, or government, they represent the direct interests of thousands of people. Without organization these interests are just raw demands, difficult to convert into feasible action.

It is organization that formulates, systematizes, and coordinates interests so they can be readied for decision making.

Corporatism is a way of rationalizing large-scale interests and making them consonant with the larger polity. Collective bargaining, concertation of interests, and planning are the tools for achieving generalized goals. The corporatist mood sets the parameters for the major actors—the politicians, technocrats, and interest groups. It conditions the things they do—their interaction, their pressures, their choices, and even their values.

Just the same, there is considerable diversity within corporatist politics. The societies, economies, and environments of New York, Paris, and London differ. The interaction, pressures, choices, and values of the major actors also differ. Much as earlier studies of elitism and pluralism showed important variations from society to society, so too does this one.[50] Each city has grown out of its particular roots and yields its particular variations. Over time, the political economies of New York, Paris, and London have created precedents that continue to shape current practice.[51] New York's pluralist-corporatist hybrid comes out of a history of fragmented government, an admiration for political entrepreneurship, and a reverence for capitalism. The politics of personality also make an imprint upon contemporary New York. In Paris, corporatism has grown out of monarchical rule and the power of bureaucracy. Private capital was less independent and the free market less sacrosanct. France is a nation in which tying capital to statist objectives is a political norm. London's liberal corporatism is drawn from an altogether different history. Its politics has been caught in an ambivalence between a respect for local democracy and a commitment to central authority. London has also inherited an ambivalence toward capitalism, drawn on the one hand from the naked industrial competition of Dickens's London and, on the other, from the moderating influence of Fabian Socialism.

Just as we rely on these traditions to understand variations between each city, so too can we make sense of continuity and change within New York, Paris, and London. The roots of urban precedent bend the branches of the contemporary city.

As New York moves into the next decade, its politics continues to revolve around two individuals—Koch and Cuomo—and around the magnetism of the marketplace. In 1986, charges of corruption rocked New York's City Hall. Though not personally connected with corruption, Koch's approval rating plummeted,[52] and along with that fall came a rise of protest against some of the city's most treasured projects, including Times Square.[53]

Scandals are not a novelty in New York; they plague the city the way locusts hit farmers. They arrive every ten years or so, do damage, and disappear until it is time to return. The significance of corruption lies not as much in its discovery as in the revelation that New York politics is exceedingly fragile. The system's reliance on political stars who link themselves, early in the decision stage, to private investors makes that relationship suspect. Even when scandal occurs elsewhere, land-use projects fall under a shadow of mistrust. Years of honest work may be tied to the fate of a single person (is any principal under indictment?), or may fall prey to the vagaries of public perception (politics is a crooked business), or may be vulnerable to a predominant mood (can we trust government to do anything?).

Fortunately for City Hall, these scandals have begun to abate. The big projects have resumed, though politicians and technocrats carry on with uncharacteristic hesitation. Some of that hesitation stems from a caution about sparking future scandals. Some derives from a spreading popular belief that areas within the urban core may have laid themselves open to excessive development. The conviction has begun to seep in that it is time to rein in the builders, preserve what little open space remains, and respect the zoning laws. Although we can expect this caution to materialize in the most densely developed parts of Manhattan, post-industrial development is likely to proceed elsewhere. Manhattan's west perimeter will continue to be suffused with residential and office towers. Planners anticipate that Manhattan's prosperity will spill into surrounding counties. Indeed, the shortage of space in Manhattan has brought about higher demands in parts of Kings County and western Queens. There are even small islands of resurgence in the Bronx.

In Paris, the centripetal forces of the system are still powerful. Chirac's role as party leader has not taken him very far from city government. He continues to reside at the Hôtel de Ville and chooses to do much of his work there. For Chirac, the mayoralty is a power base. Holding onto it means that he can dart in and out of the national government as political needs dictate. Surprisingly, Chirac continues to direct key initiatives in land-use planning. He meets regularly with top technocrats and constantly exhorts them to promote projects.

The cohesion between the political-technocratic elite that bridges state and city will bring future payoffs. The impetus toward prestige and grandeur gains momentum. On the eastern side of Paris, a new Opera House was planned by the Socialist government and criticized by the Parisian Gaullists. When the Gaullists controlled the government, they completed the project. Other public works will endow the city with more eminence. New museums dot the city, La Défense grows, and Paris heightens its appeal for international acclaim.

Of the three cities, London has traditionally been the most politically staid. Today it is the most politically dynamic. The abolition of the GLC was a first attack in a protracted Tory offensive. It deprived Labour of the chance to win over a London-wide constituency and reduced its platform for appealing against the central government. Abolition also cut off a string of benefits that tied the Labour constituency together. These included the GLC's "overspill housing" and its programs for land acquisition and conservation (the Green Belt, Covent Garden).[54]

Thatcher's 1987 victory refueled her push toward radical rightist change. The second attack against Labour is aimed directly at its borough strongholds. The Tories have led the ideological charge with their own nostrum of a "capital-owning democracy." Applied to post-industrial change, its logistics begin with tax reductions for corporations and homeowners. This is supposed to prevent high-spending Socialist councils from siphoning off private capital. The conservatives also want to create a new class of property owners. Where possible, the Tories plan to sell off public housing to tenants and other private buyers. Those renters who cannot afford to purchase their own shelter will be given the opportunity to manage public housing through tenant cooperatives or transfer housing ownership to special associations or independent landlords. In land development, the success of the LDDC stands as a Tory model. New development corporations will go into some areas, acquire property, supply infrastructure, and sell off the prepared product to private investors. The Tories intend to change the economic system. Not satisfied with tinkering with the welfare state, they aim to get rid of it—by cutting off Labour's roots in "municipal Socialism" and by starving its branches of political sustenance.

The Tory program may be more easily announced than accomplished. True, Thatcher has been an unwavering partisan who has moved onto ground where her predecessors dared not tread. It is also true that Thatcher's plans for housing hold a powerful appeal and, if successful, would greatly weaken Labour. Her other plans are fraught with problems. Tax reduction for the well-off, coupled to spending cuts for the poor, will increase resentment. The LDDC obtained very special property, under special conditions, and is not an easy model to follow. Other development corporations will have difficulty mimicking its success.

Post-industrial change is propelled or circumscribed by politics. Thatcher has shaken liberal corporatism and heightened its conflicts, but the regime and its opposition both continue to function. The Tories came to their 1987 victory with a scant 42 percent of the vote, in a deeply divided nation, and the opposition is not likely to wither, go away, or die. London's politics is still conducted through liberal corporatist institutions and familiar routes of participation. The parties, the central government, the bureaucracy, the boroughs, the GLCs-in-exile, forums, and publicly supported interest groups (tied to these institutions) continue as the major actors in this drama. And it is impossible to separate the actors from the performance.

Abolition may have rid the Tories of an annoyance, and it gives them some immediate advantages. But the GLC's manifest and psychological functions are missed. These functions will probably be taken up by other institutions, which grow into new roles, or by a suitable replacement. For the future, the betting in the town halls, the pubs, and the university dining rooms is that some kind of GLC will come back. One study has already predicted that abolition will begin

> to falter early on in its life, partly because of effective obstruction by Labour boroughs and partly because of disruption caused by rate-capping. . . . Policy effectiveness and service levels in transport, housing, planning and other areas begin to slip. The new organization and financial arrangements are complex to operate and badly understood. A period of policy drift ensues which leaves no clear response to London's changing overall problems. In the longer term (by the mid-1990's) measures are taken to reinstitutionalize a strategic policy-making body for Greater London.[55]

The Post-Industrial City and Change

New York, Paris, and London are world cities. Examining them, we see they have more in common with other world cities than with smaller cities in their own nations. World cities are subject to similar external pressures. They command the attention of international finance, multinational corporations, and are hot spots for media and the arts.

What brings a city to world-class status? World cities are not mere ciphers for whatever new technology comes along, but actively create their own environments. The clue to their power is that they have learned to generate growth from within. Using their own resources, they convert old uses to new ones, mix these in hundreds of permutations, and pyramid one asset upon another until they have virtually re-created themselves.

Self-transformation changed sixteenth- and seventeenth-century trading cities into eighteenth- and nineteenth-century industrial ones. It now enables industrial cities to become post-industrial models for the twentieth and twenty-first centuries. New York, Paris, and London show us, in varying ways, how worn out industrial enclaves can be converted into modern CBD's, how obsolete wharfs can be turned into luxury housing, and how fruit markets or seedy downtowns can become fancy cultural centers.

Yet for all its seeming simplicity, the road to post-industrialism is complicated. There is no single path—only detours with buried treasures and hidden pitfalls. New York, with its extraordinary successes and its wrenching traumas, is almost a caricature of self-transformation. One of its offspring is an expanded, hard-driving, white-collar class. This is the middle order of New York's post-industrial society, and much of it can be found in Queens, Richmond, and the suburbs.

Two other New York social orders are more conspicuous. They live closer to one another within the municipality. One of these, affluent and hopeful, embraces a large number of well-educated, employable, small-family or single-person households. These people enjoy a new and separate world of private, highly personalized services. If they live in Manhattan, they reside in privately owned high rises, they travel by private automobile, and they work in the private sector. They are protected by private police, educated at private schools, and socialize at private clubs. Even the letters they write and packages they mail are transported by private carriers. The other social order is poor and despairing. Either post-industrialism has bypassed them or they have bypassed it. If they avail themselves of help, it comes from public services. This order occupies the city's public housing projects, rides public transit, learns in the public schools, and survives on the public dole. If they are homeless, they sleep on the city's streets; if they are attacked, they seek protection from the city's police; and if they relax, they use the city's parks.

The two orders might as well live on different planets, but they live in the same city. Both desperately need each other. The rich need clerks, secretaries, technicians—ultimately professionals. Yet the poor are ill trained, often semi-literate and unprepared for the new economy. Just as certainly the poor need the rich—if only to pay for public services. The poor also need the rich for jobs and a better way of life. These needs are increasingly unbridgeable. As the demand for post-industrial skills increases and as the poor fall further behind, the tragic mismatch grows worse. The conundrum is part of New York's post-industrial inheritance—partly a product of rapid, careless growth—and it continues to haunt the city.

Self-transformation has been much more deliberate and controlled in Paris. The city is a piece of technocratic art—carefully arranged and mixed with preconceptions of what things are supposed to go where. Old neighborhoods have become incredibly neat and give the appearance of contrived quaintness. Almost everyone uses public services. The working and middle classes have been slotted into public housing, the trains are packed with commuters, and cultural centers are factories of mass consumption.

Paris is becoming homogenized into a post-industrial society. Its physical transformation has seeped into the social structure. The disparate social orders, so obvious in New York, are in Paris separate classes that participate in a common order.

This is not to say that the transformation has accomplished class harmony—only that the extensive and common use of public services ease the most grotesque disparities of class. Surprisingly, to Americans, it is easier to be poor in Paris than it is in New York, because the differences are not so obvious. This observation says a great deal about a transformation whose exceptions do not so much constitute an opposite stratum as involve people who are either socially integrated (unemployed workers) or who are presumed to have a temporary status (immigrants and students).

For a long time, London's self-transformation was limited. Today it is accelerated by a freer flow of market forces and the stimulation of private investment. London is at a historic juncture, and it will be another decade before we know how it fares. The most extreme result of Tory radicalism would fragment the metropolis into bits and pieces. Greater London would more resemble subgovernments fighting to enrich their own turf than a coherent metropolis. The most vigorous development would be concentrated in parts of the CBD, the Docklands, and some outer boroughs. Many of the inner boroughs would encounter a withering corrosion. Greater London might enjoy more jobs, but the celebration of its prosperity would occur amid less balance, less conservation, and a less humane society.

This scenario would place London's post-industrialism closer to the disparate social orders of New York. Although many Londoners might profit from the rapid conversion, a whole stratum would be left behind, increasingly ill equipped and psychologically incapable of sharing in the change.

The experience of other cities tells us that radical and prodigious change can hurt. A rising tide may raise a lot of ships, but it does not raise all of them and it may leave many submerged. Some of the most exuberant Tories talk about cleaning up London's "dependency ghettos" by adopting American techniques—as if London possessed New York's problems. For the time being it does not, but it is not far-fetched to see them developing.

In a perfect world, change should maximize benefits and minimize costs. Decision makers work, however, in an imperfect world, limited by precedent, circumstance, and public habit. Even when everything falls into place, change is not easy. Some are bound to be dissatisfied and believe that other cities have done a better job. This perception is not so much wrong as it is dependent upon position. The experience of New York, Paris, and London shows us just how relative those positions can be, and why politics must always mediate planning.

Appendix

THE THREE TABLES that make up this appendix are intended to aid the reader in determining what is referred to as the central business district (CBD), urban core, first ring, and second ring in the New York, Paris, and London areas. Note that the CBD is part of the urban core and is included in the latter's statistics in Tables A.1, A.2, and A.3.

Table A.1.   New York's Components: 1980

Analytic Category	Common Appellation	Size in sq. mi./ Residential Density
Central Business District (CBD)	CBD or "downtown"	9 sq. mi./ 63,333 per sq. mi.
Urban Core	Manhattan	22.3 sq. mi./ 64,014 per sq. mi.
Outer City or First Ring	Bronx, Kings, Queens, and Richmond counties, which are part of the municipality of NYC, plus Hudson, Union, and Essex counties in New Jersey.	886.4 sq. mi./ densities vary from 32,192 per sq. mi. in Kings to below 1,000 per sq. mi. in Richmond.
Second Ring	The "suburbs" or exurbs, which consist of 12 counties in N.Y. State, N.J., and Conn. These include the counties of Nassau, Suffolk Westchester, Putnam, and Rockland in N.Y.S.; Bergen, Passaic, Morris, Monmouth, Somerset, and Middlesex in N.J.; plus Fairfield in Conn.	Approx. 3,600 sq. mi./ densities vary from 4,683 per sq. mi. in the nearer suburb of Nassau to 683 per sq. mi. in the distant exurb of Morris County.

New York Standard Consolidated Area: 4,000 sq. mi.; 16,600,000 residents. New York City: 319 sq. mi.; 7,071,030 residents

Population	Notable Characteristics
570,000 residents; over 2,000,000 work force	Consists of an area south of 61st Street to the Manhattan Battery. This area contains the great financial institutions on Wall Street, the United Nations, the World Trade Center, and the theater district.
1,427,533 residents	Heterogeneous population within the urban core, but there is a sharp geographical division between rich and poor, black and white. Poorer populations, which are mostly black and Hispanic, live in Harlem, north of 96th Street. Most of the white, upper-middle-class population lives south of 96th Street.
8,410,000 residents	Conditions in the first ring are quite mixed. The counties of the Bronx, Kings, Hudson, Union, and Essex consist of old multiple-family housing and much of it is deteriorated. These counties have undergone a transition in the last two decades; white working classes have left and have been replaced by a poorer population of blacks and Hispanics. Welfare and unemployment are common in these counties. On the other hand, the county of Queens is newly developed and consists of single and two-family houses and luxury apartment complexes that have been popular settlements for the middle class.
6,795,763 residents	The second ring varies greatly in urban form and social composition. Most of the suburbs and exurbs consist of low-density, single-family units with a middle- to upper-middle-class social composition.

Table A.2.   Paris's Components: 1982

Analytic Category	Common Appellation	Size in sq. mi./ Density
Central Business District (CBD)	Ten inner arrondissements of Paris	9 sq. mi./ 50,000 per sq. mi.
Urban Core	Ville de Paris or Paris	42.16 sq. mi./ 51,430 per sq. mi.
Outer City or First Ring	Three departments immediately surrounding La Ville de Paris; "Seine-Banlieu" or La Petite Couronne	262.13 sq. mi./ 14,875 per sq. mi.
Second Ring	La Grande Couronne; four departments that surround La Petite Couronne	4,524.08 sq. mi./ 882 per sq. mi.

Ile-de-France: 4,828.16 sq. mi.; 10,000,000 residents
Ville de Paris: 42.16 sq. mi.; 2,168,300 residents

Population: resident and/or work force	Notable Characteristics
1,000,000 residents; work force is slightly higher	The CBD is near the very epicenter of the city, although it is extending westward toward La Défense. The area contains the major governmental institutions, the Paris stock exchange, major banks, museums, and national monuments as well as the CBD.
2,168,300 residents; work force of nearly 2 million	The urban core is becoming a middle- to upper-middle class city. This is particularly true of the inner arrondissements at the heart of La Ville de Paris and in the western arrondissements such as the 15th and 16th. Paris is undergoing an "embourgeoisement" or gentrification, although working classes and immigrant groups can still be found in arrondissements like the 11th, 12th, 13th, 18th, and 19th.
3,899,200 residents	The three departments are Hauts-de-Seine, Seine-St. Denis, and Val-de-Marne. Contains a heterogeneous population with large working-class populations, particularly in Seine-St. Denis. Single-family dwellings mixed with high-rise development. Housing is also proximate to large industrial zones and factories.
3,988,600 residents	These four departments are Val-d'Oise, Essonne, Yvelines, and Seine-et-Marne. Low-density area; mixed suburban and agricultural usage. Area of recent growth.

Table A.3.   London's Components: 1982

Analytic Category	Common Appellation	Size in sq. mi./ Density
Central Business District (CBD)	Central London or the Central Area*	9 sq. mi./ 25,556 per sq. mi.
Urban core	Inner London	117 sq. mi./ 20,000 per sq. mi.
Outer City or First Ring	Outer London	493 sq. mi./ 9,041 per sq. mi.
Second Ring	Outer Metropolitan Area (OMA)	3,802 sq. mi./ average density 1,391 per sq. mi.

Greater London: 610 sq. mi.; 6,817,200 residents (comprises CBD, urban core, and first ring)
* The term "Central London" is used by the Greater London Council in its *Greater London Development Plan* as approved in July 1976. The term "Central Area" is an official statistical designation. Though there are slight variations in the boundaries of Central London and the Central Area, they are roughly comparable.

Population	Notable Characteristics
230,010 residents; work force of more than 1 million	Consists of the "City of London" and the boroughs of Westminster, Kensington-Chelsea, and Camden. Also small portions of Tower Hamlets, Southwark, Lambeth, and Hackney.
2,350,000 residents	Consists of 14 "inner London boroughs" whose populations vary from 6,000 in "the City" to 261,000 in Wandsworth. Median population for the boroughs is 184,000 residents. Though many boroughs are heterogeneous, the wealthiest boroughs are Westminster, "the City," and Kensington-Chelsea. Poorer boroughs include Tower Hamlets and Hackney.
4,467,000 residents	Consists of the 18 remaining boroughs, which possess 77% of Greater London's residential land. Housing in outer London is newer and generally of a better condition with more amenities.
5,290,000 residents	Low-density area, but contains increasing number of burgeoning industrial towns and new towns.

Notes

Chapter 1

[1] For a view of one or more great cities that focuses on economics and industry, see the classic study by Edgar Hoover and Raymond Vernon, *Anatomy of a Metropolis* (Garden City, N.Y.: Anchor Books, 1962), and Raymond Vernon, *Metropolis 1985* (Garden City, N.Y.: Anchor Books, 1963). Peter Hall, *World Cities* (New York: McGraw-Hill, 1977), deals with several perspectives, including economic development, demographics, and planning.

For a strong administrative and legal perspective, see William Robson and D. E. Regan, eds., *Great Cities of the World* (Beverly Hills, Calif.: Sage, 1975), vols. 1 and 2. See also the multivolume series on major cities (Paris, Leningrad, Stockholm, Lagos, and Zagreb) published by Praeger during the 1960s. See especially Annamarie Hauck Walsh, *The Urban Challenge to Government* (New York: Praeger, 1969). For a social perspective stressing urbanization, see Sylvia Fava, ed., *Urbanism in World Perspective* (New York: Thomas Y. Crowell, 1968); Charles Tilly, ed., *An Urban World* (Boston: Little, Brown, 1974); and Lloyd Rodwin, *Nations and Cities* (Boston: Houghton Mifflin, 1970).

For a political perspective, see Wallace Sayre and Herbert Kaufman, *Governing New York City* (New York: W. W. Norton, 1960); Frank Smallwood, *Greater London: The Politics of Metropolitan Reform* (Indianapolis: Bobbs-Merrill, 1965); Gerald Rhodes, *The Government of London* (Toronto: University of Toronto Press, 1970); and M. Franc and J.-P. Leclerc, *Les Institutions de la Région Parisienne* (Paris: Berger-Levrault, 1977).

For an evolutionary perspective stressing architecture, see Norma Evenson, *Paris: A Century of Change, 1878-1978* (New Haven: Yale University Press, 1979).

[2] For broad-based multidimensional views, see Stanley Brunn and Jack Williams, *Cities of the World* (New York: Harper & Row, 1983). One book that takes a focused view of the performance of a great many cities is Robert Fried and Francine Rabinovitz, *Comparative Urban Politics: A Performance Approach* (Englewood Cliffs, N.J.: Prentice-Hall, 1980).

[3] See Daniel Bell, *The Coming of Post-Industrial Society* (New York: Basic Books, 1976), p. xii. For other studies on the evolution of industrial society, see Jonathan Gershuny, *After Industrial Society* (Totowa, N.J.: Humanities Press, 1978); John Galbraith, *The New Industrial State* (Boston: Houghton Mifflin, 1967); *Post-Industrial America*, ed. George Sternlieb and James Hughes (New Brunswick, N.J.: Center for Urban Policy Research, 1975). For an interesting paper on the subject, consult John Mollenkopf, "Paths toward the Post-Industrial Service City: The Northeast and the Southwest," Rutgers University Center for Urban Policy Research.

317

⁴ The point to be made is that post-industrialism should be taken not as a narrow but as a broad socioeconomic phenomenon. Although it contains elements of the "high technology" revolution, it should not be taken for just that. Although it contains elements of the service sector, it is not exclusively oriented toward services. Bell complains about such misinterpretations of his book and in a footnote wryly says, "To the extent that some critics identify me with the centrality of a service sector, it is either ignorance or a willful misreading of my book" (Bell, *The Coming of Post-Industrial Society*, p. ix).

⁵ Bell, *The Coming of Post-Industrial Society*, p. xvii.

⁶ For studies on the effects of post-industrialism, see *Back to the City*, ed. Shirley Laska and Daphine Spain (Elmsford, N.Y.: Pergamon Press, 1980). Consult also John Mollenkopf's ground-breaking account on the political reasons behind post-industrialism, *The Contested City* (Princeton: Princeton University Press, 1983), esp. ch. 6.

⁷ For example, contrast the Marxist accounts of James O'Connor, *The Fiscal Crisis of the State* (New York: St. Martin's Press, 1972) and Martin Carnoy, *The State and Political Theory* (Princeton: Princeton Univeristy Press, 1984), with Anthony Downs, *Opening Up the Suburbs* (New Haven: Yale University Press, 1973) and Edward Banfield, *The Unheavenly City Revisited* (Boston: Little, Brown, 1974), esp. ch. 2. For a general account of urban political economy, see William Schultze, *Urban Politics* (Englewood Cliffs, N.J.: Prentice-Hall, 1985).

⁸ There are, of course, exceptions, the most notable being Charles Lindblom, *Politics and Markets* (New York: Basic Books, 1977).

⁹ Scholars making these studies are also known as "public choice" or "rational choice" theorists. For a contemporary example, consult Robert Bish, Elinor Ostrom, and Vincent Ostrom, *Understanding Urban Government* (Washington, D.C.: American Enterprise Institute, 1973). See also Roland McKean, "The Unseen Hand in Government," *American Economic Review* 55 (June 1965): 496-506; Robert Dahl and Charles Lindblom, *Politics, Economics and Welfare* (New York: Harper & Row, 1953); and Robert Warren, "A Municipal Services Market Model of Metropolitan Organization," *Journal of the American Institute of Planners* 30 (August 1964): 193-204. A most recent and radical free-market approach is E. E. Savas, *Privatizing the Public Sector* (New York: Chatham House, 1982)

¹⁰ Robert Bish, *The Public Economy of Metropolitan Areas* (Chicago: Markham Publishing, 1971), pp. 3, 12.

¹¹ Banfield, *The Unheavenly City Revisited*, p. 48.

¹² Bish, *The Political Economy*, p. 68.

¹³ Larry Sawers, "New Perspectives on the Urban Political Econcomy," in *Marxism and the Metropolis*, ed. William Tabb and Larry Sawers, 2d. ed. (New York: Oxford University Press, 1984), pp. 9,11. Capitalism is pictured in still more stark descriptions within this volume. Note for example the following statement in Sawers, "New Perspectives," p. 12:

Capital as a whole has an interest in the continual fragmentation of the working class since a united working class would be invincible in any clash with capitalists. The continued domination of capital requires this fragmentation. Capitalists thus find it natural to segregate jobs by sex, discriminate against blacks in housing, or hire strikebreakers of a different race or ethnic group. But workers do much of the capitalists' dirty work for them. Racism, sexism, anti-semitism, nativism, the oppression of homosexuals are also ways in which workers turn on each other to the obvious advantage of capital.

[14] Susan Fainstein and Norman Fainstein, "Economic Change, National Policy and the System of Cities," in *Restructuring the City*, ed. Susan Fainstein et al. (New York: Longman, 1983), p. 3.

[15] On this question there are differences among neo-Marxists. Some believe the state can exercise a degree of autonomy and others see a division between those who direct the state and those who control capitalism. Neo-Marxists are, however, in accord that the state always serves the long-term interests of capitalism and its bourgeois proponents. For an interesting review of the literature see Carnoy, *The State and Political Theory*. See also the original essays by Claus Offe, "Advanced Capitalism and the Welfare State," *Politics and Society* (Summer 1972): 479-88, and "The Theory of the Capitalist State and the Problem of Policy Formulation," in *Stress and Contradiction in Modern Capitalism*, ed. Leon Lindberg et al. (Lexington, Mass.: Lexington Books, 1973), pp. 125-43; and by Nicos Poulantzas, "The Problem of the Capitalist State," *New Left Review*, no. 58 (1969): 67-78 (reprinted in *Ideology and Social Science*, ed. Robin Blackburn [New York: Vintage Books, 1973]).

[16] Eric Nordlinger argues that the state quite frequently acts in a manner contrary to social wishes and possesses the capability of ignoring social preferences (called Type I State Autonomy). Although Nordlinger's point is well taken, it may be overstated. My own conclusions concerning land-use politics are that Type I State Autonomy occurs in Paris under a system of mobilizing corporatism. It is, however, rare in New York's corporatist-pluralist hybrid and in London's liberal corporatism. For particulars on different types of political outcomes, see Eric A. Nordlinger, *On the Autonomy of the Democratic State* (Cambridge: Harvard University Press, 1981).

[17] The conception of a "state interest" can differ from that of a "public interest." State interest applies to the collective institutions of government. Public interest comes closer to the interests of "the nation" and emphasizes the collective well-being of society. When discussing the subject, free-market theorists address a public (social) interest rather than a state (government) interest. For a free-market exegesis on the subject, see Martin Meyerson and Edward Banfield, *Politics, Planning and the Public Interest* (New York: Free Press, 1955), esp. pp. 285-302, 322-29.

[18] Interesting as the neo-Marxist explanations may be, many of them are conjectural, self-validating, and lack a footing on which to conduct empirical analyses. Neo-Marxist interpretations on the role of the state are subtle and complex. One interpretation, known as instrumentalism, argues that private capitalists occupy privileged positions both inside and outside the state and therefore hold overwhelming influence over state policy. Instrumentalists argue that even without this unique access, the sheer magnitude of capitalism

puts sufficient pressure on the state so that the preferences of capitalist investors are irresistible.

Another interpretation, known as structuralism, explains that the connection between capitalists and the state is an "objective relation." This means that as long as the relations of production are capitalistic, the state will *automatically* respond to its needs. For structuralists, capitalism is deeply embedded in the system of things, and public actors reflexively act to stabilize economic relationships. That stabilization could include new investment opportunities, new ways of employing labor, or even new housing for a citizen underclass. Almost any action that would prevent, ward off, or mitigate capitalist contradictions is construed by structuralists as a remedy against continual crises.

A third Marxist interpretation, writes Theda Skocpol, emphasizes a "division of labor between those who accumulate capital and those who manage the state apparatus." According to this interpretation, capitalists act to maximize short-term profits and are not capable of appreciating the long-term interests of the economic system. The task is therefore left to "state managers" to stabilize the economy, often in the face of capitalist resistance.

In considering each of these interpretations, instrumentalists do offer manageable hypotheses that can be empirically tested. That is, relations between capitalists and public actors can be examined and policy outcomes analyzed. Here, we are interested in unique access that may be granted to capitalists, pressure that capitalists may exert on public actors, and benefits capitalists may acquire through public policy. The political side of instrumentalism has been subsumed under our own typology of elitism and its characteristics tested in nine cases.

Structuralist and division of labor interpretations are far more elusive. These interpretations are part of a closed, if not circular, set of propositions, which can be neither verified nor rejected. Thus, if one finds that public actors took measures to maximize the profits of capitalist investors, neo-Marxists conclude that the state operates to foster capital accumulation. If one arrives at an opposite finding that shows that public actors curbed or disregarded the profits of capitalists, neo-Marxists conclude that state managers needed to save the capitalists from themselves. State actions on behalf of capitalists are interpreted as a verification of class rule, and state actions against capitalists are rationalized as necessary for the long-term stabilizing of class rule. Short of the state turning around and destroying capitalism, there is nothing that can validate a structuralist or "state manager" explanation.

For an example of instrumentalism, consult Ralph Miliband, *The State in Capitalist Society* (New York: Basic Books, 1969). For neo-Marxist structuralism, see Nicos Poulantzas, *Political Power and Social Classes* (London: New Left Books, 1973) as well as his "The Problem of the Capitalist State." For a "state manager" explanation, see Fred Block, "The Ruling Class Does Not Rule: Notes on the Marxist Theory of the State," *Socialist Revolution*, no. 33 (May-June 1977): 6-28. For an overall account of these interpretations, see Theda Skocpol, "Political Response to Capitalist Crisis: Neo-Marxist Theories of the State and the Case of the New Deal," *Politics and Society* 10, no. 2 (1980): 155-201.

[19] Some Marxist scholars disagree and argue that it is better to accept decline than to accept domination by business interests. Thus two scholars write:

For declining cities the most that . . . government could hope to do would be to use whatever resources it had to mitigate uneven development. Such cities undoubtedly would face a bleak future, but the costs of decline would be distributed more equitably.

Norman Fainstein and Susan Fainstein, "Regime Strategies, Communal Resistance and Economic Forces" in *Restructuring the City*, ed. Fainstein et al., p. 273.

[20] The most incisive and, by now, controversial work in this area is Paul Peterson's, *City Limits* (Chicago: University of Chicago Press, 1981). Another recent and comparative example of how national pressures shape cities is Ted Gurr and Desmond King, *The State and the City* (Chicago: University of Chicago Press, 1987). Although the external pressures on cities should not be underestimated, they are generally "systemic" in nature and difficult to undo. For a full investigation of external pressures on American cities, see H. V. Savitch, *Urban Policy and the Exterior City* (Elmsford, N.Y.: Pergamon Press, 1979).

[21] Ironically, the point is made by a Soviet scholar and quoted in Gregory Andrusz, *Housing and Urban Development in the USSR* (Albany, N.Y.: State University of New York Press, 1985), p. 269.

[22] For the uses and techniques of "ideal types," see Max Weber, *The Theory of Social and Economic Organization*, ed. Talcott Parsons (New York: Free Press, 1984), ch. 2 and pt. 1. See also *From Max Weber: Essays in Sociology*, ed. H. H. Gerth and C. Wright Mills (New York: Oxford University Press, 1946), chs. 2, 7.

[23] The best-known elite studies are C. Wright Mills, *The Power Elite* (New York: Oxford University Press, 1959); G. William Domhoff, *Who Rules America?* (Englewood Cliffs, N.J.: Prentice-Hall, 1967); and Floyd Hunter, *Community Power Structure* (Garden City, N.Y.: Anchor Books, 1963).

Some of the best-known pluralist studies are Robert Dahl, *Who Governs?* (New Haven: Yale University Press, 1961); Sayre and Kaufman, *Governing New York City*; David B. Truman, *The Governmental Process* (New York: Alfred Knopf, 1960); and Edward Banfield, *Political Influence* (New York: Free Press, 1961).

For useful corporatist studies, see *Comparative Political Studies* 10, no. 1, ed. Philippe Schmitter (April 1977); *Organizing Interests in Western Europe*, ed. Suzanne Berger (New York: Cambridge University Press, 1981); James Simmie, *Power, Property and Corporatism* (London: Macmillan, 1981). In particular, see an article by J. T. Winkler, "Corporatism," *European Journal of Sociology* 1, no. 17 (1976): 100-136.

[24] The descriptions of elitism are distilled from Mills, *The Power Elite*; Hunter, *The Power Structure*; and Domhoff, *Who Rules?* A more contemporary

account of the elitist rebuttal to pluralism can be found in G. William Dom-hoff, *New Haven and Community Power Re-examined* (New Brunswick, N.J.: Transaction, 1978).

²⁵ There are elitist accounts that maintain that everyone who has power is part of an elite. These power holders may include labor union leaders, politicians, and others. Since all government by its nature is representative and must consist of very few individuals, it is impossible to disprove this type of claim. The claim is therefore tautological and lacks explanatory value. For an example, see Jack Newfield and Paul Dubrul, *The Abuse of Power* (New York: Viking Press, 1977), esp. ch. 4.

²⁶ The idea belongs to Hunter, *The Power Structure*, pp. 62ff.

²⁷ Thus, says Hunter's *The Power Structure*, p. 100:

It is true that there is no formal tie between economic interests and government, but the structure of policy determining committees . . . make government subservient to the interests of these combined groups. The governmental departments . . . are loathe to act before consulting and "clearing" with these interests.

²⁸ Karl Marx, *The Communist Manifesto* (Chicago: Henry Regnery, 1954), p. 18. We should emphasize that although elite theorists may share some common conceptions with Marxists, they are not necessarily Marxist. The elitist and neo-elitist analysis focuses on *power relations*; Marxist and neo-Marxist studies focus on the broader aspect of the *political economy*. This distinction also distinguishes the discussion of "typologies" from the "contextual themes" of the previous section.

²⁹ The descriptions of pluralism are distilled from Dahl, *Who Governs?*; Sayre and Kaufman, *Governing New York City*; Banfield, *Political Influence*; and Truman, *The Governmental Process*. For a contemporary discussion of pluralism and its variations, consult John Manley, "New Pluralism: A Class Analysis of Pluralism I and Pluralism II," *American Political Science Review* 77 (June 1983): 368–83.

³⁰ Thus Dahl speaks of democratic values being upheld by a "democratic creed" (Dahl, *Who Governs?* ch. 28) and Truman speaks in similar terms about the "habit background" of the American people and "potential interest groups" (Truman, *The Governmental Process*, pp. 158–59).

³¹ Truman, *The Governmental Process*, p. 159. For another pluralist orientation that stresses overlapping membership and consensus, see Seymour Martin Lipset, *Political Man* (1960; Baltimore: Johns Hopkins University Press, 1981), ch. 1.

³² On the importance of "access," see Dahl, *Who Governs?* ch. 24; Truman, *The Governmental Process*, ch. 9; and Sayre and Kaufman, *Governing New York City*, ch. 14. Note also the following from Sayre and Kaufman, *Governing New York City*, p. 720:

No part of the city's large and varied population is alienated from participation in the system. . . . All the diverse elements in the city, in competition with each other, can and do partake of the stakes of politics.

And compare this with Banfield, *Political Influence*, p. 339:

Nothing of importance is done in Chicago without its first being discovered what interests will be affected and how they will be affected and without the losses that will accrue to some being weighed carefully against the gains that will accrue to others.

33 For the importance of state "umpirage" and "broker" roles, see Sayre and Kaufman, *Governing New York City*, "Introduction to the Paperback Edition," and chs. 1, 18, 19.

The image cast by pluralists was that politicians were neutral intermediaries who waited for private initiatives to well up out of the social structure before acting. Consider the following from Banfield, *Political Influence*, p. 253:

The political head, therefore, neither fights for a program of his own making nor endeavors to find a solution to the conflicts that are brought before him. Instead he waits for the community to agree upon a project. When agreement is reached . . . he ratifies the agreement and carries it into effect.

Alan Altshuler observed the same phenomenon in Minneapolis, where he noted that the mayor ". . . does not actively sponsor anything. He waits for private groups to agree on a project. If he likes it he endorses it." Alan Altshuler, *The City Planning Process* (Ithaca: Cornell University Press, 1965), p. 362.

34 The descriptions of corporatism are largely distilled from the April 1977 issue of *Comparative Political Studies*, ed. Schmitter; *Organizing Interests*, ed. Berger; Simmie, *Power, Property and Corporatism*; and Winkler, "Corporatism."

35 Schmitter, ed., *Comparative Political Studies* 10, no. 1 (1977): 9-10.

36 Winkler, "Corporatism," p. 103, defines corporatism as "an economic system in which the state directs and controls predominantly privately owned business according to four principles: unity, order, nationalism, and success."

37 Jean Lojkine, *La Politique Urbaine dans la Région Parisienne, 1945-1972* (Paris: Mouton, 1976), p. 8.

38 On this account, Hunter, *The Power Structure*, p. 111, takes a similar position, albeit in scholarly language:

The top group of the power hierarchy has been isolated and defined. . . . These men are drawn largely from the business class. . . . They form cliques or crowds . . . which formulate policy. . . . The structure is held together by common interests, money, habit, delegated responsibilities, and in some cases by coercion and force.

39 Newfield and Dubrul, *The Abuse of Power*, p. 75.

40 Sayre and Kaufman, *Governing New York City*, p. xii.

41 Ibid., p. 658. Again the same observation is confirmed in Banfield, *Political Influence*, p. 250. Note Banfield's comment there about Chicago's mayor:

The political head is not likely to take a lively interest in the content of policy or to be specially gifted in the development of ideas.

Robert Dahl's study shows multiple patterns of leadership. Dahl sees the mayor playing a more active and energetic role, but Dahl too conveys a sense of restraint about political leadership. Dahl (*Who Governs?* p. 209) says about the mayor's "executive-centered coalition":

[The mayor] was a negotiator rather than a hierarchical executive. He could rarely command, but he could apply his political resources and skills to the task of negotiating and bargaining.

⁴² Winkler, "Corporatism," p. 105.

⁴³ Simmie, *Power, Property and Corporatism*, p. 305.

⁴⁴ For the idea of liberal corporatism, I am indebted to Leo Panitch, "The Development of Corporatism in Liberal Democracies," *Comparative Political Studies* 10, no. 1, ed. Schmitter (April 1977).

⁴⁵ Cuomo was elected Governor in 1982 and in 1986. Koch was elected Mayor in 1977, 1981, and 1985.

⁴⁶ For a rare, useful, and enlightening discussion of pluralism vis-à-vis corporatism, see Reginald Harrison, *Pluralism and Corporatism* (London: George Allen & Unwin, 1980). Another volume that deals with how the modern state copes with the pluralist-corporatist issue is Alan Wolfe, *The Limits of Legitimacy* (New York: Free Press, 1977). See especially Wolfe's discussion of the "franchise state" in chs. 4 and 5.

⁴⁷ Thus there were strong conflicts between machine and reform politicians, between Governor Nelson Rockefeller and Mayor John Lindsay, and between Governor Rockefeller and Robert Moses.

For studies on the machine conflict, see James Wilson, *The Amateur Democrat* (Chicago: University of Chicago Press, 1962) and Theodore Lowi, *At the Pleasure of the Mayor* (New York: Free Press, 1964). For an account of controversies among top politicians during the Lindsay mayoralty, see *Race and Politics in New York City*, ed. Jewell Bellush and Stephen David (New York: Praeger Publishers, 1971). For the Rockefeller-Moses controversy, see Robert Caro, *The Power Broker* (New York: Vintage Books, 1975), especially chs. 46-50. For a general and classic account about the passivity of government in the New York region during the 1950s, consult Robert Wood, *1400 Governments* (Garden City, N.Y.: Anchor Books, 1961).

⁴⁸ Douglas Yates, "Urban Government as a Policy Making System," in *The New Urban Politics*, ed. Louis Masotti and Robert Lineberry (Cambridge, Mass.: Ballinger Publishing, 1976), p. 246.

⁴⁹ Thus Teune and Przeworski ask rhetorically whether we can compare apples and oranges. They answer, yes, of course we can, because comparability depends on the level of generality that is applied to a given subject. Apples and oranges are fruits and on that level these objects can be compared. See Henry Teune and Adam Przeworski, *The Logic of Comparative Social Inquiry* (New York: John Wiley & Sons, 1970), p. 10. On the idea of "functional equivalents," see the excellent account by Mattei Dogan and Dominique Pelassy, *How to Compare Nations* (Chatham, N.J.: Chatham House, 1984), ch. 5.

⁵⁰ It is hoped that the threefold typology offered in this volume will have a stronger explanatory power than the familiar pluralist–elitist dichotomy. This dichotomy often leads to a debate over whether the system is "democratic" or not. Though that debate has value, it falls short on satisfactory explanations about the absence of overt conflict. The pluralists interpret the absence of an opposition (i.e., conflict) as a sign of political acquiescence to (or apathy about)

a decision. Elite theorists interpret the same absence as a result of biases in the system that exclude certain individuals—hence silence has been interpreted as antipathy and closure to lines of access. By itself the absence of conflict is insufficient to make such a judgment. But corporatist theorists would cast a different light on the issue and argue that the absence or presence of conflict is immaterial. What is most important, they would say, is which organizations are negotiating, how they are splitting their differences, and which ones have privileged access to decision making. In short, overt conflict does not have to occur for people to be included or excluded and for politics to take place.

[51] See Peter Bachrach and Morton Baratz, *Power and Poverty* (New York: Oxford University Press, 1970), pp. 47-49.

A generatiion of "neo-elitist" scholarship has arisen to press the issue of "hidden biases" and "nondecisions." The most outstanding example is Bachrach and Baratz, *Power and Poverty*. The strongest defense of pluralism can be found in Nelson Polsby, *Community Power and Political Theory*, 2d ed. (New Haven: Yale University Press, 1980).

For other methodological discussions, see Jack Walker, "A Critique of the Elitist Theory of Democracy," and Robert Dahl, "Further Reflections on the Elitist Theory of Democracy," both in *American Political Science Review* 60 (June 1966): 285-305; and Richard Merelman, "On the Neo-Elitist Critique of Community Power," *American Political Science Review* 62 (June 1968): 451-60.

[52] For such a "functional" approach to the city, consult Peter Hall and D. Hay, *Growth Centers in the European Urban System* (London: Heinemann, 1980), and Manuel Castells, *The Urban Question* (Cambridge: MIT Press, 1977). Castells argues that there is no such thing as the "city" and that it is merely a manifestation of conflicts in particular frames of space. A "functional" view might therefore disregard the political bounds of a city, because it bears little relation to how land is actually settled by industry, workers, or the owners of production. I find this point of view to be inappropriate. Political boundaries are important because zoning laws, planning policies, and transportation lines are established within them. Major decisions are made within the framework of the "political city," and many of these decisions are determined by "power structures" that are indigenous to the political city. Although the importance of political boundaries may be relative to each city (very important in New York, important in Paris, less important for Greater London), they have a general significance that should be appreciated.

[53] The spatial arrangements selected are the conventional boundaries used to make planning and political decisions in all three cities. There may be slight modifications from study to study, but the boundaries selected for *Post-Industrial Cities* are commonly used by scholarly and government sources. Thus, the New York Standard Consolidated Area is a designation used by the Bureau of the Census, U.S. Department of Commerce. The Regional Plan Association uses a larger region (31 counties and 12,788 square miles) but relies upon similar spatial categories (CBD, Rest of Core, Inner Ring, Intermediate Ring, and Outer Ring). See Regina Belz Armstrong, *Regional Accounts* (Blooming-

ton: Indiana University Press, 1980), p. 8, and Regina Belz Armstrong, *The Office Industry: Patterns of Growth and Location* (Cambridge: MIT Press, 1972). For Paris, the spatial areas conform to those used by governmental sources such as the Préfecture de la Région d'Ile-de-France, L'Institut d'Aménagement et d'Urbanisme de la Région d'Ile-de-France, and INSEE (the official repository for statistics in France), and *La Population d'Ile-de-France* (Paris: Préfecture de la Région d'Ile-de-France). For London there is some slight variation in boundaries between different sources, but most conventional accounts use similar designations to those here. See, for example, the designations of the Greater London Council, *Greater London Development Plan: Statement and Report of Studies* (London: Greater London Council, 1969). Of particular use is L. Weatheritt and O. N. John, *Office Development and Employment in Greater London, 1967 to 1976* (London: Greater London Council, 1979). Another useful source for designating spatial areas in London is Maurice Ash, *A Guide to the Structure of London* (London: Adams and Dart, 1972) which is cited by D. E. Eversley (former Chief Planner for Greater London), in "Urban Problems in Britain Today," GLC intelligence Unit Quarterly Bulletin, no. 19, June 1972. Finally, the official planning agency for the Paris Region (Institut d'Aménagement d'Urbanisme de la Région d'Ile-de-France) has carried out a brief demographic study of New York, Paris, and London. It relied upon spatial areas and boundaries that were the same or very similar to the ones used in this volume. See *Essai de Comparison entre les Trois Grandes Métropoles Mondiales: Paris, Londres, New York* (Paris: IAURIF, 1979).

54 In New York the counties are also called "boroughs," though they are much smaller than London's boroughs and perform entirely different functions. Kings County is more popularly called Brooklyn. Richmond County is commonly known as Staten Island. Also, Manhattan's official name is New York County.

55 Historically, Inner London consists of twelve boroughs and Outer London consists of twenty boroughs. For purposes of analysis, however, the boundaries relied upon by GLC staff have been used. These boundaries are based on the likeness of demographic features and housing conditions. See Office of Population Censuses and Surveys, *Census 1981 County Report, Greater London Part 1*, CEN 81 CR 17 (London: Her Majesty's Stationery Office), Table 2.14, Figure 2.13.

Chapter 2

1 Nelson Rockefeller created an Urban Development Corporation (UDC) and, with extraordinary cajolery, managed to provide the UDC with special powers to override local zoning laws. Those powers were eventually rescinded by angry state legislators who saw the UDC as violating the traditions of home rule. See *Restoring Credit and Confidence* (New York: Report to the Governor by the New York State Moreland Commission on the Urban Development Corporation, 1976).

2 For an unauthorized biography on Moses see Caro, *The Power Broker*.

3 *New York Times*, April 12, 1982.

4 For a fuller discussion of the post-industrial revolution see Bell, *The Coming Post-Industrial Society*; Gershuny, *After Industrial Society* and Sternlieb and Hughes, eds., *Post-Industrial America*.

5 The statistics are adapted from *County Business Patterns: 1971 and 1982* (Washington, D.C.: U.S. Department of Commerce, Bureau of the Census). Hereafter referred to as *County Business Patterns: 1971 and 1982*.

6 Committee on the Future, Port Authority of New York and New Jersey, *Regional and Economic Development Strategies for the 1980's* (New York: Port Authority of New York and New Jersey, 1979), p. 39.

7 *County Business Patterns: 1971 and 1982*.

8 Ibid.

9 Ibid.

10 Armstrong, *The Office Industry*, p. 130.

11 Statistical verification can be found by consulting firm size and settlement patterns for Manhattan in *County Business Patterns: 1971 and 1982*. For a fuller representation of firm size and firm location (including tables), see H. V. Savitch, "Politics, Planning and Urban Formation in London, New York and Paris: A Comparative Approach," paper presented at the London School of Economics and Political Science, February 1, 1982.

12 For a fuller discussion of corporate leapfrogging in New York, see H. V. Savitch, "Boom and Bust in the New York Region: Implications for Government Policy," in *Economic Prospects for the Northeast*, ed. Harry Richardson and Joseph Turek (Philadelphia: Temple University Press, 1985). For a discussion of federal policies and fiscal policies leading toward suburbanization, see H. V. Savitch, *Urban Policy and the Exterior City*.

13 See *1980 Census of Population, Characteristics of People and Housing*, New York State Data Center, New York State Department of Commerce, Summary Tape, File 3.

14 In 1980, the "poverty line" for a family of four was defined as annual earnings of $7,412 or less. The term living close to or below the poverty line is defined as 75 percent to 125 percent of this figure.

15 Department of Commerce, U.S. Bureau of the Census, "Characteristics of New York City's Population" (26 Federal Plaza, New York, N.Y., 1981).

16 *New York Times*, April 12, 1982.

17 There are a number of sources that support this. See Armstrong, *The Office Industry*; and Department of City Planning, "Environmental Impact Statement," October 1981, mimeo, p. 9.

18 See Emanuel Tobier, "Manhattan's Central Business District," *City Almanac* 12, no. 3 (October 1977); Peter Goldmark, "Foreign Business in the Economy of the New York–New Jersey Metropolitan Region," *City Almanac*, 14, no. 2 (August 1979); and Armstrong, *Regional Accounts*.

19 *Le Monde*, December 2, 1980, p. 26.

20 For detailed statistics and a fuller account of this trend see Goldmark, "Foreign Business."

²¹ For a discussion of the design and architectural implications of this trend see Paul Goldberger, "The Limits of Urban Growth," *New York Times Magazine*, November 14, 1982, pp. 46-68.

²² The phenomenon of gentrification is ably discussed in a reader on the subject, *Back to the City*, ed. Laska and Spain; in it see especially S. Gregory Lipton's article, "Evidence of Central City Revival," as well as Dennis Gale's "Neighborhood Resettlement."

²³ There are any number of accounts of New York City that vary in their interpretation of the city's future. For a bleak interpretation, see *The Fiscal Crisis of American Cities*, ed. Roger Alcaly and David Mermelstein (New York: Random House, 1976). For a more optimistic view, see Eli Ginsburg, *New York Is Very Much Alive and Well* (New York: McGraw-Hill, 1974). For more neutral and often technical accounts of New York's condition, consult *Setting Municipal Priorities: 1983*, ed. Raymond Horton and Charles Brecher (New York: New York University Press, 1983). These accounts vary so much because they examine different aspects of a very complicated system.

²⁴ In New York City, average property assessments are at approximately 50 percent of true market value. Usually one- and two-family houses are assessed at 20 percent of market value; commercial properties run at 60 percent of market value.

Chapter 3

¹ For journalistic accounts of this phenomenon, see *New York Times*, July 13, 1980, Section 2, p. 25, and Section 1, p. 1, as well as *New York Times*, April 24, 1973, p. 45.

² For a critical viewpoint, see Jane Jacobs, "How Westway Will Destroy New York," *New York Magazine*, February 6, 1978, pp. 30-34.

³ *Midtown Development: A Report of the Department of City Planning* (New York: Department of City Planning, June 1981), p. 11. The Midtown Zoning Resolution of 1982 will expire in 1988 and is scheduled for renewal. Given the anti-development sentiment that has occurred since its original passage, the fight over renewal could be intense.

⁴ Ibid., p. 16.

⁵ I am indebted to two students for excellent research papers on Times Square. They are Ellen Morosoff, for her paper "Times Square Redevelopment: Plan, Politics and Power in New York," State University of New York at Purchase, unpublished paper, May 1984; and Christopher Wright, "The 42nd Street Redevelopment Project: The Implementation of Public Policy," New York, New York University, Master's Essay, June 1984.

⁶ For basic documentation, see New York Public Development Corporation, *Forty-Second Street Development Project* (New York: Public Development Corporation, February 1985); New York State Urban Development Corporation, *Forty-Second Street Development Project: Final Environmental Impact Statement* (New York: New York State Urban Development Corporation, August 1984); Board of Estimate, City of New York, *Calendar No. 31*.

⁷ For the authoritative text on New York politics see, Sayre and Kaufman, *Governing New York City*.

⁸ Ibid., Chapter 16.

⁹ In 1986 a federal judge ruled the Board of Estimate's voting procedure to be unconstitutional and in violation of the Supreme Court's "one man, one vote" rule. It is now up to the Mayor and the Board to determine whether to appeal the ruling, take measures to change the Board's voting procedure, or initiate still other measures that would abolish the Board and assign its functions to the City Council. None of these actions is simple, though a Charter Revision Commission has begun work that could result in the diminution of the Board's power.

¹⁰ Glenn Fowler, "Community Board Wrap-Up" *New York Affairs* 6, no. 1 (1980): 8. For other articles on New York's community boards see this same issue of *New York Affairs*. Also see H. V. Savitch, "New York City's Crisis and the Politics of Charter Revision," *New York Affairs* 3, no. 2 (1980).

¹¹ *New York City Charter, Amended to April 1, 1981*, Section 197.

¹² For a journalist's acount of the West Side, see Joseph Lyford, *The Airtight Cage* (New York: Harper & Row, 1968).

¹³ *New York Times*, November 8, 1982, p. B1.

¹⁴ City Planning Commission, *Calendar No. 9*, July 19, 1982. See also *City Planning News*, July 19, 1982, and Lincoln West Associates, *Lincoln West* (New York: Lincoln West Associates, n.d.).

¹⁵ "Community Board Resolution," *The West Sider*, February 11, 1982.

¹⁶ Ibid.

¹⁷ William Price, "The 62 Acre Billion Dollar Question," *City Limits*, March 1982.

¹⁸ *New York Daily News*, March 28, 1982, p. 1.

¹⁹ *City Planning News*, July 19, 1982, p. 2; Lincoln West Associates, *Lincoln West*; and *New York Times*, August 29, 1982, Section 8.

²⁰ City Planning Commission, *Calendar No. 8*, July 19, 1982, p. 54.

²¹ *City Planning News*, July 19, 1982, p. 1, and *New York Times*, August 29, 1982, Section 8.

²² *Village Voice*, August 17, 1982, p. 28; *Village Voice*, August 21, 1982, p. 28; and *Village Voice*, August 31, 1982.

²³ For newspaper stories on Lincoln West, see Joyce Purnick, "Lincoln West: A Classic Tale of Politics and Power," *New York Times*, November 11, 1982, pp. B1-B8, and Eve Ottenberg, "Condos vs. Jobs," *Village Voice*, July 13, 1982, p. 1.

²⁴ *New York Times*, November 11, 1982, p. B1.

²⁵ *New York Times*, September 18, 1982, p. 1.

²⁶ Ibid.

²⁷ *New York Times*, September 17, 1982, p. 1.

²⁸ Purnick, "Lincoln West."

²⁹ *New York Times*, September 18, 1982.

³⁰ Purnick, "Lincoln West," and *New York Times*, September 17, 1982, p. 1.

[31] Author's interview, September 26, 1986.

[32] Ibid.

[33] *The West Sider*, through May 27, 1985, p. 28.

[34] The details of the Trump-Koch exchange are drawn from the following: Donald Trump, "Letter to Edward I. Koch, Mayor of the City of New York," New York, May 28, 1987, mimeo, and "Memorandum from Jay Biggins to Edward I. Koch, Mayor," New York, N.Y., June 1, 1987, mimeo.

[35] Edward I. Koch, "Letter to Donald Trump, President, The Trump Organization," New York, N.Y., May 28, 1987. A summary of these events and remarks can be found in "Statement by Mayor Edward I. Koch," New York, N.Y., June 1, 1987, mimeo, and a partial account can be found in *New York Daily News*, June 4, 1987, p. 7, and *New York Times*, June 1, 1987, p. B1.

[36] Coalition Against Lincoln West, *Community Letter*, May 23, 1985.

[37] New York State Urban Development Corporation, *42nd Street Development Project: Final Environmental Impact Statement*, vol. 1 (New York: Urban Development Corporation, August 1984), pp. 2-120, 121, and 123. Hereafter referred to as *Environmental Impact Statement*.

[38] Ibid., pp. 2-121.

[39] Ibid.

[40] Ibid.

[41] Ibid., pp. 1-22.

[42] Ibid.

[43] *New York Times*, June 8, 1980, Section 4, p. 6.

[44] See "Memorandum of Understanding Between the City of New York and the New York State Urban Development Corporation," New York, N.Y., June 1980, mimeo. I am indebted to Christopher Wright, "The 42nd Street Redevelopment Project," for highlighting and analyzing the UDC role in the redevelopment of Times Square.

[45] Cooper, Eckstut Associates. For the New York State Urban Development Corporation, the New York City Department of City Planning and the New York City Public Development Corporation, *42nd Street Development Project: Design Guidelines* (New York, May 1981), p. 1.

[46] *New York Times*, March 26, 1984, p. B6.

[47] *Village Voice*, May 7, 1985, p. 16.

[48] See the op-ed article by Thomas Bender, "Ruining Times Square," *New York Times*, March 3, 1984.

[49] *New York Times*, April 22, 1984.

[50] *New York Magazine*, April 2, 1984, p. 32.

[51] For legal and financial particulars on the Times Square project, consult Board of Estimate, City of New York, *Calendar No. 31*, November 8, 1984 [hereafter referred to as *Calendar No. 31*]. Also see New York City Public Development Corporation, *Forty-Second Street Development Project: Fact Sheet*, New York, revised February 1, 1985, mimeo [hereafter referred to as *Forty-Second Street Project Fact Sheet*]. Finally, the reader searching for the most recent details should consult New York State Urban Development Corporation,

New York City Department of City Planning, and the New York City Public Development Corporation, *42nd Street Development Project: Update*, New York, October 22, 1984, mimeo [hereafter referred as *42nd Street Project Update*].

52 *Calendar No. 31* and *Forty-Second Street Project Fact Sheet*, p. 6.

53 *Forty-Second Street Project Fact Sheet*, p. 6.

54 *New York Times*, March 26, 1984, p. B1, and Office of the Mayor, "Press Release," New York, N.Y., April 6, 1982, mimeo. Hereafter referred to as "Press Release," April 6, 1982.

55 *42nd Street Project Update*, p. 12.

56 *Environmental Impact Statement*, vol. 1 (Summary), p. S13. An earlier press release projected a slightly higher employment figure of 26,000 additional jobs. See "Press Release," April 6, 1982, p. 4.

57 It is difficult to estimate the real amount of the tax abatement or the real value of property in Times Square during the next decade. Assertions on all sides are conjectural, and we should be cautious about quick and glib assessments. Thus, during the project's fifteen year buildup, its tax abatement has been estimated at $650 million. This is calculated by assuming that if the project were built without public support, it would yield $1.13 billion in taxes. This amount is then deducted from estimated PILOT payments of $480 million over the next fifteen years. Such calculations beg the question, because they suppose that the project would have been built without UDC or could even have been constructed in the same magnitude. It is ironic that those who are most critical of the project's size and of its worthiness assume its largest dimensions in order to hypothesize that the city is not taking proper advantage of the project's size and worth. For details, see "The Redevelopment of 42nd Street," *City Almanac* 18 (Summer 1985), edited by Susan Fainstein. There are also many sides to the question of payment for and ownership of Times Square's new skyscrapers. Defenders of the existing arrangement point out that the developers are paying twice for the same piece of property—once for the initial acquisition and reconstruction and another time if developers exercise an option to purchase. Critics counter that the final selling price will amount to one-twentieth the market value and the developers are getting it all "for a song." For a critical viewpoint, consult *Village Voice*, May 7, 1985, pp. 13-19.

58 The garment manufacturers' own study showed far greater losses. In jobs alone the count was several thousand. In addition, the wholesale merchandise mart threatened a way of economic life for the industry. As it now exists, the garment industry rests on "integrated production," in which factory, showroom, and office are located in the same place. The merchandise mart would have separated factory from office and from showroom, because it precluded manufacturing operations. The most optimistic hopes were that factories would not leave New York City and, instead, would relocate to the Bronx. See *New York Times*, June 28, 1984, p. B1, and October 22, 1984, p. B3.

59 Formal decisions were taken by a subsidiary of UDC, the Times Square Redevelopment Corporation. Three members of this subsidiary were ap-

pointed by the UDC and, by inference, were spokesmen for the state. Two members were appointed by the Mayor's office. The vote that evoked Koch's protest was 3–0. The two city delegates abstained, but would have been outvoted anyway. *New York Times*, March 9, 1984, p. B4.

⁶⁰ For investigative stories on the Times Square case, see Martin Gottlieb, "Times Square Development Plan: A Lesson in Politics and Power," *New York Times*, March 8, 1984, p. B1, and Martin Gottlieb, "Pressure and Compromise Saved Times Square Project," *New York Times*, March 10, 1984, p. 25. A reading of Gottlieb's two-part series lends itself to a highly pluralistic interpretation of the Times Square case. Indeed, Gottlieb uses the language of pluralism to describe the interaction between the city, the state, and developers. Gottlieb reported on only a fragment of the Times Square story and missed the full context. Another investigative account can be found in D. D. Guttenplan, "Debacle on 42nd Street," *Village Voice*, May 7, 1985, pp. 13-19. This story also presents a snapshot of a long train of events. Its interpretation is more Cassandra-like and uses the language of elitist theory to describe the issue.

⁶¹ Gottlieb, "Times Square Development," March 10, 1984, p. 25.

⁶² Ibid., p. 28.

⁶³ Ibid.

⁶⁴ Ibid.

⁶⁵ *New York Daily News*, March 27, 1984.

⁶⁶ *New York Times*, October 26, 1984, p. B1.

⁶⁷ *New York Times*, November 4, 1985, p. E5.

⁶⁸ *New York Times*, November 9, 1984, Section 4, p. E5.

⁶⁹ *Clinton Community Press*, January 1985. For a viewpoint that takes the community's perspective of the final decision, see Robert Neuwirth, "Behind Closed Doors," *City Limits* (December 1984): 9-13.

⁷⁰ The most serious legal challenges to the Times Square project involved environmental issues. For cases on this subject, consult *Jackson v. N.Y. State Urban Development Corporation*, 110 A.D.2d 304, 494 N.Y.S.2d 700 (1st Dept. 1985) *affirmed*, 67 N.Y.2d 400, 503 N.Y.S.2d 298 (1986) and *Stephen F. Wilder v. Lee M. Thomas*, 85 Civ. 8356, United States District Court, Southern District of New York (1987). Interestingly, the same judge who decided against the plaintiffs on environmental issues in the Times Square suit (thereby permitting development) decided for the plaintiffs on environmental issues in the Westway case (thereby blocking development). See *Wilder v. Thomas*. For summary accounts of the earliest cases on the Times Square project, consult New York State Urban Development Corporation, "Second Times Square Suit Dismissed," February 5, 1985; "Court Dismisses 42nd. Street Development Project Suits," December 22, 1985; "Times Square Ruling Upheld," February 14, 1986; "Times Square Decision Upheld in State's Highest Court," May 8, 1986; "Second Circuit Court Upholds 42nd. Street Project," and "Federal Judge Dismisses Times Square Suit," June 26, 1986 (New York, N.Y.: The New York State Urban Development Corporation).

71 For a thorough account of Moses' role in the building of the West Side Highway and nearby routes, consult Caro, *The Power Broker*, pp. 552-62.

72 The idea belonged to Samuel Ratensky of the New York City Housing Administration and Edward Logue of the New York State Urban Development Corporation. See *New York Times*, May 6, 1984, p. B4, and Regina Herzlinger, "Costs, Benefits and the West Side Highway," *The Public Interest*, no. 55 (Spring 1979), pp. 77-98.

73 Herzlinger, "Costs, Benefits and The West Side Highway," p. 78.

74 Ibid., pp. 80-81.

75 Ibid., p. 81.

76 Ibid., pp. 85-86.

77 *New York Times*, May 20, 1985. For original documents that support these figures and for assessments on costs and design, consult Michael Lazar, Administrator Transportation Administration, City of New York, and John Zuccotti, Chairman, City Planning Commission, City of New York, A Report to the Working Committee of the West Side Highway Project, *Land Use and the West Side Highway* (New York, 1974). For a well-executed, critical study, see Michael Gerrard, *How Public Works Projects Affect Employment: A Case Study of Westway and Its Transit Alternatives* (New York: Sierra Club, 1977). Critics place the cost of Westway much higher. These costs range from $6 billion and one report claims costs would reach $10 billion. See "Westway Fact Sheet," N.Y.C. Clean Air Campaign, New York, June 26, 1984, mimeo, and *Newark Star-Ledger*, March 17, 1985, p. 1. Critics also claim that Westway is not six to eight lanes, but twelve to fourteen lanes. From what can be determined, the critics count the avenues and service lanes that run parallel to Westway and that would be rebuilt under the terms of the project. See "Westway's Actual Design," N.Y.C. Clean Air Campaign, New York, June 26, 1984, mimeo.

78 The figure of $7 billion in offshoot benefits was bandied about by Westway's proponents, notable personalities like David Rockefeller and former State Transportation Commissioner, James Larocca. Westway's opponents say the real indirect infusion of funds from Westway would have been only $300 million. For varying positions on the issue see Gerrard, *How Public Works Projects Affect Employment*, and James Larocca, "Remarks by the New York State Transportation Commissioner at the Meeting of the General Contractors of New York, Incorporated," presented at the Hemsley Palace, New York, April 12, 1984, mimeo.

79 David Rockefeller and Harry Van Arsdale, "Letter to the Secretary of Transportation, William Coleman," New York, December 30, 1976, mimeo.

80 Ibid., p. 2.

81 For a laudatory profile of Marcy Benstock, see Jack Newfield, "The Woman Who Blocked Westway," *Village Voice*, August 3, 1982, pp. 1ff.

82 Author's interview, December 9, 1985. Westway did not fall under the ULURP process, and this left the community boards with considerably less leverage. Some members of the Board of Estimate argued that since it was responsible for providing "rights of way" for the superhighway, the issue de-

served to be placed within the Board's purview. In pursuit of this alleged right, some members of the Board of Estimate brought the matter to court. Before this issue could be fully litigated, other events had already precipitated Westway's fall.

[83] Author's interviews, December 5 and 6, 1985.

[84] Author's interviews, December 5 and 6, 1985. Also consult "Resolutions regarding The Westway Project," New York Community Board Two, July 1982 and October 1983, mimeo.

[85] See John Oakes's op-ed column, "Instead Call It Wasteway," *New York Times*, June 2, 1984. There are also a host of other columns on Westway. One journalist who turned a critical eye on the project is Sydney Schanberg. For his columns see *New York Times*, December 14, 1982; March 22, 1983, p. 25; May 3, 1983; May 10, 1983; June 9, 1984, p. 23; July 2, 1985, p. 19; and June 6, 1985. For a more positive view of Westway, see "What Is Westway?" and "Westway Trade-In: An Unreliable Source of Funds," New York, Citizens For Balanced Transportation, December 8, 1980, mimeos.

[86] When Koch first ran for mayor in 1977 he called Westway "an environmental disaster," and said the superhighway was promoted by the "David Rockefellers and a lot of real estate interests." But just a few months after his inauguration, Koch referred to Westway as "inevitable." Ostensibly, Koch changed his mind because Governor Carey promised the city additional revenue for mass transit. Most knowledgeables believe Koch wanted to be gracefully released from his earlier campaign promises. See *New York Times*, October 29, 1977, p. 11, and October 30, 1977. Also see *New York Daily News*, November 3, 1977, and *The Joint Agreement of Mayor Edward I. Koch and Governor Hugh Carey*, State of New York Executive Chambers, April 19, 1976, mimeo.

[87] "Press Release, September 27, 1983," State of New York, Executive Chamber, Mario M. Cuomo, Governor (Albany, N.Y., September 27, 1983), mimeo. See also Mario M. Cuomo, "Letter to John O. Marsh, Secretary of the Army," September 23, 1983, Albany, N.Y., mimeo; and Mario M. Cuomo, "Letter to Ronald Reagan, President of the United States," September 26, 1983, mimeo.

[88] For a legal analysis of Westway, see Thomas Puccio, "Memorandum to Governor Mario M. Cuomo," Fisher, Puccio and Wilker, New York, April 25, 1983, mimeo. Newspaper accounts on the Westway's judicial proceedings are extensive. For the recent decision by the Federal District Court, see *New York Times*, August 8, 1985, p. 1.

[89] *New York Times*, June 12, 1984, p. 24.

[90] *New York Times*, September 13, 1985, p. B2.

[91] *New York Times*, September 12, 1985.

[92] *New York Times*, September 19, 1985, p. B9.

[93] *New York Times*, September 20, 1985, p. B2.

[94] For details on modest Westway alternatives, see "West Side Highway Replacement Study," New York State Department of Transportation, August 6, 1986, mimeo.

⁹⁵ For the more ambitious plan on Westway's alternative, see "The West Side Task Force, Preliminary Report," The West Side Task Force, State and City of New York, December 8, 1986, mimeo.

⁹⁶ Ibid., p. 14.

⁹⁷ The phrase *phased construction* is taken from an early study of the West Side. See "Wateredge Development Study: Hudson River Edge Development Proposal," New York State Urban Development Corporation, May 1971, mimeo. There is concern that recent plans for development will revive more aggressive activities on the waterfront by public and private sectors.

⁹⁸ *New York Times*, December 1, 1985, p. 44, and *Village Voice*, December 23, 1986, p. 13.

⁹⁹ Author's interview, October 9, 1986.

¹⁰⁰ *Village Voice*, December 23, 1986 p. 13.

¹⁰¹ *New York Times*, October 7, 1985, p. B8.

¹⁰² For an illustration of how corporatist organizations differ in content from pluralist groups, consider the following line-up in the case of Westway. *For Westway*: AFL-CIO, Chase Manhattan Bank, *New York Times*, Regional Plan Association; *Against Westway*: Bicycle Commuters of New York, East 10th Street Block Association, Friends of the Earth, Riverside Towers Tenant Association.

¹⁰³ *Meade Data Central*, New York, 1984, p. 20. Also quoted in *New York Times*, October 24, 1982.

¹⁰⁴ Robert Dahl, *A Preface to Democratic Theory* (Chicago: University of Chicago Press, 1956), ch. 4.

¹⁰⁵ Author's interview, June 6, 1985.

Chapter 4

¹ For descriptive accounts of the reorganization of the Paris region, see Annmarie Hauck Walsh, *Urban Government and the Paris Region* (New York: Praeger, 1968) and Paul Delouvrier, "Paris," in *Great Cities of the World*, vol. 2, ed. Robson and Regan. For a comprehensive history of the Paris region, see Michel Carmona, *Le Grand Paris*, 2 vols. (Paris: Girotypo, 1979). For a fine overview, consult J. Beaujeu-Garnier *Paris et l'Ile-de-France* (Paris: Flammarion, 1977).

² Carmona, *Le Grand Paris*, 1:79.

³ Ibid., p. 80.

⁴ Ibid.

⁵ For discussions of Plan d'Aménagement et d'Organisation Général de la Région Parisienne (PADOG), see Delouvrier, "Paris," and James Sundquist, *Dispersing Population* (Washington, D.C.: Brookings Institution, 1975).

⁶ Carmona, *Le Grand Paris*, 1:98.

⁷ Ibid., p. 88.

⁸ *Schéma Directeur d'Aménagement et d'Urbanisme de la Région de Paris* (Paris: La Documentation française, 1965).

⁹ Carmona, *Le Grand Paris*, 1:105.

¹⁰ See Phillippe Pinchemel, *La Région Parisienne* (Paris: Presses Universi-

taires de France, 1979). For a synopsis of the Statute of Reform for Paris, consult M. Etienne, *Le Statut de Paris* (Nancy: Berger-Levrault, 1975).

[11] The quote is taken from a manuscript by Jean-Paul Alduy and Monique Dagnaud, *La Vème République et l'Aménagement de la Région de Paris*, vol. 1 (Paris: Institut d'Aménagement d'Urbanisme de la Région d'Ile-de-France, September 1977), p. 128. Throughout this lengthy work, Alduy and Dagnaud make the point that territorial reorganizations were initiated to break the power of the Left and of leftist localities. They also point out that the Right wanted to break the power of the Department of the Seine.

[12] See Carmona, *Le Grand Paris*, vol. 1, ch. 3, and Delouvrier, "Paris." The announced eight new towns of the master plan of 1965 were later reduced to five and their anticipated populations were also reduced. Delouvrier's power to acquire land and to build was also qualified. First, local governments would have to be consulted before any action took place. Second, new developments, such as new towns, would eventually revert to the jurisdiction of the local authority.

[13] Carmona, *Le Grand Paris*, 2:72.

[14] Maurice Doublet, *Paris en Procès* (Paris: Hachette, 1976), p. 128.

[15] We should not overestimate the effect of decentralization on the power of prefects. Decentralization has modified—perhaps diminished—the prefect's role in decision making. But it is still an important role. The Prefect of Paris still prepares the regional budget and submits it for approval to the regional council. The Prefect still prepares the master plan for the region, which guides urban development. The Prefect's role as guardian of state interests vis-à-vis the localities is still very much intact, and this can entail formidable powers of discretion. Moreover, within the City of Paris, nearly 70 percent of the land is considered to be a matter of state concern. This puts a sizable hunk of terrain within the Prefect's purview. On a less formal level, local politicians often rely on the good will of the Prefect and are especially vulnerable to prefectoral influence when there is no clear majority. For a defense of current prefectoral privileges, see "La Fonction Préfectorale après la Décentralisation," *Le Dossier du Mois: ENA* April 1985, pp. 1-19, and "Le Rétour des Préfets," *Valeur Actuelles*, May 5, 1986, pp. 6-8.

[16] For an excellent historical treatment of one notable prefect, see David Pinkney, *Napoleon III and the Rebuilding of Paris* (Princeton: Princeton University Press, 1958). Pinkney recounts the relationship between Georges Haussmann, the great Prefect of the Seine, and Napoleon III. For an autobiographical account emphasizing the problems and limitations of the job, see Doublet, *Paris en Procès*.

[17] There are a number of interesting articles and interviews with recent prefects. For different perspectives on the position, consult *Le Monde*, March 29, 1977, p. 34, and *L'Aurore*, March 17, 1977, p. 11, as well as "Le Maire et Ses Préfets," *Valeurs Actuelles*, March 21, 1977. See also a brief tribute to Delouvrier in *Le Monde*, October 5, 1984, p. 7.

[18] Calculations are made by place of work and by population figures for the years indicated. Place-of-work statistics are taken from Table 4.1 and its

sources. Population is taken from *La Population d'Ile-de-France: Résultats Provisoires du Récensement* (Paris: INSEE, 1982) and from *Essai de Comparison entre les Trois Grandes Métropoles Mondiales: Paris, Londres, New York* (Paris: IAURIF, March 1979).

[19] *Annuaire Statistique Sommaire, Avril 1978 et 1982* (Paris: IAURIF, 1982).

[20] *La Population d'Ile-de-France: Résultats Provisoires du Récensement* (Paris: INSEE, 1982) [hereafter referred to as *La Population d'Ile de France* (1982)].

[21] *Paris Projét*, #19.20, p. 19.

[22] *Premiers Résultats du Récensement de 1982 à Paris* (Paris: Atelier Parisien d'Urbanisme, 1983), p. 34.

[23] Ibid., Annexe 7.

[24] Monique Dagnaud, *Histoire de la Planification en Région Parisienne: Du Schéma de la Croissance (1965) au Schéma de la Préservation (1980)* (Paris: Centre d'Etudes des Mouvements Sociaux, November 1980), p. 18.

[25] *Vingt Ans d'Evolution de Paris* (Paris: Atelier Parisien d'Urbanisme, n.d.), Table 2, 4th arrondissement.

[26] *Paris Projét,* #19.20, p. 13, and *Premiers Résultats du Récensement de 1982 à Paris*, p. 4.

[27] *Paris Projét*, p. 13.

[28] Ibid.

[29] *Premiers Résultats du Récensement de 1982 à Paris*, p. 18.

[30] *Logements Terminés à Paris*, mimeo. (Paris: Bureau d'Information sur la Construction), and *Paris Projét*, p. 13.

[31] *Vingts Ans d'Evolution de Paris*, Figure 3, and *Premiers Résultats du Récensement de 1982 à Paris*, pp. 39, 40.

[32] Guy Loinger and Patrick Venny, "Rénovation Urbaine et Réhabilitation à Paris: Bilan Social," *Métropolis*, 1980, pp. 9-16.

[33] There is a considerable literature on this subject that focuses on the displacement of the working classes of Paris. See F. Godard et al., *La Rénovation Urbaine à Paris: Structure Urbaine et Logique de Classe* (Paris: Mouton, 1973). For a journalistic account, see Marcel Cornu, *La Conquête de Paris* (Paris: Mercure de France, 1972). The Communist Party is strongly in favor of building high-rise residential towers and has decried conservation measures as an insidious effort to get rid of the working classes.

[34] *Le Marché des Bureaux en France en 1980* (Paris: IAURIF, 1980), p. 30.

[35] *Les Bureaux à Paris: 1970-1980* (Paris: Atelier Parisien d'Urbanisme, 1980), 3.

[36] *Le Figaro* Magazine, March 23, 1981.

Chapter 5

[1] The claim is more verbal than found in the literature. For critical studies on the subject, see Jean Lojkine, *La Politique Urbaine*, and Godard et al., *La Rénovation Urbaine à Paris*.

[2] In 1954, 55 percent of the housing units did not possess a bathroom. Twenty years later the number of apartments without a bathroom was reduced to 30 percent and by 1982 that number had fallen to 21 percent. Consult *Vingt*

Ans d'Evolution de Paris and *Premiers Résultats du Récensement de 1982 à Paris,* pp. 39, 40.

³ For critical studies, see Lojkine, *La Politique Urbaine,* and Castells, *The Urban Question.*

⁴ For histories of planning see Carmona, *Le Grand Paris;* Alduy and Dagnaud, *La Vᵉᵐᵉ République et l'Aménagement de la Région de Paris,* vol. 1; and Dagnaud, *Histoire de la Planification en Région Parisienne.*

⁵ For an account in English of this process, written by the former Prefect of the Paris Region, see Delouvrier, "Paris," in *Great Cities of the World,* ed. Robson and Regan.

⁶ For an official account of the strategy behind French new towns, consult *Villes Nouvelles: Dossier Administratif,* Ministère de l'Équipement, 1970 and 1971. See also *L'Aménagement et la Gestion du Cadre de Vie dans les Villes Nouvelles,* Premier Ministère, December 1980.

⁷ Originally eight new towns were each supposed to contain 350,000 residents for a total of 2.8 million people. That figure was later reduced to five new towns, each containing 200,000 residents, for a total of one million. Today there are five new towns in the Ile-de-France, each containing between 70,000 and 150,000 residents, for a total of 572,000 people. For an elaboration, see *Villes Nouvelles de France* (Paris: Secrétariat Général du Groupe Centrale des Villes Nouvelles, n.d.).

⁸ Malcolm Moseley, "Strategic Planning and the Paris Agglomeration in the 1960's and 1970's: The Quest for Balance and Structure," *Geoforum* 3 (1980): 216-19.

⁹ *Vingt Ans d'Evolution de Paris* and *La Population d'Ile-de-France* (1982).

¹⁰ Evenson, *Paris: A Century of Change,* p. 309.

¹¹ *Le Monde,* October 5, 1984, p. 7.

¹² *Le Nouveau Statut de Paris* (Paris: Maire de Paris, Direction Générale de l'Information et de Relations Extérieures, March 1977), p. 9. See also Etienne, *Le Statut de Paris.*

¹³ Michel Carmona, untitled manuscript, pp. 7-11.

¹⁴ *Paris Projét: Aménagement Urbanisme Avenir,* no. 1 (July 1969), p. 11.

¹⁵ The incident is aptly described in Pinkey, *Napoleon III and the Rebuilding of Paris.*

¹⁶ Robert Franc, *Le Scandale de Paris* (Paris: Editions Bernard Grasset, 1971), p. 146. Les Halles is a territory of 43 hectares (107.5 acres) comprising a geographic rectangle around the pavilions. This includes the boundaries of rue de Rivoli (south), rue Etienne Marcel (north), the Louvre (west), and rue de Renard (east). See Figure 5.4 for a detailed plan of the area.

¹⁷ *Etude d'Opinion auprès de Leaders de Participation a l'Aménagement des Halles* (Paris: COPRAS, September, 1968), p. 17.

¹⁸ Ibid., p. 18.

¹⁹ *Paris Projét,* no. 1 (July 1969), p. 21.

²⁰ An incident that would later set the mood for Les Halles involved the wife of President de Gaulle. One day Madame de Gaulle happened across rue St.

Denis and was horrified by the hordes of prostitutes along the streets. The President was soon confronted by his wife, who recounted her day's experience. The police quickly descended upon the quarter to camouflage its atmosphere. The streetwalkers were pushed into hallways and smaller sidestreets, and Les Halles was scrutinized night and day. Although the incident disturbed only the most prudish officials, it bolstered a growing feeling that Les Halles needed to be sanitized. See Franc, *Le Scandale de Paris*, p. 149.

[21] Very little has been written about the politics of Les Halles' demolition and renewal. Most of the information contained herein is drawn from interviews and from bits and pieces of documents. For partial newspaper accounts, consult *Le Monde*, October 23, 1968, p. 9, and October 24, 1968, p. 16. There are also annual reports released by SEMAH (the managing corporation of Les Halles), which are useful. For further information, see *L'Operation des Halles à Fin 1972, Rapport à l'Assemblée Générale Ordinaire sur l'Exercice 1972*, and *Présentation de la Société d'Economie Mixte d'Aménagement de Rénovation et de Restauration du Secteur des Halles* (Paris: Société Anonyme d'Economie Mixte d'Aménagement de Rénovation et de Restauration du Secteur des Halles, 1972 and 1973). There is also a short chronology of events available; see *Aménagement du Quartier des Halles de Paris: Chronologies de l'Action des Associations,* Union des Champeaux, Paris, undated [hereafter referred to as *Chronologies*].

[22] *Chronologies*. See also *Le Monde*, October 23, 1968, p. 9.

[23] *L'Operation des Halles à Fin 1972*, pp. 3, 6, 8.

[24] There was a short reprieve for the demolition of the pavilions, and for some time after the fruit and vegetable vendors left, the pavilions were used by local artists. One pavilion has also been salvaged and moved to Nogent-sur-Marne, just outside Paris.

[25] The Prefect of Paris and the Prefect of the region were decisive at this stage, partly because of their authority and also because they had a monopoly of information and technical expertise concerning Les Halles. Most of this information was kept out of public view. One of the ostensible reasons for destroying the pavilions was that the construction of underground transport facilities made it impossible to preserve them. The argument appears to be a specious rationale that could be promoted without criticism because the opposition lacked engineering and other assistance. This was picked up by one lone letter writer; see "Pas de quartier pour Les Halles," *Le Nouveau Journal*, April 14, 1969.

[26] For an extensive article on the planning and technical aspects of Les Halles, and for an account of Chirac's role, see *Le Monde*, February 18-19, 1979, p. 18. In addition to winning two terms as Mayor of Paris, Chirac has been Prime Minister twice. His first tenure as Prime Minister occurred between 1974 and 1976, while Giscard d'Estaing was President. His second tenure as Prime Minister began in 1986 under President François Mitterrand.

[27] For a good account of Les Halles' contemporary design, see "Filling the Hole at Les Halles," *Urban Design International* 1, no. 3 (March-April 1980): 32-33.

[28] *10 Ans d'Activité: Les Halles* (Paris: Société Anonyme d'Economie Mixte d'Aménagement de Rénovation et de Restauration du Secteur des Halles, 1979), p. 14.

[29] Author's interview, October 2, 1984.

[30] *Etudes d'Opinion*, p. 28.

[31] *Rapport à l'Assemblée Générale sur l'Exercice 1972*, p. 4.

[32] Of those individuals displaced, only 27.8 percent were rehoused in Les Halles. The majority went to other arrondissements in Paris; a smaller proportion moved to the suburbs. See *L'Operation Les Halles à Fin 1972*, p. 18.

[33] Evenson, *Paris*, p. 18.

[34] "La Défense d'Henri IV à Charles De Gaulle," *Le Monde*, November 6, 1986, p. 29.

[35] Lojkine, *La Politique Urbaine*, pp. 31-32.

[36] Ibid., pp. 33-35.

[37] Ibid., p. 214. Lojkine interprets the events surrounding the making of La Défense differently and draws different conclusions. Although he concedes that the state took the initiative in the making of La Défense, he argues that private developers found it to be a profitable venture by the late 1960s, and exploited it. From this vantage point Lojkine sees La Défense as having been prepared by the French government for a capitalist elite to exploit. In my opinion, Lojkine's interpretation ignores the controls exercized by EPAD over La Défense, the taxes and the income that accrued to both EPAD and the communes from the operation, and the independent role played by political actors. See Chapter 8 for further discussion.

[38] Thus permissions were granted in 1971 to construct a total of 268,000 square meters (2.9 million square feet) of office space in Paris. By the mid 1970s that number had plummeted to 18,100 square meters (201,000 square feet) of office space. Note this represents permissions or *agréements* given to builders and not the amount actually constructed. See Carmona, *Le Grand Paris*, vol. 2, annex 4, p. 222.

[39] See "Ce Sera le plus grandes Centres d'Affaires d'Europe," *Le Figaro* Magazine, July 4, 1981, pp. 54-56 (hereafter referred to as "Ce Sera le plus grandes"). The figures cited in the text can also be found in *La Défense* (Paris–La Défense: EPAD, 1982), pp. 26, 28.

[40] Figures are derived from "De La Bute de Chantecog au Quartier de La Défense" (Paris–La Défense: EPAD, 1983), n.p.

[41] See Marc Clairvois, "La Défense contre-attaque," *l'Expansion*, December 4-17, 1981 and "Ce sera le plus grandes," p. 54.

[42] See *La Défense*, p. 28, and "Ce sera le plus grandes."

[43] *Le Nouveau Journal*, April 29, 1982.

[44] *Le Nouveau Journal*, January 24, 1980.

[45] "Hommes et Enterprises," *Le Moniteur*, October 6, 1980, p. 4.

[46] *Le Monde*, March 9, 1978, p. 2.

[47] Author's interview, October 23, 1984.

[48] "Plan-Programme de l'Est de Paris," *Communication au Conseil de Paris* (Paris: Atelier Parisien d'Urbanisme, November 23, 1983), p. 7.

[49] Ibid., p. 9.

[50] Ibid., p. 13. Chirac plainly declared that as Mayor, his goal was to make "neighborhoods in the east of Paris as desirable as those in the west." "Nouvelles Infrastructures de Voirie dans le Secteur Seine Sud-Est" (Paris: Mairie de Paris, January 17, 1986, mimeo.), p. 3.

[51] *Paris Projét*, no. 12, p. 19.

[52] Ibid., p. 16.

[53] *Bulletin Municipal Officiel de La Ville de Paris*, Débats du Conseil de Paris, 2 Session Ordinaire de 1972, June 29, 1973, p. 630.

[54] *Paris Projét*, no. 12, p. 33.

[55] See *Bulletin Municipal Officiel*, p. 626.

[56] Ibid., p. 628.

[57] See *Paris Projét*, no. 12, p. 33.

[58] Ibid., p. 33.

[59] Ibid., p. 33.

[60] *Bulletin Municipal Officiel*, p. 625.

[61] Ibid., p. 638.

[62] Ibid., p. 638.

[63] Ibid., pp. 639-40.

[64] Quarrels over the Secteur occurred over an effort to make it a seat for a World's Fair. Mayor Chirac wanted the state to pay for much of the cost; President Mitterrand resisted. Chirac and Mitterrand also disagreed over what to develop and how development should be carried out. In the National Assembly, Gaullists and Socialists accused one another of sabotaging the project and by 1983 the idea for a World's Fair had collapsed. Nonetheless, the controversy brought the Secteur to Chirac's attention and prompted him to initiate action for control over more of its land. See *Valeurs Actuelles*, July 4, 1983, pp. 32-35.

[65] Author's interview, October 26, 1984.

[66] Author's interview, January 4, 1985.

Chapter 6

[1] See, for example, Ken Young and Patricia Garside, *Metropolitan London* (New York: Holmes & Meier, 1982); Rhodes, *The Government of London*; and Ash, *A Guide to the Structure of London*, pp. 1-13.

[2] Public Information Service, *Survey of London's Knowledge of the Council and Its Work* (London: Greater London Council General Purposes Committee, November 21, 1966), p. 2.

[3] See Department of the Environment, *Streamlining the Cities: Government Proposals for Reorganizing Local Government and Metropolitan Counties* (London: HMSO, October 1983).

[4] Consult Donald Foley, *Governing the London Region* (Berkeley: University of California Press, 1972).

[5] Young and Garside, *Metropolitan London*, p. 163.

[6] Ibid., p. 214.

[7] Hall, *World Cities*, p. 39. One group that began the early planning of Lon-

don was the Barlow Commission, established in 1937, which made an inquiry about the future of London's growth and issued a report.

[8] Patrick Abercrombie, *Greater London Plan, 1944*, A Report Prepared on Behalf of the Standing Conference on London Regional Planning at the Request of the Minister of Town and Country Planning (London: Her Majesty's Stationery Office, 1945).

[9] Young and Garside, *Metropolitan London*, p. 233.

[10] *Greater London Development Plan* (London: Greater London Council, 1976), p. 8.

[11] Young and Garside, *Metropolitan London*, p. 218.

[12] William Robson, *The Government and Misgovernment of London* (London: Allen & Unwin, 1939).

[13] Lipsky's ideas are an imaginative adaptation to American cities and a contemporary idea. Although Lipsky makes no recommendations about reorganizing government along different tiers, other scholars have done so, and Robson was a great proponent of the idea. See Michael Lipsky, *Street-Level Bureaucracy* (New York: Basic Books, 1980), and Robson, *The Government and Misgovernment of London*.

[14] Young and Garside, *Metropolitan London*, p. 247. See also Robson's comments in William Robson, "The Greater London Plan," *Political Quarterly* 16 (April 1945): 106-116.

[15] Figures are garnered from *London Facts and Figures* (London: Greater London Council, 1983), Figure 6, and Young and Garside, *Metropolitan London*, p. 342.

[16] Hall, *World Cities*, p. 41.

[17] *London Facts and Figures*, Figure 30.

[18] *The Future of London: Draft Alterations to the GLDP* (London: Greater London Council, 1983), p. 21.

[19] See *Economic Statistics from the 1981 Census: Statistical Series, No. 31* (London: Greater London Council, 1984), Tables 20 and 21.

[20] Jane Jacobs, *The Death and Life of Great American Cities* (New York: Vintage, 1961), p. 50.

[21] Hall, *World Cities*, p. 40.

[22] *Greater London Development Plan* (1976), p. 12.

[23] Quoted in Young and Garside, *Metropolitan London*, p. 299.

[24] There are a number of accounts that agree with this prognosis. See, for example, Smallwood, *Greater London*; Rhodes, *The Government of London*; and Young and Garside, *Metropolitan London*, esp. p. 309. A group organized by Robson from the London School of Economics had been active during the Herbert Commission's inquiry and had given testimony. According to most histories of the event, that testimony was decisive. As told in Smallwood, *Greater London*, p. 196:

What was really of importance here, was the fact that the London School of Economics testimony offered the Royal [Herbert] Commission the very thing it so desperately needed if it was to advance any comprehensive proposals at all: namely, a solid base of support upon which it could plead its case. The entire reorganization . . . came into clear focus once the LSE had presented its evidence. The Royal Commission finally had a peg upon which it could hang its reform hat.

[25] See Dick Netzer, "Local Government in Heaven and Hell," *New York Affairs*, 1 (Summer 1973), and Paul Kantor, "The Governable City," *Polity* 7 (1974).

[26] Quoted in Rhodes, *The Government of London*, p. 175.

[27] The positions on abolition of all three political parties can be found in their party manifestos. For the Conservative statement, see "The Next Moves Forward," *The Conservative Manifesto* (Milton Keynes, United Kingdom: The Conservative Central Office, 1987), p. 62. For the Labour statement, see "Britain Will Win," *Labour Manifesto* (London: The Labour Party, 1987), p. 11. For the Alliance statement, see "Britain United," *The SDP/Liberal Alliance Programme for Government* (London: Hebden Royal, 1987), n.p.

At the time the Thatcher government proposed abolition, most Conservative members of the GLC opposed outright abolition. These Tories favored a modification of the GLC's powers, but eventually came around to supporting Thatcher's position. See *Streamlining the Cities: Response by the GLC Conservative Group* (London: Office of the Leader of the Opposition, Greater London Council, January, 1984).

[28] *1981 Census Results for Greater London and the London Boroughs: Small Area Statistics and Historical Comparisons, Statistical Series, No. 19* (London: Greater London Council, 1983), Table 2.

[29] Wealth or poverty can be assessed by "rateables" (property assessments) of a borough as well as by its socioeconomic composition. It is true that many wealthy boroughs in Outer London (Bromley, Sutton) lost very little population. Other well-off areas (Kingston, Richmond), however, lost appreciable amounts of population. For measures on borough wealth or poverty within Greater London and specific data for each borough, consult *London Boroughs Association Handbook, 1982-86* (London: London Boroughs Association, 1982), Tables 1 and 2.

[30] Nicholas Falk, "First Steps in Regenerating London's Inner Areas," in *London Looks Forward*, Greater London Conference Paper no. 6 (London: April 1977), p. 6.12.

[31] Ibid., pp. 6.13 and 6.14.

[32] Firms with fewer than 250 employees are considered to be "small." See Falk, "First Steps." For unemployment rates in Islington and other boroughs, consult *Economic Statistics from the 1981 Census: Statistical Series, No. 31* (London: Greater London Council, 1984), Table 6.

[33] For details on New York, consult *1980 Census of Population and Housing*, prepared by the New York State Data Center, New York State Department of Commerce, Summary Tape File 3. For Paris, see *Récensement de la Population de 1975 et 1982: Région d'Ile-de-France* (Paris: INSEE, 1984).

[34] *1981 Census Results for Greater London and the London Boroughs: Small Area Statistics and Historical Comparisons, Statistical Series, No. 19*, p. 10, and *Demo-*

graphic Review of Greater London: 1983 Statistical Series, No. 20 (London: Greater London Council, 1983), p. 24.

35 *1981 Census Results for Greater London and the London Boroughs: Small Area Statistics and Historical Comparisons, Statistical Series, No. 19*, Table 6.

36 Ibid., p. 10. Economic conditions for ethnic minorities are different. The poorest of NCWP immigrants are the West Indians. One-third of all households classified as West Indian found its chief breadwinner in unskilled or semi-skilled work. West Indians took jobs that the native population no longer wanted. Today they can be found in semi-skilled municipal jobs such as transport services.

Asians are better off. Indians and Pakistanis can be seen working as professionals and shopkeepers along many of the retail strips in London.

In comparison with New Commonwealth immigrants, those from the ROW category have an easier time. As a rule they are economically heterogeneous and found in service occupations. Immigrants from the Iberian peninsula often find work in Central London's hotel industry; those from Greece and Egypt function as shopkeepers; and still others from Iran and Poland are in the professions. For particulars on the West Indian population, see *Draft Alterations to the Greater London Development Plan: 1983* (London: Greater London Council, 1983), pp. 19, 48-50.

37 *London Facts and Figures*, n.p.

38 Ibid., Figure 29, and *Planning for the Future of London* (London: Greater London Council, 1984), p. 8.

39 See Oliver Marriott, *The Property Boom* (London: Hamish Hamilton, 1967), p. 1.

40 Ibid., p. 1. See also Peter Ambrose and Bob Colenutt, *The Property Machine* (London: Penguin, 1975).

41 James Sundquist, *Dispersing Population* (Washington, D.C.: Brookings Institution, 1975), p. 54.

42 Ibid.

43 Foley, *Governing the London Region*, p. 97.

44 Sundquist, *Dispersing Population*, p. 55.

45 Ibid., p. 55.

46 *London Facts and Figures*, Figure 19. We cannot attribute all of Greater London's economic problems to the imposition of controls, but they were of significance. Apart from controls, firm bankruptcies also rose during the 1970s.

47 Sundquist, *Dispersing Population*, p. 56.

48 See the *Office Development Pipeline in Greater London*, Item 6, P 939 (London: Greater London Council, Planning Committee, December 15, 1983), adapted from Table 1.

49 N. Starkman, *Les Bureaux à Londres: 1983 Document Provisoire* (Paris: Atelier Parisien d'Urbanisme, 1984). See also GLC Planning Committee Report, "Office Development in Greater London," Item 11, P 1193 (May 16, 1984), p. 5. GLC planners argue that London has an abundance of office space and that the loss of white-collar jobs can go hand in hand with an increase in office

stock. Thus they claim it is not a lack of supply but a lack of demand that is at the root of London's problems. Without rebutting this point, it can be argued that creating a viable CBD means more than just offices. A positive business climate, a solid infrastructure, and aggressive salesmanship are elements that can make a difference. For a viewpoint that emphasizes the desirability of a slowdown in construction, see *Review of Office Policy in Central London* (London: Greater London Council Planning Committee, July 17, 1981), Item 3, P63, pp. 2–6.

Chapter 7

¹ *Planning for the Future of London: Alterations to the Greater London Development Plan*, proposed by the Greater London Council under the Town and Country Planning Act 1971, Part II, Appendix A (London: Greater London Council, 1984), p. 1.6 [hereafter referred to as *Alterations to the GLDP, 1984*].

² *Planning for the Future of London: Draft Alterations to the Greater London Development Plan, 1983* (London: Greater London Council, 1983), p. 86 [hereafter referred to as *Draft Alterations to the GLDP, 1983*]. The history of the Greater London Development Plan (GLDP) and the CAZ–Community Area Plan is contorted. The plan had never been accepted by the central government and was never adopted into law, but it was treated as a "submitted plan," which meant that it could be used as a guide. With abolition the GLDP was withdrawn. However, a number of boroughs adopted concepts like the CAZ–Community Area Plan into their own structure plans, thereby giving it force in parts of London. The London Planning Advisory Committee (LPAC) also now uses the CAZ–Community Area Plan as a starting point for constructing its own recommendations.

³ *Alterations to the GLDP, 1984*, p. 8.11.

⁴ Normally and over the long haul, the central government is quite willing to let the locals decide. There have been a number of occasions, however, when central authorities have exercised decisive authority with little regard for local wishes. One of these occurred in 1964, when the conservative government established the GLC over the wishes of County Hall. Other occasions have occurred more recently, in 1984 and in 1986, with the abolition of the GLC.

Comparing Great Britain and France, one scholar sees government in Britain as more dogmatic, rigid, and in effect more centralized. My own view is that relative to interest groups, French government is far more centralized and monolithic than British government. Relationships between central and local governments are a different matter in Britain and France. Viewed from the perspective of intergovernmental relations, the French are more flexible than the British. This is due, in part, to the opportunities for consultation and cooperation between French political elites. For a formidable account of local government in each of these nations, consult Douglas Ashford, *British Dogmatism and French Pragmatism* (London: Allen & Unwin, 1983).

⁵ Since abolition, the phrase "GLCs-in-exile" has been used in a variety of ways. Here I employ the phrase in its broadest meaning, to refer to any organ-

ization that in some way fulfills the function, policy making, or political role of the original GLC. As a result of abolition, the Inner London Educational Authority (ILEA), which governs primary and secondary schools in twelve Inner London boroughs, is now directly elected and more autonomous. As the ILEA becomes more politicized, its informal alliance with the ALA and the Inner London boroughs will become more apparent.

6 Douglas Hart, *Strategic Planning in London* (London: Pergamon Press, 1976), p. 5. A good deal of the background for the case study on Motorways has been derived from Hart's excellent volume on the subject.

7 Author's interview, June 5, 1984.

8 Author's interview, June 5, 1984.

9 *Greater London Council Election 9, April 1970* (London: Greater London Council, Intelligence Unit, 1970), and *Times of London*, April 10, 1970, p. 1.

10 Hart, *Strategic Planning in London*, p. 172.

11 Simon Jenkins, "The Politics of London Motorways," *Political Quarterly* 44 (July-September 1973): 263.

12 Hart, *Strategic Planning in London*, p. 168.

13 Jenkins, "The Politics of London Motorways," p. 260.

14 Young and Garside, *Metropolitan London*, p. 343.

15 Jenkins, "The Politics of London Motorways," p. 270.

16 For a good contemporary account of Covent Garden, see Terry Christensen, *Neighbourhood Survival* (London: Prism Press, 1979).

17 David Triesman, "The Covent Garden Comprehensive Development Area," *Proof of Evidence*, unpublished manuscript.

18 Ibid. and see Christensen, *Neighbourhood Survival*, introduction and ch. 1.

19 Christensen, *Neighbourhood Survival*, p. 25.

20 For example, see Lewis Mumford, *The Culture of Cities* (New York: Harcourt Brace, 1938) and *The City in History* (New York: Harcourt Brace, 1961); Jane Jacobs, *The Death and Life of Great American Cities* (New York: Vintage, 1961); and Kevin Lynch, *Image of the City* (Cambridge: MIT Press, 1960). There was more than one "plan" for Covent Garden and there have been modifications to different plans. The major plans were *Covent Garden's Moving* (1968), *Covent Garden* (1971), and the most recent and final plan, *Covent Garden Action Area Plan* (1978). For purposes of discussion the most salient features of different plans have been taken up for analysis.

21 Triesman, "The Covent Garden Development," p. 79.

22 For newspaper accounts of Rippon's decision, see *Financial Times, London*, January 16, 1973; *Evening Mail*, January 16, 1973; and *Northamptonshire Evening Telegraph*, January 16, 1973.

23 Christensen, *Neighbourhood Survival*, pp. 47-48.

24 Author's interview, May 25, 1984.

25 Author's interview, May 28, 1984.

26 Author's interview, June 4, 1984.

27 *Covent Garden Action Area Plan* (London: Greater London Council, January 24, 1978), p. 17 [hereafter referred to as *Action Area Plan*].

28 Activists on the CGCA believe the community has been sold out. For views of the outcome more critical than presented here, consult *Putting the Record Straight* (Covent Garden Community Association, June 1980) and *Covent Garden Fightback: What's in a Plan* (London: Covent Garden Community Association, February 1979). These contrast with the official and generally accepted interpretation of the *Action Area Plan*.

There are allegations, some of which are well founded, that dwellings have been illegally converted. This is coupled to a charge that structures set up for flats are being used for offices. Although this may be true, it appears that it is a relatively small part of the total picture and that the GLC lived up to its basic promise that the old community would be given housing and social facilities.

29 For an account of London's East End, see Peter Wilsher, "East End or East Beginning," *Sunday Times of London*, January 23, 1977.

30 Ibid.

31 *Times of London*, August 12, 1975, p. 13.

32 Ibid.

33 For a factual account of contemporary events in The Docklands, consult the *Report from the Select Committee of the House of Lords on the London Docklands Development Corporation Area and Constitution Order 1980* (London: HMSO, 1980) [hereafter referred to as the *Select Committee Report*].

34 *The London Docklands Strategic Plan* (London: Docklands Joint Committee, 1976).

35 *Select Committee Report*, pp. 5.1 and 5.2.

36 For refutations of the *Select Committee Report* and criticisms of the LDDC, consult *London Docklands: Review of the First Two Years of Operation of the LDDC* (London: Greater London Council, 1984). See also *Heseltine's Docklands: The First Six Months* (London: Joint Docklands Action Group, May 1982) and *Docklands Fights Back: 18 Months of the LDDC* (London: Joint Docklands Action Group, June 1983).

37 *London Docklands Development Corporation, Annual Report and Accounts 1985-86* (London: London Docklands Development Corporation, 1986), p. 5. For a brief and imaginative essay on the LDDC's future, consult John Shepherd, *Land, Landholders and the Regeneration of London Docklands*, mimeo., n.d.

38 During its early years of operation, the LDDC was very wary of public participation. Since the early 1980s, the corporation has softened its stand. Note, however, the following quote from the Chairman:

The LDDC is prepared to explain, listen, and discuss. Nevertheless, it is not prepared then to sit back and do nothing in the hope that some ideal solution will emerge which will accommodate everyone's objectives. Consultation can too easily become an excuse for inaction in the face of lack of agreement since human beings are individuals and individuals rarely hold the same point of view or beliefs.

See the *London Docklands Development Corporation Annual Report and Accounts, 1982-83* (London: London Docklands Development Corporation, July 1983), p. 26.

39 *London Borough of Southwark, Planning Committee, North Southwark Plan:*

Toward Adoption, mimeo., July 26, 1985, p. 84, and consult *Report of the House of Lords, Select Committee on the 1980 Order* (London: Her Majesty's Printing Office, 1980).

[40] For an example of borough resistance to the LDDC and the central government, consult *Four Year Review of the LDDC* (London: The Docklands Consultative Committee, 1985), *Memorandum on the Docklands Development Corporation* (London: The Docklands Consultative Committee, August 1985), and a community newsletter called the *Docklander*.

[41] *London Borough of Southwark, Planning Committee*, p. 8.

[42] Ibid., p. 81.

[43] Ibid., p. 85.

[44] Ibid., p. 80.

[45] As of this writing, two "GLCs-in-exile" maintain offices in County Hall. These are the Association of Labor Authorities (ALA) and the Inner London Educational Authority (ILEA).

[46] There are any number of accounts that deal with the conservative and gradualist features of British politics. A seminal and incisive portrayal can be found in Walter Bagehot, *The English Constitution* (Garden City, N.Y.: Doubleday, n.d.). An account that uses survey data is the well-known comparative study of five political cultures by Gabriel Almond and Sidney Verba, *The Civic Culture* (Princeton: Princeton University Press, 1963). A more recent volume is Max Beloff and Gillian Peele, *The Government of the United Kingdom* (New York: W. W. Norton, 1980).

[47] Two of the most outstanding examples are James MacGregor Burns, *The Deadlock of Democracy* (Englewood Cliffs, N.J.: Prentice-Hall, 1963), and Theodore Lowi, *The End of Liberalism* (New York: W. W. Norton, 1969).

[48] For an account of how corporatism works in another British city (Oxford), consult Simmie, *Power, Property and Corporatism*. Simmie draws a distinction between established organizations that have special access to decision making (corporatism) and unorganized groups that have limited access to decision making.

Chapter 8

[1] Lasswell's book is inspirational, and he follows in the path of other seminal thinkers. Cf. Harold Lasswell, *Politics: Who Gets, What, When, How* (New York: Meridian, 1963); Gaetano Mosca, *The Ruling Class* (New York: McGraw-Hill, 1939); Weber, *From Max Weber*, ed. Gerth and Mills, esp. pt. 2; and Talcott Parsons, "The Distribution of Power in American Society," *World Politics* 10 (1957): 123-43.

[2] There are any number of ways in which to break down the components of a decision. The method used here follows standard procedures and is relatively uncomplicated. For some ideas, see James Robinson, *Congress and Foreign Policy Making* (Homewood, Ill.: Dorsey Press, 1967), chs. 1 and 6, esp. p. 178; the classic article by Robert Dahl, "The Concept of Power," *Behavioral Science* 2 (1957): 201-215; Harold Lasswell, *The Decision Process* (College Park, Md.:

Bureau of Governmental Research, University of Maryland, 1956); Richard Snyder et al., *Foreign Policy and Decision Making* (New York: Free Press, 1962). Bachrach and Baratz also deal with this issue extensively in *Power and Poverty*, chs. 1-4.

In addition there are some excellent articles on decision making that have a closely focused, methodological orientation. Consult, for example, Richard Snyder, "A Decision-Making Approach to the Study of Political Phenomena," in *Approaches to the Study of Politics*, ed. Roland Young (Evanston: Northwestern University Press, 1958); Edward Banfield, "The Decision-Making Schema," *Public Administration Review* 17 (Autumn 1957); and Herbert Simon, "Theories of Decision Making," *American Economic Review* 49 (June 1959).

[3] Frank L. Wilson, "French Interest Group Politics: Pluralist or Neocorporatist?" *American Political Science Review* 77, no. 4 (December 1983): 896. There are, of course, other essential differences between pluralism and corporatism. Wilson points out that under pluralism "whom you know" is important to groups seeking to influence policy. This is because there "are no institutionalized channels for group access to policy making." By comparison, "whom you know" is less important in a corporatist system, because group access is put within an "institutional frame of government." Thus, the group and its demands become a legitimate part of the governmental mechanism, and the group can stake its claims as a normal feature of decision making.

[4] The notion that politicians have been playing a more prominent role in public development is not new. Robert Salisbury pointed this out in an article entitled, "Urban Politics: The New Convergence of Power," *Journal of Politics* 26 (November 1964): 775-97. More recently, John Mollenkopf has brought political entrepreneurs to light in *The Contested City*. Mayoral biographies have also been written that point up this occurrence. See, for example, Alan Talbot, *The Mayor's Game* (New York: Praeger, 1970). Also see a compendium edited by Leonard Ruchelman, *Big City Mayors* (Bloomington: Indiana University Press, 1969). What is new about the treatment in this volume is the contextual setting of activist mayors within the power structure argument as well as the specification of methods and alliances used by mayors to wage their struggle.

[5] The same point is very ably made in Douglas Ashford's study of central-local relations in France and Great Britain. See Ashford, *British Dogmatism and French Pragmatism*. His argument, however, is different from the one offered here. Ashford claims that French pragmatism allows a formally centralized system to bring about a de facto decentralization of relationships. This is true, and the analysis here confirms the collaborative efforts of central and local officials. When the system is viewed in terms of interest groups lobbying government, however, the formal apparatus of centralization is borne out. In short, the centralist or decentralist tendencies of the system depend on what relations are being examined and who is being studied.

[6] French officials are not anxious to admit that such collaboration takes place. This is particularly true for partisans who want to blame the Left or the Right for their problems or who are anxious to gain political capital at the

expense of their opponents. After one denial that such collaboration took place at Secteur Seine Sud-Est, I undertook a lengthy investigation and confirmed that collaboration occurs with great (almost invariable) frequency. For a broad view of community decision making in a number of French cities, consult P. Kukawa, C. Mingasson, and C. Roig, *Recherche sur la Structure du Pouvoir Local en Milieu Urbain* (Grenoble: Institut d'Etudes Politiques, 1969).

7 The picture has largely been painted by Banfield and Meyerson as well as by Banfield in descriptions of politics in Chicago. See Meyerson and Banfield, *Politics, Planning and the Public Interest*, especially chapter 11, which discusses the notion of "the public interest." For a sequel to these themes see Banfield, *Political Influence*, especially chapters 11 and 12. An early treatise on metropolitan New York also sees the public sector as weak: cf. Wood, *1400 Governments*. The magnum opus on New York, Sayre and Kaufman, *Governing New York City*, takes a somewhat broader view of political actors, though they are not considered as particularly strong or proactive. A more recent work on the subject takes issue with earlier findings and argues that the public sector is central to regional development. Consult Michael Danielson and Jameson Doig, *New York: The Politics of Urban Regional Development* (Berkeley: University of California Press, 1982).

8 For an explanation and elaboration of this, see Evenson, *Paris: A Century of Change*.

9 This occurs on practically all issues of government. See Ashford, *British Dogmatism*, as well as H. V. Savitch and Madeleine Adler, *Decentralization at the Grass Roots*, Sage Administrative and Policy Series (Beverly Hills, Calif.: Sage, 1974).

10 The literature is extensive. Consult, for example, *Urban Bosses, Machines and Progressive Reformers*, ed. Bruce Stave (Lexington, Mass.: D. C. Heath, 1972). Harold Gosnell, *Machine Politics* (Chicago: University of Chicago Press, 1937). For an idea of how the "spoils system" has persisted, see Martin and Susan Tolchin, *To the Victor . . .* (New York: Random House, 1971) and an excellent article by Raymond Wolfinger, "Why Political Machines Have Not Withered Away and Other Revisionist Thoughts," *Journal of Politics* 34, no. 2 (May 1972).

11 In New York, ad hoc collaborators are frequently drawn from the Presidents of each borough who sit on the Board of Estimate or from other members of the Board of Estimate (Comptroller, President of the City Council). Borough Presidents play a strong role when decisions involve their particular domain. Because all the decisions we examined for New York dealt with the urban core or Manhattan, the President of that borough must be counted as an influential leader.

12 The literature on New York politics is replete with the theme of changing governmental coalitions. Sayre and Kaufman, *Governing New York*, describe changing coalitions for the period of the 1950s. A similar period is covered in Edward Costikyan, *Behind Closed Doors* (New York: Harcourt, Brace and World, 1966). Costikyan deals exclusively with party politics and nomina-

tions. For the 1960s, five major issues (police, housing, welfare, education, and health) are examined in *Race and Politics in New York City*, ed. Bellush and David. On the issue of education, consult David Rogers, *110 Livingston Street* (New York: Random House, 1969). More recently, Mayor Ed Koch was at the forefront of shifting party coalitions when a heated debate occurred over the appointment of a school chancellor. Koch found himself the target of antagonistic coalitions arrayed against him for the mayoral race of 1985. See Sam Roberts, "Coalition Maneuvers," *New York Times*, February 13, 1985, p. B4.

13 Author's interview, October 24, 1984.

14 Christensen, *Neighbourhood Survival*, pp. 25-26.

15 Ibid. The planner who was fired went on to write a book about the Covent Garden episode; see Brian Anson, *I'll Fight You For It* (London: Jonathan Cape, 1981). Anson's book is regarded by participants on both sides of the issue as highly prejudiced, and some have claimed it was filled with inaccuracies.

16 In New York City, much is made of political contributions given to politicians. The charge is often leveled against top politicians that they are bought by developer interests. Mayor Koch, in particular, is often said to be in the hands of developers. The following is a brief compilation of money given to top politicians by Times Square development interests over the five-year period (1980-1984) that was the most critical for deciding Times Square's future.

Cuomo (Governor)	$ 5,000
Koch (Mayor)	80,500
Goldin (Comptroller)	154,500
Bellamy (Pres., City Council)	12,250
Stein (Borough Pres., Manhattan)	114,440
Simon (Borough Pres., Bronx)	12,625
Mannis (Borough Pres., Queens)	4,200
Gaeta (Borough Pres., Richmond)	0
Total	$383,515

Although some of these amounts are not insubstantial, they constitute only a fraction of a campaign treasury fund, which usually runs into millions of dollars for a top political office. Mayor Koch, for example, raised $5.3 million during his 1985 election campaign. Moreover, the total contributions by individual developers are relatively small. The developer for the office towers at Times Square (George Klein) contributed a total of $50,200, the Trade Mart developer (Tishman-Speyer) contributed $27,650, and the theater developers (Lazar and Nederlander) contributed $35,565. The highest single contributor (Jacob Milstein) contributed $118,750 and he was *not* awarded a construction contract and is suing the city. Although campaign contributions do bolster private influence, their impact should not be exaggerated. (Source: Board of Elections, City of New York, April 1985.)

17 There has been a great debate among political scientists about the nature and definition of the "public interest" and indeed about whether a "public interest" exists or not. For a skeptics' view, see Meyerson and Banfield, *Politics,*

Planning and the Public Interest, ch. 11. See also Glendon Schubert, "The Public Interest in Administrative Decision Making: Theorem, Theosophy or Theory," *American Political Science Review* 41 (June 1957), and Emmette Redford, "The Never-Ending Search for the Public Interest," in *Ideals and Practice in Public Administration* (Birmingham: University of Alabama Press, 1958). So deep has been the cynicism about the existence of a public interest that it has come to be defined through its obverse. Thus David Truman defines the public interest as an equilibrium of private interests in *The Governmental Process.* A more recent book has sought to redefine the "public interest" by abolishing large parts of the public sector. See Savas, *Privatizing the Public Sector.*

[18] Ashford, *British Dogmatism,* p. 7, and Mark Kesselman, *The Ambiguous Consensus* (New York: Knopf, 1967). With recent reforms, French politicians are now limited to holding two political offices at the same time.

[19] Author's interview, May 27, 1984.

[20] Stephen Elkin, *Politics and Land Use Planning* (London: Cambridge University Press, 1974), p. 131.

[21] *Architectural Design* 41, no. 7 (July 1971): 404.

[22] Ibid.

[23] Ian Christie, "Covent Garden: Approaches to Urban Renewal," *Town Planning Review* (January 1974): 57. Also see a critical volume on British planners by David Eversley, *The Planner in Society* (London: Faber, 1973).

[24] Christie, "Covent Garden," p. 57.

[25] For a succinct and impressive account of Motorways, see Hart, *Strategic Planning in Central London.*

[26] There are numerous kinds of typologies that can be generated about a political system and about its actors. In *City Politics and Planning* (New York: Atherton, 1969), Francine Rabinovitz distinguishes different roles (technician, broker, mobilizer). John Kotter and Paul Lawrence, *Mayors in Action* (New York: John Wiley, 1984), develop an elaborate schema for analyzing the behavior of mayors. The idea of political entrepreneurship is replete in the literature and has been used recently by Mollenkopf in *The Contested City.* An excellent article on decision making and its theoretical dilemmas is Graham Allison, "Conceptual Models and the Cuban Missile Crisis," *American Political Science Review* 63, no. 3 (September 1969): 689–718.

[27] David Braybrooke and Charles Lindblom, *A Strategy of Decision* (New York: Free Press, 1963). The concept is noted frequently in the literature and used by such diverse scholars as Kotter and Lawrence, *Mayors in Action,* to explain decision making.

[28] The concept of a "veto group" has been used to describe American politics. This concept is, however, more valid for other cities or for national politics than it is for New York. New York politics is too unpredictable and too fluid to sustain the "veto group" concept. Veto groups need fixed junctures at which to exert their power. The idea of "veto groups" belongs to sociologist David Riesman, who describes them "as a series of groups each of which has struggled for and finally attained a power to stop things conceivably inimical to its interests" (David Riesman, *The Lonely Crowd* [New Haven: Yale Uni-

versity Press, 1950], p. 213). It has been used sporadically in political science. For example, see Harmon Ziegler, *Interest Groups in American Society* (Englewood Cliffs, N.J.: Prentice-Hall, 1964), p. 284, and Ira Katznelson and Mark Kesselman, *The Politics of Power* (New York: Harcourt Brace Jovanovich, 1975), p. 131. William Schultze's *Urban Politics* used the term "business veto" in analyzing the ability of commercial classes to block pieces of legislation. Schultze argues that businesses do not need to be active in politics, because cities need their investments and tax revenues. The only time business does become active is when there is a perceived threat. According to Schultze, this is "analogous to the veto process" (p. 110). Schultze's statement is at variance with the experience of our case studies.

[29] For a partial account of Haussmann's career, see Pinkney, *Napoleon III and the Rebuilding of Paris.*

[30] Author's interview, November 5, 1984.

[31] Author's interview, December 14, 1984.

[32] The question can be raised, how can we account for decisional change? The answer is that the planning decisions are blocked or modified by reversing the route they took in the first place—that is, by replacing one set of values with another and following those values with a new plan. Again, the rational decision reigns and again it is changed from the top—perhaps as a reflection of a shift in mass attitudes.

The era of the late 1960s and the 1970s reveals much about the process. In the late 1960s Paris was on its way to large-scale construction and making itself Europe's premier post-industrial city. Office towers, grand auto routes, and a World Trade Center were scheduled for the city. This was reversed neither by the gnawing of pressure groups nor by the protest of grass-roots politicians. It was the election of Giscard d'Estaing in 1974 that blocked radical transformation of the built environment. Giscard was determined to guard his place as an urban conservationist. The President and his new entourage stopped the building of an expressway on the Left Bank, put a halt to the planning of office and residential skyscrapers, and scrubbed the planning for a World Trade Center.

Giscard's critics are often reluctant to admit this, because they are prone to see conspiratorial forces at work. Consult, for example, Louis Chevalier, *L'Assassinat de Paris* (Paris: Fayard, 1977); Franc, *Le Scandale de Paris*; Georges Pillement, *Du Paris des Rois au Paris des Promoteurs* (Paris: Entente, 1976). A more restrained view of how the built environment is created can be found in a book by a former Prefect of Paris, Maurice Doublet, *Paris en Procès.*

[33] For a history, see Young and Garside, *Metropolitan London.*

[34] The biography of Moses goes into this subject in detail. Consult Caro, *The Power Broker*, chs. 10, 11, 12, and 13.

[35] Televised interview, Public Broadcasting System, 1976.

[36] Moses's biographer, Robert Caro, relates that Governor Nelson Rockefeller wanted to relieve Moses of one of his posts and that Moses thought he could rely on his many connections to thwart the Governor. Here is how Caro describes the confrontation between Moses and Rockefeller:

The Boss [Moses] comes out of the building and there's the Governor coming out after him and tugging at his arm, really pulling at him, trying to get him to come back inside and let's discuss it. Moses pulls his arm away from him and gets inside, saying, "Come on let's go," and we pull away leaving the Governor of the State of New York, just standing there on the sidewalk, and there are members of the public just standing and staring at this scene.

Moses lost anyway. But before he accepted defeat, he used the media and organized labor in an attempt to retrieve his position. See Caro, *The Power Broker*, pp. 1074-81.

³⁷ Author's interview, January 4, 1985.

³⁸ Ibid.

³⁹ See, for example, Abercrombie's collaborative work with J. H. Forshaw, *County of London Plan*, prepared for the London County Council (London: Macmillan & Co., 1944), and Abercrombie, *Greater London Plan, 1944*.

⁴⁰ William Robson published a large number of works on local government, law, and the civil service. His influential work on London was *The Government and Misgovernment of London*.

⁴¹ For Robson's impact, see Smallwood, *Greater London: The Politics of Metropolitan Reform*, especially p. 196, and consult Young and Garside, *Metropolitan London*, passim.

⁴² Robert Moses, "Mr. Moses Dissects the Long-Haired Planners," *New York Times Magazine*, June 15, 1944, p. 17.

⁴³ Ibid., p. 38.

⁴⁴ Author's interview, January 4, 1985.

⁴⁵ Forshaw, *County of London Plan*, p. 2.

⁴⁶ Robson, *The Government and Misgovernment of London*, esp. ch. 14.

⁴⁷ Moses reveals his personal philosophy in his own book, *Public Works: A Dangerous Trade* (New York: McGraw-Hill, 1970) and in a rebuttal to Robert Caro, *Comment on a New Yorker Profile and Biography*, August 26, 1974, mimeo.

Chapter 9

¹ See *The Politics of Aristotle* (Oxford: Oxford University Press, 1962), edited by Ernest Barker, especially Books IV and VI, where Aristotle talks about the varieties of constitutional orders as well as methods for constructing democracies and oligarchies. For an eighteenth-century sequel to Aristotle, see Alexander Hamilton, John Jay, and James Madison, *The Federalist Papers* (New York: Modern Library, 1937). In particular, consult nos. 10, 49, and 51. For a twentieth-century view, consult E. E. Schattschneider, *The Semisovereign People* (New York: Holt, Rinehart and Winston), especially chapters 3 and 4.

² For the political impact of how positions and timing shape outcomes, consult Harold Seidman, *Position and Power* (New York: Oxford University Press, 1980); and Bachrach and Baratz, *Power and Poverty*. Several writers who discuss how access may differ between issue areas are Roger Cobb, Jennie Keith-Ross, and Marc Howard Ross, "Agenda Building as a Comparative Political Process," *American Political Science Review* 70 (March 1976): 126-38.

³ Thomas Galloway and J. Terry Edwards, "Freedom and Equality: Dimen-

sions of Political Ideology and City Managers," *Urban Affairs Quarterly* 17, no. 2 (December 1981): 176. See also Altshuler, *The City Planning Process*; John Dyckman, "Planning and Decision Theory," *Journal of the American Institute of Planners* 35 (1961): 335-45; and D. N. Rothblatt, "Rational Planning Reexamined," *Journal of the American Institute of Planners* 37 (1971): 26-37.

4 This is not to cast aspersions at interest groups or to congratulate the planners. Decades of experience have taught us that "comprehension" is not always worthy, and "piecemeal" development is not necessarily invidious to the public interest. The point is ably made in Robert Goodman, *After the Planners* (New York: Simon & Schuster, 1971).

5 By "legislative structures," I mean deliberative bodies made up of legislators whose main purpose is to hold hearings, examine the facts, and pass laws. New York City's Board of Estimate is a strong institution, but it is not a true legislative body. Of its eight members, seven are executives whose power base is either in the office of the Borough President or in a citywide office (Mayor or Comptroller). The eighth member is President of the City Council, which is a legislative body, albeit a weak one.

It is the strength of interest groups that gives the city its hybrid of pluralism and corporatism. The force of interest groups gives them a power to organize and press for their cause. Yet at nonexecutive levels there is little structure into which they can plug.

6 My own observation clashes with the standard literature on French politics, which views interest groups as powerful actors in the political process. See, for example, H. W. Ehrmann, "French Bureaucracy and Organized Interests," *Administrative Science Quarterly* 5 (1961): 534-55. Perhaps the major reason for this clash is that most of the research on French politics has been done on such issues as trade, taxation, and subsidies. Relatively little has been published on the politics of the built environment. Most research on the built environment has been undertaken by geographers and sociologists—many of whom tend to overlook interest group activity. When research does focus on the political aspects of the built environment, the role of the interest group is very much diminished. See, for example, Carmona, *Le Grand Paris*. Even Marxist scholars see little action by interest groups during the process of decision making. Consult, for example, Godard, et al., *La Renovation Urbaine à Paris*; Lojkine, *La Politique Urbaine dans La Région Parisienne, 1945-1972*. The Marxists do, however, see political outcomes as favoring upper classes and developers. The cause is attributed to the imperatives of economics rather than to interest-group advocacy.

7 For an idea of how this works, see H. V. Savitch and Madeline Adler, *Decentralization at the Grass Roots: Political Innovation in New York and London* (Beverly Hills: Sage, 1974).

8 For insight and inspiration on this subject I am indebted to Charles Lindblom, *Politics and Markets*.

9 For a more broadly based assessment on this subject consult Lindblom, *Politics and Markets*.

10 This does not mean that private investors do not build. They, of course,

do a great deal of development. On the most crucial projects, however, the public sector is dominant, and on somewhat less crucial projects, private investors build under public guidance.

[11] The pattern of majority rule in the GLC is as follows: Labour (captured majority in 1964), Conservative (1967), Conservative (1970), Labour (1973), Conservative (1977), Labour (1981).

[12] *Docklands Fights Back: Eighteen Months of the LDDC*, pp. 3-5.

[13] For studies on national planning that support this thesis, see John McArthur and Bruce Scott, *Industrial Planning in France* (Boston: Division of Research, Harvard Business School, 1969), and Stephen Cohen, *Modern Capitalist Planning: The French Model* (Berkeley: University of California Press, 1977).

[14] Pierre Gremion, *Le Pouvoir Peripherique: Bureaucrats et Notables dans le Systèm Politique Français* (Paris: Le Seuil, 1976).

[15] The point is quite rightly made by Stephen Cohen, in *Modern Capitalist Planning: The French Model*, p. xvii.

[16] A host of studies, both "empirical" and "impressionistic," support this observation. For examples, consult the classics by Seymour Martin Lipset, *Political Man* (1960: Baltimore: Johns Hopkins University Press, 1981), and Robert Lane, *Political Ideology* (Glencoe, Ill.: Free Press, 1962). Other well-known accounts include Gabriel Almond and Sidney Verba, *The Civic Culture* (Princeton: Princeton University Press, 1963), and Angus Campbell et al., *The American Voter* (New York: John Wiley & Sons, 1964).

[17] Republicans had some success in electing mayors before the 1970s, but they had to rely on endorsements from other political parties in order to win. This occurred most notably with Fiorello La Guardia in elections between 1933 and 1941 and with John V. Lindsay in 1965. For an elaboration, see Lowi, *At the Pleasure of the Mayor*, esp. pp. 183-87.

For a general account of the partisan nature of New York consult Sayre and Kaufman, *Governing New York City*, esp. chs. 5 and 6 (parties and elections), ch. 16 (the Council), and ch. 17 (the Board). Recent data sustain the trend toward Democratic voting. For example in 1973, 65 percent of the votes cast for the City Council were made on the Democratic line. See *Preliminary Recommendations of the State Charter Revision Commission for New York City* (New York: State Charter Revision Commission, 1975), p. 69. Of the more than 1.5 million votes cast in the city for the gubernatorial race of 1982, Democrat Mario Cuomo captured 68 percent of the vote. See the *New York Post*, November 3, 1982. Even more impressive Democratic victories occur when lesser offices are at stake. In two city-wide races during 1981, the Democratic candidates for Comptroller and President of the City Council rolled up more than 80 percent of the total vote. See the *New York Times*, November 5, 1981.

[18] Until the charter reforms of 1975, the New York City Charter stated that "the City Planning Commission shall prepare and adopt in one or more parts, and from time to time modify a master plan for the physical development of the city" (*The New York City Charter, Effective January 1, 1963 As Amended to January 1969*). Attempting to fulfill that provision was fraught with so many difficulties that it had to be dropped.

¹⁹ A version of this trichotomized strategy of development can be found in H. V. Savitch, "Toward a Post-Industrial Order: Planning in New York, Paris and London," paper presented at the Annual Conference of the Urban Affairs Association, Norfolk, Virginia, April 1985.

²⁰ A good generalized version of containment can be found in Peter Hall, *The Containment of Urban England* (London: George Allen & Unwin, 1973). Although it is not Hall's intent to outline a containment strategy as such, his book illustrates British attitudes toward growth, planning, and development.

²¹ Danielson and Doig, *New York: The Politics of Regional Development*, p. 4. This volume is a worthy companion to the classic work by Wood, *1400 Governments*.

²² Altshuler, *The City Planning Process*.

²³ Not only does fragmented government give strength to a free marketplace, but there are cultural factors that contribute to this strength. The American belief structure places a high value on private property, capitalism, and individualism.

²⁴ Martin Schain, *French Communism and Local Power* (London: France Pinter, 1985), p. 3.

²⁵ See Mark Kesselman, *The Ambiguous Consensus* (New York: Knopf, 1967).

²⁶ *Informations d'Ile-de-France, Numero 23, October 1976* (Paris: IAURIF, 1976), pp. 13-14.

Chapter 10

¹ See the classic by James Bryce, *The American Commonwealth*, vol. 1 (New York: Macmillan, 1893), p. 637.

² Ibid., p. 642.

³ Quoted in David Hammack, *Power and Society* (New York: Russell Sage, 1982), p. 16. The original quote is from *The Banker's Magazine*, 53, 1896.

⁴ Ibid.

⁵ Pinkney, *Napoleon III and the Rebuilding of Paris*, p. 36. See also Evenson, *Paris: A Century of Change*, esp. ch. 1.

⁶ Young and Garside, *Metropolitan London*, p. 47.

⁷ Pinkney, *Napoleon III and the Rebuilding of Paris*, p. 36.

⁸ The thesis of the "private city" can be found in Sam Bass Warner's classic, *The Private City* (Philadelphia: University of Pennsylvania Press, 1968).

⁹ Quoted in Lester Salamon, "Urban Politics, Urban Policy, Case Studies" *Public Administration Review* 37 (July/August 1977): 423. Salamon presents an interesting conceptual framework that uses the idea of the "private city," the "bureaucratic city," and the "policy-planning" city.

¹⁰ For how this was done in Paris, see Evenson, *Paris: A Century of Change*. For London, see Donald Olsen, *The Growth of Victorian London* (New York: Holmes & Meier, 1976).

¹¹ For an excellent discussion of pluralism and corporatism as well as "concertation," see Harrison, *Pluralism and Corporatism*, esp. ch. 5.

¹² For an extended political analysis see the landmark study on America's

transformation by Theodore Lowi, *The End of Liberalism* (New York: W. W. Norton, 1969). See also Yair Aharoni, *The No Risk Society* (Chatham, N.J.: Chatham House, 1981).

[13] Quoted in Susan Fainstein et al., *Restructuring the City*, p. 252.

[14] *Le Monde*, April 30, 1977, p. 98.

[15] *New York Times*, August 2, 1982, p. A2.

[16] The analysis of "caretaker politics" comes out of an earlier era of urban scholarship and can be found in Oliver Williams and Charles Adrian, *Four Cities: A Study in Comparative Policy Making* (Philadelphia: University of Pennsylvania Press, 1963).

[17] The tradition is an old one, brought into vogue during the 1970s by the Bachrach and Baratz classic, *Power and Poverty*, and revitalized most recently in John Mollenkopf, *The Contested City*, and Clarence Stone, "Systemic Power in Community Decision Making: A Restatement of Stratification Theory," *American Political Science Review* 74 (December 1980): 978-90.

[18] Stone, "Systemic Power in Community Decision Making," p. 985.

[19] Ibid., pp. 980, 982 and passim. Another way of analyzing "situational dependencies" is to view them in terms of the things a city must do in order to function, survive, or prosper. It can be argued, for instance, that since cities must turn to private business for income, employment, and economic vitality, they must *always* favor those who are economically well off. See H. V. Savitch, *Urban Policy and the Exterior City*, pp. 61-63. Frederick Wirt makes a similar point by quoting Machiavelli's admonition about "the compulsion of necessity." See Frederick Wirt, *Power in the City* (Berkeley: University of California Press, 1973), p. 352.

[20] Regarding the application to land use of the concept of prevailing coalitions, see the formidable collection of articles edited by Clarence Stone and Heywood Sanders, *The Politics of Urban Development* (Lawrence, Kansas: University Press of Kansas, 1987); for a general treatment, see John Mollenkopf, *The Contested City*. For the application of this idea to non–land use issues, see Martin Shefter, *Political Crisis/Fiscal Crisis* (New York: Basic Books, 1985).

[21] Peter Blau, *Exchange and Power in Social Life* (New York: John Wiley & Sons, 1967), p. 5.

[22] *1980 Census of Population, Characteristics of People and Housing*, New York State Data Center, New York State Department of Commerce, Summary Tape File 3.

[23] Statistics for Paris can be found in *Récensement de la Population de 1975 et 1982: Région d'Ile-de-France* (Paris: INSEE, 1984). Statistics for New York can be obtained from New York State Data Center, Summary Tape File 3.

[24] INSEE, Observatoire Economique de Paris.

[25] New York State Data Center, Summary Tape File 3.

[26] For London, consult *ECONDAT Y67: 1971 and 1981* (London: Greater London Council), Tables 26 and 27 [hereafter referred to as ECONDAT]. For New York, consult *1980 Census of the Population, Characteristics of People and Housing*, Summary Tape File 3. For Paris, consult Institut National de la Statistique et des Etudes Economique (INSEE), *Récensement de la Population Région d'Ile-de-France 1982* (Paris: Observatoire Economique de Paris, n.d.).

[27] ECONDAT.

[28] See Hall, *World Cities*, pp. 39–44.

[29] Sundquist, *Dispersing Population*, ch. 3.

[30] One study that appears to substantiate this thesis is Richard Knight and Thierry Noyelle, *The Economic Transformation of American Cities* (New York: Rowman & Allenheld, 1984).

[31] See, for example, Falk, "First Steps," p. 6.12.

[32] Savitch and Adler, *Decentralization at the Grass Roots*.

[33] London began to construct similar kinds of facilities during the late 1960s, mostly on the dilapidated East End. After several years' experience with this kind of construction, it was abruptly halted. London's flirtation with megastructure housing was relatively brief and it reverted to the practice of building human-scale public (council) housing. In New York, megastructure-type housing was built for the poor and for the middle class shortly after World War II and in the 1960s.

[34] *42nd Street Development Project: Update*, p. 12.

[35] *Covent Garden Action Area Plan* (London: The Greater London Council, January 24, 1978), p. 19.

[36] For estimated costs, see *Forty-Second Street Development Project Fact Sheet*, p. 6, and Tim Wacher and Alan Flint, "How Covent Garden Became a Specialty Shopping Center," in *The Chartered Surveyor*, July 1980, p. 1 (reprinted by the GLC, Covent Garden Team).

[37] *Covent Garden Action Area Plan*, p. 27.

[38] *New York Times*, October 22, 1984, p. 63.

[39] *Environmental Impact Statement*, p. S14.

[40] *Covent Garden Action Area Plan*, p. 27.

[41] *Rapport à l'Assemblée Générale Ordinaire sur l'Exercice 1972*, p. 6.

[42] *10 Ans d'Activité: Les Halles*, p. 49.

[43] The quotes for Times Square, in order of presentation, are drawn from the *New York Times*, March 26, 1984, p. B1; *Environmental Impact Statement*, p. S8; and the *New York Times*, March 26, 1984, p. B1. For Covent Garden the quotes are drawn from *Action Area Plan*, pp. 13, 26, and from the *Birmingham Evening Mail*, January 16, 1979. For Paris, the quotes are taken from *Le Monde*, February 18/19, 1979, *10 Ans d'Activité: Les Halles*, p. 13, and a personal interview, December 14, 1984.

[44] *Environment Impact Statement*, pp. S13, S14. A press release by the Mayor's office states that the project will furnish "26,000 new permanent jobs," *Press Release*, Office of the Mayor, New York, April 6, 1982, p. 4.

[45] Wacher and Flint, "How Covent Garden Became," n.p. Before abolition, the GLC owned the Covent Garden's renovated market building. Since abolition, GLC property has been managed by the London Residuary Body (LRB). The LRB is supposed to function for a transitional period until all GLC affairs are terminated. GLC property is normally transferred to the boroughs, so they are likely to become Covent Garden's landlord.

[46] *Covent Garden Action Area Plan*, p. 18.

[47] The results can be seen in the financial accounting of Les Halles. In 1979 revenues amounted to $3.2 million, of which private developers contributed

only 27 percent. The rest came from concessions granted to other public authorities, state assistance, and user fees. See *10 Ans d'Activité: Les Halles*, p. 51.

⁴⁸ Precise comparisons between the three sites are difficult to make because of different systems of accounting and different modes of payment. They can also be misleading because of different territorial definitions and because the figures are often estimates. With these caveats in mind I have constructed a brief table of comparison. The reader can note the major contrasts between Times Square and Covent Garden. Les Halles' statistics fall somewhere in between.

	Size of Commercial Target (sq. acres)	Cost of Reconstruction (millions)	Direct Revenue Paid Annually to Public Sector (millions)	Increase or Decrease in Employment (percentage)	New Office Space (thousands of sq. ft.)
Times Square	13	2,400	35.27	+ 500%	4,000
Covent Garden	34	22.5	1.25	− 27	434
Les Halles	16	1,000	3.22	not avail.	1,666

SOURCE: Adapted from *42nd Street Redevelopment Project: Final Environmental Impact Statement* (New York: Urban Development Corporation, August 1984); *Covent Garden Action Area Plan* (London: Covent Garden Committee, 1978); and *10 Ans d'Activité: Les Halles* (Paris: Société d'Economie Mixte d'Aménagement des Halles, 1979). Cost and revenues for Times Square are estimated figures derived from the Urban Development Corporation (author's interview, July 23, 1987).

⁴⁹ Samuel Beer, "Group Representation in Britain and the United States," *Annals of the American Academy of Political and Social Science* 319 (September 1958). Also see Beer's later work, *British Politics in the Collectivist Age* (New York: Alfred Knopf, 1967).

⁵⁰ For examples of these differences, compare C. Wright Mills, *The Power Elite* (New York: Oxford University Press, 1959), with Floyd Hunter, *Community Power Structure* (New York: Doubleday, 1963), and still further with the "neo-elitist" critique by Bachrach and Baratz, *Power and Poverty*. In pluralist literature there are significant differences between Sayre and Kaufman's study of New York City, *Governing New York*, and Wirt's study of San Francisco, *Power in the City*. Within this school a whole new wave of "neo pluralist literature" has surfaced. For an explanation see John Manley, "Neo-Pluralism: A Class Analysis of Pluralism I and Pluralism II," *American Political Science Review* 77 (June 1983): 368-83.

⁵¹ For an appreciation of how historical precedent shapes different kinds of corporatism, consult Philip Cerny, "The Missing Linkage: Putting the State Back into Neo-Corporatism," paper presented at the Annual Meeting of the American Political Science Association, Washington, D.C., August 1986.

⁵² Thus in a six-month period corresponding to before and after the revelation of the scandal, those who approved of Koch's performance as Mayor fell from 71 percent to 61 percent, while those who disapproved of his performance jumped from 23 percent to 32 percent. See *New York Daily News*, June 4, 1986, p. 5.

⁵³ See the appeal for public support on Times Square by a former head of

the Urban Development Corporation, William Stern, "Don't Punish Times Square," *New York Times*, May 22, 1986, p. A31.

⁵⁴ For a critical prognosis of GLC abolition that is co-authored by a former member of the GLC, consult George Nicholson and Leith Penny, "Strategic Planning in London: The Past and the Future," *Viewpoint*, May 1986.

A "GLC comeback" could take any number of forms, as long as it consisted of a comprehensive government for a substantial part of what we know as London. These forms might include a return to three-tier government, an elected regional assembly, a council for Inner London, or the evolution of an existing institution into a broad-purpose authority.

⁵⁵ Thomas Clegg, Roger Crouch, Patrick Dunleavy, and Alan Harding, *The Future of London Government* (London: London School of Economics and Political Science, 1985), p. 104.

Index

Abercrombie, Sir Patrick, 171–178, 192, 198, 207–208, 239, 261–264, 268
Administrative Council of La Défense, 152–153. *See also* La Défense
Aristotle, 265
Association of London Authorities, 204, 228
Atelier Parisien d'Urbanisme (APUR): form of power, 249–250; role in Secteur Seine Sud-Est, 154
axes strategy, 277–279, 281–282

Bachrach, Peter, 24–25. *See also* decisions: as crucial issues
Baltard Pavilions, 138–139, 142–143, 160. *See also* Baltard, Victor
Baltard, Victor, 138
Baratz, Morton, 24–25. *See also* decisions: as crucial issues
Battery Park City (BPC), 51–53. *See also* public authorities in New York
Beame, Abe, 82, 249
Beaubourg. *See* Plateau Beaubourg
Bell, Daniel, 3–5
Bellamy, Carol. *See* City Council and Council President of New York City
Benstock, Marcy, 85, 87. *See also* Westway
Berra, Yogi, 258
Bish, Robert, 6
Blau, Peter, 290
Board of Estimate of New York City: case decisions, 249; functions and status, 57–59; Lincoln West, 65–67; partisan control, 274; Times Square, 78
Bridwell, Lowell, 81, 85–87
British planning tools: Brown Office Ban, 193; Central Activities Zone (CAZ), 199–201, 278–279, 282; Community Areas, 199–201, 277–279, 282; Comprehensive Development Area (CDA), 214, 219–220; Forums, 203,

221–222, 261; Green Belt, 172–178, 181, 183, 197–198, 201, 261, 277–279, 282, 303; Industrial Development Certificates (IDCs), 192–193, 197; Office Development Permits (ODPS), 193, 197; public inquiries, 203–204, 212, 219, 228; Royal Commissions, 203; strategic centers, 194–195, 199, 200, 279
Brown Office Ban. *See* British planning tools
Bryce, Lord, 284

Carey, Hugh, 65, 82, 86, 249, 253
Central Activities Zone (CAZ). *See* British planning tools
Centre Français de Commerce International (CCI) (World Trade Center in Paris), 142, 145, 161
Centre Pompidou. *See* Plateau Beaubourg
Chalandon, Albin, 105–106
Chirac, Jacques, 107, 125, 134, 144, 158, 249, 254, 272, 287, 302
City Council and Council President of New York City: Bellamy, Carol, 66–67, 78; partisan control, 274; role, 57; Times Square, 70
Clore, Charles, 192
Comité de Recherche et d'Action Sociale (COPRAS), 141
Comité d'Initiative pour l'Aménagement des Halles (CIAH), 141, 143, 161
Communists. *See* political parties
Community Areas. *See* British planning tools
community boards in New York City: ability to prevail, 89; functions and role, 57–59; Lincoln West, 63; Westway, 86
Comprehensive Development Area (CDA). *See* British planning tools
Comptroller of New York City, 57